Nnedi Okorafor

Critical Explorations in Science Fiction and Fantasy
A series edited by Donald E. Palumbo and C.W. Sullivan III
Earlier Works: www.mcfarlandpub.com

57 *Wells Meets Deleuze: The Scientific Romances Reconsidered* (Michael Starr, 2017)

58 *Science Fiction and Futurism: Their Terms and Ideas* (Ace G. Pilkington, 2017)

59 *Science Fiction in Classic Rock: Musical Explorations of Space, Technology and the Imagination, 1967–1982* (Robert McParland, 2017)

60 *Patricia A. McKillip and the Art of Fantasy World-Building* (Audrey Isabel Taylor, 2017)

61 *The Fabulous Journeys of Alice and Pinocchio: Exploring Their Parallel Worlds* (Laura Tosi with Peter Hunt, 2018)

62 *A* Dune *Companion: Characters, Places and Terms in Frank Herbert's Original Six Novels* (Donald E. Palumbo, 2018)

63 *Fantasy Literature and Christianity: A Study of the Mistborn, Coldfire, Fionavar Tapestry and Chronicles of Thomas Covenant Series* (Weronika Łaszkiewicz, 2018)

64 *The British Comic Invasion: Alan Moore, Warren Ellis, Grant Morrison and the Evolution of the American Style* (Jochen Ecke, 2019)

65 *The Archive Incarnate: The Embodiment and Transmission of Knowledge in Science Fiction* (Joseph Hurtgen, 2018)

66 *Women's Space: Essays on Female Characters in the 21st Century Science Fiction Western* (ed. Melanie A. Marotta, 2019)

67 *"Hailing frequencies open": Communication in* Star Trek: The Next Generation (Thomas D. Parham III, 2019)

68 *The Global Vampire: Essays on the Undead in Popular Culture Around the World* (ed. Cait Coker, 2019)

69 *Philip K. Dick: Essays of the Here and Now* (ed. David Sandner, 2019)

70 *Michael Bishop and the Persistence of Wonder: A Critical Study of the Writings* (Joe Sanders, 2020)

71 *Caitlín R. Kiernan: A Critical Study of Her Dark Fiction* (James Goho, 2020)

72 *In* Frankenstein's *Wake: Mary Shelley, Morality and Science Fiction* (Alison Bedford, 2020)

73 *The Fortean Influence on Science Fiction: Charles Fort and the Evolution of the Genre* (Tanner F. Boyle, 2020)

74 *Arab and Muslim Science Fiction* (eds. Hosam A. Ibrahim Elzembely and Emad El-Din Aysha, 2020)

75 *The Mythopoeic Code of Tolkien: A Christian Platonic Reading of the Legendarium* (Jyrki Korpua, 2021)

76 *The Truth of Monsters: Coming of Age with Fantastic Media* (Ildikó Limpár, 2021)

77 *Speculative Modernism: How Science Fiction, Fantasy and Horror Conceived the Twentieth Century* (William Gillard, James Reitter and Robert Stauffer, 2021)

78 *English Magic and Imperial Madness: The Anti-Colonial Politics of Susanna Clarke's* Jonathan Strange & Mr. Norrell (Peter D. Mathews, 2021)

79 *The Self and Community in* Star Trek: Voyager (Susan M. Bernardo, 2022)

80 *Magic Words, Magic Worlds: Form and Style in Epic Fantasy* (Matthew Oliver, 2022)

81 *Discovering* Dune: *Essays on Frank Herbert's Epic Saga* (eds. Dominic J. Nardi and N. Trevor Brierly, 2022)

82 *Nnedi Okorafor: Magic, Myth, Morality and the Future* (Sandra J. Lindow, 2023)

83 *Science, Technology and Magic in* The Witcher: *A Medievalist Spin on Modern Monsters* (Kristine Larsen, 2023)

Nnedi Okorafor
Magic, Myth, Morality and the Future

SANDRA J. LINDOW

CRITICAL EXPLORATIONS
IN SCIENCE FICTION AND FANTASY, 82
Series Editors Donald E. Palumbo *and* C.W. Sullivan III

McFarland & Company, Inc., Publishers
Jefferson, North Carolina

This book has undergone peer review.

ISBN (print) 978-1-4766-8332-4
ISBN (ebook) 978-1-4766-4888-0

Library of Congress and British Library
cataloguing data are available

Library of Congress Control Number 2022052201

© 2023 Sandra J. Lindow. All rights reserved

No part of this book may be reproduced or transmitted in any form or by any means, electronic or mechanical, including photocopying or recording, or by any information storage and retrieval system, without permission in writing from the publisher.

Front cover image by Mike Orlov (Shutterstock)

Printed in the United States of America

*McFarland & Company, Inc., Publishers
Box 611, Jefferson, North Carolina 28640
www.mcfarlandpub.com*

To MICHAEL LEVY for his loving guidance through
the Greeny Jungle of Academic Scholarship

Acknowledgments

I would like to thank my late husband Michael Levy whose encouragement, lovely insights, critical commentary, and historical knowledge of the field made early conference papers a pleasure to write and whose last words to me were to keep writing. I want to thank my beta readers, especially Jonna Gjevre and Mark Decker, for their incisive comments and my editors, Kevin Maroney at the *New York Review of Science Fiction* and Brian Attebery at the *Journal of the Fantastic in the Arts,* for liking my work enough to publish it, thereby providing me with insights and the confidence to keep writing after Michael died on April 4, 2017.

I want to thank Nisi Shawl for encouraging me to continue with my book despite my late-in-life awareness of invisible privilege; Scott McDonald for his insight on Okorafor's comics and graphic novel; Kelly McCullough for introducing me to the word *kyriarchy,* which became a unifying concept in my manuscript; Elena Marshall for her thoughtful discussion of aging and moral maturity; the Rev. Kathleen Reymond for her insights on privilege and moral decision-making and for sharing her books on reconciliation; and the Writers' Group at the Library (now Zoom) for providing critical response to important parts of this book when I was developing my arguments and needed others' insights.

Finally, I want to thank all my friends and family for their patience when my words became waterfalls of all the things circling in my mind, things I needed to say about literature, moral development, and what's wrong and right in the world.

Table of Contents

Acknowledgments vi

Preface 1

Introduction to Reading Okorafor 5

1. Exploring the Empire of Girls' Moral Development 17

2. Watching Windseekers: Wonder, Anger, Intimacy, Independence and Transformation 41

3. Mythology and Sacrifice in *Who Fears Death* 58

4. *The Book of Phoenix,* Motherless Monsters and the Morality of Abomination 76

5. Tomorrow Is Now: An Evolution of Young Women's Rights, Trauma and Resilience 98

6. Magic, Masquerades and Morality 118

7. Degrowth in the Anthropocene Worlds of Le Guin and Okorafor 139

8. Black to Okorafor: Entering the Intersection of Afrofuturism, Comics and the Women's Movement 152

9. Conclusions About Morality, Technology, Magic and the Lessons of History 173

Appendix: Motherlessness, Anger, Agency and Inspiration in the Life of Mary Shelley 189

Chapter Notes 193

Works Cited 217

Index 229

Preface

I first became interested in Nnedi Okorafor when she was a guest of honor at SF Minnesota's 2008 Diversicon, a yearly convention held in the St. Paul–Minneapolis area. Okorafor's appearance was striking, and her fiction took me to a place I had never been before. When her YA novel *Zarah, the Windseeker* won the 2008 Wole Soyinka award for literature written in English by a writer of African descent, I bought a copy and started reading. Wole Soyinka was Africa's first Nobel Laureate, and receiving this award gave Okorafor's work considerable gravitas. I was immediately fascinated by her secondary world of Ginen, as well as by her depiction of girls' decision-making and moral development. Two years earlier I had semi-retired after thirty-five years of teaching, twenty-five of them as a reading and writing specialist in a treatment center for emotionally disturbed children and adolescents. During that time, I had worked with many emotionally damaged African American girls, their hopes for the future destroyed through neglect and physical and sexual abuse. Some of them had been prostituted by their parents. Many had been homeless at least once. Most had grown up in the war zones of inner cities. One young woman's mother had been shot and killed while they were walking through a city park together. A few were immigrants from Cuba and Somalia. These girls were angry for good reasons, but it was an anger that needed to be understood before they could have better lives. Part of my job was to help them channel their anger through the written word. Thus, I applauded Okorafor's depiction of anger in response to the culturally imposed silencing of women's voices, the limitations of gender roles, and the damage lookism causes to young women's self-esteem. Pioneering critic Gayatri Chakravorty Spivak explains:

> Why not develop a certain degree of rage against the history that has written such an abject script for you that you are silenced? Then you begin to investigate what it is that silences you, rather than take this very deterministic position—since my skin colour is this, since my sex is this, I cannot speak [Landry, 5].

I was at that time completing the final chapters of *Dancing the Tao: Le Guin and Moral Development*, 2012, my first scholarly book, and I realized that Okorafor followed in Le Guin's feminist footsteps but was able to depict girls' emotions and heroism in an intimate way that Le Guin could not. I immediately wanted to write about what I was seeing in Okorafor's work. The first chapter, "Exploring the Empire of Girls' Moral Development," began as a conference paper that was presented at the International Conference of the Fantastic in the Arts and later published in *The Journal of Fantastic in the Arts*. Other conference papers followed.

Okorafor's emergence as a Nigerian American writer has allowed her considerable international attention through her juxtaposition of traditional African magic with futuristic science and technology. In a 2016 article in *Pivot,* Nigerian scholars Mary Bosede Aiyetoro and Elizabeth Olubukola Olaoye explain:

> The idea of a Nigerian science fiction is relatively new, as the genre is still bourgeoning in the country. Authors like Adebayo Williams, Biyi Bandele Thomas, and Ben Okri have transgressed the shores of realism in their narratives by experimenting with magical and pseudo-realism in their work, but no writer has dared to engage with the idea of science fiction in Nigerian literature in that way that Okorafor has [228].

To better understand Okorafor's breadth of vision, this book accesses African and African American writers, beginning with W. E. B. Du Bois, and scholarship, inside and outside the field of science fiction and fantasy, including recent criticism.

Chapter 1, "Exploring the Empire of Girls' Moral Development," cites Erik Erikson, Lawrence Kohlberg, Carol Gilligan, Nancy Rule Goldberger, and Mary Field Belenky on moral development, Maureen Murdock on *The Heroine's Journey,* and Gloria Steinem on girls' self-esteem. It begins a discussion of Elizabeth Schlüsser Fiorenza's conception of kyriarchy that continues throughout the rest of the book.

Chapter 2, "Watching Windseekers," follows the development of second wave feminism, drawing insight from Alice Walker's understanding of Womanist Feminism, the Combahee River Collective, Rebecca Walker's origin of third wave feminism, Sami Schalk's examination of disability in speculative fiction by Black women writers, and Donna Haraway's conception of the cyborg.

Chapter 3, "Mythology and Sacrifice in *Who Fears Death*," references Lenore Terr's work on childhood trauma, Mary Pipher's ground-breaking study of girl's self-esteem, and critiques Thomas Carlyle's concept of the Great Man.

Chapter 4, "*The Book of Phoenix,* Motherless Monsters and the Morality of Abomination," compares *Phoenix* with Mary Shelley's *Frankenstein*. Particularly valuable here is work on surveillance by Bill Ashcroft, 2000; colonialism and neo-colonialism by John Rieder, 2008; Isabel Wilkerson's work on *Caste,* 2020; and Istvan Csicsery-Ronay's 2008 examination of the sublime and the grotesque.

Chapter 5, "Tomorrow Is Now: An Evolution of Young Women's Rights, Trauma and Resilience," returns to Pipher and Gilligan with further insight from Audre Lorde and Alice Walker as well as theologian Michael Battle's work on reconciliation.

Chapter 6, "Magic, Masquerades and Morality," applies Carol Pearson's classification of heroes.

Chapter 7, "Degrowth in the Anthropocene Worlds of Le Guin and Okorafor," employs recent Marxist degrowth scholarship and looks back at Aldo Leopold's citizenship to the land.

Chapter 8, "Black to Okorafor: Entering the Intersection of Afrofuturism, Comics and the Women's Movement," looks back at recent work by Ytasha Womack, Isiah Lavender, Lisa Yaszek, and Alex Zamalin.

Chapter 9, "Conclusions About Morality, Technology, Magic and the Lessons of History," reconsiders continually relevant scholarship by historians Will and Ariel Durant, 1968, in order to provide a historical overview.

Throughout this book, my intent is to be genre attentive, text specific and informed by theories of human development and intersectionality. *Intersectionality* is the term generally used to describe how multiple social systems connect to create a multiplicity of "identities, oppressions, and privileges" (Schalk, 7). The term was initially conceptualized in 1989 by Professor of Law Kimberlé Crenshaw,[1] to explain how Black women were doubly damaged by an intersection of racism and sexism. Okorafor has much to offer in this regard.

This book has been over ten years in the making. Much has changed in that time, and I have come to a clearer understanding of the way Black Feminism merges into Afrofuturism and Africanfuturism. I want to clarify that I do not wish to co-opt any part of the field. I simply want to celebrate the importance of these books to young women. Although I have tried to touch on the major themes in Okorafor's work as it relates to feminism, racism, and moral development, more work can be done, particularly in the areas of disability studies and queer theory—and in the areas in which her work responds to police brutality, right-wing insurrection, violence in the streets, and global pandemic (see Chapter 9). Furthermore, Okorafor, only in mid-career, continues to write, grow, and broaden as a writer.

Parts of this book were previously published in earlier versions:

Lindow, Sandra. "Nnedi Okorafor: *The Book of the Phoenix*, the Morality of Abomination." *New York Review of Science Fiction*, January 2016, No. 329, Vol. 28, #5.

_____. "Nnedi Okorafor: Exploring the Empire of Girls' Moral Development." *Journal of the Fantastic in the Arts,* Vol. 28, #1, 2017.

_____. "Black to Okorafor: Entering an Intersection of Afrofuturism, Comics, and the Women's Movement." *New York Review of Science Fiction*, December 2017.

Introduction to Reading Okorafor

"I am an outcast and I dwell on top of many borders in so many ways, I guess. Oh, let me count the ways. I embrace and own these things rather than try to hide them, regardless of what society tries to push on me. It shows in my work" (Okorafor, *Mosaic Magazine*, 2014).

Award-winning Nigerian American novelist Nnedimma Nkemdili[1] "Nnedi" Okorafor, writes speculative fiction that is both politically adept and developmentally aware. Since the beginning of her writing career, her predominant focus has been on the challenges faced by young people in difficult, often dangerous worlds. She was initially recognized to write at the forefront of the Afrofuturist subgenre of science fiction. Daily life in her futuristic secondary world of Ginen depicts environmentally based egalitarian communities, what South African writer Mohale Mashigo, 2018, describes as "a place in our imaginations that is the opposite of our present reality where a small minority owns most of the land and lives better lives than the rest" (np). In Okorafor's Ginen the land belongs to itself, and its ecology is vigorously protected by its human inhabitants. Clearly Ginen offers a hopeful design for a sustainable African future that includes healthy possibilities for inner and outer space.

The term *Afrofuturist* was first coined by columnist Mark Dery, 1993, to refer to an emerging movement of art and music and writing. Nalo Hopkinson suggests that the term initially functioned as a kind of carrier bag to describe a wide range of work by individuals of African descent, including Africentrist work (set in the present or past) by African writers such as Kenyan author Minister Faust; however, considerable discussion, definition, and evolution has narrowed the terminology somewhat to focus on a dynamic community of writers and artists who depict fantastic futures where privilege is not determined by skin color (Lavender, 25, 27). Nevertheless, Okorafor began to see that much of the energy of the movement surrounded the diaspora and the long-term damage caused by slavery in America (blog October 19, 2019). Since 2017, she has identified as an *Africanfuturist* or an *Africanjujuist* in that her internal camera has always been on the devastating effects of colonialism on Africa, its cosmology, its continental life, and its present and future potential to become an international power. In a 2017 essay, Nisi Shawl calls Okorafor's separation from the community of Afrofuturism "troubling" because it ignores "years of scholarship and creativity that focus on Afrofuturism as an artistic expression of Africa's diaspora" (np). It is understandable that Okorafor wants to self-define, thus avoiding scholarly definition, and another not-quite-right category that "society tries to push on" her, but she was born and educated in the United States. Far from a solo work of imagination alone, her fiction has grown through conscious and unconscious dialogue with postcolonial and Afrofuturistic scholarship. Definitive aspects of both continue to apply to her work.

Yaszek, 2005, has written that "Afrofuturism is not just about reclaiming the history of the past, but reclaiming the history of the future as well" (300). Nigerian writer Suyi Davies Okungbowa, 2021, further adds, "For us, the future is always the past is always the present—the embodiment of Afrofuturist consciousness—and telling our stories means we are always looking through this prism" (np). The future will be different by definition, but contemporary Afro and Africanfuturists assert that the future may well depend on how and where the lens is set for viewing the past and present. Furthermore, Okorafor suggests that unless humans become more accepting of difference and change, there may be no future.

Okorafor's Oeuvre

In a remarkable series of books that range from picture and chapter books for children to middle grade, young adult, adult novels and comics, Okorafor's work has primarily focused on girls and women who struggle with damaging cultural and sexist traditions, although recently she has begun to explore the complications of becoming a fair-minded man in a world where male privilege and sexism are commonly shared like air. When she writes about overcoming obstacles to empowerment, she examines the underlying politics of race, skin color, gender, privilege, ability, capitalism and ecology, demonstrating a kyriarchal connection between damage to the environment and damage to women's bodies and self-esteem.

In *Locus*, Gary K. Wolfe writes that "Okorafor's genius has been to find the iconic images and traditions of African culture ... and tweak them just enough to become a seamless part of her vocabulary of fantastika" (17). Like the windseeker's dadalocks that entwine living vines and a legacy of magic in utero, Okorafor uses this vocabulary interstitially to slip somewhere between genres, slyly entwining fantasy, science fiction and magical realism. In her essay "Organic Fantasy," 2009, she relates that her stories emerge organically out of an African story-telling tradition. For her, fantasy "is the most truthful way of telling the truth" (279). It is "the most accurate way of describing reality" (279). An intuitive writer and a fast typist, she describes how she sometimes does not know what will happen in a scene until her hands write the words (Rasheed, np). To her, the magic seems to emerge organically:

> I see the world as a magical place. Therefore, it was only natural that magic wafted from my fiction like smoke. It wasn't something I purposely did. I would try to write "realistic" fiction, and someone would fly or there would be a black hole full of demons or a girl who attracted frogs [Rejectionist, np].

Early Influences

Okorafor's fantastic fiction emerged out of early experiences in Africa where she was profoundly affected by the flora, fauna, folklore and culture, in her words, "the place where I have experienced my life's greatest joys and greatest terrors" ("Organic," 276). The joys were those of interspecies connection in a natural world often incredible in its beauty. The terrors were of the known and the unknown with stories often set in the liminal spaces between.

Although she was born in 1974, five years after her parents immigrated to the United States, her family made frequent trips back to Arondizuogu, her father's Igbo village: The trips themselves were surreal culture-entwining multi-sensory experiences that required the accompaniment of armed guards because the roads were not safe. "Organic Fantasy" describes driving through a Nigerian forest with her family. She reads *The Talisman*, 1984, by Stephen King and Peter Straub, while her uncle tells horrific, probably apocryphal, tales about headhunters, and she listens to a new Guns 'n' Roses album to drown him out until singer Axl Rose uses the word "niggers" and she stops listening in disgust (277). In grade school back in the United States, she has been called "nigger" (Pen, 370).

The Talisman fascinated her because it describes a young boy's heroic quest between parallel worlds to find a magic crystal that can save his dying mother. Okorafor suggests that this definitive multi-cultural, multi-media reading experience sets the pattern for her writing.

Later African trips also involved the intersection of culture and gender: As a teenager, she was heckled by adult men for wearing baggy knee length shorts in a marketplace in Muslim Abuja ("Organic," 278). Furthermore, in her father's home village, she and her sisters were harassed and whipped by men and boys disguised as masquerades, a secret society that believed they embodied (and gained permission from) deceased ancestors when they wore secretly created masquerade costumes. Her father, a cardiovascular surgeon, had been initiated into the village masquerade society as a young man and ostensibly allowed the harassment to occur. From an educated western parenting point of view, this would be considered a serious betrayal of trust, which in turn could cause cognitive dissonance regarding the rights of women to make their own decisions, but Okorafor loved her father, respected his beliefs, and saw evading the masquerades as a kind of challenge, a way to engage in early warrior training. This resilience training also helped in dealing with racial prejudice at home in the United States "where issues of race continue to lurk around corners" and she was frequently bullied for being different ("Organic" 277).

It is not surprising then that Okorafor does not take women's rights for granted, but rather as part of a continuing battle against invisible systems of male privilege that must be fought and refought in various times and places (see Chapter 2: "Watching Windseekers"). Presently this war continues to be fought in the science fiction and fantasy community where conservative white male fans, such as Brad R. Torgerson and Theodore Beale (aka Vox Day), have furiously asserted that Hugo and Nebula award-winning women such as Okorafor, Hopkinson, and N.K. Jemisin are "half-savages," despite their advanced degrees and university positions (Dowdall, 150). These fans suggest that the popularity of African American speculative fiction is due to "literary affirmative action" and reassert long-disproved theories of racial inequities, as Dowdall, 2020, suggests, "the dehumanizing ideologies that justified colonialism and slavery" (150).

Likewise, the continuing war between contemporary and traditional values creates a dramatic tension throughout Okorafor's work, with human rights abuses, such as the 2014 Boko Haram kidnapping of the Chibok school girls, providing inciting action for several of her stories (see Chapter 5, "Tomorrow Is Now"). Early 20th Century socialist W.E.B. Du Bois once explained that African Americans look at the world through a "double consciousness," which suggests that at any given time they can observe events through the binocular perspectives of being both African and American (Souls, 8).[2] Okorafor adds to this a third consciousness: that of being a woman who has been sexually harassed and frequently undervalued, her voice ignored by those who have been privileged with power.³ Correspondingly, she has a deep compassion for those who have been othered, and this compassion extends to the flora and fauna of the ecosystem and beyond into outer space.

Like other writers such as Maxine Hong Kingston in *The Woman Warrior: Memoirs of a Girlhood among Ghosts*, 1976, Okorafor grew up with no clear cognitive boundaries between the magical and the mundane. The result is an ingrained acceptance of and interest in the Other and a blurring of boundaries between human, plant and animal. In a 2009 interview in *Clarkesworld* magazine, Okorafor writes that when a story comes to her, it won't let her rest; the characters and their worlds are real: "I've felt the sting of their sandstorms and smelled their forests. The creatures really do bite, snarl, sing, spit, sting, etc." (np).

Okorafor as Rudimentary Cyborg, the Dynamics of (Dis)Ability

As a child, Okorafor was fascinated by insects and originally intended to be an entomologist, but when she was nineteen, a spinal surgery to correct her scoliosis went horribly wrong, In May 1993, between her freshman and sophomore years in college, surgery to straighten her spine resulted in paralysis. The surgeons decreased the correction, fused two vertebrae and "lashed" a stainless-steel rod to her spine to keep everything in place (*Broken*, 35). After the surgery, she was temporarily paralyzed from the waist down: "It was as if half of me had teleported to another dimension" (*Broken*, 34). She saw herself as "a rusted robot":

> A machine with no waterproofing caught out in the rain, with no shelter nearby. No options. Vulnerable. I was now malfunctioning. I needed a hard reset [*Broken*, 23].

Afterwards, as she lay in a haze of pain medication, her hospital room was infested by enormous "fluorescent" insects, bigger than the ones she caught in Nigeria (*Broken*, 17). In an unpublished verse from *Earthseed: The Books of the Living*, Octavia Butler has written that "Sanity is the tool with which we build worlds around ourselves. The smoother our interface between our personal world and those of others, the more sane, the more human, we perceive those others to be" (Schalk, 59), but what if our experience of reality is defined by otherness? Okorafor's postanesthetic vision reflects an essential part of her internal world. Similar insects eventually populate the Greeny Jungle of Ginen, her secondary world.

Okorafor's slow recovery gave her time to reevaluate her plans for the future. While she was in the hospital, she attended a craft therapy activity. First, she constructed a woman out of blue clay and later drew that woman with long blue dreadlocks (*Broken*, 45). Drawn out of the depths of despair, this picture became an inspiration for her Windseeker stories as well as Binti's *okuoko* tentacles. Her memoir, *Broken Places, Outer Spaces*, describes her recognition that this was a Nigerian woman who lived a long time ago, and the reason the woman is not "all sweaty" in her long dress is that she could fly (45). This conclusion has been significant for Okorafor. Although at the time, she was in considerable pain and could not feel her legs and feet, she still retained the confidence and resilience of a top-ranked athlete: a fast runner and a champion tennis player. Despite her shock and anger at being paralyzed, a deep part of her personal mindset believed that there must be a way to transcend, to fly above her problems. Her scribblings in the margins of a used paperback of Isaac Asimov's *I, Robot* describe the adventures of the flying woman:

> It was April 1925, Eighty degrees with a nice breeze. She was twenty years old. Hovering above in the dark, she looked down at her village with disgust. But she didn't fly off just yet [*Broken*, 83].

With those first words, her life changed irrevocably. She took her first creative writing class in the fall of her sophomore year. Eventually these scribblings led to the Windseeker stories, and were incorporated in her short story, "How Inyang Got Her Wings." The 2013 introduction to the story concludes with these lines: "She shed no tears. Instead, she looked ahead. To the east. The sun was rising" (61). The rising sun symbolizes a chance for a better life, less controlled by societal values that keep women in their place. Like Octavia Butler before her, Okorafor is deeply interested in autonomy and agency. Also, like Butler, she sees autonomy, suffering, and freedom to be interconnected. It is not possible to earn one's freedom and get away unscathed.

Coming of Age as a Cyborg

Physical pain and abuse are major threads that run throughout her fiction, as are prosthetic enhancement. It is important to note that Okorafor's physical recovery was not complete. More often than not, her YA and adult literary tapestries are also interwoven with pain and metaphysical horror. "The House of Deformities," her first short story written in 1993 in her first creative writing class,[4] may psychologically relate to the shock of her paralysis and slow recovery. At the time the story was written, she was still using a cane and learning to deal with disability. Based on an experience she and her sisters had while traveling in Nigeria, the story depicts a backyard outhouse that may or may not open into an underworld of horrific suffering ("House," 38–51). She considers this magic realist tale "nine parts nonfiction and one part fantasy" (*Broken*, 75). The story tells how Grace, one of four sisters, mentions a newspaper article about evil men practicing black magic by "kidnapping children and cutting off their heads and using their brains and grinding up their skulls for powerful potions"; when a child disappears, there is always "a man wearing a black hat hanging around" (*Kabu*, 41–42). In westerns, comic books, and anime, black hats often indicate villains. When the girls dare each other to go behind a restaurant, they enter a surreal backyard with an outhouse surrounded by "foul-smelling air" and buzzing insects (49). Because a man wearing a black hat is sitting nearby, the girls imagine that the lost children have been buried beneath the outhouse and that their "high-pitched" voices can be heard from far beneath the pit (49). Within Nigerian culture, blackness, particularly at night, is linked to ancient supernatural dangers that exist outside of Christian belief systems.[5] Thus, in her first story, Okorafor has established a premise that the "blue-eyed blond Jesus" of Christianity is ineffectual against Africa's old animistic religions[6] (41). This theme continues throughout her work and is particularly explored in *Lagoon*. Black Hat will reappear in *Akata Witch*.

Decades later she continues to have difficulty with balance and foot control, requiring accommodation when driving her specially designed Tesla. Thus, her work can be read as a dynamic between ableism and disability, what disability scholarship identifies as (dis)ability, referring to the "overarching social system of bodily and mental norms that includes ability and disability" (Schalk, 6). All of her young protagonists suffer from *bodymind*[7] issues that initially mark and separate them from others, and despite their ability to attain agency by overcoming marginalization through fight and flight, pain, both physical and emotional, continues to be a driving force.[8] More often than not transcendence depends on personal resilience and problem solving combined with advanced technology.

High technology is one of the defining aspects of Afro and Africanfuturism. In "Tumaki," a coming-of-age sequel[9] to *Shadow Speaker*, Dikéogu, the viewpoint character, carries a multi-purpose e-legba computer. It connects him to a hip-hop radio station, offers a Hausa/Arabic dictionary, and includes a copy of *My Cyborg Manifesto* (219). It is an obvious reference to Donna Haraway's essay "A Cyborg Manifesto,"[10] 1983, a pioneering essay that rejects rigid boundaries between human, animal and machine. As demonstrated throughout her fiction, Okorafor has been profoundly influenced by Haraway's cyborg. James and Mendlesohn, 2003, assert that Haraway reconceptualizes the cyborg in a way that has fused "the sf imagination" (122). Certainly, the word "My" in "My Cyborg Manifesto" is personally significant to Okorafor. She describes herself as a cultural shapeshifter ("Organic," 278). Her Twitter account describes her as a "naijiamerican professor and rudimentary cyborg." The word "rudimentary" implies that with her spinal surgery, complexly braided hair, large dark-rimmed glasses, and various net connections, she sees herself involved in a process of becoming increasingly assisted and augmented. This process is also reflected in her fiction with the cyborg interface between flesh and prosthetic machine providing the impetus for her 2021 novella, *Noor*.[11]

Now, with a master's degree in Journalism from Michigan State and a PhD in English and creative writing from the University of Illinois–Chicago, Okorafor uses memory and research to create sensory rich stories about a past, present and future Africa that is endangered by environmental collapse, violence, corruption, and bigotry, but also contains powerful seeds for rebirth and renewal. This Africa connects to Ginen, a fantastic parallel world with vast, intentionally unexplored areas. The intersection of magical and mundane worlds and the liminal lands between provides literary space for Okorafor's thought experiments regarding young women who challenge hierarchical power structures and the cultural traditions that hinder their moral development and self-actualization.

For the most part, Okorafor negates the influence of Europeans and Americans. The residents of Ginen "look like black Africans" because the first people chose not to explore the rest of their planet and kept their population small and sustainable (*Shadow*, 216). In his article "Beyond the History We Know," Dewitt Kilgore suggests that she uses "the realist strategies of modern science fiction and fantasy" to create a post-apocalyptic Africa where "a powerful place for women is essential to its endurance" (122–123). What we consider traditionally feminine endeavors such as homemaking, gardening, neighborhood markets, and small businesses are essential to the ecological and economic structure of Ginen's communities, making women as important as men. In Ginen, computers are botanical and biological, and magic is powerful enough to slip dimensional bonds and leak into the mundane world. As her series progresses, Earth and Ginen begin to merge in various ways, causing dissonance and political unrest as well as enrichment. Magical metahuman talents such as windseeking, shape shifting, and shadow speaking emerge causing personal and interpersonal conflict. These challenges incite action for heroic journeys in which powerful alliances are created and moral choices are made that effect long-term cultural change.

Brown's Tools for Using Speculative Fiction to Explore Social Justice

Throughout her work, Okorafor champions social justice issues. In "Outro," the conclusion to the *Octavia's Brood* anthology of Butler-inspired short stories, Adrienne Maree Brown provides three tools for writing fiction that explores current social justice issues through a speculative lens. The first tool is to write visionary fiction that evinces "power inequalities" and is "conscious of identity and intersecting identities" by centering on those who have been marginalized. With her emphasis on the *Bildungsroman* adventures of young women from minority cultures, Okorafor's work clearly represents this focus; for instance, microaggression, bullying and harassment for being different (or just for being) incites action in her early short story "Amphibious Green,"[12] 2001, and her novels *Zahrah the Windseeker*, 2005; *Shadow Speaker*, 2007; *Who Fears Death*, 2010; *Akata Witch*, 2011; *Binti*, 2015; *Akata Warrior*, 2018, and *Noor*, 2021.

Brown's second tool is "emergence" which looks at providing strategies for change that is *not* "linear, hierarchical," "outcome oriented" or developed in ways that cannot adapt to changing conditions (*Brood*, 280). Emergence describes the way "complex systems and patterns" can arise out of a multiplicity of "relatively simple interactions" (*Emergent*, 3). Brown also suggests that an emergent strategy reflects "intentional change," a way to grow "our capacity to embody the just and liberated world we long for" (*Emergent*, 3). It respects and valorizes natural change as emphasized in Butler's *Parable of the Sower* where the protagonist, Lauren Olamina's, mantra has become an SF cultural icon: "All that you touch, you change. All that you change, changes you. The only lasting truth is change" (1).

Beginning with her early short stories, Okorafor consistently depicts emergent magic that challenges the status quo, using talent and collaboration to move young women into positions powerful enough to effect change. Butler's mantra is particularly reflected in the second chapter of *Shadow Speaker* which begins "History is change" (10). Okorafor's ideal for change is primarily that of natural sustainable emergence although *Who Fears Death* and *Lagoon* explore radical deconstruction and the nature of personal sacrifice while *The Book of Phoenix*, 2016, provides a near-future cautionary tale where out-of-control techno-capitalist totalitarian evil is met with revolutionary violence. As *Shadow Speaker* demonstrates, change that is based on coercion cannot last (see Chapter 1, "Exploring the Empire of Girls' Moral Development"), but change that is built on an understanding of nature and human nature has a chance (see Chapter 7: "Degrowth in the Anthropocene Worlds of Le Guin and Okorafor"). Throughout her fiction, there is a thread of utopian progression that can be observed, a "place that was too far ever to get to. But maybe someday it would not be" (*Who*, 286), a future that may become accessible through an intentional process of what Dowdall, 2013, calls "willed transformation" (186). She concludes that "The potential of the future lies within us, in the present, and must be activated in a determined and meaningful way" (186). This determined intentionality is present in all of Okorafor's writing. Finally, emergence requires inclusion of the unexpected and uncontrollable. Although preparedness is essential (and all her protagonists prepare for their journeys), there is always an aspect of life that cannot be controlled, either because of chaotic natural forces or unfathomable divine design. Throughout her work, a mythopoetic evolving Trickster tendency exists that is always at work generating serendipitous events and unexpected answers; therein lies a sly cosmic humor. Okorafor implies that we must expect the unexpected and then hold onto our roots when it appears.

Brown's final tool is networking. Recent Afro/Africanfuturist fiction has flowered in part due to effective mentorship and communication. Samuel R. Delany, whose apocalyptic landscapes defined early Afrofuturist fiction, began publishing in 1962, and in 1970, Delany mentored Octavia Butler at Clarion. Since 1968, Clarion has consistently provided literary midwifery for the genre. Butler's first story was workshopped at Clarion and published in 1971. Later, Butler taught at Clarion, and in 1995 she was the recipient of the prestigious McArthur Genius Award. After Butler died in 2006, WisCon's Carl Brandon Society[13] established a Clarion scholarship for writers of color in her name. Afrofuturist writer Steven Barnes first published in 1974 and later became a teacher at Clarion. Many of Okorafor's early stories were written in 2000 and workshopped at the 2001 Clarion SF Writers Workshop in Lansing, Michigan: "The Future (Re-) Envisioned." Prior to Clarion, many of Okorafor's university instructors had tried to warn her away from genre fiction, but after Clarion, she found her place in a vibrant community. Barnes was one of her teachers; another was WisCon Motherboard member Pat Murphy who encouraged connection with WisCon's diverse community of feminists.[14]

In 2001 Okorafor received the Hurston/Wright literary award for her short story "Amphibious Green," and her children's book *Long Juju Man* was the 2007–08 winner of the Macmillan Writer's Prize for Africa. In 2008, her YA novel, *Zahrah the Windseeker*, was awarded the Wole Soyinka Prize for Literature in Africa.[15]

At the beginning of the 21st Century, writers of color were drawing considerable critical attention, and many of them were women. Part of this attention was due to WisCon's role as literary doula. In 2005, its Carl Brandon Society initiated two $1000 awards, the Parallax for speculative work by writers of color and the Kindred for works that examine race, ethnicity and culture. In 2007, Okorafor won the Parallax Award for *Shadow Speaker,* and in 2010, she received the Kindred for *Who Fears Death.* In 2010, she was a WisCon guest of honor along with writer/editor Mary Anne Mohanraj. Her other awards include the 2011 World Fantasy Award for *Who Fears Death,* the 2012 Black Excellence Award for Outstanding Achievement in Literature; the 2016 Nebula Award for *Binti,* the 2016 Children's Africana Book Award for Best Book for Young Readers for *Chicken in the Kitchen,* and the 2016 Hugo Award for Best Novella for *Binti.* In 2018, *Akata Warrior* won both the Hugo[16] Lodestar Award and the Locus Award for Best Young Adult Novel. In 2020 her graphic novel *LaGuardia* won Hugo and Eisner awards. In 2021, she accepted a position at Arizona State University as a Professor of Practice in its Interplanetary Initiative and College of Liberal Arts and Sciences.

Okorafor is, however, more than the sum of her education and awards. Beyond the novel ideas and intimate details of domestic life depicted in her stories is a vision that aligns her with Marxism and radical feminism. This vision recognizes that changing the social system from within is not possible; there must be radical change that comes from outside the system. In 1977, three years after Okorafor was born, the Combahee River Collective of Black feminists wrote:

> We realize that the liberation of all oppressed peoples necessitates the destruction of the political-economic systems of capitalism and imperialism as well as patriarchy. We are socialists because we believe that work must be organized for the collective benefit of those who do the work and create the products, and not for the profit of the bosses [Taylor, 19–20].

Overall, Okorafor's fiction demonstrates radical destruction as well as creative rebuilding, revealing a past and future history that moves beyond the status quo of capitalism and kyriarchy to envision a far future world where human equality actually becomes possible and material resources are equitably available. The winds of success lift her onward.

1

Exploring the Empire of Girls' Moral Development

> "A new world has just been born and we are on the brink of war" (*Shadow*, 41).
>
> "Yes, Nkolika," [Queen] Jaa countered. "It's known that shadow speakers are born with leadership potential, and she's your daughter. She's strong. I want her to come with me" (*Shadow*, 41).
>
> "—*walkabout*. She read it over and over, her sense of foreboding increasing every time she read it" (*Shadow*, 43).

Throughout her fiction Okorafor struggles with various postcolonial questions regarding how a girl can maintain healthy relationships within family and community while confronting aspects of what theologian Elisabeth Schlüsser Fiorenza identifies as a kyriarchal power structure—a structure that links sexist and bullying behaviors with war, environmental degradation and political corruption.

Postcolonialism refers to the multidimensional and frequently disputatious critical study of the colonial process and the corresponding struggle of indigenous peoples for independence and identity after the breakdown of empire. Empire is usually defined as a multi-ethnic or multinational state with political and/or military dominion over populations that are culturally and ethnically distinct from the imperial (ruling) ethnic group and its culture. The leadership of the imperial group is traditionally seen as male, and the role of the female within an imperialist structure is essentially male defined, whether she be a queen or a milkmaid. Within an empire, feminism, if it exists at all, exists in reaction to male-defined hierarchical structures; however, within a postcolonial context, feminism attempts wider self-definition. In *Wisdom Ways*, 2001, Fiorenza explains that "postcolonial feminism intensifies arguments" and points to "the impact of Western imperialism and colonialism on wo/men's[1] self-identity and social-cultural location. It investigates the interconnection between empire and the discourse of empire and wrestles with the question of how to negotiate solidarity and alliances between different social formations and interests" (62–63).

In Okorafor's YA novels—*Zahrah the Windseeker*, 2005; *The Shadow Speaker*, 2007; and *Akata Witch*, 2011, *Akata Warrior*, 2017, and the *Binti* trilogy 2015-2018[2]—her secondary world of Ginen[3] offers a social system in which the influence of the Western World and Global North has been subtracted, along with the unconsciously racialized settings and characters that have been central in science fiction and fantasy, but patriarchy and hierarchy remain.[4] *Ginen*, an early unpublished novel, unwinds from an initial vision "of a bloated overly patriarchal chief" and his "miserable wives," a vision that eventually informs *The Shadow Speaker* (Jones). Thus, the entire series of stories and novels appears to be a reaction to the negative excesses of patriarchy (among other things). The stories function as ways to explore and decolonize visible and invisible patriarchal constructs.[5]

Despite its patriarchal roots, the role of women in Ginen is changing, partly because an ancient magic is working to undermine traditional hierarchical structures and partly because women are becoming more educated and politically aware.[6] As evidenced in *Shadow Speaker*, women are learning linguistic terminology for identifying the nature of their suppression. Through magical talents such as flight, shape-changing and communication with ancestral spirits, the balance of power has slowly begun to shift toward gender equality. A girl's moral development then exists as an empire to be mapped. Deserts and jungles can be explored because times are changing, and girls are gaining physical abilities and psychological permissions that previously belonged only to boys. Thus, girls with enhanced abilities can make a difference on a larger community scale if they succeed in their quests.

These novels can be seen as *Bildungsroman*,[7] coming-of-age stories that psychologically and geographically intersect in various ways, describing an Africa that does and does not exist. They follow a similar pattern in which young adult protagonists, who do not fit well in their communities, overcome negative self-images, learn to channel anger, establish alliances, gain agency, and begin to understand sexual intimacy. Although her first YA novels focus on early adolescence (possibly responding to her daughter's age at the time of the writing), *Akata Warrior* and the *Binti* trilogy focus on older adolescence when girls begin to understand who they are as women.[8] This chapter examines Okorafor's depiction of early adolescence in *Zahrah*, *Shadow Speaker*, and *Akata Witch*, in which girl protagonists are just beginning to explore the world outside their families.

Okorafor's approach to girl development will be viewed via historically evolving work by Erik Erikson, Lawrence Kohlberg, Carol Gilligan, and Mary Field Belenky, and also in relation to Carol Pearson's hero archetypes and Maureen Murdock's Heroine Journeys Project, which explores life-affirming alternatives to the hero's journey as originally explicated by Joseph Campbell.

The protagonists of Okorafor's YA novels have physical appearances that identify them as Other and set them up to be bullied and excluded. From Piaget onward, psychologists have found that children as young as four recognize physical differences between themselves and others. During adolescence, awareness of difficult-to-change physical characteristics such as eye shape, skin color and hair texture can lead to self-abnegation and toxic despair. Adolescent girls, in particular, are negatively affected by *lookism*, social judgments made on the basis of how well or poorly they meet cultural standards for physical attractiveness. Thirteen-year-old Zahrah has vine-entwined, thick dada hair. Bullies at her school call her "vine head," "snake lady," "swamp witch" and "freak" (3). They identify her as a "witch" and ask her about her "juju" (259). Zahrah's menarche corresponds with a sudden ability to levitate, a secret that further isolates her. Eventually she learns that she is a windseeker, an identity that carries a fair amount of cultural baggage. In *The Shadow Speaker,* Ejii has golden eyes like a cat. Her half brothers and sisters call her "goat girl," and when she is eight, her father makes plans to marry her to his cook's son, a lazy man three times her age who is known for harassing women (16). In early adolescence, she begins hearing voices. Sunny, the viewpoint character of *Akata Witch*, is an albino[9] and an excellent writer; her classmates call her *akata*, which means "foreign-born" or "bush animal" (11). Once again, bigotry identifies difference as being less than human. Although people of Caucasian ancestry no longer live in Africa,[10] the effects of colonization remain in its ecology, tradition, and discarded technology. The stigma of having light skin and other Caucasian characteristics remains. Ejii and Sunny suffer because of it. As cultural outsiders,[11] Okorafor's protagonists are well positioned to question cultural values, a step that is essential in moral development. As her novels progress, the words used in taunting are gradually repositioned as positive attributes.

When Okorafor suggests that "fantasy is the most accurate way of describing reality," she implies that sensitive subjects like girl development are easier to tackle when they are clothed in the fantastic (Organic, 277). As Lacey, 2014, remarks, "The fantastic is a form of intervention into narrative that often accompanies other types of interventions that relate directly to social control" (174). The cultural challenge to control women has historically been a major social issue. Perhaps it is easier to analyze the damage that traditional culture can do to girls when the story is defamiliarized by setting it in a faraway and magical world. Magical intervention of reality interrupts the status quo of the mundane and allows a new set of rules to emerge. Writers like Ursula K. Le Guin, Suzi McKee Charnas, Margaret Atwood, Octavia Butler, N.K. Jemisin, Nalo Hopkinson, and Nisi Shawl have all used fantasy when exploring sexism and cultural attempts to control girls' agency. Okorafor's characters may have magical talent, but their self-esteem problems are clearly endemic in our world, and they provide impetus, the emotional drive trains for Okorafor's plot vehicles.

According to pioneering research such as Gilligan's *A Different Voice*, 1982, and Belenky et al. in *Women's Ways of Knowing*, 1986, young women's moral development often begins in a state of silence in which perceived morality depends on obedience—and they lack awareness of their own rights to opinions and separate selves. In the absence of internal voices, they rely upon external authority for direction (24). Okorafor's hero journeys[12] start at home when her characters first find their own voices in order to evaluate and question unfairness in their cultures. Zahrah recognizes cultural prejudices against individuals like herself who are deemed to be "rebellious" because of their dada hair. She also sees differences between how boys and girls are treated: "I was a girl, and only boys and men were supposed to be rebellious. Girls were supposed to be soft, quiet and pleasant[13]" (vii). In *Akata Witch*, Sunny is acutely aware that her father does not want her because she is different: "Sometimes I hated my father. Sometimes I felt he hated me, too. I couldn't help that I wasn't the son he wanted or the pretty daughter he'd have accepted instead" (5). *The Shadow Speaker* begins with Ejii writing an essay about her father's violent death. When encouraged by a friend to write a lighter version for the teacher, Ejii responds, "It's what happened and where I fit into it. ... I don't care if she's shocked or doesn't understand. The truth hurts and doesn't always make sense" (8). The protagonists in these novels tend to be close to their mothers. Their fathers represent their cultures and range from benign parental acceptance in Zahrah's case to genuinely evil in Ejii's case. Having a distant or abusive father is a clear detriment to a girl's moral development. In *Reviving Ophelia: Saving the Selves of Adolescent Girls*, clinical psychologist Mary Pipher writes:

> Fathers ... have great power to do harm. If they act as socializing agents for the culture, they can crush their daughters' spirits. Rigid fathers limit their daughters' dreams. Sexist fathers teach their daughters that their value lies in pleasing men [117].

Despite cultural and paternal opposition, Okorafor's protagonists passionately believe in the truth of their own experiences as well as their right to give voice to them. Their explorations evolve from a desire to know where they fit within their own worlds.

Heroine Journeys and Moral Development

Joseph Campbell has written that a traditional hero journey includes separation, initiation, trials of valor, and a return to community, but Campbell did not believe that heroic quests were appropriate for girls. When in 1981 psychologist Maureen Murdock asked him why, he replied, "In the whole mythological tradition the woman is *there*," implying that women were already "at the place people" (i.e., men) were "trying to get to" (Murdock, 2). By this, Campbell implied that women function as a kind of prize for men who succeed in their quests. He then suggested that young women shouldn't "get messed up with the notion of being pseudo-male" (2). In *The Heroine's Journey*, 1990, Murdock reports being "stunned," finding his response "deeply unsatisfying" and recognizing the need for women to have heroic agency in a quest to heal the "physical and emotional damage" that traditional patriarchal cultures have inflicted on women (1–2). She then began to explore ways to help women become "whole" human beings rather than simply tokens of men's success (3).

Okorafor recognizes the right for young women to be the heroes of their own stories and structures her YA novels to reflect how girls can go on adventures that seek solutions to problems in a dangerous world. Her protagonists leave home because of an urgent danger to their communities. They enter the wilderness to learn self-esteem and agency while fighting archetypal dragon-like monsters. Her viewpoint characters all have a powerful calling to travel and explore, but all are initially conflicted about leaving. The social contracts of caring keep them from leaving until departure becomes an emotional necessity. Their journeys require physical and cognitive exertion as well as moral decision-making. Ejii calls it "walkabout," borrowing a term from Australian aborigines (43). Lacking reliable maps, they follow the song lines of an intuitive process, discovering their own weaknesses and emerging strengths and learning to work through them. In order to do this, each must learn traditionally masculine skills because their feminine skillsets are insufficient for what they must do (Murdock, 5). To succeed they must endure a series of trials, facing dangerous confrontations that cause them to question their worthiness, but courage in the face of danger earns them tools to use as they continue with their quests. Overall, their successful hero journeys allow them to challenge ignorance, fear, and anger and to take the first steps toward a better understanding of adult responsibilities.

According to Kohlberg, 1976, conventional morality can be seen as the shared values that sustain relationships and community (Gilligan, 73). Kohlberg describes this as "being good" (*Philosophy*, 410). In sociological terms, the "being good" empire includes an unconscious acceptance of local traditions, shared norms, mores and attitudes; contingent is a set of local beliefs regarding how girls should behave. At a conventional level of morality, authority is internalized and remains unquestioned. Moral reasoning is based on the norms of the group to which the person belongs. Initially children want to be good to gain approval from those around them, but a change occurs when children become aware of differences in the fairness of social values. They begin to recognize issues of rights and inequities in caring and justice. In her essay, "Cultural Imperatives and Diversity in Ways of Knowing," Nancy Rule Goldberger reveals that cultural minorities seem "to develop a way of knowing that seems to evolve through their marginality and life struggles." For them, "Knowledge and knowing are [...] a matter of strategy and survival" (356).

Although selfishness is typical of toddler behavior, brain development causes an increasing awareness of others that can lead to empathy and the recognition of mutual cooperation and generosity. At Kohlberg's Conventional level of morality, individuals don't see morality as a system that can be questioned or that can vary from community to community (*Philosophy*, 410). Recognizing a social perspective regarding how others think indicates a transition to a higher level of moral development that eventually becomes Post Conventional and then Principled levels, at which moral interaction is driven by "Social Contract" instead of unquestioned internalized rules (411). Okorafor depicts her YA protagonists at a place where they are beginning their transition to Post Conventional moral development. They have a gut-level recognition that the social norms of their communities are narrow-minded and prejudicial, but initially they don't know other possibilities. Furthermore, their behavior is routinely affected by cascading adolescent emotions that initially hamper their decision-making. Zahrah reflects on her earlier ignorance, "If I only knew what I know now" (11). Central to these novels is learning to redirect powerful emotions such as anger and fear so that higher levels of confidence and moral development are attained.[14] Gilligan's pioneering work, *In a Different Voice*, calls this entering the "moral domain" and points out that such exploration can eventually lead to moral insight characterized by a "fusion of justice and love" (*Voice*, 173).[15]

Gilligan describes adolescence as a time of "epistemological crisis" (vii). By this, she means that adolescents experience considerable cognitive dissonance regarding cultural beliefs and personal truth. Throughout her novels, Okorafor explores how adolescents interrogate local mores.

Their development takes place at the edges of the moral empire in that place where a lack of adult guidance necessitates a leap of faith and a trust in their own decision-making processes. In each case, her girl protagonists make decisions that counter prevalent cultural mores regarding what girls are supposed to do. In *Zahrah* and *Shadow Speaker*, Okorafor sends them into a wilderness alone, but in *Akata Witch*, Sunny must cross a bridge of unknown magical terrors in order to reach the village of Leopard Knocks. These girls leave home to fulfill their destinies and protect communities that have alienated them. The desire to leave home is initially based on a partial awareness that a change of personal geography will help in resolving their epistemological crises. Entering a jungle or desert becomes symbolic of exploring the unknown psychological terrain of adulthood, and in each case, a change in local community culture also occurs because they succeed in their quests.

In "The Way of the Wilderness," Steven Harper remarks that "wilderness begins teaching as soon as we plan the adventure. We must decide what to take with us and what to leave behind" (188). In each case, Okorafor's YA protagonists have support from their friends as they prepare to enter the unknown.[16] In *Shadow Speaker*, the ghost of a tree says, "A friend is like a source of water during a long voyage. Without water, you'll wither away" (205). Throughout Okorafor's fiction, her young protagonists need to distance themselves from their birth families, overcome isolation, and create new, interdependent alliances. Distancing from parental and societal authority is an essential part of adolescent hero journeys and *Bildungsroman*. Identity formation depends upon it[17] (*Mapping*, 145). In *Mapping the Moral Domain*, Gilligan calls preparation for developmental journeys as "exit" strategies and explains that "seeing the possibility of leaving, the adolescent may become freer in speaking, more willing to take perspective and voice opinions that diverge from accepted family truths" (143). Since preparing to enter the wilderness alone is seen as a masculine endeavor, Murdock calls this stage of the heroine's journey "Identification with the masculine and gathering of allies" (Murdock, 1990, 5). In *Akata Witch*, the guide book, *Fast Facts for Free Agents*, explains that "home will never be the same once you know what you are. Your whole life will change" (18).

Okorafor's use of believable adolescent voices that contemplate separation is part of what makes her narratives so compelling: her protagonists know they could die. Zahrah and her friend Dari join hands as they enter the Borderlands of the Greeny Jungle for the first time. Their only guidance is a *Field Guide*, a computer digi-book that works only intermittently.[18] Their innocent joining of hands is a symbolic first step of emotional and sexual intimacy. Zahrah describes it as a "shift," a change in how she sees the world: "At the time it reminded me of what a snake must feel like after it has shed its first skin—wet, new, strong and vulnerable.... Different" (97).[19]

Jungian psychologist Carol S. Pearson, 1986, describes six hero archetypes that identify developmental stages in life's journey as individuals learn resilience, develop independence, achieve goals, sacrifice for the sake of others, find happiness, and change the world: the Innocent, the Orphan, the Wanderer, the Warrior, the Magician, and the Altruist (*Hero Within*, 18). Innocents want the world to stay as it is, but in order to grow, they must risk losing the safety of home and face an adventurous world. Orphans lose innocence when they experience mistreatment. To move onward, Orphans must recognize that suffering, pain, scarcity, and death are inevitable parts of life (41). Although they have families, Okorafor's protagonists often begin their journeys as emotional Orphans. Because of the bigotry and abuse they have experienced, they believe that their worlds must be changed. To do this, they must leave home. Wanderers' identities come from being outsiders (67). They are seekers who believe that knowledge, meaning and treasure can be found in the unknown world. Warriors learn courage, fortitude, self-discipline, and endurance. Zahrah and Dari's desire to venture into the unknown exemplifies the Wanderer archetype. It typifies most of Okorafor's protagonists. Pearson explains:

> Consciously taking one's journey, setting out to confront the unknown, marks the beginning of life lived on a new level. For one thing, the Wanderer makes the radical assertion that life is not primarily suffering; it is an adventure [65].

In her memoir, *Broken Places and Outer Spaces,* Okorafor remarks, "There is often a sentiment that we must remain new, unscathed, unscarred, but in order to do this, you must never leave home, never experience, never risk or be harmed, and thus never grow" (9). The growth to which Okorafor alludes comes from making mistakes, learning from them, and carrying the scars. Pearson explains that "maturity comes with that curious mixture of taking responsibility for our prior choices while being as imaginative as possible in finding ways to continue our journeys" (79). That crux of responsibility and creative engagement is at the center of Okorafor's YA fiction.

Later Zahrah becomes brave enough to enter the Forbidden Greeny Jungle alone, even though it terrifies her, risking her own life to save Dari's after he is bitten by a war snake.[20] Her journey indicates the need to fulfill an essential social contract. During her journey, she gains unusual allies including a village of intelligent gorillas who become extended family for her.[21] In *Shadow Speaker,* when disembodied voices tell Ejii that she must cross the desert and attend a Golden[22] Meeting to keep a war from starting, she leaves without her mother's permission, but Ejii's friends Arif and Sammy help her prepare for her journey. She heeds a social contract that has been initiated by the voices of her ancestors.

Akata Witch describes how Sunny and her friends Chichi, Sasha, and Orlu must work together to stop the wizard Black Hat Otokoto from murdering children to increase his own magical power. Black Hat's crime is a fantastic retelling of the Botswanan *dipheko* superstition: murdering bright, innocent children so that their parts can be used as *muti* or medicine to ensure the success of a business deal (Beukes, *Slipping*, 239). The coven must keep their mission a secret from their parents. Their social contract is with their Leopard Society[23] sorcerer/mentors, leaders who are desperate enough to endanger their students' innocent lives to stop a serial killer whose depth of corruption seems to confound them.[24] In working together to do what adults cannot or will not do, Okorafor's protagonists take the first steps toward intimacy. Intimacy is built on knowing, talk and trust, and they cannot do what they need to do without these essential behaviors. Gilligan explains, "The concept of identity expands to include the experience of interconnection. The moral domain is similarly enlarged by the inclusion of responsibility and care in relationships" (*Voice*, 173).

Okorafor's protagonists' magical talents develop through study, practice and interaction with difficult environments. They gain what *Women's Ways of Knowing* calls "procedural knowledge," in other words, skills regarding how to do things. They know that truth is not always "immediately accessible" and that "knowing requires careful observation and analysis" (Belenky, 94). Truth often lies hidden beneath the surface of daily life. Magic may be an unfamiliar realm of knowledge for them, but rules can be learned for using magic safely.[25] Although their departures from parental authority may seem impulsive, their goals are exemplary.[26] They have typically idealistic adolescent passion for correcting societal inequalities. Ejii asserts, "That above all things, we do what has to be done to make things better … [so] that we leave this earth having made it better than when we came to it" (*Shadow*, 210).

Mentors, Guides and Initiations

Because their goals are worthy, Okorafor's protagonists earn the help of unusual spiritual guides, doorkeepers who provide emotional support and essential, often secret information. In many cases, these are embodiments of the Yoruba trickster god Legba ("Organic," 280). Although they take different forms,[27] these mentors can be identified by liminal qualities that allow them to mediate between worlds, not only between the mystical and the mundane but also between conflicting human factions. For instance, after a hard day at school, when Zahrah simply wants to be left alone, Papa Grip, chief of her village, provides emotional intervention:

> Papa Grip knew how to mediate between groups. He knew how to organize and make sure everyone was happy. He wove peace and understanding with his bare hands [3].

The word "wove" is significant. He takes the concepts of "peace and understanding" and makes them concrete with his "bare hands." In a symbolic sense, Papa Grip helps Zahrah get a "grip" on her life when all she wants to do is hide under her bed covers. His idiosyncratic dress identifies him as something beyond a local politician, and his words are those of a shaman who works to heal the mind as well as the body:

> "Mark my words there is nothing wrong with being different."
> ..."Look at me. I am the chief of Kirki, but I like to wear pink caftans!" he exclaimed, dancing over to the large mirror that spanned my bedroom wall. He danced in a circle, his bright pink clothing billowing out as he twirled [4].

Grip's intervention with Zahrah is an example of shamanic healing. As Leslie Gray explains in "Shamanic Counseling and Ecopsychology," "shamanism seeks to change human behavior" not through extended talk therapy but "through techniques of personal empowerment" (174). Through Grip's eccentric support, Zahrah is freed to begin her hero quest.

Belenky observes that during adolescence many young women regard "words as *central* to the knowing process" (36). Language is essential to moral development, but the physical aspect of gender performance is important as well. Grip represents moral maturity and universal wisdom—what Kohlberg calls "agape," borrowing the Greco-Christian term for the highest form of charity (*Philosophy*, 351). Grip has gone beyond the challenges of lower-level moral development and is dedicated to the good of community. His choice of clothing indicates ability to transcend gender. He offers Zahrah verbal approval and self-acceptance; then initiates her for her journey of self-realization. When Zahrah listens to him she "receives" knowledge that is essential to her moral development; she is at an age when what respected authorities say is very important.

Later, without parental permission, Zahrah enters the Dark Market and meets a new mentor. Nsibidi, who is also dada, is able to give Zahrah insight into her windseeker identity: "People will always be difficult when it comes to being dada" ... "We're more connected to the trees and plants" ... "And the sky. We are born with memories of long ago" (35). Nsibidi's name refers to a system of artistically fluid, ideographic script native to what is now southeastern Nigeria.[28] Her windseeking parents appear in Okorafor's earlier short stories. Through Nsibidi, Zahrah receives a

1. Exploring the Empire of Girls' Moral Development 27

secret personal history that also reinforces her gut-level recognition of her own otherness. Thus, Okorafor creates a lineage based on shared personal qualities.

Akata Witch describes how a giant named Anatov initiates 12-year-old Sunny so that she can enter the spirit world with her friends Chichi, Orlu, and Sasha. Sunny's initiation is a near-death experience in which she is pulled through a hut's dirt floor and into the "sweet-smelling" earth below (49):

> As she was pulled downward, Sunny's mouth filled with earth. She couldn't scream! The earth was pushing its way down her throat, pulling up her eyelids, scratching her eyeballs, grating her clothes away, and pressing at her skin. It got worse [49].

The filling of the mouth with "sweet" earth is significant. The Heroine's Journey Project describes this type of initiation as a "descent to the Goddess" (Murdock, 5). As in the Persephone myth, it implies death and rebirth along with a corresponding change in voice and an increased sense of identity and inner awareness. This rite of passage also symbolizes a rebirth of community.[29] Unlike the male initiations described in Bruce Lincoln's *Emerging from the Chrysalis*, Sunny's loss of clothing and temporary nakedness does not imply shame and negative status but validation of her worth for herself alone (Lincoln, 103–104).[30] After passing her initiation, she is allowed to enter the spirit world village of Leopard Knocks where she can buy valuable items such as charms, knives, and guidebooks, boons awarded for her courage.

In *The Shadow Speaker*,[31] Ejii is mentored by Mazi[32] Godwin,[33] a Shadow Speaker born in "what used to be the United States" (51). When Ejii begins to hear shadowy ancestral voices, they tell her to take her mother's mysterious egg stone and follow Jaa,[34] the Red Queen, to Ginen. These voices are symbolic of the inner voices that adolescents must recognize in order to achieve moral development. Simone Weil defines morality as a paradoxical "silence in which one can hear the unheard voices" (Gilligan, 151). The egg's womb shape suggests womanpower. When Ejii leaves, she wears a silver amulet with symbols that tell the story of her family back to her "great-great-great-grandparents" (87).[35] In the desert, she meets Dikéogu, a soul mate, whose fits of uncontrolled rain-making have caused him to be shamed and sold into slavery by his embarrassed celebrity parents.[36] The storms he creates and gradually learns to control may represent hormone-enhanced adolescent emotions.

Together, Ejii and Dikéogu earn the respect of sand-dune cats and meet the shape-changing Desert Magician who goads them into being more assertive, "Wah, Wah. I know you're a girl, but get some balls. Stand up tall and say, 'Give it to me or I'll kill you with my bare hands'" (151).

The Desert Magician, who purports to be "older than time," is actually an incarnation of Legba ("Organic", 281). His trickster/mentorship actively encourages assertiveness and aggression in opposition to the norms for girls in Ejii's culture (147). Murdock asserts that healing the "wounded masculine" (the damage a repressive culture does to girls' natural adventurousness) and integrating "masculine and feminine" are essential parts of the Heroine's Journey (5). Because he is really a *jinn* with access to future knowledge, he knows that soon the two friends will have to fight for their lives in a masculine-defined space, what Campbell calls "The Road of Trials" (5). Like Papa Grip, the Magician's shiny metallic pink tent, perfectly manicured toenails and long red caftan mark him as being beyond gender, a doorkeeper of secret knowledge. Through newfound friendship and mentoring, Okorafor's YA protagonists create webs of friendship that begin "a chronicle of expanding connection" (Gilligan, 156).[37] This expanding connection provides them with the confidence to assert their own powers and make decisions that may be contrary to the dictates of their mentors.

The Anger Advantage vs. Depression and Rage

The authors of *Women's Ways of Knowing* remark that "conventional feminine goodness means being voiceless as well as selfless" (167). Okorafor's protagonists are essentially good, but they are not conventional. What stands out about young women's moral development in these novels is that Okorafor allows her protagonists to be angry. They believe they have the right to speak out against authorities. Because of the prejudice they experience, her protagonists are angry for good reason. Their intelligence allows them to see all the inequities in the world as well as in adults' commonplace, imperialistic attitudes toward children. According to Gilligan, many women perceive aggression as "a fracture of human connection" (43), but Okorafor's protagonists live in communities where emotional connection is breaking down (at least for them). In such circumstances, the ability to speak up and fight back gives them an edge in the battles for survival that will follow. In *Akata Witch*, Sunny is an aggressive soccer player with the gumption to talk back to her elders when she thinks they are wrong. She confronts the scholar Taiwo:

> "You expect us to capture this Black Hat, who is like you, one of the people who has passed the highest level of juju ability? That's—I mean no disrespect—" She paused, the irritation that had been brewing in her for weeks suddenly flaring bright. She felt used. "That's insane! And I am beginning to

know how you people think! You'll just find some other kids to do it if we're all murdered" [170].[38]

Here Sunny is demonstrating the beginnings of what Kohlberg and Gilligan call Post Conventional logic, the ability to recognize conventional logic patterns and weigh the ramifications of certain lines of thought and behaviors,[39] thereby reaching what Gilligan describes as a "reconstructed moral understanding" (Gilligan, 73, 102). Despite mistrusting her mentors, Sunny is willing to continue training for their mission because ultimately it is right to risk her own life to rid the world of a great evil. It is an act of conscience rather than conformity.

Socially acknowledged anger eventually can be channeled and used in the development of a healthy self-esteem. *Shadow Speaker's* 14-year-old Ejii gets the better of her half-brother, Fadio, in a fight after he threatens her, calling her a "curse" and a "mistake"—and calling her mother a "whore" (27–28). They punch, scratch, and bite:

> It was not a children's fight. This was a fight poisoned with hate and resentment that was older than both Ejii and Fadio combined [28].

The long-term "hate and resentment" mentioned above are the result of the jealousy, scapegoating and rigid cultural stereotyping endemic in the community. When bullying is accepted and even condoned, discrimination can lead to anger that constantly simmers beneath the surface of daily life. Left unacknowledged, anger can become toxic; however, young women who are allowed to recognize and express anger have an edge when it comes to survival. Okorafor explains:

> Ejii is a bit more hardcore than Zahrah. I especially learned this when she gets into a fist fight [...]. This was not an innocent fight. It was absolutely vicious. And getting into it, Ejii was throwing off all the cultural baggage that normally should have stopped her from doing such a thing. She eventually, by her own choice, goes out into a dangerous environment—in this case a post-apocalyptic Sahara Desert. She, too, possesses deep, deep courage [Ottinger, np].

Correspondingly, determination gives Ejii an advantage when, with only her talking camel for protection, she goes into the desert knowing full well she might die.

Initially, all three protagonists are pressured by their cultures to mask their intelligence and independence. Pipher suggests that "bright and sensitive girls are most at risk for problems [....]. They have the mental equipment to pick up our cultural ambivalence about women, and yet don't have the emotional and social skills to handle this information" (43). Pipher explains that

> girls have four general ways in which they can react to the cultural pressures

to abandon the self. They can conform, withdraw, be depressed or get angry. Whether girls feel depression or anger is a matter of attribution—those who blame themselves feel depressed, while those who blame others feel angry [43].

Depression is anger turned inward. It occurs when individuals feel that solving their problems has become hopeless. Gloria Steinem, 1992, has written that

> the little girl who is discouraged from strength and exploring, or is punished for willfulness and praised for assuming a docility and smiling sweetness she doesn't feel, often begins to construct a "deflated" self, which results in the mostly female problem of depression [67].

All three protagonists initially hover on the edge of depression regarding the social stigmatization they experience. They internalize external events and blame themselves, a response common in adolescent girls. For instance, Zahrah says, "I'd given up on being accepted and just wanted to be left alone. I wanted to blend in so I wouldn't be noticed. But my hair wouldn't let me" (xii). Social withdrawal is a primary indicator of oncoming depression. In *Akata Witch*, Sunny is shamed that her grandmother Ozoemena was Black Hat Otokoto's mentor before he was corrupted by his own power:

> And it was Otokoto who killed your grandmother in a ritual to steal her abilities as he stole her life. You want to know why he is powerful? All you need to look at is who your grandmother *was* and who Otokoto was before he became the infamous Black Hat [190–191].

Like Ejii, whose father was an evil wizard/politician, Sunny has an inherited guilt that becomes her responsibility through no fault of her own. She feels "unworthy, childish, stupid and worthless" because her grandmother taught "a murderous psychopath" (191). Such responsibility can be crushing to an adolescent. Okorafor's narratives follow her girl protagonists as they learn their own strengths and free themselves to be angry with purpose.

In his groundbreaking book, *Childhood and Society*, Erikson maintains that initiative is the healthy response to guilt. It is characterized by "the quality of undertaking planning and 'attacking' a task for the sake of being active and on the move" (255). In other words, initiative means doing something rather than nothing when obstacles are experienced. Fortunately, Okorafor's YA protagonists have the energy and moral resilience to overcome temporary despair and move on.[40] They are able to see their imperfect selves as "good enough" and seek out experiences of "authentic relationship or responsive engagement with others" (Gilligan, *Mapping*, xxxiii).

Although anger can energize critical thinking, destructive rage can evolve from an anger that has been suppressed. Rage can be differentiated from anger because rage becomes difficult to control. In *Zahrah*, rage is symbolized by the Elgort, the terrifying creature that Zahrah must overcome in order to save Dari:

> "Elgorts are raging with life, angry with it. The rage is transferred from mother to baby through the egg. For some reason, or so it says in this book, the extracted yolk reverses the effects of the [war snake] venom" [115].

Thus, in Okorafor's universe, "angry" life can overcome "poison," but acquiring it can be lethal. In *Shadow Speaker*, Okorafor personifies rage as the Aejej,[41] a giant desert storm: its whirlwinds combine rage and confusion with sand and air, sounding "like a thousand women screaming. They may be mad, but they are also very conscious. Too conscious. It's human life they seek to destroy ..." (98). The Aejej is like a bully that chooses victims who have been physically and socially isolated. It is pertinent that it sounds like "women screaming." Fortunately, Ejii is able to recognize its danger and find shelter from it.

Rage is also personified in *Akata Witch* by the screaming masquerades that, similar to the Aejej, rise out of the angry earth. As they spin, they emit "a deep thick sound that seemed to come from another place" (325). Likewise, when individuals experience rage it seems to come from a place beyond the self. On a symbolic level, all of these raging creatures represent a dangerous part of the self that must be redirected in order to reach moral maturity. Okorafor examines rage further in YA novels *Ikenga* and *Remote Control*.

Identity in Okorafor's Moral Universe

Erikson, 1963, has asserted that adolescents develop identity between the ages of twelve and eighteen. He explains that in adolescence, identity is the opposite of role confusion (261). Because of their physical differences from the norm, Okorafor's protagonists develop a sense of identity early.[42] That they are not crushed by their otherness is primarily due to good parenting. Because their mothers have nurtured them, they have good instincts and a sense of enduring personal connection that is able to sustain them during crises. To survive the Greeny Jungle, Zahrah combines what she has learned in the *Field Guide* with stress management techniques she has learned through her parents' care. When she is attacked by a carnivorous gourd, she remembers that it responds to music and begins singing "A World of Our Own" by the Seekers (1965), a song her mother sang to her when she was very young: "Close the Door, Light the light ..." (190). The Seekers' name, the title of the song, and the lyrics all fit Zahrah's predicament. When the plant listens, it stops pulling her into its mouth, and she is able to unwind herself and escape. Her survival requires a combination of book learning and independent critical thinking.[43] She takes an important step in moral development when she concludes that "you could never fully trust anything you read or that was told to you. Human beings simply weren't perfect" (194–5). Belenky calls the ability to recognize and accept human imperfection "separate knowing" (102).

Women's Ways of Knowing asserts that "separate knowing" is characterized by the ability to evaluate and doubt at a time when critical thinking has become autonomous, while "connected knowing" is problem-solving characterized by accessing others' relevant knowledge in order to better understand the world. The latter strategy is strongly associated with an epistemological process that can differentiate young women's problem-solving techniques from young men's because it is interactive and informed by an ethic of care (101–102, 113).[44] Okorafor's protagonists need both separate and connected knowing in order to develop dependable cognitive structures regarding which sources they can trust and which beliefs they can hold onto.

Facing Death

Facing the reality of death is an essential part of the Hero Journey. Zahrah's nemesis, the birdlike Elgort, is described as "living death"; Sunny's masquerades embody immortal evil; and Ejii is caught in the middle of a civil war ((*Zahrah*, 232). Erikson suggests that "healthy children will not fear life if their elders have integrity enough not to fear death" (*Childhood*, 269). However, throughout her fiction, Okorafor depicts adult authority with questionable integrity and a physical and moral powerlessness that can reflect a "spiritual aridity" (Murdock, 5). Her protagonists feel betrayed, experience a loss of innocence, and are pushed to the edge of despair when they realize they must fight against evil on their own.

Exploring the Matter of Ginen

In *Akata Witch*, the children of the Oha coven are being taught to be warriors as well as magicians. Psychologist Carol Pearson asserts that "warriors strive to channel their feelings as a resource for their power, enabling them to perform the action" (101). They claim their power and

1. Exploring the Empire of Girls' Moral Development 33

assert their identity in the world (102). The Magician archetype helps people take responsibility for existential choice. Pearson explains:

> We step into the point of power inside our own magic circles when we act on the knowledge that we have as much right as does anyone else to determine the world's future. There are many possible outcomes for humankind. Nothing is locked in. We cast our vote for the world we prefer for ourselves and our children with every choice we make every day [184].

Pearson concludes that Magicians frequently add "a revolutionary consciousness to the hero's journey." They say: "When things are not all right, I will stand and be counted" (186). When Okorafor's young protagonists make conscious decisions not to be afraid all the time, they set themselves on a course of disciplined study and practice that sometimes necessitates entering danger in order to motivate change.[45]

Historically, myths of glory are created to support the goodness of belonging to a certain locality. They are intended to rally support for wars against outsiders. In classic fantasies, there is, however, an underlying evil in the world that is sapping its vitality from within that makes utopia approachable but ultimately unreachable—the matter of Britain, the rotten in Denmark, the death-denying wizards in Earthsea. In C. S. Lewis's *The Lion, the Witch, and the Wardrobe*, for instance, the children enter the world of the wardrobe and symbolically encounter the evils of World War II. Good triumphs over evil, but at a cost, and the war between good and evil is never completely won.

The underlying evil is a tragic flaw that undermines moral leadership. It has to do with the addictive nature of success and the corruption of power. Sometimes this flaw is seen as sexual, but the corruption of moral leadership is deeper and more complex than adultery. Rather, powerful people begin to believe that they are above the rules they set for others. In *Akata Witch*, Leopard community moral leadership is embedded and self-protective. Mentor behavior seems morally ambiguous especially since the leadership previously lost other covens to Otokoto, the sorcerer they once educated. Black Hat Otokota is kidnapping and killing children to increase his own magical power, but the teachers who taught him don't endanger themselves to arrest him, nor do they seek out the moral flaws in the system of education that allowed Black Hat to reach a pinnacle of power. Instead, they choose to sacrifice children to stop him from sacrificing children. Sunny, the child of Lamb parents, must learn to act as a Leopard to be strong enough to confront this evil.

The system of punishment that supports Leopard power structure has been corrupted by a callous attitude toward suffering. Apprentices are whipped for using magic without permission or locked in a demon-haunted basement overnight. Like generals and Congressmen who start wars, Leopard leadership wants to eliminate evil without looking at themselves first, fully believing that innocent blood needs to be shed to stop the loss of innocent blood. Otokoto's crimes then can be seen as "only one leg of the centipede and the centipede's head is yet to emerge" (*Akata Witch*, 306). His crimes symbolize a much greater emerging evil to come, an evil that may include nuclear holocaust (307). Okorafor further explores the deadly combination of hierarchy, intelligence and arrogance in *Akata Warrior*, *Who Fears Death* and *The Book of Phoenix*.

A complicating issue is that, although suffering, pain, and death are real, the children are being taught a cultural myth of possible transcendence. Death is not entirely final (which may explain the apparent imperialistic callousness of Leopard leadership regarding the lives of the children). As part of their training, Sunny and her friends are brought by their mentors to watch two wrestlers, Saye and Miknikstic, fight to the death for the Zuma International Wrestling Championship. Both wrestlers have metahuman characteristics. After an amputation caused by an auto accident, Saye has an actual phantom arm that can be used for fighting. Miknikstic can see the near future (233). When Miknikstic is killed, he becomes a guardian angel, sprouts brown-feathered wings and leaps into the sky like a rocket while the audience applauds (239).[46] Learning to fight as a team is considered essential to the coven's education. Perhaps this shared experience is intended to convince them that if they fight honorably, risk themselves fully, and fail, there will be a possibility of transformation in the afterlife.

Throughout Okorafor's fiction, the corruption of leadership seems to be directly linked to various resource-destructive industries—clear-cutting forests, mining for precious metals, and particularly production of petroleum. Black Hat Otokota owns a gas station. When Sunny, Chichi, Sasha and Orlu first confront him, he seems to be winning: the children he kidnapped appear to be dead, and he may have killed Sasha with a bolt of red lightning from his juju knife (321), but Chichi counters with her own spell:

> "*I am a princess of Nimm!*" Chichi screamed, standing at the front entrance. She slashed her knife from left to right and shouted some words in Efik....
> "This charm is from Sunny's grandmother Ozoemena, to my mother, to you, Black Hat Otokoto." [...] "Past sins will always come back to haunt you," Chichi said[47] [321–322].

In her introduction to *School Girls: Young Women, Self Esteem and the Confidence Gap*, Peggy Orenstein asserts:

> Girls with healthy self-esteem have an appropriate sense of their potential,

their competence, and their innate value as individuals. They feel a sense of entitlement: license to take up space in the world, a right to be heard and to express a full spectrum of human emotions [xix].

Chichi's courage comes out of her awareness of a spiritual lineage of strong women and of what they have taught her about right and wrong. Later, when Sunny must face Ekwensu, the evil masquerade Otokoto has summoned, her thoughts are of her family as she recognizes and comes to terms with her own mortality: "She knew how the world would end. She knew that someday she would die. She knew that her family would live on if she died right now" (326). Thus, Sunny's moral thinking demonstrates a maturity and universal awareness unexpected in adolescents her age.

Ginen, the Gaia Hypothesis and Ecofeminism

The freedom of the wilderness allows young women to reclaim their agency and assertiveness, but Okorafor has created another way toward healing women's wounded bodies by revisioning the body of Africa as sacred and feminine.[48] Her protagonists must cross the Sahara's hot, dry wounded masculine desert to reach the fertile and feminine neighborhoods of Ooni Kingdom of Ginen, which has been constructed based on ecofeminist principles[49]—what is described in *Akata Witch* as "a logical blueprint for a new order" (307–308).

An alternative to a post-apocalyptic, increasingly dystopian Earth, Ginen can be seen as a living ecosystem similar to Lynn Margulis's "Gaia Hypothesis," 1974. Margulis, a microbiologist, maintains that everything on earth is complex, self-regulating system symbolized by the body of the Goddess. In Ginen, oil flowing through pipelines is pink rather than black (Spider, 113). There is a liminal, vagina-like quality to Ginen's tree houses,[50] in which interior space is an extension of the exterior world, a controlled, protected atmosphere in which people live comfortably with symbiotic creatures like grasshoppers and geckos[51]:

> Ejii looked more closely at the plant wall. It was so green. She could see the individual green bits inside each cell, chloroplasts she thought.... She pressed her finger against the wall. It was tough but not like wood or concrete. It felt alive. (*Shadow*, 252)

Even the name "Ginen" suggests the Greek word for "woman," as in "gynecology."[52] City buildings are enormous flowering trees, reflecting a sacred wholeness. Like a giant Georgia O'Keeffe flower painting, the Ooni Palace Tower stands 4,188 feet high and is topped by "a giant blue flower with purple petals" (*Zahrah*, ix–x). "The skyline glowed as if the buildings themselves were made of a luminous material.... Thick green-brown vines linked every building like veins and arteries" (*Shadow*, 241). Furthermore, the word Ooni sounds like *yoni*, the Sanskrit word for womb, or like the orgasmic "O" of "Molly Bloom's Soliloquy," the circle being a womb symbol.

Exploring Ginen's exterior spaces is a way for Okorafor's protagonists to discover a universal feminine that exists in opposition to masculine patriarchy, venture capitalism, and militarism. All of her girl heroes have experienced abuse from these forces. Gilligan's "Exit-Voice Dilemmas in Adolescent Development" suggests that feelings of powerlessness and vulnerability can cause young people to envision a world that offers protection.

> This ideal or utopian vision, laid out along the coordinates of justice and care, depicts a world where self and other will be treated as of equal worth, where, despite differences in power, things will be fair, a world where everyone will be included, where no one will be left alone or hurt [144].

As originally envisioned, Ginen is clearly not a utopia where everyone is happy and equal but a utopia-in-progress where humans behave no better or worse than they do in our contemporary world. It is, however, a world with potential to be a fairer and more ecologically balanced than our own.

The paternal/masculinist gaze views natural resources (including women) as there for the taking, but ecofeminism seeks to live within nature and restore equality and agency to women and other living creatures. Fiorenza explains that

> not just sentient life but all living things, present and future, form one sacred Body, and that in the evolutionary creative process we all become manifestations of it. The feminine is not strictly identified with the female but it is an energy or power in all living things [62].

In "The Spirit of the Goddess," Betty Rozak explains that "Ecofeminism" is an ecological awareness that "rejects the outmoded dualism of the scientific mode in favor of a sense of unity with all living things, for a world view that emphasizes process, dynamic change, and the interrelatedness of all beings" (295). Okorafor's Ginen is informed by ecofeminist awareness of the Chief's five miserable wives but then establishes a *yin/yang* balance of ecological progressiveness. In the Ooni Kingdom of Ginen, bioluminescent light bulbs grow in pots and can be transplanted into the walls of a house *(Zahrah*, 23). Computers grow from CPU seeds and pull energy from the sun and from body heat. A vine wrapped around users' ears allows these very personal computers to read brain waves (*Zahrah*, 38).

1. Exploring the Empire of Girls' Moral Development

Okorafor describes Ooni as a clean place—the "perfect marriage between the ancient and the modern, nature and technology" ("Organic," 281). For instance, very sophisticated technology exists, but to lower the carbon footprint, transportation is mostly by foot. Nevertheless, like many real-world marriages, this marriage has some serious problems to overcome. Biological warfare has linked Earth and Ginen, creating chaos where the dimensions intersect. After the Peace Bomb, described at the beginning of *Shadow Speaker* as a magical "green wave" that destroys nuclear weapons and smells like "thousands of types of flowers," an increasing number of people are born with metahuman skills; windseekers can learn to fly, faders can disappear, and speakers can communicate with animals or ghosts (56). The Peace Bomb was created by the Grand Bois, an enviro-militant group, to level the field of human aggression, but once loosed, a domino effect of collapsing natural laws begins to undermine the boundaries between alternate realities. Magic no longer looms underneath things. "It floods everything" (56). (Like the phrase "Good Old Boys," the term "Grand Bois" is a sly attack on patriarchal assumptions that they know best, bringing to mind immature boys of all ages heedlessly playing with chemicals in the basement.) Okorafor intimates:

> I love the idea of the earth rebelling. I love the idea of human beings having no clue WTF is going on. I love the idea of the laws of physics going haywire. Human beings seek to control, they seek to be at the top of their self-created hierarchy, above all creatures. We're arrogant as hell even though we don't know what's going on half the time [Jones].

In *Dawn*, Octavia Butler asserts that the human fatal flaw is "a combination of hierarchy and intelligence" (*Emergent*, 6), and Okorafor adds arrogance to the genetic self-destructive cocktail. She concludes:

> In Ejii's world, one must learn to move with the earth, by its rules to survive, as opposed to forcing the earth to conform to one's own rules as we do today. This makes for a different kind of story and different kinds of characters [Jones].

Moving with the earth represents a high level of moral development; it is an indigenous concept that undermines the capitalist ethic of being able to control and own the Earth. In an ecofeminist environmental sense, it involves recognition of otherness and an awareness of the mutual care concerns that are essential in women's knowing. Poet Mary Oliver has described her own girlhood as an interaction of otherness and the environment as follows:

> ...the world's *otherness* is antidote to confusion—that standing *within* this otherness—the beauty and the mystery of the world, out in the fields or deep inside books—can re-dignify the worst-stung heart [64].

Thus, achieving balance with the natural world works in opposition to the role of confusion that Erikson describes as a threat to identity during adolescence.

Although Ginen has an ecological edge over Earth in its privileging of sustainable resources, its politics remain hierarchical and sexist. In *Shadow Speaker*, Ooni's Chief Ette tells Ejii that her talents are wasted because "femininity is the destroyer of greatness" (289–290). Furthermore, even with the well-meaning but impatient Queen Jaa, diplomacy is quickly abandoned for skullduggery and warmongering, causing a summit conference to turn into a deadly free-for-all. As Ejii concludes, "Even those with the best intentions can be corrupted by power" (319). Responding to this violence creates a moral dilemma for Ejii because of her desire to do no harm, even to her enemies.

Despite its patriarchal traditions, Ginen contains aspects of an intrinsic morality, a magical system in which hard intellectual work and good moral choices are immediately rewarded. This gives intellect and spirit an edge over brute force. In *Shadow Speaker*, flowers magically fall from the air when individuals demonstrate strength of character or make good choices (21, 246). In *Akata Witch*, "fist-size horseshoe-shaped rods" called *chittim* appear whenever individuals master certain magical skills (51). These rods can be used to purchase food, clothing and magical items in Leopard Knocks. Furthermore, copper is more valuable than gold because it seems to have more magical power.[53] Repositioning value attribution of a common metal over a rare one may, in fact, eventually have an impact on cultural values as a whole. Likewise, scholars and librarians are leaders (82), a revisioning that could eventually shift cultural apprehension of personal power toward learning and away from the traditional interlocking system of money, power, and physical punishment (224).

Journey and Transformation

Okorafor's protagonists do not embark on their journeys seeking treasure, but when they complete their quests, the treasure they have found is themselves. In *The Female Hero*, Pearson and Pope write:

> At the end of her quest, the female hero returns to enjoy a new community with herself, with the natural and spiritual worlds, and frequently with other people. To some degree, she also embodies the power necessary to revitalize the entire kingdom—to rid it of dragons as her classical predecessors did [260].

At the end of her journey, Zahrah has become a local celebrity, bringing local attention and perhaps acceptance to windseekers through her independent heroism. Zahrah herself has been transformed by her journey, losing her fear of heights and learning to fly. The novel concludes for Zahrah and Dari with a mutual affirmation of wanderlust and recognition of possibly unspoken hierarchical issues. Both want to learn more about Earth, and when Dari suggests they sit in their usual tree and watch the sunset, Zahrah replies, "Okay, but don't expect me to sit on the lowest branch anymore" (308).

As *Akata Witch* ends, Sunny has gained considerable self-esteem through ridding the community of a great evil. As a Free Agent, she has a new mentor, Sugar Cream, a powerful librarian whose name reflects a lighter skin color similar to hers. Sunny is learning to balance living a life divided between schooling in both the mundane and spiritual realms (perhaps similar to a writer's necessity to balance time between writing and other real word efforts). In *Shadow Speaker,* Ejii heals what Murdock defines as "the mother/daughter split" by returning to the arms of her loving mother (Murdock, 5). In a corresponding healing of community, her mother has also had her own adventures fighting for rights that were lost to patriarchal authority.

Erikson asserts that "Intimacy vs. Isolation" is the stage of development that occurs in early adulthood (263). A young person who overcomes isolation and achieves identity is ready for intimacy with others. Okorafor's young protagonists, Zahrah, Sunny, and Ejii, confirm their own gender and take the first steps toward developing healthy intimate relationships. Their comings-of-age are supported by realizing Ginen's ecological foundation of utopian feminine principles.

Conclusions About Okorafor's Empire of Adolescent Moral Development

The chorus of The Seekers' song, "World of Our Own" begins, "We'll build a world of our own that no one else can share / All our sorrows we'll leave far behind us there / And I know you will find there'll be peace of mind / When we live in a world of our own." Okorafor has built a world of her own where girls can succeed through intelligence and courage. It grew fantastically out of her own experience ("Organic," 277–279). In an interview with *Fantasy Faction,* 2013, she explains that she mines a lot from her own life, plucking "the gender, generational and non-violent cultural issues" from her own experiences and those of her Nigerian relatives and family friends (np).

As a third-wave feminist, Okorafor believes that fighting for women's rights must be ongoing. From her real-life experience in Africa and

America, she developed the idea of Ginen as a thought experiment, a place to fight against the invisible interlocking empire of predatory capitalism, bigotry and prejudice—a hierarchical cognitive mindset as Hairston describes it: "Invisible, taken for granted, running constantly in the background, normal is the default setting for the empire of the mind" ("Dismantling," np).

At the end of her YA novels, it is apparent that Okorafor's protagonists have resolved important issues of identity and role confusion. They are aware that "all knowledge is constructed and the knower is an intimate part of the known" (Belenky, 137). They integrate feelings and care into their decisions, and they are able to share knowledge to achieve goals. Their initial explorations of the moral domain have ended in success; they have challenged various kyriarchal power structures and won. The triumph of their moral development is that the protagonists and their friends have successfully taken care of each other at the risk of their own lives. They are, however, still young. They are still in process of becoming who they will be as adults. The independence, autonomy and generativity of adult work are yet to come. Although they have gained insight into the social contracts of adulthood, they still lack the emotional stability of morally developed adults. Their exploration of intimacy has just begun, but it has begun in a world that has become a little better because of their efforts. Furthermore, they have consciously explored how a feminine-inspired ecology is a far better choice than the ecologically damaging results of kyriarchy. This is symbolized at the end of *The Shadow Speaker* when Jaa's sword sprouts a soft round end and the egg stone Ejii has carried throughout her journey hatches into an insect that burrows through dimensions of time and space to reveal a ravaged New York[54] City, on a Freudian level, a symbolic act of sex. The egg stone emblematically balances the "green egg" of the technology-destroying Peace Bomb seen above the Sahara Desert in the beginning of the novel (3). Correspondingly, the hole the egg stone creates may then provide a way for Ginen's utopian potential to infect post-apocalyptic Earth's ruined ecology with new life, nature's womb once again proving more enduring than the sword (*Shadow*, 326).

2

Watching Windseekers: Wonder, Anger, Intimacy, Independence and Transformation

> When I was born, my mother took one look at me and laughed.
> "She's ... dada," said the doctor, looking surprised.
> "I can see that," my mother replied with a smile. She took me in her arms and gently touched one of the thick clumps of hair growing from my little head. I had dadalocks, and woven inside each one of those clumps was a skinny light green vine. Contrary to what a lot of people think, these vines didn't sprout directly from my head. Instead, they were more like plants that had attached themselves to my hair as I grew inside my mother's womb [*Zahrah*, vii].

Throughout Nnedi Okorafor's fiction, flight is an evolving motif that eventually symbolizes transcendence, the ability to rise above repressive attitudes and stereotypes to become one's truest self. As a child, Okorafor dreamed of flying[1] and loved African and African American folk tales, particularly Virginia Hamilton's[2] Coretta Scott King award-winning anthology *The People Could Fly*. *Zahrah the Windseeker*, 2005, is dedicated to Hamilton, "who showed me that people could fly," and to her parents "who gave me the means to soar" (np). She concludes, "The eyes of eagles see far," an astonishingly predictive statement regarding the series of books that were to follow (np).

In "Her Pen Could Fly," Okorafor writes that she "inhaled" Hamilton's stories, especially those that describe transformation and physical flight to escape slavery (370). Slavery originally provided the backbone of capitalist production. Since slavery in America was defined by skin color, it was nearly impossible to escape. Although realists might argue that the captured slaves "flew away" by dying, Okorafor concluded that literal flight might have occurred. She cites accounts of "Flying Africans" from sources like *Drums and Shadows*, a 1940 collection of stories from the Gullah Island people: "Dey sho lef duh hoe stannin in duh fiel an dey riz right up an fly right back tuh Africa" ("Organic," 280). In a 2010 interview on *Tor.com*, Okorafor responds that she hopes readers will receive the following "takeaway" from her work:

> That Africa will be part of the future. That women can be great complex warriors. That people can fly. That sometimes leaves are not leaves. That tradition is alive and some parts of it are dead. That the end is sometimes a beginning. And that stories are powerful juju [np].

Throughout her fiction, flight, though wondrous, is often achieved as a response to horrific events. Within her universe, the ability to fly is a genetic predisposition that accompanies vine-entwined "dadalocks[3]" (tightly curled hair). There is, however, considerable difference between the depiction of flight in her young adult novels and that in her much darker adult novels and short stories. Early short stories such as "Windseekers," "Asuquo or the Winds of Harmattan" and "How Inyang Got Her Wings" connect flight with repressive patriarchal systems and the sometimes-deadly battle of the sexes that is triggered by powerful conflicting desires for intimacy, sexual attachment, and the safety of home versus freedom, independence and travel. These stories, which are included in her 2013 *Kabu-Kabu* collection, recreate a history of human and posthuman rights that parallels the pendulum swings of human racial conflict from the early slave trade through the 21st Century. Thematically, they fit together as a series of interwoven thought experiments similar to Le Guin's Earthsea Cycle and Hainish series.

One legend that particularly influenced Okorafor was the 1803 Ebo[4] landing story about a shipload of slaves who "flew away"—walked into Georgia's swampy Dunbar Creek—rather than allowing themselves to be enslaved (280). In her essay "Organic Fantasy," Okorafor mentions reading Hamilton's version of the tale. The story begins:

> They say the people could fly. Say that long ago in Africa, some of the people knew magic. And they would walk up on the air like climbin up on a gate. And they flew like blackbirds over the fields. Black shiny wings flappin against the blue up there [Hamilton, 166].

In her end notes to *The People Could Fly*, Hamilton calls the flying stories "wish fulfillment" and a secret language about running away from slavery (Hamilton, 272), but Okorafor creates a reality for "black shiny wings" that is more than metaphoric.[5]

Flying Through Feminism

Because Okorafor's Windseeker stories begin in the late 1800s, they follow the evolving issues of the struggle for women's rights and equality.

First Wave Feminism focused on suffrage and overcoming obstacles to legal equality. Okorafor's depictions of flight show a transition that follows the history of women's rights. Her short story "The Winds of Harmattan" is an African variant of a witch trial. The Harmattan is the cold, dry trade wind that blows northeasterly over West Africa from the Gulf of Guinea between the end of November and the middle of March. It blows during the dry season, which occurs during the lowest-sun months. On its passage over the Sahara, it picks up fine dust[6] and sand particles. Corresponding temperature variations create sandstorms and sometimes tornadoes, events that become important in Okorafor's later work. In this story, the Harmattan becomes a metaphor for a cooling marital relationship and the desire to escape from it. Asuquo, the fourth daughter of the chief's third wife,[7] lacks privilege but has acute senses and an untrained ability to levitate. Her seven locks of dada hair identify her as a "wind girl," a Windseeker, at a time when very few are born (121). In a storytelling diction similar to Hamilton's, Okorafor connects the decrease in Windseekers with colonization:

> There was a time when Windseekers in the skies were as common as tree frogs in the trees. Then came the centuries of the foreigners with their huge boats, sweet words, weapons and chains. After that, Windseeker sightings grew scarce ["Winds,"128].

Windseekers were a socially marked minority, but it is not clear why they disappeared. Perhaps amidst colonial repression, they found safe haven in the parallel world of Ginen. Perhaps they were murdered or sold into slavery by their own people.[8]

Since women with dada hair are considered undesirable, Asuquo's parents do not circumcise or fatten her, as is the custom with other young women when they are being prepared for marriage. She is sexually experienced when she marries and knows the flight of sexual pleasure. On their wedding night the traditional roles are reversed:

> That night Asuquo had her way with him in ways that left his body tingling and sore and helpless, though she'd have preferred to be outside under the sky [126].

Okon, her young husband, is unprepared to find her hovering horizontally above the bed on the morning after their wedding night:

> ...there was something gentle about how she floated. He could feel a soft breeze circulating around her. He sniffed. It smelled like the arid winds during Harmattan. He sneezed three times and had to wipe his nose ["Winds,"126].

Although her undamaged sexuality initially strengthens her marriage, and her abilities as gardener, herbalist, and mother of healthy sons make her the envy of people in the village, her husband and sons develop an allergy to her. This allergy is indicative of Asuquo's otherness. With her vine-entwined hair,[9] she is clearly cyborg and evolutionarily posthuman, what Okorafor identifies in "Tumaki" as meta-human[10] (*Kabu*, 225).

Asuquo[11] can be considered a budding first wave feminist. She recognizes the imbalance of power between men and women, but she lacks the education and experience to envision a life beyond the village. Although she attempts to repress her powerful, creative self to be a selfless wife and mother, doing so represents a kind of martyrdom that cannot last. Her honest sexuality is reminiscent of other rebellious first wave feminists of the time, such as George Sand (July 1, 1804–June 8, 1876), but she is hampered by the insularity of village culture. Although she is not alien, she is different; her symbiotic hybridity eludes the kind of stereotypical categorization that makes for comfortable social relationships in traditional cultures. Finally, her husband condemns her as *Amuosu*, witch, and the village elders decide to kill her in a trial by forcing her to eat a poisonous chop nut. Although Asuquo has the ability to leave, she is "weighed down by sadness" and so demoralized that she allows the murder to occur (134). She dies dreaming of her soul mate, a man in purple who flies above the clouds looking for her.

Inyang

In her groundbreaking book, *Sexual Politics*, 1969, Kate Millett identifies the First Wave of Feminism as lasting from 1830 to 1930 (91). "How Inyang Got Her Wings" is an origin story set in the 1920s, an era of increasing freedoms that provides a bridge between first and second wave feminism. Inyang, the main character, would be a contemporary of European writers such as Collette (January 28, 1873–August 3, 1954) and Anaïs Nin (February 21, 1903–January 14, 1977). She is angry about women's inequality and uses her sexuality to get back at the men in her village.[12] This story was originally conceived in 2000 as part of an unpublished novel, *The Legend of Arrö-yo*, but was not published until 2013. It begins in 1929. Inyang,[13] whose great grandmother was Asuquo's sister, is forced to leave her home in Calabar, Nigeria, forever because of her dadalocks: "All the important things about her life were decided upon her birth" (74). Her hair marks her as "bizarre, potential bad luck, and unmarriageable," so, like her great aunt, she is not ritually fattened and circumcised to prepare her for marriage (64). Like other windseekers, Inyang is tall, strong, and healthy[14]: her behavior characterizes feminist rebellion against cultural stereotypes. In *Revolution from Within*, Gloria Steinem wrote:

Rich cultures may prefer thin women and poor cultures may prefer fat ones—because as far as possessions go (and women *are* still possessions) whatever is rarest confers the most status—but all patriarchal cultures idealize, sexualize, and generally prefer weak women [217].

Whereas Asuquo dreams of romantic rescue by a man in purple, Inyang simply discards romantic love as being an impossibility (66). Angry regarding her limited circumstances, she takes pleasure in using her undamaged sexuality by having sex without emotional attachment or commitment. Already at fourteen she secretly has had five lovers, the power of sexual pleasure corresponding with a desire for flight (68). When, with menarche, her ability to unconsciously levitate develops into controlled flight through the window curtains and into the air above the village, her grandmother relates Asuquo's story as a cautionary tale and encourages her to leave before it is too late. Girls are supposed to be sweet and passive, but Inyang is willful and adventurous. Deep-seated rage attracts her to Koofrey, the chief's son, a young man with "violent tendencies" (75). When Koofrey tries to rape her, she fights him off. Her restless sexuality and rebelliousness make her a problem in the village, especially after she beds the chief: "She'd purposely played with him, vengefully so" (76). Eventually she is forced to choose exile over death. The narrator concludes, "Even a bird can't fly away from what is expected of it. Inyang would see war, death, love and life. But always it came back to a fundamental problem of tradition. And above tradition, her fixed inevitable fate" (80). The supposed inevitability of fate is a theme that runs throughout Okorafor's fiction. Overall, Inyang's story reflects the young woman's hero journey, different from the young man's because girls who leave repressive traditional families and cultures do not immediately return to community celebration following their coming-of-age quest; instead, they confront and reinterpret the myths of virginity, romantic love, and self-sacrifice and continue onward to more adventures,[15] a *manymyth* instead of a monomyth.[16]

Second Wave Feminism

In *Passages,* her 1976 bestseller, Gail Sheehy writes that traditionally boys were defined by seeking and girls by merging. "Girls could seek scholarship as long as it didn't interfere with popularity" (92). Sheehy concludes that giftedness could force a choice between marriage and mastery of an art (92). Gifted and ahead of her time, Inyang is enraged by societal attempts to make her demure, acquiescent and dependent and plunges headlong into adventure. She seeks the wind of change, fully believing that she has the right to pleasure, sexuality and independence. Early second wave feminism examined the intersecting nature of gender and culture, widening beyond women's legal rights to their rights to control their own minds and bodies. It focused on workplace equality and control of sexual reproductivity, lengthening the time that women worked outside the home before they had children and needed to balance families with careers. Despite their efforts, sexism and pay inequality persisted. The primary goal of early second wave feminism was to raise consciousness of women's rights to equality and an identity that is separate from family caregiver.

Nevertheless, second wave feminist writers like Ursula K. Le Guin initially had difficulty imagining ways that women could be truly heroic on their own and often wrote through the agency of a male perspective. In her essay, "Earthsea Revisioned," 1992, Le Guin writes, "I couldn't continue my hero-tale [*Earthsea*] until I had, as a woman and an artist, wrestled with the angels of the feminist consciousness. It took me a long time to get their blessing" (Le Guin, 984). Betty Friedan in *The Feminine Mystique,* 1963, Joanna Russ in *The Female Man,* 1975, and Erica Jong in *The Fear of Flying,* 1974, write that women of their generation were trapped by lookism and the willingness to exchange agency for the stability and protection of marriage. In the mid–20th century, the cosmetically-co-opted status quo for women required perfect bodies to attract perfect men who would then allow them to fly slipstream to self-actualization and shared goals; however, the end result for many women was exhaustion, disillusionment, and shattered dreams. Growing up, Okorafor surely saw many examples of women who were encumbered by traditionally defined relationships, lacked the equality of shared domestic chores, and tried to do too much.

Second wave feminists vowed to make things different for their daughters and to revise the messages that girls were given. These new messages included some essential freedoms: the right to be angry, the right to act assertively and fight for a cause, and the right to love boldly in ways that might conflict with community and family expectations. Thus, many third wave feminists have grown up believing that women can be heroes—strong, fit, and confident. Beginning in 1972, public schools and universities were required to support women's sports equality. The U.S. Department of Education's Title IX Amendment states that "No person in the United States shall, on the basis of sex, be excluded from participation in, be denied the benefits of, or be subjected to discrimination under any education program or activity receiving Federal financial assistance" (U.S.D.E.). Feminist writers were revising folk and fairy tales for their daughters, allowing girls to see themselves as the heroes of their own lives. Jack Zipes's critically acclaimed *Don't Bet on the Prince: Contemporary Feminist Fairy Tales in North America and England*, 1986, collected revisionist fairy tales that had been published beginning in 1970. What stands out in these tales is the freedom for young women to make their own choices and not be limited by traditional expectations. For example, Judith Viorst's "…And Then the Prince Knelt Down and Tried to Put the Glass Slipper on Cinderella's Foot," 1982, is a poem of just four lines:

> I really didn't notice that he had a funny nose.
> And he certainly looked better all dressed up in fancy clothes.
> He's not nearly as attractive as he seemed the other night.
> So I think I'll just pretend that this glass slipper feels too tight [72].

Viorst's Cinderella is not ready to get married, and that's okay. Likewise, Okorafor's protagonists all find the constraints of essentialist female behavior to be "too tight" and initially are not sure that they will ever want to wear any glass slipper[17] of total commitment to another person. Like Robert Munsch's *The Paper Bag Princess,* 1980, Okorafor grew up believing that a princess could rescue a prince from a dragon. In the decades that followed Black women writers were learning how Black feminism could inform and shape a believable Black heroine.

Black Feminism

In the '70s and '80s, when Okorafor was growing up in Chicago, the glass ceiling for women was beginning to look breakable, but Black women were still finding it very difficult to achieve equality in the workplace and described "feelings of craziness" before becoming aware of feminism, sexual politics, patriarchal rule, and what is now identified as critical race theory[18] (Taylor, 17). However, many could not identify with the apparently white middle class values of second wave feminist consciousness-raising groups. For them, there were more serious considerations—poverty, rape, marital abuse, abortion, and enforced sterilization of low-income women of color. Even today Keeanga-Yamahtta Taylor, 2017, writes that "in 80 percent of Black families, Black women are either the sole provider or the main provider," which brings into focus the economic hardship of most Black families [3].) Many Black feminists were drawn to the Marxist explorations of the Combahee River Collective, 1977, which argued "for the reorganization of society based on the needs of the most oppressed" (Taylor, 5). Finding it difficult to organize other Black women, they consciously moved away from feminism, seeking to create a movement that, after centuries of erasure, would restore and redefine Black women's role in the past, present and future. Alice Walker, whose novel *The Color Purple*, 1982, drew popular attention to violence against Black women, coined the term *womanist* in 1972. Later in her "Introduction" to *In Search of Our Mothers' Gardens: Womanist Prose*, Walker remarked that "womanist is to feminist as purple is to lavender" (xii). In other words, to be a Womanist is to have a deeper, darker, wider, more visceral feminist ideology and commitment. Thomas, 2020, suggests that Black woman writers like Toni Morrison, Gayl Jones, and Jewelle Gomez defined a "womanist aesthetic" that focused on and celebrated Black women's experience, "creating a space where ancient and modern systems coexist" (Thomas, 44). Certainly, Okorafor's Ginen is such a place.

Third Wave Feminism

Nevertheless, Okorafor seems to have more in common with present-day third wave feminists. The term third wave feminist was first introduced in *Ms.* magazine in 1992 in an essay by Rebecca Walker, Alice Walker's daughter, a 22-year-old, bisexual African American woman from Jackson, Mississippi. In response to the Anita Hill case, Walker asks the question, "Can a woman's voice, a woman's sense of self-worth and injustice challenge a structure predicated on the subjugation of our gender?" (86). She concludes with a plea to women hesitant to take action:

> Do not have sex with them. Do not break bread with them. Do not nurture them if they don't prioritize our freedom to control our bodies and our lives. // I am not a postfeminism feminist. I am the Third Wave [87].

In the introduction of *To Be Real: Telling the Truth and Changing the Face of Feminism*, Rebecca Walker asserts that third wave feminists believe that women have a right to empowerment and that empowerment can be self-defined. The notion that empowered women should "look, act, or think" in any particular way "is simply another impossible contrivance of perfect womanhood, another scripted role to perform in the name of biology and virtue" (Walker). Beginning in the late '90s popular fantastic media commonly showed girls in heroic roles such as the *Buffy the Vampire Slayer* series (1997–2003). Even Disney moved away from passive heroines with the warrior princess, *Mulan*, 1998. Throughout her fiction, Okorafor depicts powerful young women whose looks depart from the cultural norm, and although they initially struggle with being different, their beauty, grace, and heroic potential are eventually revealed.

Windseekers Exploring Attachment and Separation

As third wave feminist, Okorafor writes fiction that flies away from the frequently hesitant first steps toward self-reliance that typified early second wave feminism. Windseeking is not simply an ability, like quilt making or gardening: it is character and lifestyle. It comes with health, heightened senses and an intrinsic desire to travel. "Windseekers," 2002, the first Windseeker story to be published, explores the dynamics of inevitability, anger, sexuality, violence, and free will. Here, repeated incarnations of male and female Windseekers, Arro-yo[19] and Ruwan, meet, love, and kill each other:

> "If you let me love you, you would never leave me."
> "You'll never leave me and that's why I have to kill you" [184].

Arro-yo is from Earth, and Ruwan is from Okorafor's alternate universe, Ginen[20]; they are supposedly twin souls, but each wants to explore the world alone (186). Flight symbolizes freedom, yet each selfishly believes that only one should have that power, possibly mirroring the anger some young couples experience when balancing careers and chores or when a baby limits their freedom to work and travel. At the heart of this story is a very deep anger that defines the battle of the sexes, a solipsistic sense that in becoming part of a couple, an essential part of the self is lost that must be retrieved at all costs in order to be whole rather than half. (A more positive exploration of attachment appears in "Asunder," 2007.) Arro-yo's ability to deal with her attachment to Ruwan has been diminished by unexamined cultural norms such as the nature of female beauty: "*Women like me are never beautiful*," she thinks with obvious self-defeating resentment (181). Furthermore, because she lives in a repressive time, she knows that if she were to fly in public, she could be "plucked from the sky and tied to a tree until death came" (177).

Windseekers are drawn to living and sleeping outdoors, but that alone is not what makes windseeking so problematic. Their tendency to cause allergic reactions is both symbolic and indicative of vine-entwined hybridity.[21] Innate restlessness creates attachment and separation issues, a social disability. Generally, the ability to attach is developed in infancy when babies and mothers create a strong bond of mutual attachment (see "Motherless Monsters"). Babies who are secure in their attachment are able to begin to explore the world knowing they can return to their mothers when needed. Infant/Mother attachment ensures the long-term evolutionary continuation of human beings. It is also a pattern that repeats in adult intimate relationships. In "The Winds of Harmattan" the soul mate is identified as a *chi*, a mate mystically assigned at birth. An old woman in the market tells Asuquo, "Even your father is probably allergic to you, wind girl." She continues, "All except one. You watch for him. Don't listen to what they all say. He's your *chi*. All your kind are born with one" ("Winds," 122).

Through a psychological lens, the existence of the one perfect love is a myth. Girls who grow up with a secure attachment to their fathers recognize that lasting love is a matter of good-faith negotiation. Within the context of the series, it is easy to hypothesize that windseeking girls may attach naturally to mothers who fed and nurtured them but not to traditional fathers who believed child care to be unmanly. This distancing from their fathers can result in difficulties with long-term marital intimacy and in resolving the inevitable conflicts that will occur in every relationship. Okorafor examines traditional attitudes about sexual attraction and attachment throughout her fiction, expanding on allergy and untouchability in her later novel, *Who Fears Death*. It is clear that the concept of the one true soul mate is a conceit that her protagonists must confront and adapt to their own needs.

For Asuquo, the perfect match remains a romantic dream, but other characters in Okorafor's early stories have difficulty maintaining long-term connection even when a soul mate has been found. In *Shadow Speaker*, Ejii and Dikéogu part after their journey is completed. In "Asunder," 2007, Nourbese and her husband Osaze have been close since early childhood, so close that their hair has knitted together "like honey and root tea" (213). But after their child is born, Nourbese asks her father to separate them. At thirty years of age, she has begun to see the value of personal boundaries. In "From the Lost Diary of TreeFrog7,"[22] the protagonist and her husband explore the Forbidden Greeny Jungle, adding species information to the *Greeny Jungle Field Guide*,[23] even though she is eight months pregnant—an irresponsible time to be in the field, but the desire to explore overpowers prudency and parental responsibility. The two are not windseekers, but they exhibit windseeking personality traits such as restlessness and obsession with exploration and discovery. When resentments build up between the two, they lack ability to reconcile through discussion. Treefrog writes in her diary:

> But Morituri36[24] needs to remember that he is a human being, and that *I* am a human being, too. When he gets in his moods, he speaks to me as if I'm a piece of meat. As if I'm lower than his servant. He speaks to me the way the Ooni chief speaks to his wives. How dare him. I am carrying our child. I have done as much work as he has [np].

Okorafor, who was born in 1974, was only twenty-six when these stories were conceived at the Clarion Writers Workshop at Michigan State

University in 2000.[25] Her daughter Anyaugo was born in 2003. Five years later, her blog for October 17, 2008, announced that she had been "ecstatically divorced since February '08." The difficulties of relationship building were obviously fresh in her mind when she was writing these tales. In an interview with John Ottinger, Okorafor explains that she finds tragic stories to be important:

> Life doesn't always end happily. And the ending is not often the purpose of the story. Sometimes it's how you got there. Also, the purpose of stories shouldn't only be to opiate. There is darkness in the world, as there is light. Sometimes the light wins. And sometimes the darkness does, too [np].

Initially, Arro-yo and Ruwan are not soulmates in the Celtic sense. In Celtic spiritual tradition the soul mate is called the *anam cara*, "a soul-friend." It describes a relationship that works against dualism and allows individuals to get in touch with their own stories, their own voices, through sharing in a non-judgmental way (Murphy, n.p.). This deeply felt bond is dependent on the recognition of inner beauty and light. Soul friends create long-term relationships when they accept each other as whole persons who have the right to disagree as well as to be different and imperfect. According to Erik Erikson, 1959, achieving intimacy is the major developmental goal of young adulthood, and he suggests that intimacy depends on spontaneity, warmth, fellowship, and conversation regarding plans, wishes and expectations (101). True intimacy is not characterized by lockstep agreement. Essentially, the inability to compromise and share is a problem of moral development. To achieve moral maturity, it is necessary to accept the rights of others: to set aside selfishness and be part of something good and productive while still feeling whole. Okorafor's protagonists have the ability to find talented soul mates but their windseeking natures draw them toward dangerous adventures and cultural conflicts, activities that can strain or break even the strongest interpersonal bonds.

Kyriarchy and the Windseeker Stories

Kyriarchy is a word coined by Harvard Divinity professor Elisabeth Schüssler Fiorenza in 1992 to describe an interconnected system built around domination, oppression, and submission (210). It is an intersectional extension of patriarchy that includes various power differentials related to ableism, classism, homophobia, racism, sexism, xenophobia, and economic injustice. These invisible privileges manifest through an interlocking pyramidal structure that includes the remnants of colonialism, as well as present-day neocolonialism, militarism, the prison-industrial complex, ethnocentrism, anthropocentrism, speciesism and other forms of dominating hierarchies that make it possible for those in power to remain in power (Fiorenza, 118, 210).

Okorafor grew up in America, but because of her Nigerian heritage, she could observe, firsthand, traditional cultures in which young women were still considered property and forced into subservient roles. She also saw many ways that America was (and still is) failing young women. Sexism and sexual abuse remain common. Kyriarchy prevails in a nation that, while pretending to embrace democratic values, still criticizes women for being too smart and competitive.[26] Much of Okorafor's fiction has been written in angry response to kyriarchy. Okorafor's anger at destructive kyriarchal values is palpable, and it is a driving force throughout her work.[27] "Biafra," 2005, is a windseeker story set in 1967 during an alternate-history Biafran Civil War.[28] When Biafra declared its independence from Nigeria, a brutal war followed. The war was a direct result of colonialism in that Nigeria had not been prepared to govern itself.[29] When the British granted so-called independence to Nigeria, "false boundaries" were "strategically sketched and strictly enforced" (241): Many of the new rulers that were selected by the British "were magicians and sorcerers gone wrong" (241).

Along with the kyriarchal hierarchies of neocolonialism and the interconnected corporate/military/prison/industrial complex, Okorafor adds another hierarchy of evil magicians who have "intercourse with woman after woman, sapping their feminine lifeforce and throwing away their shriveled, sad bodies" (241). (This great evil is further explored in *Who Fears Death*.) In "Biafra," Arro-yo returns home to try to help, but it is a country ruled by political corruption, Nigerians and Biafrans are fighting each other with machetes and self-guided surface-to-air missiles.[30] Starvation, rape and murder are epidemic (242). Arro-yo decides to provide humanitarian aid wherever she can. She has reached a level of moral development that is not limited to tribal loyalties:

> She no longer heard the different languages people spoke. She didn't see the tribal markings on their cheeks or the styles of their uniforms. The people fighting all looked the same to her. She made her decisions according to who was hurt and who was doing the hurting [244].

Arro-yo provides care wherever she can until her blue dress is stained with others' blood and her own sweat (246).

World peace begins at home. As long as interpersonal greed, bigotry, prejudice, superstition and violence exist, there will always be war. It is clear, though, that in "Biafra," Arro-yo herself has changed: she has discovered a way to help others while still protecting herself. Although the issues in "Windseekers" remain unresolved, there are a few answers in Okorafor's later fiction in which the back-story implies that Arro-yo and Ruwan eventually find enough balance together to raise healthy windseeking children. Zahrah is saved and mentored by their daughter Nsibidi,[31] and Ejii, the main character of *The Shadow Speaker*, is rescued by their son, Sunrise.

Flight in Okorafor's Young Adult Novels

The bitterly competitive nature of windseeking is modified and softened in Okorafor's young adult novels. *Zahrah the Windseeker, Akata Warrior*, and the *Binti* series all depict flight in noncompetitive ways. *Zahrah* is set in the small town of Kirki in the Ooni Kingdom of Ginen, a utopia-in-progress. As is appropriate for early YA novels, Okorafor sets this novel in a gentler, more progressive community than is depicted in her earlier short stories. It is an advanced, ecological world in which biological computers are nurtured from CPU seeds to mature PCs. However, the novel still evolves from bigotry and bullying. As Zahrah explains, "Despite all our diverse knowledge and progress here in Ooni, my dada nature and hair will never be truly accepted, nowhere in the north or anywhere else in Ooni" (*Zarah*, xi). However, Nsibidi provides Zahrah with a model for self-acceptance and nearly effortless flight: "She was like a bird, except more graceful. She moved through the air with more ease" (241).

For Zahrah, learning flight takes practice and corresponds with a desire to transcend the traditional female stereotypes, as well as the limiting nature of community expectations. She begins by making small forays into the Forbidden Greeny Jungle, "a vast untamed wilderness that covers thousands of miles"[32] (xii), so that she can practice levitating without observation. The Jungle is forbidden because it is dangerous, but similar to the forest in Nathaniel Hawthorne's "Young Goodman Brown," 1835, going there is also symbolic of exploring the unconscious. Those with dada hair seem more in touch with the archetypical. Zahrah's dreamlike encounters with increasingly dangerous magical creatures allow her to develop initial flying skills as well as self-confidence and independence. Eventually, she is able to steal the unfertilized egg of the terrifying elgort in order to save her friend Dari from death. Escaping from the enraged elgort allows her to truly fly for the first time. She is relaxed, energized and ready:

The elgort's trunk touched my ear again, this time more firmly, and I knocked it away. Then, as if I had always done it, I took to the sky. Yes, I knew how to fly.

> It had been in the back of my mind for weeks. An unthinkable, unspoken possibility. But in that moment, I chose to fly, not die [260].

At the end of the novel, it appears that Zahrah's future, like that of all Windseekers, will be shaped by her wanderlust, but it is also clear that flight will not result in cutting ties with her community as it does in Okorafor's earlier short stories. She has no reason to abandon her loving and accepting parents. It also seems likely that her friend Dari, who shares her desire to explore, will "dare" to travel with her. Furthermore, her computer and shared net addresses will go with her, a concept unimaginable in Inyang's 1929, a triumph for cyborg integration.

Although the ability to fly is a genetic predisposition in Okorafor's universe, it is also clear that such posthuman talents become stronger more quickly when paired with adversity and abuse. As in Susan Palwick's 1992 novel, *Flying in Place*, psychological need to separate from emotionally unacceptable circumstances can be a post-traumatic dissociative response that manifests through flight, a psychological splitting from severe pain and hardship. Nevertheless, although Okorafor's windseekers embrace their right to be themselves, to be different, to be angry, and to be free from cultural subjugation, they cannot escape cultural conflict. Flight simply provides a reprieve or time-out to reconsider options for handling personal and political conflicts on the ground.

Black Feminism, Flight and Warrior Windseekers

When Okorafor suggests that she wants her writing to demonstrate how women could be "great complex warriors," it may be intended as inspiration to young women whose everyday lives are battles to survive. Psychologists say that individuals respond to threat with flight or fight. *Akata Witch*[33] and *Akata Warrior*[34] tell the story of Sunny Nwazue as she explores the nature of good and evil and learns to fight as part of a team. Okorafor realizes that the ability to fight back is essential for a woman in a sexist world in which physical violence and sexual abuse are common. According to the National Center on Violence Against Women in the Black Community:

- For every black woman who reports rape, at least 15 black women do not report.
- One in four black girls will be sexually abused before the age of 18.
- One in five black women are survivors of rape.
- Thirty-five percent of black women experienced some form of sexual violence during their lifetime.

- Forty to sixty percent of black women report being subjected to coercive sexual contact by age 18.
- Seventeen percent of black women experienced sexual violence other than rape by an intimate partner during their lifetime [Barlow, np].

Historian Barbara Ransby, initiator of the 1991 *African American Women in Defense of Ourselves Campaign* and a co-convenor of the 1998 Black Radical Congress, writes:

1. Never be afraid to speak truth to power.
2. In the face of racist, misogynistic threats of violence and attacks, when you have the impulse to either fight or flight, [...] Fight.
3. Always ally yourself with those on the bottom, on the margins, and at the periphery of the centers of power. And in doing so, you will land yourself at the very center of some of the most important struggles of our society and our history [Taylor, 183].

As Ransby advises, Okorafor's windseekers identify with "the periphery of the centers of power" but "land" at the center of important historical conflicts. Although Sunny is not a windseeker, she does have a definitive need to speak truth to power and do good in the world. In *Akata Warrior*, she is driven to delay the end of the world that she envisioned in the previous novel, a city ravaged by fire and flood. As she begins to learn warrior self-discipline, personal identity as a good person becomes an essential driver. Psychologist Erik Erikson's ground-breaking work on moral development explains that identity depends on "learning effective steps toward a tangible future" that is based on "whole-hearted and consistent recognition of real accomplishment" (95).

Although flight, for Sunny, is not as personally compelling as it is for windseekers, it is directly connected with a story Sunny tells the giant story-weaving spider, Udide, about being bullied when she was in grade school in Manhattan. African American sixth-grade girls bully her because she is small, light-skinned, and speaks with a slight Nigerian accent. Bullying reflects a kyriarchal attempt by those on low levels of gender, economic, educational and racial hierarchies to express their anger against someone who has a limited ability to fight back. At age eight, Sunny does not yet understand the mechanics of bigotry: "I don't know why they hated me so much. They truly hated me. I think if I had been hit by a car and was dying in the street, they'd point and laugh and watch my slow death" (337). The older girls focus on shaming difference, creating a false otherness. One of them hits Sunny hard enough for her to see stars, possibly indicating a minor concussion[35] (339):

> "Dirty African booty scratcher," Faye spat. "Filthy diseased Shaka Zulu bitch. Yo' mama probably got AIDS and yo' daddy got syphilis, that's why you came out looking like that" [*Warrior*, 339].

Sunny wonders why people of African descent call each other "dirty" (341). Through a postcolonial lens, "dirty" reflects norms for physical beauty set by the dominant white culture. Although only a third-grader, Sunny recognizes there is something not right about Faye's obsessive use of whitening creams to fade her very dark skin.

Because Sunny's true story reveals honesty, identity, and narrative power, Udide weaves Grashcoatah, a grasscutter with periwinkle eyes the color of "an alien ocean" (356). Grashcoatah is an intelligent "van-sized rodent" with a sly sense of humor and the power to become invisible (357); its allegiance must be won before it allows them to fly on its back through a timeless, other-dimensional wilderness to Osisi in Ginen. Like the giant space-faring insects in the *Shuri* series, Grashcoatah likes music, particularly hip-hop. Throughout her fiction, Okorafor uses music as an important vehicle for creating shared interspecies communication. Although Sunny is worried that her developing warrior skills are making her into a monster, flying with her friends calms her as she feels the wind blowing on her face:

> "Whatever it was, it caused the veil of sadness and doom to lift from her shoulders. And soon she, too, was in awe of the whole experience" [381].

This healthy sharing of flight's pleasure represents a kind of compensation for her earlier suffering. It stands in contrast to "Windseekers," who jealously guarded flight as a personal privilege, an immature identity that does not acknowledge shared inheritance, refuses interdependence, and feeds into the interlocking hierarchies of kyriarchal privilege. The four friends of the Oha Coven share the pleasure of flight as equals; each has talents the others respect.

In *Binti: The Night Masquerade*, flight becomes completely cyborged. Her spaceships are intelligent living creatures, genetically designed to withstand the dangers of outer space and faster-than-light travel. After Binti dies trying to mediate a truce between two warring cultures, she is reincarnated as a symbiotic extension of the infant spaceship New Fish. Her flight becomes an out-of-body experience that allows her to engage in spaceflight with pleasure as New Fish protects her from the freezing cold of absolute zero:

> I was flying forward. I flipped and flew what my body perceived as down. I laughed with glee and flew faster and stopped. The feeling of floating in space made me euphoric. It was such freedom [161].

Windseeking Conclusions

Throughout her fiction, windseeking is a response to various aspects of abuse and suppression. It is liminal by nature, an almost out-of-body experience that breaks the laws of physics. Flight makes personal freedom possible when the forces of repression are too powerful to fight. Eventually flight evolves into a way a woman warrior can comfort the afflicted and fight for others' freedom. Although originally inspired by African American mythology, Okorafor's depictions of flight all involve a cyborged evolution of increased meta-human differences from vine-entwined hair to symbiotic interconnection with a sentient spaceship. Originally imagined while Okorafor was recovering from paralysis due to a spinal surgery, human flight becomes an aspect of cyborg-enhanced freedom, a way to rise above the physical and psychological disabilities that occur in response to long-term social repression. The political rights of the cyborg are declared in "My Cyborg Manifesto" a digi-book that is carried and referenced by her protagonists. *To manifest* means to disclose what is secret, unseen, or obscure.

"My Cyborg Manifesto" evolves as a fantastic idiosyncratic response to Donna Haraway's "Cyborg Manifesto." Borrowing from Karl Marx and Friedrich Engels' *Communist Manifesto*, 1848, Haraway's groundbreaking work envisions a more fluid system of biology and gender where categories and stereotypes are broken down, and the cyborg becomes "a positive agent of historical transformation" (James and Mendlesohn, 123). Throughout her fiction, Okorafor uses her windseekers as agents of cultural transformation, combining genetic inheritance with an unexplainable component of magic.

There is, however, a dark side of flight, an unavoidable contingency of danger. In Okorafor's universe, the winds themselves have a kind of awareness, and an emotionally ill ecology can manifest in various ways, including the raging semi-sentient, bone-carrying desert sandstorm, the Aejej. "My Cyborg Manifesto" provides guidance to these manifestations (*Shadow*, 98). Thus, seeking the wind seems to be tied to the windseeker's potential for explosive rage that must be controlled and redirected in flight. Okorafor's young windseekers have experienced abuse and repression. They are angry at a world in which so much inhumanity occurs. It is an anger that begins in the distant past and extends into the future. It is an anger that transcends the bounds of a single universe, an anger that becomes more radical and dangerous as her adult stories evolve, and yet it is an anger tempered by human connection and the pleasure of flight.

3

Mythology and Sacrifice in *Who Fears Death*

> What happened when those rocks hit her head? I'm still asking that. There was light that flowed from her, a mixture of blue and green. The sand surrounding her buried body began to melt [Who, 380].

All mythology is problematic. It depends on story, and story is both truth and lie. If we look at world mythology, we see a lot of problematic behavior by powerful individuals: privileged mindsets that rationalize rapes, murders, unnecessary heroics, and impulsive solutions to problems that may in some cases be exemplary and in others, morally bereft. Mythology also depends on context and interpretation. Chasing the moneylenders out of the temple sounds exemplary, but vandalizing the shopping mall does not. It is the same story either way but dependent on viewpoint. It can be argued that stories become great myths *because* they are problematic. As well as explaining complexities like creation, great myths generate discussion due to sacrificial behavior. Having supper with friends isn't usually a matter for mythology, but having supper with friends while being betrayed (and accepting that betrayal as part of a higher plan) has a certain cachet and makes a lasting impression. In creating her adult novel *Who Fears Death*, 2010, Okorafor tells a problematic story while specifically examining the nature of sacrifice and myth. In doing so, she continues to develop a symbolic universe, entering into it both as an insider and as an outsider.

In *Stories about Stories: Fantasy and the Remaking of Myth*, 2014, Brian Attebery writes that "myths are dangerous" (11). Myths are powerful narratives that can change lives even when an audience believes that the events depicted didn't occur or occurred differently. Myths remain dangerous because their events can work in ways that are "hidden, coded," or "unconscious" (Attebery, 19). Myths often relate dynamic metamorphoses, attempting to explain cultural transitions or the confluence of traditions and civilizations. Attebery explains that "the most powerful claims [in mythic literary fantasy] have traditionally been based on blood: both the blood ties of ancestry and the blood shed as one civilization encroaches on or enslaves another" (20). Warner, 2002, describes these turning points as "moments of clash and conflict between one intellectual hegemony and another" (18). During these conflicts, pivotal individuals arise at focal points of change. When powerful individuals behave in fantastic, world-changing ways, their behavior triggers awe. Carl Jung first outlined this response in his explanation of the death and resurrection of the hero as an archetype of the collective unconscious, through which *Apokatastasis* or restitution[1] is made possible (Jung, 60). An easy example is William Butler Yeats's retelling of "Leda and the Swan" which begins:

> A sudden blow: the great wings beating still
> Above the staggering girl, her thighs caressed
> By the dark webs, her nape caught in his bill,
> He holds her helpless upon his breast [np].

The poem, told through the male gaze, suggests rapture and concludes with the suggestion of Leda gaining godly "knowledge" and "power" such that Troy was destroyed through the complex interactions of the twins she birthed as eggs: Helen, Clytemnestra, Castor, and Pollux.

Mythology, Atrocity, Kyriarchy and the Great Man

In *Who Fears Death*, Okorafor tells a similar tale, but told through women's experience, a story that begins with a rape and ends with the destruction of an army. In between are nurture, friendship, metamorphosis, the destruction of innocence, haunting and horror, finally informing a myth that becomes central to an emerging, more egalitarian culture. Onyesonwu, the protagonist of *Who Fears Death*, is the child of a rape and "born of pain" (31). Her mother, Najeeba, was raped by a techno-savvy evil sorcerer who records the rape for posterity with a tiny "coin-shaped[2]" recording device, a further dehumanizing, high-tech extension of the male gaze (19). He sings as he pulls her legs apart and speaks snarling words that Najeeba doesn't understand. After awhile, Najeeba spits and snarls right back at him. (19) No rapture here. Okorafor asserts that "women's bodies are a war zone in every culture" (Zoboi). In a 2010 interview with Mikki Kendall, she explains that the character Onyesonwu was inspired by a *Washington Post* news story "Arab Militiamen in Sudan Said to Use Rape as Weapon of Ethnic Cleansing" (np), in which a Janjaweed militiaman tells the woman he rapes, "We want to make a light baby." Okorafor "wondered what these children would be like, what would their struggles be, how would they survive, who would they grow up to be" (np).[3]

Onyesonwu's name in Igbo literally means "who fears death." Her mother chooses not to die in the desert so that her daughter can be born to fight against the evil she has experienced. Onye and her mother live in a post-apocalyptic vision of the Sudan in which the lighter-skinned Nuru have enslaved and oppressed the darker-skinned Okeke for many years before deciding to follow their *Great Book* and exterminate them for good. *The Great Book* is local mythology, accepted as truth by both Okeke and Nuru. Children read it in school. It is similar to *The New England Primer*, 1690, which begins "In Adam's fall, we sinned all." According to *The Great Book*, the goddess Ani brought the sun closer to the earth, scorching it, reducing most of Africa to desert, a mythologized event that Okorafor depicts at the end of her apocalyptic prequel, *The Book of Phoenix,* a story that begins in a New York City that is partially flooded because of anthropogenic climate change and ends in holocaust. Similar to the Jews being blamed for killing Christ, the Okeke are blamed for their technological progress, their "juju-working machines"[4] (92). "They were aggressive like the rushing rivers, forever wanting to move forward," an act of hubris that angers Ani and justifies enslavement (92).

This cultural transgression has the ring of Old Testament mythology with its various punishments for attempting to co-opt Yahweh's designated powers. According to feminist theologian Elisabeth Schlüsser Fiorenza, 2016, most of the world's major religions are based on a kyriarchal power structure with God, the Father, at the top of a hierarchy of religious officials followed by male property owners who have dominion. Everyone else is subordinate and othered based on race, gender and economic ability in "a gradated system of dominations" (8). Selfhood is defined by what one owns. In *Primate Visions*, 1989, Donna Haraway calls this "the construction of the self from the raw material of the other" (11). Most major religions traditionally hypothesize a God-given right to exploit the environment until something disastrous happens, which is then seen as an expression of God's wrath and usually blamed on someone else. Thus, patriarchal religion conveniently creates God in man's image, but even though Okorafor's goddess Ani[5] personifies the environment, both Okeke and Nuru still see her in a reflection of the male gaze. The role of woman, for example, is to do whatever it takes to make the world easier for the Great Man as depicted in the Great Book's story of Tia and Zoubeir, a tale that highlights the importance of female self-sacrifice (242–244).

Attributed to the Scottish philosopher Thomas Carlyle,[6] the Great

Man theory is a 19th-century idea that asserts that human history can be largely explained by the impact of great men, or heroes—highly influential and unique individuals who, due to their natural attributes, such as superior intellect, heroic courage, or divine inspiration, have a decisive historical effect. Jung, 1964, writes that "the universal hero myth [...] always refers to a powerful man or god-man who vanquishes evil [...] and who liberates his people from destruction and death" (68). The Great Man/Hero, however, when viewed through lenses of feminism, postcolonialism and post modernism, is revealed as a greatly sanitized Great Myth precariously balanced on a great many participatory evils and erasures.[7] In her groundbreaking essay, "The Carrier Bag Theory of Fiction," 1986, Le Guin writes that the Hero's "imperial nature and uncontrollable impulse" continually tries "to take everything over and run it while making stern decrees and laws to control his uncontrollable impulse to kill it" (168–169). This constant hierarchical restructuring can be revealed as the reason that peace never lasts. There is always another "Great Hero" with a personal vision of a better world.

Ani's theagenic dictates, as seen via the Great Book, are as capricious as the Old Testament Yahweh when he theogenically fires Sodom and Gomorrah with brimstone or dices with Satan over Job's ability to be righteous under stress. Nevertheless, we know that there is usually some essential truth behind any myth. Techno-industrial progress has environmental limits. Too much environmental heat unbalances the ecology, eventually causing catastrophic results, as we in the 21st century have recently experienced.[8] Presently, the Sahara Desert covers an area of northern Africa larger than the lower 48 United States, and in the last one hundred years, it has grown larger by over ten percent. Due to global warming, rainfall levels have decreased along the southern edge of the Sahara, causing some areas that were once semi-arid grassland to become desert (Madson, np). Furthermore, as I write this in January of 2020, much of central Australia, an area twice the size of the state of Maryland, is on fire due to a succession of exceedingly dry years. Over a billion wild animals are feared dead (Doyle, np). Scientists are warning that the earth will endure our experiment with run-amok techno-capitalism, but humans and other animals may be extinct. In her 1984 essay "The Woman Without Answers," Ursula K. Le Guin muses that myth marries contemporary history "all the time"[9] (129). It is easy to mythologize Ani's anger.

The Nature of Scapegoating

Onye's mixed-race, sand-colored skin identifies her as *Ewu*, halfbreed (25). Being Ewu is in itself a crime sufficient to earn punishment by stoning. *Ewu* literally means *goat* (Dowdall, 178): connotatively, *Ewu* suggests scapegoating, a societal unwillingness to avoid social problems by blaming the victims, part of a kyriarchal mindset despite the absence of Western colonization in Okorafor's revisioned Africa. Onye is born angry, "shrieking" even before she enters the world (24).

Desert provides the structural symbology for *Who Fears Death*. A historical rivalry for limited desert resources has escalated into a genocidal war between the Nuru and the Okeke peoples; Nuru terrorists systematically rape and impregnate Okeke women, slaughtering their husbands and burning their villages. Onye is born in the desert and figuratively represents the desert. She glows like a star. Her skin is like camel's milk, sand-colored and freckled. Her eyes resemble a desert cat's, and her hair is like a cloud of dried grass (9). She looks more like a desert spirit than either of her parents. Whenever Najeeba and Onye enter a village, Onye's light skin puts them at risk. The eastern village people do not want to face the reality of rape and murder in the west and choose to blame the victims in true kyriarchal style: the increasingly angry and agitated crowd accosts Najeeba and her *Ewu* child. "They grew bold and self-righteous. Finally, they struck" (28). Infant Onye is literally marked by violence when she is struck by a stone. In fantasy, a mark on the forehead is a common indicator of magical power. We see it in Patricia A. McKillip's *Riddle Master of Hed* and in J. K. Rowling's *Harry Potter* series.

Like other Okorafor protagonists with atypical appearances, Onye grows up tall and strong. She recognizes very early that people find her oddly beautiful but unmarriageable because of her mixed-race identity (9). Yet despite some central struggles with self-esteem, she initially develops a feisty resilience. When her appearance draws attention from the wrong kind of men, she is able to evade them because she is always quicker and knows how to scratch.[10] She has learned from desert cats (10). Her young life characterizes both the damage that has been done to the desert ecology by humans and by the desert's latent power to recover from that damage; however, within her town, belittling, blaming and shunning the innocent are easier than dealing with the prejudices and territoriality that separate the two peoples. Neither Okeke nor Nuru are innocent of prejudice: both reflect the casual bigotry of seeing physical difference as ugly. Furthermore, many individuals consider Onye to be potentially violent. Her mother, however, attempts to counter this bigotry by explaining: "People believe that *Ewu*-born eventually become violent. They think that an act of violence can only beget more violence. I know this isn't true, as you should" (31).

Onye spends her first years living in the desert with her mother until it is time for her to go to school. When they decide to make their home in the town of Jwahir, "Home of the Golden Lady," they are fortunate to find a stable homelife with Fadil, a talented blacksmith, whom Onye loves as a father. His very dark skin and his artistic bending of iron are significant symbols of the emotional protection he provides, but he dies when she is sixteen. The novel begins: "MY LIFE FELL APART WHEN I WAS SIXTEEN." Papa died. "He had such a strong heart, yet he died" (3). These lines reflect Okorafor's feelings about the death of her own father, Godwin Okorafor, a heart surgeon who died of congestive heart failure, March 14, 2004, at age 63. In his youth, Godwin had been a champion hurdler and high jumper. In a 2015 interview published in *Locus Online*, Okorafor explains that she started writing this novel while she was grieving his death[11]: "I was very angry and there was a lot flying around in my head." This angry flight of ideas was to correspond with actual flight in *Who Fears Death*.

Clitorectomy and Sexual Repression

Onye grows up feeling ashamed that she has brought "dishonor" to her mother "by existing" and scandal to her adopted father "by entering his life" (35). When Onye overhears town gossips saying that there would be "no point" for her to undergo the Eleventh Year Rite of circumcision because "no one will marry her" (9), she is angered. This kind of information can be crushing to a child's self-esteem, and strong-willed girls can be determined to prove adults wrong. Onye explains, "Humiliation and confusion were staples of my childhood. Is it a wonder that anger was never far behind?" (15).

Dowdall, 2013, describes female adolescence as "a space of resistance" (7). Although young women can use their anger to gain strength to overcome adversity, too much anger can become toxic. In *Reviving Ophelia: Saving the Selves of Adolescent Girls*, clinical psychologist Mary Pipher explains that depression is "anguish turned inward" (158). Dangerous, it can lead to poor decisions and illness. Pipher asserts that "self-mutilation can be described as psychic pain turned inward in the most physical way. Girls who are in pain deal with that by harming themselves" (158). The problem is characteristic of a "girl-piercing culture" in which girls experience considerable pressure to be perfect (Pipher, 158).

Even though her mother, Najeeba, is nurturing and wise, Onye, who desperately wants to fit in with her peers, disregards her mother's guidance and secretly undergoes a "magic" (nano)-enhanced Eleventh Year clitorectomy. The rite is intended "to align a woman's intelligence with her emotions" (74). The most respected women in Jwahir, a wise woman, a healer, a seamstress, and an architect, attend the clitorectomy, indicating the persistence of repressive traditions even though women are receiving higher education. It is an invisible system of privilege that functions in response to male dominance. Furthermore, a sexually predatory culture exists where prepubescent girls are routinely the victims of sexual pressure and abuse. Of the four girls undergoing the rite, only Onye remains sexually untouched. One of the girls, Binta, is being sexually abused by her own father. The older women are not surprised and promise protection henceforth. Afterwards, Binta's father is punished, and her family is ordered to receive counseling for three years, although it is difficult for this reader not to be skeptical since the cultural concept of femininity is constructed as an adaptation to male privilege and nothing is being done to change the kyriarchal combo of systematic scapegoating of difference paired with repressive cultural attitudes toward women.

From a Western, second-wave feminist perspective, it is difficult to imagine why educated women would not recognize the damage being done by sexually predatory male attitudes and work together to protect their daughters from having to pay with their bodies before they are ready for a fully consensual relationship, but it continues to happen. Small children can feel sexual pleasure, but sexual behavior with adults, especially adult caregivers, is confusing. Children lack the ability to make informed decisions regarding safe and unsafe touch unless they are explicitly taught. Removing the ability to feel pleasure does not solve the problem of sexual victimization—it only complicates it. Of the two sexually experienced girls in Onye's group, neither knows why sexual contact is occurring. It has not been her decision. Prior to puberty, children's affection is not sexually focused unless they have been sexualized by adults—despite the common pederast's rationalization that a child "is asking for it." Prepubescent girls and boys want healthy touch, attention, affection, and love from both their parents, and they want acceptance and admiration from their peers.

Clitorectomies damage women's ability to feel sexual pleasure, permanently otherizing them and reducing them to reproductive vessels; however, even in the 21st century, genital mutilation continues to occur in many parts of the world although it is officially illegal. In 2016, UNICEF estimated that 200 million women currently living in 30 countries—27 African countries, Indonesia, Iraq, Kurdistan, and Yemen—have undergone the procedure (UNICEF). In the Igbo language of eastern Nigeria, it is called *isa aru* or *iwu aru* ("having your bath"), as if the loss of pleasure were an act of cleansing (Abusharaf, 1). This sacrificial cleansing comes through in the text when Onye calls the clitorectomy *ana m-bobi*, believing that her parents would no longer be shamed because she is no longer unmarriageable (41). The word "sacrificial" comes from the Latin word

3. Mythology and Sacrifice in Who Fears Death 65

sacer, which means "untouchable" in the dual sense of being both holy and unclean. According to Walker, 1983, in Biblical times, menstruating and parturient women were considered "unclean" because they were "filled with a mysterious, dangerous magic" (876). "Leviticus 15" describes menstruation as a sin that separates women from God/Yahweh that requires seven days of confinement followed by the sacrifice of two turtle doves or two pigeons. Through a patriarchal lens, what is natural to being a woman is seen as sinful because men cannot control it. Although none of the world's religious texts prescribe female genital mutilation, the cultural mindset in some communities suggests that it reduces libido and helps young women resist extramarital sexual activity (World Health Organization, np). Male desire is seen as natural and expected while female desire is considered unnatural and licentious. In *Revolution from Within,* 1992, Gloria Steinem concludes that

> in many parts of the world, cutting out the clitoris is done at about eight, usually brutally and without anesthetic, as a traumatic lesson in social ownership and the excision of sexual will [...] [F]emales rarely own their own bodies [224].

In *Who Fears Death,* the circumcised girls become magically untouchable: any sexual response will cause them considerable pain,[12] but since males don't feel the pain, the protective juju only works if girls have no contact. It is important to remember that advances in technology and moral development do not necessarily go hand in hand into the future. Other writers such as Ursula K. Le Guin, in *Four Ways to Forgiveness,* have dealt with repressive coming-of-age tribal traditions in otherwise technologically advanced cultures (Lindow, 144–146). It is also important to note that history and mythology provide many examples of young women who choose to undergo painful practices such as fasting and flagellation because of heartbreaking shame.

When Onye experiences the excruciating pain of the clitorectomy, the shock briefly separates her mind from her body, and she becomes translucent like water. This physical manifestation is similar to what can occur psychologically during sexual abuse when a victim's awareness separates from the physical experience. Freud first called this *Ich-Spaltung* or "I-splitting" (Terr, 124). Onye teleports briefly into the wilderness of the spirit world, "a place of periwinkle and yellow and mostly green," briefly crossing the boundary between dimensions[13] (41). She then sees the room below her and something like the "giant eye of a jinni" (41) It is clitoris-shaped, "red and oval shaped with a white oval in the center" (41). It sizzles and hisses, snakelike, as it comes closer to her. "The red was bitter venom. The white was like the sun's worst heat" (41). Later it becomes apparent that this is her first contact with the evil sorcerer who raped her mother, an extension of his male gaze.

In a 2010 interview, Okorafor explains that this part of the novel evolved out of the fury she felt when she first heard about female genital mutilation. Her mother, Helen Okorafor, was educated as a nurse midwife in Nigeria and England. It is likely that Helen would have had first-hand knowledge of a clitorectomy's long-term damage to women's reproductive health. Nevertheless, Okorafor felt compelled to explore why a girl would willingly accept this maiming:

> The [ritual circumcision] was horribly difficult to write, mainly because it was Onyesonwu's story and therefore her actions were her own, not mine. I was just the writer, so I had to watch, with horror, this girl makes some very brave, bold, naive, guilt-riddled choices [Ottinger].

Suicidal Shame

Adolescence is a time of comparatively rapid physical change. Insecure girls often respond to their changing bodies with shame, sometimes self-cutting or becoming anorexic. Bradshaw, 1988, writes, "As a state of being, shame takes over one's whole identity. To have shame as an identity is to believe that one's being is flawed, that one is defective as a human being" (vii). Too early, Onye concludes that she should not exist because of her violent conception: "I was poison" (30). However, Onye has an inborn ability to escape when shame becomes overpowering. Like Octavia Butler's *Wild Seed*[14] (1980) protagonist, Anyanwu,[15] she is a shapeshifter. Onye, who identifies with birds, lacks the vine-entwined dadalocks of a windseeker, but flight becomes possible for her when she takes the shape of a bird. The first time it happens, she identifies with a sparrow and ends up naked in a giant iroko tree, remembering nothing of how she got there. Mwita, an older boy who is apprenticing as a healer, sees her and later becomes her friend. In the African Swahili language, Mwita means "summoner" or "the one who is calling" (*BabyNamesPedia*, np). Mwita is also Ewu and, unknown to them, initially learned magical skills from Onye's evil father, Daib, although they do not know this until much later. Talking with Mwita provides Onye with perspective and a way of establishing a new normalcy. Mwita identifies her as *Eshu*, shape changer (55). Initially, Onye's shape changing corresponds with attacks of shame that are accompanied by a vision of the red eye that connects her to her the violence of her conception (70). The depth of her despair is further expressed later in a sexually symbolic event when she is standing in her mother's garden and a giant cobra rises up to her face, triggering self-loathing so deep that she raises her hands to gouge out her own eyes: "*I am awful. I am evil. I am filth. I should not be*" (55).

The cobra personifies her underlying fears and negative self-image. Its evil messages are hypnotic, but a deep resilience allows her to resist self-harm. She shifts into the oily black body of a vulture and pecks at the snake until it slithers away; afterwards, she finds herself naked and lying next to her clothes (55). The carrion-eating vulture has been Onye's spirit animal since she first started shifting. Like a fallen angel, it exists somewhere between the sublime and the grotesque. She has internalized the negative self-denying traditions of her culture, but identifying with the vulture provides a certain stubborn resistance. Although the cobra stands for the suicidal shame that binds her, the vulture is temporarily more powerful.

Later, she learns to control her transformation although being within a bird mind is compelling and difficult to return from: "All I wanted to do was ride the wind, search out carrion[16] and not return home" (82). The power of transformation allows her the confidence needed to leave home and fight against a genocidal uprising that is being led by her father; however, Onye never fully learns how to use this talent as a warrior.

The Female Body, Forbidden Knowledge and Power

Although *Who Fears Death* was marketed as an adult novel, its structure is that of a *Bildungsroman*. Like Okorafor herself, her girl protagonists are challenged by forbidden knowledge. The greatest secret for Onye is that of the Mystic Points, a system of magical knowledge only taught to the most powerful seekers of the arcane and are "only for the pure of spirit" (66). They represent the physical world (*Uwa*), the "wilderness" of the spirit world[17] (*Mmuo*), the masquerades and other spirit beings that move between worlds (*Alusi*), and the Creator (*Okike*),[18] suggesting in the three-to-one ratio of the compass-like points that there is much more happening than what individuals perceive as the real world. Onye believes that learning the points holds the key to ridding herself of her father's evil surveillance and ending the violence between the two cultures. When she is thirteen, her friendship with Mwita provides her with incentive to seek learning from his teacher Aro, who refuses to teach her because she is a girl. Once again, menstruation is viewed as unnatural and unclean. Aro says, "You're filthy with woman blood as we speak," […] "How dare you come here in this state" (66).

Aro,[19] who is publicly known as "Aro the Worker," is actively involved in Jwahir politics, having crafted the "fairest" governmental structure Jwahir has had, although this fairness is informed by an unquestioned patriarchal system of otherizing (72). Supposedly "objective" male behavior is the pattern for normalcy in the governmental system. Mwita tells Onye, "You act like a woman. You run on emotions. You are dangerous" (74). Aro, himself, has "treated" the scalpel used in the clitorectomies so that sexual arousal would cause pain until marriage (76). An emerging recognition of unfairness in the local traditions makes it easier for Onye to continue to ask Aro to teach her his secrets, and three years later, she attacks his spirit in rage and frustration, becoming phoenix-like:

> I was searing light determined to burn his very soul from inside out. I felt his shock.
> I forgot my purpose in coming. I was tearing and clawing and burning. The smell of smoldering hair [105].

(Although she doesn't believe in Ani, Ani may be working through her without her knowing it.) She almost kills Aro, but after he recovers, he agrees to teach her since he now acknowledges her powerful untrained talent makes her "a danger to us all if I don't" (109). Aro is a complex character, and he is beginning to rethink former decisions and revise his opinion of women although he remains stuck in sexist attitudes regarding sexual responsibility as indicated when Aro confronts Onye and Mwita about their developing physical relationship:

> "I'm sorry," Mwita said.
> "Sorry for what? You're a man and this woman is yours."
> "I'm sorry," I said, looking at my feet, knowing that this was what he expected,
> "You should be" he said. "Once we start, you're to keep him off of you. If you became pregnant while still learning, you could get us all killed" [118].

Hypermasculinity and Kyriarchy

In *Who Fears Death*, Onye's mother acts as a sensible feminine balance to the Aro/arrow of masculine power, but there are things Najeeba continues to hide from her daughter. Daib, the rapist, wanted his only child to be a boy, but Najeeba used untrained magical power to create a girl. As a result, Onye was born with a complex combination of male and female qualities, a male assertiveness that sometimes results in fist fights, paired with a feminine love for colorful clothing.[20] Like the children of Holocaust survivors, Onye has inherited a toxic situation that becomes much worse as Daib stalks her through her dreams, attempting to induce her to kill herself. In Daib, Okorafor explores the handsome, charismatic evil leader who is able to influence others to join his cause. Onye can hear his laughter from miles away (70).

Kyriarchy depends on hyper-masculinity where male size, strength, loudness, rhetorical ability, and wealth are set as ideals. (Ejii's father in *Shadow Speaker* has similarly compelling, Hitler-like talents.) In *Who Fears Death*, the masculine gaze is extended through technological surveillance:

> He wore a blue caftan. He was turning to me ... all I could see were his eyes. They were red with searing white undulating centers. They merged into one giant eye [70].

As in *The Book of Phoenix*, intrusive surveillance inspires desperation. As the vision of her father becomes clearer in her mind, Onye begins to make plans to confront and destroy him.

Mythic Journey and Sacrifice

One of the drivers in Okorafor's writing is to identify her own fears and write through them. In the 2009 *Clarkesworld* interview "If It Scares You, Write It," she explains:

> If it scares you to write it, then you should definitely write it. My forthcoming novel W*ho Fears Death* is full of moments and situations that I wanted to pull back from or skip over. I didn't want to look at certain issues, practices or situations. But I knew that if I was feeling that way then that's where the good stuff was, so I faced it. When I wrote these parts, I was plagued with nightmares, felt depressed, etc., it was pretty awful [Jones, np].

Onye's journey into the western desert is a journey into fear. What differentiates Okorafor's YA novels from *Who Fears Death* is that Okorafor's YA heroines—Zahrah, Ejii, and Sunny—return home after their adventures overcoming evil while Onye does not. Okorafor is remythologizing the messianic tradition that most often ends in death and glorious transcendence. As in the *Harry Potter* series and Okorafor's *Akata Witch*, powerful elders manipulate prophesy and create young warriors to use as weapons in the mythic war between good and evil. The albino sorcerer Sola, who has been Aro's teacher, was also Daib's teacher before Daib[21] became corrupted by power and intoxicated by his power to cause unnatural violence (316). Although Sola refuses to recognize any personal responsibility for Daib's inebriation and fall into darkness, he maintains an unhealthy sexual boundary himself, bragging about Daib's mother's hips and "mischievous smile," thus implying that he has had sexual intercourse with her (and may possibly be Daib's father and Onye's grandfather) (318).

Onye recognizes the inappropriateness of Sola's comment but does not take the next step of recognizing his long-term complicity in the Okeke/Nuru conflict, which allows him to remain at the top of the sorcerers' hierarchy without endangering himself.

Although believable as a traumatized teenager, Onye is too violent to be considered saintly, but by nature of prophesy, she believes that she has been chosen to sacrifice herself to save the world. Whether she has a choice is debatable. The prophesies could be read as subtle manipulation. Onye accepts her fate and the nature of her preordained death. Later she describes fate as "cold" and "brittle," seemingly the opposite of a living body that is warm and flexible (276). The words *cold* and *brittle* could also be used to describe the ancient and incredibly powerful sorcerer Sola, a complex kyriarchal figure whose name in Yoruba means "God made my wealth" or "God has given me wealth," suggesting some kind of kyriarchal divine power when he shows Onye her own death. The power of this vision compels Onye to go out into the desert to face the mounting danger spearheaded by her evil father, leaving home without any clear plan for stopping him. She returns to the desert of her early childhood with Mwita and friends she has had since her Eleventh Year Rite, having inspired them to accompany her by showing them the violence and carnage of her conception. Throughout her journey, Onye, as sacrificial lamb, experiences various levels of untouchability, at one point giving off electrical shocks that only a small child and Mwita, her soul mate, do not feel. Throughout history, various cultures have required that sacrificial offerings not be touched. Frazer, 1922, writes that "primitive man believes that what is sacred is dangerous; it is pervaded by a sort of electrical sanctity which communicates a shock to, even if it does not kill, whatever comes in contact with it" (549). Okorafor makes this "electrical sanctity" physical as well as metaphysical.

Although Onye has powerful magic, she is still very young, and sometimes the cascading catastrophes of personal loss can cause trauma survivors to lose the will to keep trying. What follows later in the novel has much to do with the shame and anger of her unresolved issues. In *Mighty Be Our Powers*, Liberian Nobel prize winner Leymah Gbowee writes:

> When you're depressed, you get trapped inside yourself and lose the energy to take the actions that might make you feel better. You hate yourself for that. You see the suffering of others but feel incapable of helping them, and that makes you hate yourself, too. The hate makes you sadder, the sadness makes you more helpless, the helplessness fills you with more self-hate [85].

In an interview, Okorafor concludes, "There is darkness in the world, as there is light. Sometimes the light wins. And sometimes the darkness does, too" (Ottinger).

In describing Onye's dilemma, Okorafor is purposely pushing the limits of what is acceptable to her readers. Jesus Christ's death on the cross and his resurrection are acceptable to Christians partially because they are distanced in time and place. As God's favorite son, Jesus is seen as adult, schooled in scripture and ancient in his wisdom. In mainline Protestant churches, his suffering is seen as temporary compared to his eventual joyous eternal reunion with God, the Father. For many contemporary Christians, Christ's life and his moral example as a pacifist are far more important than the details of his death.

Onye, although powerful enough to heal, reincarnate the dead, and control the weather, lacks a philosophical system to support her decisions. Her moral education has been brief. She is neither scholarly nor wise. She means well but sometimes lacks empathy, often acting impulsively and/or in anger, believing others are "stupid," and she recklessly enters an impossible situation with a group of untrained, sexually entangled, often bickering young adults[22] (235). After her rages, she is overcome by remorse. It is important to note, however, that individuals in their late teens are commonly used in combat worldwide. The average age of Viet Nam era draftees was nineteen. Of those killed, 61 percent were younger than age twenty-one (Hack, np). The kidnapped Chibok schoolgirls were sixteen to eighteen years old when some of them were forced to fight in the Nigerian guerrilla war. Overall, young adults are more likely to take risks because their brain development is incomplete (Galvan, 165–167). Even though they are capable of making rational decisions, they are more likely to throw caution aside and act on emotion when they are under stress, especially when they are encouraged and accompanied by other young adults (Galvan, 174).

Remythologizing Myths Over Time Through Juju

As an alternative to kyriarchy, Okorafor offers a vision of a postcrisis utopia based on the Vah, a nomadic people who own no land and live protected in the heart of a sandstorm, carrying their plants "in large sacks of a fragrant substance" (256). The Vah, similar to Le Guin's Kesh, appear to live in harmony without sexual jealousy, women equal in power to men, children loved and cared for by all, a cultural green space in the heart of the desert. To counteract Daib's toxic influence, the Vah sorceress Ving covers Onye's hands with magical Nsibidi script. Toward the end of her time with the Vah, Onye's spirit is taken on a vision quest by a *Kponyungo*,[23] a magical fire-spitting lizard who speaks with her mother's voice. It is as if she rides the wings of the wind. Okorafor bases the Kponyungo on a mythological creature depicted in Ivory Coast funeral masks. When Onye sees Ginen, it gives her "a deep sense of hope" that "true forest" exists somewhere, even if it is very far away (287): "It meant there was life *outside* the Great Book. It was like being blessed, cleansed." (287)

Whereas clitorectomy is revealed as a corrupted version of cleansing and blessing, Ginen is revealed as a true blessing and cleansing. It is Onye's destiny to end the enslavement of her people, the subordination of women, and the scapegoating of difference by revisioning Ani, a deity she initially considers "a weak human idea" (301–302). However, when the Vah women come together to hold a "conversation" with Ani, Onye is anointed with Nsibidi script written in a mixture of menstrual blood and desert flora and fauna; it proves to be a powerful, transfiguring event. Onye's wordless "conversation" reveals that the true Ani is neither weak nor defined within the context of the male gaze.

On October 19, 2019, after much consideration, Okorafor publicly redefined herself as an Africanfuturist and Africanjujuist (blog). She identifies Africanfuturism as a subcategory of science fiction and Africanjujuism as a subcategory of fantasy (blog). In this way, she centers her work on the future and magic of Africa. Critics such as O'Connell, 2019, contend that her work is more precisely a hybridization of SF[24] and fantasy; however, Okorafor has created a system of fantastic magic (juju) that is distinctly African. When she writes that "fantasy is the most accurate way of describing reality," it becomes possible to see *Who Fears Death* as a very complex juju spell set in motion to work against kyriarchy ("Organic" 277). Although Onye's martyrdom is troubling, it does serve a purpose. The mythology of the androcentric Great Book is remythologized, erasing adulation of the Great Man and recreating an ecofeminist utopian green where it was lost to environmental apocalypse. Furthermore, it may eventually work to undermine the sorcerer hierarchy that manipulated Onye's self-sacrifice.

If violence could solve the problem of violence, the world would be a peaceful place. In the 21st century alone, the United States has executed, assassinated, or enabled the killing of a number of evil men—Saddam Hussein, December 30, 2006; Osama Bin Laden, May 2, 2011; Muammar Gaddafi, October 20, 2011; and most recently Iran's General Qassem Suleimani, January 6, 2020. However, there have always been other military leaders ready to take the place of those that have been killed. Killing Daib is not the reason that Onye's world changes: it is her rewriting of the Great Book. The rewriting is a task wherein the reader participates by seeing through various aspects of Onye's limited first-person narrative. The juju is completed by rewriting the Book in Nsibidi, the magical symbolic script of the liminal crossroads. The transformation that follows revisions a world in which Okeke, Nuru, and Ewu children can play together, a world in which windseekers, shadow speakers and rain makers can openly demonstrate their talents.[25] The invisibly rewritten Great Book causes a paradigm shift in how the world is seen, lifting the curse of the Okeke because it "never existed" (378). Dowdall suggests that "Nsibidi is a metaphor for the power of writing itself to explore alterity, to promote difference" (12). Because translations of Nsibidi are elusive, the symbols work neurologically to evoke visions of whatever is needed. Okorafor explores this throughout her work, with particular emphasis in the *Akata* books. Dowdall further asserts that

> while in dystopian literature, language is often coerced into an authoritarian system of control that ensures the interpellation and subjugation of its citizens, Okorafor's fluid symbols avoid the hegemonic reduction of meaning, encouraging an open dialectic of hope [12].

Within Okorafor's context, Nsibidi is not graffiti. It cannot be used to lie; nor can it be used to support the various unconscious lies of the patriarchy, particularly those assertions that everyone is better off within hegemonic structures headed by Great Men. Dowdall concludes that by "using Nsibidi, Okorafor writes against ontological closure and avoids the false conclusions and 'happy endings' of the Western fantasy canon" (12).

Conclusions About Myth and Remythology

Despite the promise of what is depicted as a greener afterlife in the spirit world, Onye's prolonged suffering and death, intimately experienced by readers, are angering. It feels wrong for her to be faced with such heavy moral choices when she is barely out of her teens. (The elders who created the problem should risk themselves, not watch from the sidelines as they do throughout the novel.) It feels wrong for her to doom the innocent lovechild she and Mwita have created. Like Onye herself, conception becomes a weapon to be used. Furthermore, her death is avoidable because she has the power to transform and fly away from it all. An alternate ending is offered, but it feels tacked on, like a mythic appeasement of the audience. Rather than a sacrificial lamb, she becomes a *Kponyungo*, a firespitter, and blasts out "a ball of flames," entering the wilderness of the afterlife in a more violent version of Christ's ascension to Heaven,[26] but the horror and agony of her death remains (385).

Okorafor's purpose is to explore the nature of myth and remythology, demonstrating how myths and stories are collected and repurposed.[27] Despite her extraordinary talents, Onye becomes an everyyoungwoman, symbolizing all those who have died because their behavior has conflicted with kyriarchal authority. Death by stoning is a particularly kyriarchal punishment because no one in the crowd of stone throwers needs to take moral responsibility for the death. Presented in the *Torah* and *Talmud* as suitable punishment for various crimes, it continues in the 21st century as punishment primarily for women, unmarried couples, or homosexuals who behave outside of patriarchal control. Today it remains a legal or customary punishment in the United Arab Emirates, Iran, Iraq, Qatar, Mauritania, Saudi Arabia, Somalia, Sudan, Northern Nigeria, Yemen, Afghanistan, Brunei, and parts of tribal Pakistan (Batha, np).

In *Stories about Stories,* Attebery writes:

> Myths are not timeless; like the individuals who perform them, they reflect historical processes, and they change over time as the cultures that maintain them change. They are not universal, for the full significance of a myth depends on a web of associations and social interactions shared by storyteller and listeners [20].

Who Fears Death does indeed reflect historical processes, but I would quibble with Attebery in that the essential deep structure of myth reveals coming-of-age journeys to be timeless and universal because they are based on young adult development. Self-sacrifice also maintains a deep mythic structure. Furthermore, jealousy, rape, adultery, murder, and war versus altruism, loyalty, fidelity, love and peace are all aspects of the human condition. They inform myths in every culture in every age, triggering a catharsis when the truth of a story is understood; otherwise, myths would not continue to be retold. What Attebery is really saying is that due to the oral nature of storytelling, myths are flexible rather than being set in stone. They adjust to fit the needs of the storyteller and the audience. Remythology is made possible by changing the lens through which mythic events are viewed.

When Okorafor remythologizes African myths, landscape, values, and experience, her inside-Africa experience guides her, but she also grew up in America, reading a wide range of fantasy and horror from the Tove Jansson *Moomintroll* series children's fantasy books to adult literary horror by Stephen King, Clive Barker, and Charles Stross. Her academic education in English, creative writing, and the sciences weaves in and out of her writing, adeptly managing its intricately crafted postcolonial, postmodernist self-driving luggage.[28] The structure of *Who Fears Death* reflects the tropes of science fiction, fantasy, horror, and myth, plus a sophisticated academic mindset, but it is the dynamic of her binocular insider/outsider lenses that gives her work depth. This combination has captured the imagination of a wide audience such that *Who Fears Death* won the 2011 World Fantasy Award for best novel as well as the Carl Brandon Kindred Award in 2010 for outstanding work of speculative fiction dealing with race and ethnicity." In July 2017 it was optioned by HBO to be produced as a series with George R.R. Martin as its executive producer.

4

The Book of Phoenix, Motherless Monsters and the Morality of Abomination

> My beginnings were in the dark. We all dwelled in the dark, mad scientist and SpeciMen alike [*The Book of Phoenix*, 6].

On her Twitter account page, Nnedi Okorafor includes a picture of herself atop a building with huge black wings behind her. She appears composed and confident in her ability to lift into the air. The photo is an obvious reference to *The Book of Phoenix*,[1] 2015, (henceforth *Phoenix*). A finalist for the Sputnik, Clarke and Campbell awards, it was written as a prequel to her World Fantasy Award winner *Who Fears Death*, 2010.[2] Thematically, it parallels Mary Shelley's *Frankenstein*,[3] while continuing Okorafor's examination of abuse, flight, apocalypse, and renewal. Composed in a series of vignettes similar to that of a graphic novel, *Phoenix* is a troubling mythology that rises again and again from its own ashes.

Considered to be the first science fiction novel, *Frankenstein* was a book Okorafor read in high school and reconsidered later,[4] wondering if Shelley wrote out of trauma regarding her loss of essential relationships: Shelley's mother, Mary Wollstonecraft, died of peritonitis after giving birth to her. Shelley's first premature baby (possibly conceived while visiting her mother's grave) died shortly after birth (Hoobler, 73). She was just seventeen. In *Broken Places & Outer Spaces*, Okorafor connects Shelley's creation of her monster with her own creation of a clay lady while she was recovering from her spinal surgery:

> Could it be that Mary wrote *Frankenstein* as a way of facing her pain and fears? That she produced something so great and beyond herself from the grief she suffered? If this is true, then not only did Mary Shelley have her own "clay lady" (Frankenstein's monster) but an entire genre of literature (science fiction) was launched by the Breaking [*Broken*, 48].

Naturale, 2015, suggests that "in the library of the mind," *Phoenix* should be shelved "between *The X-Men* and *Frankenstein*," indicating that Okorafor takes Shelley's theme of scientific hubris and abomination and adds superpowers born of mad-scientist, near-future technology[5] (np).

Although written 200 years apart, both novels examine how human morality can lag behind scientific knowledge and technological advancement. Both focus on the necessity of human bonding, demonstrating how a lack of early attachment can create individuals capable of doing great harm. Both focus on the use and abuse of power, exploring how the triple trauma of motherlessness, rejection, and abuse can contribute to the mindset of a serial killer. Together the novels parallel, in a rotating yin-yang of symbolism, male/female, light/dark, hot /cold, natural/unnatural.

Industrial Slavery and the Temptations of "Modern" Unregulated Science

SF historian Edward James, 1994, writes that there was "never a time in history of sf when the scientist appeared unambiguously as the hero and the herald of progress. The scientist has always had the capacity to wreak evil, consciously or by accident, as well as to bring good" (24). Written during the European Industrial Age that began around 1760, *Frankenstein: The Modern Prometheus* demonstrates a remarkable prescience regarding the danger of scientific advancement. The glorification of modernity in the title should be viewed ironically. Prometheus, a Titan,[6] made humans from clay and then brought them natural light in defiance of old-guard deistic authority—but "modern" artificial lighting would enable factory owners to make workers toil harder and longer, consequently spawning overcrowded industrial centers, pollution, environmental degradation, and child workers completing repetitive, sometimes dangerous tasks ten to sixteen hours a day (Waldo, 183). The end result was a functional neo-slavery where machines could distance owners from human responsibilities. The meta-slave[7] doctrine of the Industrial Age regarded lower-class workers as natural machines and machine extensions, essential for producing wealth and progress.

The hazards of unregulated industrialism were so considerable that many saw it akin to the destruction of Eden. Charles Dickens, 1852, describes a factory town of machines and tall chimneys "out of which interminable serpents of smoke trailed themselves for ever and ever, and never got uncoiled," a persistent proliferation of temptation for industrialists motivated by greed (30). As industrialization progressed, science became increasingly competent, with increasingly repeatable results making possible increasingly widespread harm as well as innovation. This, in itself, may be the reason science fiction emerged and became so important.⁸ Waldo, 1994, writes that "perhaps no thematic concern in *Frankenstein* is more significant to science fiction than the idea that the technology we create becomes our destroyer"⁹ (187). This, too, is true of *Phoenix*.

Frankenstein and the Making of a Monster

Mary Shelley (1797–1851) was nineteen when she envisioned *Frankenstein*. In 1816, "the year without a summer," Mary, her common-law husband Percy, and her stepsister Claire had gone to Lake Geneva, Switzerland, to spend time with Lord Byron, the most famous poet of the era. At the time, she was still breastfeeding her second child, William. The cold, rainy weather of that summer may have evoked the gloomy setting for the novel, as well as for its arctic ending, but there were other factors as well. Claire was pregnant by Byron but keeping it a secret. It's not surprising that Mary's anxieties may have informed her writing. It may also be that she had a teenage attraction to the monstrous.

Anyone who has attended a horror movie knows how some can be drawn to the monstrous, the carnal, and the grisly. In *Monsters of Our Own Making: The Peculiar Pleasures of Fear*, Warner, 1998, explains that the first public dissection of a human body occurred as early as 1302 (132). Paintings of public dissections like William Hogarth's *The Reward of Cruelty*, 1751, were publicly displayed (133). At the time *Frankenstein* was written, artistic depictions of hybrid creatures such as Egyptian deities with human bodies and animal heads were part of the British Museum's collections, and paintings such as those by Hieronymus Bosch (1450–1516) and Arcimboldo (1526 or 1527–1593) had been displayed for centuries.

Although it is not stated explicitly in the novel, Shelley's 1831 "Introduction" suggests that Victor Frankenstein uses electricity, the cutting-edge technology of the time, to animate his creation. She explains that when Lord Byron challenged the group to write ghost stories, she mused that perhaps a corpse could be reanimated by galvanism (viii). Early experiments by Galvani, Volta, and Aldini had fascinated her. Humphry Davy and William Nicholson, the era's leading electrical researchers, were friends of her father (Hoobler 46, 88, 120, 142). In 1814, Mary and Percy had attended a demonstration of electricity using early batteries called Leyden jars, and Percy had experimented with generating electricity (Hoobler, 88). Her first vision of the scientist and his monster was of a pale student of the unhallowed arts kneeling beside the thing he had put together. I saw the hideous phantasm of a man stretched out, and then, on the working of some powerful engine, show signs of life, and stir with an uneasy, half vital motion [Shelley, viii].

The term half *vital energy* is key here. This is, after all, a ghost story: the monster is alive but not morally mature. The *élan vital* of soul energy is only half there.

Nineteenth-century tales of alchemists involved reanimation of the dead using the philosopher's stone, magic words, secret formulas, circles, and arcane symbols. In a popular legend of the ruined Castle Frankenstein[10] in Germany, Konrad Dippel (1673–1734), the son of a Lutheran minister, was accused of robbing graveyards and making a deal with the devil (Hoobler, 82). However, Shelley's monster may well be literature's first technological hybrid. Like the alchemists who built blast furnaces in hopes of making gold from lead, Victor Frankenstein wants to create life through science and engineering, thus usurping the role of the loving mother. It is an obsession that essentially becomes an act of scientific rape, an aggressive theft of personal volition. Blindered by privilege, he steals human parts from the graveyard without concern for the grieving families who laid them to rest. Then, reflecting a misguided "bigger is better" idea of progress,[11] he uses bones from the slaughterhouse, believing that a creature "eight feet in height, and proportionally large" would "bless" him for it (32).

Phoenix and the Making of a Monster

Okorafor's reconsideration of the *Frankenstein* story is historically important to Afro and African futurism. The history of scientific experimentation on black bodies has been one of abomination, a soulless requisitioning that includes the Tuskegee Institute Syphilis Study (1932–1972) and the case of Henrietta Lacks. James Marion Sims (1813–1883), Father of American Gynecology, perfected his surgical techniques by operating on unanesthetized, enslaved Black women. Dr. Albert Kligman, (1916–2010), infamous for biochemical and radioactive experimentation on inmates in Holmesburg Prison from 1951 to 1974, recounted entering the prison for the first time, "All I saw before me were acres of skin. It was like a farmer seeing a fertile field for the first time" (Meyer).

In *Phoenix*, the "workshop of filthy creation" is a sterile lab in a skyscraper in a Manhattan that is largely underwater because the Arctic ice has melted. Working under the innocuous company name of LifeGen, Bumi, a childless female doctor, leads a multi-national team of neo–Nazi-like industrial scientists to create mutant soldiers for the military and an underclass of worker cyborgs.[12] Initially an American biomedical research and pharmaceutical company, LifeGen has evolved into a multinational, fully militarized shadow government. Reflecting the moral disregard of corporations that are too big to fail, LifeGen's intention is to create a monstrous weapon that is resistant to temperature extremes and capable of explosive violence. At age two, Phoenix has the physical development of a 40-year-old, perimenopausal woman.

Phoenix is an intentional abomination, an accelerated biological organism created through "advanced and aggressive genetic manipulation and cloning" and cyborged with metal in her bones[13] (8). She was created via CRISPR recombinant DNA gene-editing, using an egg and sperm modified with genetic material from donors representing over ten West African nations. This genetic material included DNA from Henrietta Lacks's immortal cancer cells[14] and from the DNA of Lucy "the Mitochondrial Eve, the ten-year-old Ethiopian girl who carries the complete genetic blueprint of the human race"[15] (147). The zygote for Phoenix was then implanted into the womb of a surrogate mother, and Phoenix was born "glowing like a little sun" (206). LifeGen took her away from her surrogate mother as soon she was "suckling well" (147, 206, 203). Thus, Phoenix strategically represents all women who have ever been born or ever will be born.

In Igbo, the word *Bumi* means "gift of god." In Sanskrit, it means "earth." Like Victor Frankenstein, whose expectations of victory end in great personal loss and his own premature death, the name *Bumi* must be viewed ironically. The ultimate techno-evil stepmother, Bumi is the female embodiment of Victor Frankenstein's monomania, a "gift" that should have been returned. The male-identified, pistol-packing Bumi wears a synthetic wig, symbolic of her unnatural nature. Like Victor Frankenstein, she has given up normal human relationships in service of her obsession. Bumi, who was present at Phoenix's birth, was born in Nigeria and correspondingly believes that her work with Phoenix will bless her with American citizenship: "I'm legal but not a citizen. Not yet. I will be. My work with you will earn me the pull I need" (19). Consequently, she approaches Phoenix with a mixture of possessiveness and scientific detachment. Bumi's detachment reflects a variant of the Stockholm Syndrome in which lower-caste individuals "see the world not with their own eyes but as the dominant caste sees it" and learn to adjust their expectations in order to succeed (Wilkerson, 283).

Meta-Slave Surveillance, Monstrous Creation, Monstrous Education

Surveillance is an essential aspect of subjugation. For slavery to be an effective means of production, slaves must be imprisoned and watched. The residents of the Tower call LifeGen "Big Eye" because they are constantly monitored, an obvious reference to "BIG BROTHER IS WATCHING YOU" in George Orwell's groundbreaking dystopian novel *1984*, published in 1949 (Orwell, 9). In the book, Orwell creates a dismal world that is always at war, ostensibly to keep the common people powerless.[16] Ashcroft, 2000, suggests surveillance is one of the "most powerful strategies of imperial dominance" because it implies a viewer with an elevated vantage point "suggesting the power to process what is seen" in order to "fix" an othering relationship (226). Observing and recording is necessary to maintain a superior position in a power structure. LifeGen's surveillance is hard and bright, reflecting a prison watchtower, a totalitarian destruction of personal privacy rather than a mother's tender gaze and fond scribblings in a baby book. Like Iraqi War profiteers Blackwater and Halliburton, LifeGen reflects the international militarization of corporate culture and the arrogant mindset that they are above and beyond the law. Okorafor's corporate colonization is harshly lighted by new technology, but the understanding of equal rights is no more honest than in Shelley's or Orwell's worlds. All three novels evolve as meta-slave narratives, indicating an awareness of subjugation. Since technology allows fewer chances to avoid surveillance, secret noncompliance becomes harder and angrier, and civil disobedience becomes even more dangerous. Mutants have become the new slaves of industry.[17] It is a world ripe for insurrection. Phoenix explains,

All the time, they watched us, though not closely enough to realize their great error and not closely enough to prevent the inevitable [9].

Similar to the papal Doctrine of Discovery[18] of 1493, which allowed Christians to "discover" and lay claim to any land vacant of Christians, both monster and Phoenix are claimed by their creators as unmarked territory and thus undeserving of choice and personal agency. Womack, 2013, writes that "dehumanization was wrongfully encoded into laws, and falsely substantiated by inaccurate science, all to justify a swath of violent atrocities in the name of greed" (31). It can be argued that slavery, like bullying, is an intentional failure of empathy.

Historically, slaves were viewed as hardier and less affected by pain (as were children). In *Phoenix*, Okorafor explores a neo-colonial[19] meta-slavery within the hegemony of the military-industrial complex, in which college graduates must become indentured servants to pay off their expensive educations, special Black children are harvested for body parts (169), and the simmering rage of oppressed, enslaved cyborgs and genetic mutants is ready to explode into nuclear reaction. Phoenix herself only provides the fuse.

Egyptian Mythology in *Phoenix*

Both *Frankenstein* and *Phoenix* are first-person narratives set within a frame. Although Frankenstein's narrative is told to an idealistic sea captain, who has been trapped in Arctic ice while attempting an impossible northwest passage to the North Pole,[20] the *Phoenix* narrative is a memoir that is recorded and then lost. Reflecting the rapidly accumulating, potentially devastating effects of global warming and pollution (see "Degrowth"), it begins approximately eighty years into our future in a post-environmental-holocaust Manhattan Times Square that is mostly underwater, ostensibly because the Arctic ice has melted.[21] The frame story begins about two hundred years later when Sunuteel, an elderly African storyteller, finds a discarded computer with an intact audio file that contains Phoenix's story. Sunuteel's name is significant because it implies a brightness and positivity that is absent in the dark events that Phoenix relates.

The name Sunuteel also suggests the Egyptian sun god Ra as well as Herman Poole Blount (1914–1993), the 1950s Chicago avant-garde musician who called himself "Sun Ra" or "Le Sony'r Ra" (see "Black to Okorafor"). An early Afrofuturist inspiration, his music urged space travel to new planets where equality could be possible. Sun Ra incorporated Egyptian and other non-Western mythologies into his music, reminding his audience that dark-skinned people once ruled advanced societies that shaped global knowledge (Womack 81). Although he never had traditional academic training, in 1971, he taught a class at the University of California, Berkeley titled "The Black Man in the Cosmos," which included Egyptian and Nubian mythologies and encouraged students to move away from Eurocentric thinking. Sun Ra commonly called racially otherized peoples "angels," urging them to reclaim dignity and fly beyond their persistent commodification under capitalism (Zamalin, 100).

Phoenix provides a symbolic reexamination of the phoenix allegory of resurrection. Tower 7, the 200-year-old, thirty-nine-floor marble skyscraper[22] in which the scientists work, represents the Egyptian obelisk, a hubristic attempt to reach and symbolically mate with the sky. (As it was for the Tower of Babel, the corporate sky is the limit.) Their logo, painted on their helicopters, is a huge eye similar to the All-Seeing Eye of ancient

Egypt, representing the hawk warrior god, Horus, and the phallus as the "One-Eyed God." Originally, the Phoenician god Phoenix was believed to be embodied by their king. After the king died, his remains were cremated, and the god symbolically reincarnated in the new king from the ashes of the old. After his immolation and rebirth, the god was said to rise to heaven in the form of the Morning Star (Walker, 798). It is interesting to note that Lucifer, translated as "light-bringer," is the Roman name for Venus, the morning star, a name that has come to be connected with Satan, the tempter. The Egyptians identified the phoenix with their *hennu* bird, a spirit of the *benben* or phallic obelisk, which represented an erect phallus and the earth god's perpetual eagerness to mate with the Goddess of Heaven (Walker, 732, 798). In *Phoenix*, Okorafor reappropriates the phallocentric phoenix myth but gives it feminist feathers.

Proto-Feminism in Mary Shelley's *Frankenstein*

Feminism has evolved considerably since Mary Shelley penned *Frankenstein*. Like her mother, Mary Wollstonecraft, author of *A Vindication of the Rights of Woman*, 1792, Mary Shelley's novel is essentially proto feminist. Although the narrative is male driven, critique of male behavior is tacit. Victor Frankenstein, an early representation of the modern antihero, lacks foresight and Promethean wisdom. From personal experience, Shelley knew that those who create life, without considering responsibility, demonstrate a lack of foresight. Her whole life had been spent with men who maintained privileged mindsets—men who amassed great debts, financial and personal, and then tried to avoid paying them. It should be noted that Victor Frankenstein's comfortable upper-class upbringing allows him time for his experiments. The motherless monster he creates and then abandons for its ugliness[23] raises ethical questions regarding 200 years of scientific practice. Good mothers love their infants even if they are not pretty (and immediately after birth, they frequently are not), but Victor does not identify as a parent. A thin facade of scientific education distances him from his hubristic act of creation. When he rejects his creation, the nameless monster has nowhere to turn. His rightful parents, both human and animal, were not involved in his creation, thus evoking an enduring larger-than-life vision of illegitimacy and abomination. Part of the tragedy that follows is that the monster's serial murder of innocents could have been avoided if Victor had possessed more foresight,[24] empathy, and steadier mind. (For more on the effects of motherlessness and rejection, see the Appendix.)

Codedly Black

When he first awakens, the monster's need to connect and attach is great, but Frankenstein cannot bear to look at him and runs away; however, the nameless monster is neither helpless nor entirely *tabula rasa*. Frankenstein's carnal quilting has used parts of beings that were once alive. Subconsciously the monster recognizes that he has a right to eye contact and interaction with his creator and seeks him out, but Frankenstein has hysterics and runs away again. At first, the monster cannot put words to the pain of his rejection. His ugliness and the unnatural nature of his creation make his social inferiority permanently marked, and in rage he rebels against his creator. With his black hair and large, heavily muscled body, the monster can be viewed as codedly Black. Late in the novel he reflects his awareness of enslavement when he screams:

> "Slave, I before reasoned with you, but you have proved yourself unworthy of my condescension. Remember that I have power; you believe yourself miserable, but I can make you so wretched that the light of day will be hateful to you. You are my creator, but I am your master;—obey" [122].

Mary Shelley opposed slavery. As a woman in an age in which women had very few rights, she deeply understood the nature of power imbalances—that the desire to overcome helplessness and become the master can become very seductive.[25] She knew of slave rebellions that had been occurring since the 17th Century. The French Revolution (1789–1799) was of considerable importance in her diaries and letters. Her anarchist father, William Godwin, opposed all forms of coercion and advocated for "the dissolution ... of that brute engine which has been the only perennial cause of the vices of mankind" (Hoobler 31). The "powerful engine" she first envisioned to spark the monster into life may be cognitively connected to Godwin's "brute engine" of coercion. Shelley recognizes that a slave is one who is used without permission. The pervasive attitudes of white colonial privilege assumed that slaves bore "the mark of their inferiority permanently and 'naturally' on their skins" and that coercion of a lesser being was a God-given right (Rieder, 2008, 97). In her best-selling critical book, *Caste*, 2020, Isabel Wilkerson writes:

> The tyranny of caste is that we are judged on the very things we cannot change: a chemical in the epidermis, the shape of one's facial features, the signposts of gender and ancestry—superficial differences that have nothing to do with who we are inside [379–380].

Thus, within colonial and neo-colonial worlds, skin color rankings are arbitrary and intentionally constructed "to meet the needs of the larger production" (Wilkerson, 53). Frankenstein's creation, though a private, personal endeavor, reflects the widespread social acceptance of otherizing for "progress" and capitalist gain.

Anger and Agency

Both *Phoenix* and *Frankenstein* are based on an exploration of anger and agency. *Phoenix* was inspired by Okorafor's anger regarding the closely linked military, industrial, and prison systems,[26] as well as her personal experience visiting one of her students in a Chicago prison in 2011. Later in the day, she was to receive the World Fantasy Award for *Who Fears Death*,[27] an unsettling combination of events. Her anger regarding the high incarceration rate of African Americans would not let her go until she wrote the story[28] (blog, January 8, 2015). Wagner, 2015, calls it "perhaps the angriest SFF novel to broadside the genre since Joanna Russ's *The Female Man*" (np).

What differentiates *Phoenix* from *Frankenstein* is that Okorafor, older than Shelley by two decades, writes through lenses that recognize a woman's right to anger and agency. Reflecting a 19th century stereotype of the selfless ideal woman, Shelley depicts Elizabeth, Frankenstein's bride, as a delicate creature, an anger-less pawn whose absence of agency makes her an excellent victim. Correspondingly, Victor lacks the ability to be angry with a purpose. His reactions are likely modeled on Percy Shelley's tendency to be hysterical and ineffectual under stress. He lacks clear-minded strategies for ending the abomination he has created. Conversely, the rejected, unsocialized monster becomes the embodiment of rage, and he uses his agency to effect revenge.[29]

Okorafor's Phoenix quickly departs from gender stereotypes. From a helpless beginning, she develops the ability to be strong and decisive in a surprisingly short time. She learns to focus her anger and become a leader who is able to inspire others to participate in her cause. Although both novels are very dark, Okorafor's ending, though apocalyptic, holds hope for positive change (creating physical, political, and cognitive space for the utopian developments of her other novels), while Shelley's holds none.

Loss of the Mother: The Primal Wound

In "The Loss of the Mother and the Sense of Self," Nancy Newton Verrier writes that infants exist in a "dual unity" with their mothers for a year after birth (29). The relationship between mother and child is not characterized "by subject and object, but by a kind of fluidity of being, the mother/child/world transcending both time and space" (29). This primal relationship is essential to the developing infant's sense of self, and "sets the tone for all subsequent relationships" (29). Removing an infant from the mother creates what Verrier calls a "primal wound" that is so deep that the child is only semi-conscious of a sense of loss. "The loss is real and the need for mourning acute" (39).

Although it can be argued that the monster was without empathy from his awakening in Frankenstein's laboratory, the text suggests that the results might have been different if Victor had been capable of bonding with his monster. Victor's privileged education blinds him to the responsibilities he should have for his neonatal monster. The monster later remarks, "No father had watched my infant days, no mother had blessed me with smiles and caresses; or if they had, all my past life was a blot, a blind vacancy in which I distinguished nothing" (86). Bumi, however, is an intentionally toxic parent; she removes Phoenix from her mother fully aware that it will be traumatizing. To LifeGen, Phoenix is a lab animal, a "SpeciMen," and no more human than a sample taken for urinalysis (9).[30]

Child development authorities such as Piaget, 1965, Kohlberg, 1971, and Gilligan, 1982, agree that moral development is set in the first three years of life, but Phoenix, like Frankenstein's monster, lacks any preverbal intimate relationship that can become the basis for emotions such as compassion, empathy, shame and guilt: however, like most infants, she does have a basic human tendency toward facial connection and bonding. Laible and Thompson, 2000, explain that the development of a child's conscience is the effect of "a warm, supportive mother–child relationship and early conversations about the child's behavior infused with discussions of feelings and values" (1424).

Infant attachment is a three-step process, sometimes called "the soul cycle" (Cline 303). It is dependent on touch, eye contact, smiles, cuddling, and rocking. Infant experiences of discomfort such as hunger, pain, or cold are expressed by crying. When a mother's response is not immediate, crying becomes a "rage reaction" that is a combination of helplessness, hopelessness, and anger. (Cline 303). However, when caregivers are responsive to needs and restore comfort in a timely manner, infants begin to develop bonds of lasting trust. Phoenix, however, is denied any kind of support for her emotions. Although Bumi provides smiles, physical contact, storytelling and one-to-one conversation, she combines them with torture, routinely placing Phoenix in a machine that heats up like a furnace.

> Before I started to heat myself, they would place me in a heated room and watch me sweat and wheeze for hours. In my second year of life, they started burning me. With hot needles, then larger broader instruments. On my face,

4. The Book of Phoenix, *Motherless Monsters and Morality*   87

belly, legs, arms, they burned every part of me. I knew the smell, sound and sight of my cooking flesh [66].

When Phoenix screams in pain, Bumi responds with soothing aphorisms like "Nothing great comes without pain" and "Just relax" (17). Later Phoenix concludes, "She'd told me stories while she caused me pain; she was what lies were made of, even though her stories were truth" (53). This is an important moral conclusion.

Part of the horror of Phoenix's story is that she becomes aware of LifeGen's intent to use her. In "The Origins of Morality in Early Childhood Relationships," Gilligan and Wiggins write that "if recurrent childhood experiences of inequality are less mitigated by experiences of attachment ... compounded by social inequality in adolescence ... feelings of powerlessness may become heightened and the potential for violence may correspondingly increase" (116). Although explosive violence is more common in boys, Phoenix has been raised not as a girl but as an intelligent weapon. The ability to care and feel compassion for others is grounded in attachment, but her only friendship has been with her friend Saeed, another cyborg experiment who has been altered to live on refuse, rust and gravel (15). Saeed listens to her and tells her stories of his life before he was taken by LifeGen. Their developing affection for each other has been discouraged. SpeciMen are not allowed to pair unless the Big Eye deems it "good research" (131). When she is told that Saeed has died from eating an apple she gave him, she believes she has nothing left to lose. Gilligan and Wiggins, 1988, suggest that

> moral outrage can be provoked not only by oppression and injustice but also by abandonment or loss of attachment or the failure of others to respond. In a study of high school girls, moral passion marked their descriptions of situations in which someone did not listen ... [120].

Both Phoenix and the monster are children in adult bodies. Without having experienced the benefit of childhood play that merges fantasy and reality in preparation for adult responsibility, they are immediately thrust into adult dilemmas. Bruno Bettelheim has written that "besides being a means of coping with past and present concerns, play is the child's most useful tool for preparing ... for the future and its tasks" (Bettelheim, np). Play is essential for socialization and for neurological development. Through play, children rehearse future behavior, but Phoenix and monster have had no time to play. Neither has developed a sense of humor or the stress reduction of playfulness. It is all deadly serious.

Languageless at first, the monster has to relearn basic words like "fire," "milk," "bread" and "wood" (78). He, whose eventual diction is likely modeled on Lord Byron's, learns language and reading by watching through a hole in a wall as members of a poor family teach language to a beautiful "Arabian" woman named Safie (84). The unlikely, but obviously symbolic, book used for teaching is Volney's erudite *Ruins of Empires,* an essay on the philosophy of history and the contributions of non-Western cultures (84).[31] The name Safie or Sophie means "wisdom," but actual wisdom takes a lifetime to acquire, and what the monster gets from reading is the ability to rationalize his infantile rage at abandonment.

Although Phoenix has intentionally been subjected to extreme emotional neglect and repeated torture, she is also given free access to the company's digital database of literature. At age two, she responds to her LifeGen guardians with estrangement and resentment, emotions much more complicated than a 2-year-old's simplistic black-and-white binary rages. Her only source of moral education has come from the books she has read. Her brain has developed—she can read a 500-page book in two minutes—but her consciousness is slower to awaken. In two years, she has acquired the equivalent of a classical education, a combination of mythology, science, and colonial and postcolonial narratives,[32] but the complexity of world literature takes time to process.

On an affective level, Phoenix's education parallels Mary Shelley's. The stories Mary learned from her father, William Godwin, and later from Percy Shelley and Lord Byron rang with high ideals, but their real-life relationships were based on lies and rationalizations. Mary's homelife was defined by emotional neglect. Children can view neglect as normal but still feel that something essential is lacking. It is the stuff of cognitive dissonance and incomprehensible anger until it is sorted through. Likewise, Phoenix is just beginning to recognize the reality of her situation. "To them, I was like a plant they grew for the sake of harvesting" (9).[33] Phoenix's recognition reflects the historical harvesting of Black bodies for supposed scientific purposes.

In her groundbreaking book *Breaking Down the Wall of Silence*, psychotherapist Alice Miller explains that the early lives of mass murderers, such as Adolf Hitler, Rudolf Höess, and Joseph Stalin, were characterized by "a brutal upbringing aimed at enforcing unthinking obedience and total contempt for the child" (83). Miller explains that "the victims of such an upbringing ache to do to others what was done to them" (84). Miller's three principles of Nazism can describe Phoenix's early upbringing:

* Disobedience and criticism are unthinkable because they will be punished with corporal punishment and death threats.
* The lively, vital child should be turned, as early as possible, into an obedient robot and slave.
* Unwelcome feelings and real needs must, consequently, be suppressed to the maximum [Miller, 89].

4. The Book of Phoenix, *Motherless Monsters and Morality*   89

Essentially, *Phoenix* and *Frankenstein* depict authorial assaults on the walls of silence that protect fortresses of cultural power. Both narratives reveal a social masonry of awful secrets that eventually falls. It is probable that the monster speaks for Mary Shelley when he remarks:

> For a long time, I could not conceive how one man could go forth to murder his fellow, or even why there were laws and governments; but when I heard of vice and bloodshed, my wonder ceased, and I turned away with disgust and loathing [84].

Phoenix's response is similar.

Both monster and Phoenix are autodidacts, having educated themselves without benefit of interpretation and moral guidance, and the contradictory nature of what they read creates cognitive dissonance. From an educator's point of view, their rapid intellectual achievement is unlikely, but the two are fantastic embodiments of times when intellectual achievement is proceeding much more quickly than moral development. Their memoirs become counternarratives to the metanarratives that are used to define the status quo of their times. Shelley's monster remarks:

> I learned that the possessions most esteemed by your fellow creatures were high and unsullied descent united with riches. A man might be respected with only one of these advantages, but without either he was considered, except in very rare instances, as a vagabond and a slave, doomed to waste his powers for the profits of the chosen few [85].

Phoenix's diction is not as elevated as the monster's, but her distress regarding human genocide is as obvious: "The Germans killed many people because they were sure that they were inferior or a threat or both. The book I read spoke as if wiping them out was the right thing to do. It certainly looked wrong to me" (25).[34]

As the monster's diction becomes increasingly sophisticated, he becomes increasingly violent. He begins to believe that the murder of innocents is justifiable. Initially he sees himself as Adam in search of an Eve, but after reading Milton's *Paradise Lost*, he sees himself as Satan, a fallen angel.[35] The monster now sees himself as unfairly separated from the sublime bliss of Heaven. Rage reaction and monstrous behavior are all that are left.

Okorafor also evokes the Adam and Eve motif. There is a kind of Garden of Eden in the lobby where Phoenix is not allowed to go: "an earthly wonderland, full of creeping vines covering the walls and small trees growing from artistically crafted holes in the floor" (8). In the center is the Tree of Life, an apparently immortal experimental tree that has grown through the floors of the entire building. When she hears that Saeed has died supposedly, because of eating the apple she gave him to draw, she immediately sees a Biblical connection: "My mind went to one of my books. The Bible. I was Eve and he was Adam" (Okorafor 11). She believes that like Eve, she is at fault.

Unaware of having any personal rights, Phoenix's 2-year-old rage becomes internalized. In response to repeated torture by fire, her body begins heating itself, a monstrous version of menopause as well as an embodiment of phoenix mythology. Her hot flashes are so serious that her body begins to burn, and electronic devices explode in her hands: "It was as if I was harboring a sun deep within my body and that sun wanted to come out. Under the dark brown of my flesh, I was glowing, I was light" (15). Symbolically connected to Lucifer, the light-bearer, she attempts to escape from surveillance. In doing so, she discovers and awakens Seven, a winged man who is suspended in midair from the enormous undying tree[36] that grows from the lobby up through the Tower's greenhouse on its top floor, his feathered brown wings stretched wide (27).[37] A remythologized angel, Seven is connected to the mystical dimensions of the Okorafor universe. He recognizes Phoenix as the Change he has been waiting for.

Reincarnation, the Fulfillment of Purpose and the Recreation of Family

Seven, who first appeared in *Akata Witch*, is the reincarnation of a wrestler who was killed while fighting for the Zuma International Wrestling Championship. When he dies, brown feathers unfurl from his back, and he shoots up into the sky like a rocket (*Akata*, 239). For those who have fulfilled their purpose, death becomes an opportunity to achieve higher purpose in a changed form. Later in the novel, Seven tells Phoenix that as he died, he remembered a song that called him to be one with God (179). He then chose to become the Guardian of New York: "Africa bleeds, but it will be fine," he said. "I go where I am most needed" (180). Seven is to become a meta-human father figure for Phoenix.

During her escape, Phoenix is able to reach the lobby of the Tower before the Big Eye guards kill her. In dying, she explodes with heat and light, bringing down the building. Unable to die and stay dead,[38] she rises out of the rubble after a mystically important seven days and sprouts wings. Hunted like an abomination, she escapes through the streets of New York and learns to fly. After her feathers dry, they are like another set of arms—"powerful arms whose every curve, fold, muscle I could control. I could flex them, retract them, move specific parts. I ran. Then I flew for my life" (52). Whereas Frankenstein's monster escapes to the Arctic Circle, Phoenix and Seven reverse the trajectory and fly to Africa: although he is twice as large as she is, they share a hawk-like resemblance, reflecting Horus, the Egyptian hawk deity.

Africa represents a chance for Phoenix to find her roots. It represents the Global South, the economic periphery far from world centers of power. As Ferreira, 2019, suggests, since those within the center of power misjudge how those on the periphery think, the Global South is "one place to turn in searching for renewal, revision, and extension of the SF megatext" (678). Africa is the place in Okorafor's universe where the mythical and mystical naturally interweave with the techno-rational, creating a potentiality that Sun Ra describes as *"mythocracy,"* insisting that "myth speaks of the impossible, of immortality. And since everything that's possible has been tried, we need to try the impossible" (Zamalin 99–100).

Although Shelley's monster attempts to recreate family for himself, all attempts end in failure due to his hideous appearance. Phoenix is more successful. If she covers her wings, she looks fairly normal. At first, she tries to find a way to live a normal life in Ghana despite the encumbrance of her wings, but she continues to be chased by Big Eye mercenaries who consider her property that needs to be retrieved. When they kill her lover, a doctor named after Kofi Annan,[39] she explodes again, and when she reincarnates, her wings are red gold. Like Dana, the heroine of Octavia Butler's *Kindred,* she develops the ability to slip through time as well as space. Similar to Lacks' cancer, her nanotechnology appears immortal. If she is killed, the damage is healed, and she is reborn, stronger and more beautiful. Each time she rises from her own ashes, her wings have changed color, and she is more powerful.

After she reconnects with a reincarnated Saeed and his friend *Mmuo,* a Nigerian shapeshifter who has also survived the fall of the Tower, she enters a more normal time in which she is able to experience true friendship. Like Mary Shelley, Phoenix finds temporary stability in a communal living arrangement and finds time to construct a memoir of her life experiences. Her body glows with a full spectrum of light, reflecting the chakras: orange, red, yellow, and a hint of blue that symbolically relates to the throat and a nascent ability to speak with compassion (115), but it proves to be the calm before the storm.

Cyborgs and Cyborg Revolution

When the three friends become part of a cybernetically connected metahuman resistance movement of mutant slaves, she learns that her surrogate mother had wanted to keep her but wasn't allowed to do so because she is "a dangerous non-human person" (147, 206). In *Primate Visions,*

1989, Donna Haraway defines a cyborg as "the figure born of the interface of automaton and autonomy" (139). With her injected nanomites and her titanium[40] bones, Phoenix represents the "binary oppositions of meat/metal" described in Haraway's "A Cyborg Manifesto." For Haraway, the cyborg is a "myth about transgressed boundaries, potent fusions, and dangerous possibilities" (154). Both *Frankenstein* and *Phoenix* are cautionary tales in which mythology becomes reality and reality becomes mythology. Their stories transcend the eras in which they were written. In creating and abandoning his monster, Frankenstein transgresses moral boundaries, an original sin that causes the murder of innocents. In creating then torturing Phoenix, LifeGen further transgresses moral boundaries, embodying a dangerous possibility that eventually evokes a holocaust that kills millions.

As in Okorafor's earlier stories, flight becomes increasingly entwined with anger, metaphorically a moving response to bigotry and repression—sexist, cultural, political and interracial—, a response that includes both "flight" *and* "fight," a pattern of behavior commonly found in trauma and abuse survivors. Psychiatrist Judith Lewis Herman describes it as the result of a powerful need to reestablish control over bodily and emotional responses and reaffirm "a sense of power" (Herman, 199). Herman writes, "Taking power in real-life situations often involves a conscious choice to face danger" (197). She further explains that dangerous behavior may be a reenactment of earlier trauma, but "it is undertaken consciously, in a planned and methodical manner, and is therefore far more likely to succeed" (197). Unlike the monster who is simply enacting revenge, Phoenix is possessed by a vision of a possible world that exists outside of chronological time.

Throughout, Seven acts as a moral compass for Phoenix. Although Phoenix muses that Seven causes her to feel more "balanced" (180), it is necessary to note that Seven is also a lethal weapon who has clearly left most of his humanity behind. He takes a longer view of mortality and suffering. He knows things that Phoenix does not, and his perspective is farsighted rather than immediately altruistic. His advice is counterintuitive: "If you are unsure of what to do, go with the choice that hurts your heart. It is the correct one" (180). In other words, look to the long term and don't simply make a choice that avoids short-term harm.[41] He tells her that the Big Eye Towers must be destroyed to stop the experimentation and enslavement.

Gradually, Phoenix's anger becomes a weapon she can focus. The cyborgs with whom she now fights have drawn meaning from previous human rights revolutions. An angry letter rescued from the team's demolition of LifeGen Tower 5 reflects early slave rebellions as well as second wave feminism:

Do you remember the man Nat Turner? You don't because he has been erased from your files or buried in disconnected databases. Replaced with your commercials about skin, sex, hair products, food, sparkling water, and money. We tell his story by mouth. Then we sent his story amongst us by electronic file. Then the Phoenix struck, and his story came to life [192].[42]

The rebellion is a spontaneous explosion of rage against corporate neo-slavery and neo-imperialism.[43] However, it is not a *human* rights revolution. Okorafor's fiction makes clear that beyond genetic tampering, her metahumans are the product of a posthuman evolutionary movement that has always been in process. Genetic tampering simply accelerates what is already happening. With all of written history at their disposal, those in the metahuman resistance recognize this and demand the right not to be enslaved despite the capital investment that went into their creation.

LifeGen's intent was to create Phoenix as an intelligent, but biddable, weapon without morality, but what results is an avenging angel[44] who transcends human mortality, becoming an emissary and agent of animistic forces that cannot be controlled. As in *Frankenstein*, once atrocity reaches a certain velocity, it can be very difficult to stop. The triumph of the story, however, is that in Okorafor's universe, there are forces more powerful than human hubris.

Moving Between Monstrosity, the Grotesque and the Sublime

Both *Frankenstein* and *Phoenix* can be considered explorations of monstrosity, the grotesque, and the sublime. Both are warnings, cautionary tales. The Latin root for monster is *monstrum,* referring to an omen, a supernatural being or object that is the will of the gods. *Monstrum* is derived from *monere*, meaning "to warn or advise, particularly in a divine sense." Although initially referring to heraldic creatures like griffins, minotaurs, and centaurs, between the 12th and 14th centuries, monstrosity began to be used to describe physical deformity. Monstrous became frightful and shocking as well as unnatural, thus losing some of its original mystical meaning. Shelley's monster is both monstrous and grotesque, but in creating Phoenix, Okorafor returns the idea of monster as mystical emissary.

Human attempts to create bigger and better often end in the grotesque. The word *grotesque* originally referred to murals found in Roman ruins, *grotto* meaning "cave." Another word for grotesque is *diablerie* which refers to reckless mischief and sorcery assisted by the devil. In *The Seven Beauties of Science Fiction,* 2008, Istvan Csicsery-Ronay explains that the word *grotesque* is used to describe creatures with misshapen, asymmetrical ugliness, a conflation of disparate elements, things put together that shouldn't go together (146). He exemplifies Frankenstein's monster as "a carnal bricolage," something unnaturally constructed from a range of available things, and further suggests that the monster may well be literature's first example of the "techno grotesque" (246). He writes that "once nature itself is viewed as prone to violate its own rules, or when human technologies can recast them with impunity, we are in the domain of the grotesque and the techno grotesque, where fascination rules, and transcendence is unthinkable" (154).

In "The Grotesque and the Techno-Grotesque," Schütze, 1995, writes, "The grotesque body, which is coupled, hooked up and permanently, or temporarily, plugged into the technological is indicative of the arrival of a new body which no longer fits into the category of what we know as human" (np). Although Shelley's monster has what can be considered superpowers, he remains what Schütze considers an "impure construction, not quite organic anymore, and not yet altogether *technological*" (np). That the monster is grotesque is part of the monster's continuing fascination. Popular audience assumes that along with a larger-than-life body, he also has a larger-than-life potential for sexuality. In his study of the grotesque, Harpman, 1982, points out that "genre, genus and genitals are linked in our language as in our subconscious" (5). To this list I would add that the art and literature of the grotesque links a mad "genius" that parallels obsession.

Okorafor's Phoenix is an unnatural, techno-genetic bricolage that transcends the grotesque through the symmetry of her form. Born in a techno-capitalist age in which scientific temptation has become even more dangerous than it was in the industrial age, she is a new creature, having triggered a hidden genetic template that reincarnates with increasing symmetry and beauty. Her larger-than-life cyborged body embodies the posthuman. Although she was originally an "impure construction," she is not sexually impure. Serially monogamous, her explosive rage and grief at the death of loved ones induce reincarnations that exhibit an increasingly dangerous purity of purpose. She becomes a weapon that transcends the control of her creators. The wings were never part of their plan.

On a semantic level the grotesque and the sublime can be considered opposites. In *The Critique of Judgement*, 1790, Immanuel Kant explains that "the feeling of the sublime is at once a feeling of displeasure" that arises from a sense of "inadequacy" in recognition of "magnitude," [...] "and a simultaneously awakened pleasure arising from this very judgment of the inadequacy" (quoted in James, 104). Victor's memoir begins with recognition of the pristine beauty of the Italian Alps, but he sees it as unmarked territory that can be claimed: "I wept like a child. Dear mountains! My own beautiful lake! How do you welcome your wanderer?" (49) Victor refuses to accept his own inadequacy in the presence of the sublime and open himself to the pleasure inherent in a sense of wonder. He believes that he is "capable of more intense application," mastery of the sublime through the construction a creature that is huge and beautiful (18).

Unlike Victor, the monster is initially capable of appreciating the sublime for itself alone. One of his earliest memories is of the moon:

> "Soon a gentle light stole over the heavens, and gave me a sensation of pleasure. I started up and beheld a radiant form rise from among the trees. I gazed with a kind of wonder" [71].

But his perception of sublime beauty stands in stark contrast to his recognition of his own shocking ugliness. By the time he confronts Victor, he sees himself as "miserable beyond all living things ... bound by ties only dissoluble by the annihilation of one of us" (68).

Since the sublime is connected with our sense of awe, it cannot be created or controlled. Human attempts to recreate the sublime almost always end in monstrosity or collapse. Paralleling the monster's wonder at the moon, Phoenix recognizes the sublime when she first perceives the night sky:

> *Blackness. Pure. Quiet. Then pricks of tiny white, blue and yellow lights. I was seeing stars for the first time. Billions and billions of stars. As I flew through space smooth and gentle. In a vastness that made me want to weep. But I had no eyes with which to shed tears* [40–41].

Later, after Phoenix begins to fly, she sees beyond human mortality to an inherent potential for annihilation.

> ...in the sky, above and away from everything, with no one but the sun and the spiraling columns of warm air during the day and the moon and whipping cool winds at night, it was easy to be that which knew death intimately [159].

Conclusion:
The Monsters in Our Minds

Frankenstein's crime began in secrecy. Later, shame limits him to ineffectual independent action. Full disclosure and group action may well have stopped the dominoes of death from falling, but he does not ask for help until the very end when he is dying of exposure and exhaustion. The idiocy of the heroic mindset is demonstrated when the captain of the vessel remarks, "I had rather die than return shamefully,—my purpose unfulfilled" (160). Essentially, the problem throughout is the danger of solipsistic action, behavior that reflects the colonial norm of manly independence. Frankenstein, the so-called Modern Prometheus, cannot be forgiven. His foresight has been damaged by privilege, false values, and narcissism. Separated from a community's balancing input, isolation becomes desolation and insanity, metaphorically what the monster describes as "the most northern extremity of the globe" (166).

LifeGen also cannot be forgiven. Their crime begins in secrecy but ends in apocalyptic fire, an uncontrollable, cataclysmic event that levels the techno-capitalist, military-industrial playing field and sets the stage for *Who Fears Death* and the eco-utopian progress seen in Okorafor's YA novels. Like Frankenstein's monster, Phoenix is capable of determining right and wrong but rationalizes her use of violence. Late in her memoir she explains:

> Scorched earth is heartless, it's violent, it's merciless, and it usually involves fire. One of its methods, the strategy of destroying civilian food supplies in an area of conflict has been banned under Article 54 of Protocol I of the 1977 Geneva Conventions. But this is only enforceable by countries who have ratified this protocol. Only the United States and Israel have not. In this way, I am very American [218].

The implication is that everyone in America is responsible for the corruption that created Phoenix. When Phoenix finally confronts and destroys Bumi, she feels justified in taking out all of New York at the same time. Eventually, like Kali Ma, the Hindu triple goddess of creation, preservation, and destruction, Phoenix embodies Death itself, "the reaper come to reap what was sown" (221). In world mythology, life and birth are always bound up with death and destruction (Walker, 488). Okorafor's characters are frequently informed by anger at a world in which so much inhumanity occurs, but Phoenix is angry with a difference: her moral judgment comes out of a preordained ability to create change, a long-term wild card animistic morality that exists beyond human control. After Phoenix destroys the neocolonial world, her story languishes in the darkness of the junk pile, but in the mythical long view, time means next to nothing. After Sunuteel's discovery, her story rises from its ashes to become "the most read book of the last one hundred years" (230). Not an ending but a beginning, *Phoenix* can be seen as *Frankenstein* turned inside out. Victor Frankenstein attempts to create a sublime creature and gets a monster, but LifeGen's scientists attempt a monster and evoke the sublime.

In conclusion, monstrosity implies a disruption of natural design, an unnatural creature. Marina Warner remarks that modern monsters "no longer swarm in religious images, but in science fiction and children's books" (258). This paradigm shift reflects a new understanding that departs from the superstition that misshapen or unnatural creatures are messages from the divine. Beginning with Mary Shelley, science fiction has gone beyond the monstrosity of physical ugliness to examine the true monstrosity of human obsession—individual, cultural, scientific, or techno-corporate, and in doing so, the narrative once again merges with mythic horror, another kind of divine message regarding the hubristic misuse of others. If Phoenix and Frankenstein's monster were mindless, their stories would simply be seen as horror, but when their intelligent appreciation of the sublime is seen along with the atrocity of their creation and their subsequent crimes, their stories are elevated to tragedy. To fully comprehend this tragedy, we must confront the invisible monsters of hierarchy that abide in our own minds.

5

Tomorrow Is Now: An Evolution of Young Women's Rights, Trauma and Resilience

> "Five, five, five, five, five, five," I whispered. I was already treeing, numbers whipping around me like grains of sand in a sandstorm, and now I felt a deep click as something yielded in my mind. It hurt sweetly, like a knuckle cracking or a muscle stretching. I sunk deeper and there was warmth. I could smell the earthy aroma of the *otjize* I'd rubbed on my skin and the blood in my veins [*Binti: Home*, 7].

Okorafor has a "genius" for finding and using "iconic images and traditions of African culture" (Wolfe, 17). These images recur throughout her fiction to demonstrate cultural change, with some values and attributes remaining consistent through time, others evolving. Many of these icons of African culture, such as thick dada hair, palm wine, uli art, and otjize body cream are magically repurposed to be closely connected to young women's freedom and potential for social and political power. The connection between innovative talent and the agency to create change is particularly explored in "The Palm Tree Bandit," *The Girl with the Magic Hands*, 2013, and the *Binti* Trilogy 2015–2017. Together they provide a path toward a sustainable African future for everyone, but especially for girls.

Okorafor is particularly interested in creating healthy developmental rites of passage for girls. Researchers say that there is a critical time in girl development when a young woman may either begin to develop agency or alternatively may start "disavowing the self" (Stern, 105). This disavowal of the self can involve uncertainty and depression. In 1926, Karen Horney called this "gender dysphoria"[1] and linked a sudden drop in self-esteem to the loss of freedom that is culturally tied to being a young woman. Horney suggested that somewhere in early adolescence, young women begin to measure personal value based on cultural assumptions that may be male-defined—including values that are foreign to girls' biological natures (Stern 106). Attempting to be perfectly compliant and passive can be dangerous to any girl's sense of well-being. The problem is not in the girl but in the culture. Carol Gilligan, 1984, has described the result as an "erosion of self-confidence" and a deep conflict about the validity of what is seen and experienced (Gilligan 2). Okorafor, however, allows her heroines to learn from experience and trust their own inner voices regarding life choices, which results in emerging self-confidence and agency.

The Palm Tree Bandit as Teaching Story

Like Le Guin and other feminist writers from earlier generations, Okorafor is interested in how teaching stories can support women's wisdom, self-esteem, and moral education. Her short stories are often told by a mother or grandmother during hair combing and are intended to connect a girl child to her family history and thereby support her agency and self-confidence. This is particularly true of "The Palm Tree Bandit" legend, a recurring feminist trickster hero mentioned throughout Okorafor's fiction ("Palm," 252).[2] Originally published in *Strange Horizons*, "The Palm Tree Bandit," 2001, relates how a lively woman named Yaya[3] becomes a cultural hero because she is able to flaunt the social norm that women must not climb and tap palm trees because tapping is men's work. In Nigerian tradition, palm tree wine begins as a milky white sap. Because of naturally occurring yeasts, it begins fermenting as soon as it is tapped. In Okorafor's tale, palm wine is thought to give power to the first person to touch it and drink it, but women are considered weak creatures and supposedly incapable of "withstanding such power" (252).

One evening after an argument with Old Man Rum Cake, the village elder, Yaya shimmies up a palm tree and secretly carves a feminine moon symbol. (The traditional shape for tapping is a phallic-like triangle). The next week she taps a tree and leaves a jug of palm wine below it next to a carved heart, a symbol for Erzulie,[4] the village's mother goddess. Yaya's continued thefts and nonviolent resistance have a kind of aphrodisiac power. The sweetness of palm wine lingers on her body, affecting her husband and causing her coworkers to crave chocolate. Stories arise in popular culture surrounding the identity of the bandit, and although men initially revile the thefts, women start praying to the bandit for intervention in their problems. Eventually, the tradition evolves, and women are allowed to tap palm trees if first they offer sacrifices to the bandit (255). Like Prometheus stealing fire, hero tales often involve going up against the will of old-guard gods to achieve long-term good, essentially a flaunting of convention. Okorafor's message is that with courage and perseverance, seemingly set-in-stone sexist values can be challenged, and she references "The Palm Tree Bandit" story throughout her YA fiction.

The Girl with the Magic Hands

Another teaching story, "The Girl with the Magic Hands,[5]" is a portal[6] fantasy that initially follows the hero quest formula. It is told by an elderly man who describes the world as "a work of art at play" (para. 3). At the beginning, Chidera, the physically and verbally abused 11-year-old daughter of poor and unhappy parents, has "the saddest face you could imagine" (para. 7). Her father considers her worthless and wishes she were a boy. Her mother is weak, depressed and passively struggling with failure as a cook, gardener, and artist. Like many at-risk 11-year-old girls, Chidera has concluded "Maybe I'm not good at anything" (Loc 55). One day, however, Chidera hears sweet, siren-like singing at the village well, and she follows these disembodied voices deep into the forest where her vision is transformed and she sees beautiful spiraling designs all around her: "On the ground, on every tree leaf, from the top to the bottom, tree trunks, on the vines, on stones, even the backs of lizards" (Loc 124). Chidera has never seen such designs before. This transformation of sight is akin to what occurs in the movie version of *The Wizard of Oz* when the black and white of poverty and hopelessness transforms into Technicolor. There is magic in the forest, and Chidera wants to be part of the secret. The women she meets are manifestations of the Goddess—mother and crone plus one more powerful, Osisi[7] Uli, who has incarnated as a tree. Their bodies are painted with indigo blue designs. Osisi is an Igbo word for tree while Uli refers to the traditional designs of the Igbo people. Like the henna practice of North Africa and the Middle East, Uli patterns are used by women to prepare for celebrations such as festivals and marriages. The goddesses initiate and empower Chidera by igniting her artistic talent and making her part of a magical sisterhood. After they draw an indelible glowing leaf[8] on her hand, they send her off with a blessing, "Go and be fruitful, my child" (Loc 184).

In her definitive essay, "The Master's Tools Will Never Dismantle the Master's House," Audre Lorde has written that

> Interdependency between women is the only way to the freedom which allows the "I" to "be," not in order to be used, but in order to be creative. This is a difference between the passive "be" and the active "being" [Lorde, 95].

This painless initiation permits Chidera to actively "be" herself and counters the painful and destructive eleven-year rite of clitorectomy that is described in Okorafor's adult novel *Who Fears Death*. Chidera's eyes have been opened to a new world of creativity. For girls, eleven is a critical age. Block, 1990, has described a sudden drop in optimism and resiliency around age eleven that is not seen in boys of that age (Gilligan, 13). Okorafor recognizes that girls need rituals powerful enough to overcome the double-whammy emotional rollercoaster that occurs with menarche and the accompanying heavy pressure culture places on girls to be perfect. She delineates this pressure by describing how Chidera is belittled by her father who says "You move like a fat man" (Loc 72) and forces her to get water from the well when he knows it could make her late for school. Later, Chidera is publicly shamed by her male teacher for having a wet uniform. Okorafor is describing a culture in which misogyny is ingrained and toxic. Chidera's father and teacher are culturally sanctioned bullies whose hostile behavior is allowed because they are men. In *Reviving Ophelia: Saving the Selves of Adolescent Girls,* Mary Pipher writes that "Fathers ... have great power to do harm. If they act as socializing agents for the culture, they can crush their daughters' spirits. Rigid fathers limit their daughters' dreams and destroy their self-confidence" (117). The message that Chidera is receiving is that a girl's emotional and educational needs are not important; however, her encounter with the Goddess is a transformative event that battens and supports her confidence and resilience.

Although Uli art was practiced during her parents' youth, the craft died out so that only a few in the village now remember the artform. The implication is that industrial progress has artistically impoverished the culture. The leaf draws the attention of other schoolgirls, and Chidera eventually makes symbolic designs on others with an apparently magical felt tip pen she has found. The leaf functions as a symbol that inspires positive memories for those who see it, and like Lisa Goldstein's 1987 novel *A Mask for the General,* Chidera's story explores the subtly transformative nature of art. As Chidera's skills improve, she begins to see how various patterns symbolize experience, such as how linked spirals represent women's conversation at the well. After she decorates the walls of her room with a mural, her parents respond with new respect for her. By recreating the world around her, Chidera begins to identify her inner goddess. She has found her strength. When Mama Ugo, a local wise woman, teaches her to make dyes from local materials, Chidera learns to paint, and her work becomes even more beautiful. She begins to be known for her magic hands.[9] When she reconnects with her mother by helping decorate the figurines her mother sells at the market, sales flourish. This reconnection is psychologically important, what Carol Pearson describes as "crucial" to a woman's "successful hero journey" (Pearson, 178). Murdock calls it "healing the mother/daughter split" (5). Whereas her father demonstrates initiative and attachment by introducing her to Mama Ugo at a critical time, Chidera's artistic talent comes from her mother. Participation in her mother's own art demonstrates that she values her maternal connection and creates a bond of womanhood that is, in itself, transformative. To be a whole person she needs to recognize and integrate male and female qualities. As her reputation spreads, she begins to be paid for her work.

According to various Nigerian websites, the name Chidera means something like "What God has written, he has written forever," and it is a name traditionally given to boys. By giving this name to a girl, Okorafor subverts tradition and further implies that it is the Goddess who protects and revitalizes artistic practice by bringing it forth from the earth. Although Chidera's talent is her own, the story is clear that art has its own intrinsic earth magic. Cultural change occurs not violently at the point of a sword but organically at the end of a *nma uli* painting stick. As the narrator concludes, "Sometimes the magic flows from one's fingers, other times it is transferred to the person who experiences the result. Magic has always worked in mysterious ways" (Loc 711).

From Inner Space to Outer Space

In America, women were barred from astronaut training until 1978, but in 1983, Sally Ride became the first American woman to go into outer space. Young women, however, have been fascinated by space travel from the beginning,[10] and writers like Leigh Bracket and C.L. Moore began writing about women going into space decades before. Madeleine L'Engle's YA novel *A Wrinkle in Time,* 1962, portrayed Meg Murry, a 13-year-old traveling through the universe to rescue her father. (Early movie versions portray Meg as white, but the 2018 Disney film portrays her as bi-racial.)

Although Octavia Butler is a notable exception, 20th century women writers of color such as Maya Angelou, Toni Morrison, and Alice Walker focused their attention on the inner spaces of women's bodies and the struggle to find meaningful personal relationships in a culture defined by racism and sexism. In 1994, Samuel Delany suggested that Black writers were "fenced out of science fiction by a semiotic concertina wire" (Dery, 109). Delany believed that the blinking instrument panels and advanced technology presented a cognitive "No Trespass" sign to writers of color. That may have been true in the '80s and '90s, but contemporary Afrofuturist writers are venturing into outer space. Barbadian writer Karen Lord, in particular, has explored extraterrestrial landscapes and technology in her novels *The Best of All Possible Worlds,* 2013, and *The Galaxy Game,* 2015, but these books do not move African culture into outer space in the same way that her earlier novel, *Redemption in Indigo*, 2010, integrates the magic realism of an African folktale. When considering whether to write about space travel, Okorafor wanted to envision an African space program that would involve powerful mythology and earth magic. By her own admission, she had always been somewhat nervous about flying, but in 2015, she and her daughter Anyaugo went to Cape Canaveral to watch a shuttle launch.

Although personal flight was integral to the evolution of her stories, she was initially hesitant to write about space flight[11] because she saw herself as "very much an earthling," but she wondered if seeing a shuttle launch might give her momentum to move her stories into outer space (blog). On July 15, 2011, her blog describes how she and her daughter attended the final space shuttle launch from Kennedy Space Center. Later she describes the launch as a "serious" "o-m-g moment," and she concludes that "maybe I can write about space now" (blog). Her description of the launch is intensely personal:

> Once everyone saw the plumes of exhaust, people started cheering.... It was happening right in front of me.... And I was tingly with exhilaration and fear, it was so close. Then there was the noise. It was pressing on my face. Vibrating through my body. Up up up, it went. Then it punched through the thin clouds. And then it was gone. You could see its shadow reflecting on the clouds. It took less than a minute [blog].

The result was a triggering of Africanfuturist imagination that led to her Hugo Award winning novella *Binti*.

Binti: Exit Strategy, Trauma and Resilience

The immediacy of the shuttle launch seems to have overcome Okorafor's hesitancy to write about space. *Binti*, 2015, a novella mostly set in outer space, received both the 2015 Nebula and 2016 Hugo awards. With *Binti*, Okorafor takes the inner spaces of a girl's life into outer space. Its sequels, *Binti: Home* and *Binti: The Night Masquerade*, 2017, also award-finalists, continue this journey. *Binti* begins like a futuristic wagon train saga. It describes a 16-year-old Himba woman's travel between the stars, leaving home among strangers who do not share her ways or respect her customs. In this novella, the cultural artifacts and red clay earth that she takes with her are essential in resolving a deadly interstellar conflict. One of them, the *edan*, is an alien artifact found in the desert. It is both weapon and universal translator, perhaps reflecting the utopian peace and ecological sufficiency of the Biblical Eden. Binti is a mathematical genius, a lightning calculator. When she takes a spaceship to a university on another planet, her ship is attacked, and her fellow students are murdered by Meduse warriors from a spear-wielding, alien culture who have a legitimate grudge against the university. Through intelligence, quick wits, and endurance, Binti is able to overcome her fears enough to communicate and negotiate with the jellyfish-like aliens who murdered her friends.

For Binti, the saving agent is otjize, a red clay mixture that she uses on her hair and body to protect it from the harsh desert climate of her home village and for hygienic purposes due to the region's scarcity of water. Still used today by the women of the Himba tribe of Namibia, otjize is a combination of butterfat and ochre pigment. This paste is often perfumed with the aromatic resin from the *Omuzumba* shrub. The mixture gives skin a deep orange or reddish tinge. For the Himba, this symbolizes the earth's rich red color and blood which is the essence of life. The Himba women use otjize in their hair, which is long and plaited and rolled into intricate designs. When the paste dries, the hair resembles a clay sculpture, providing an ideal for feminine beauty. Over time, the paste flakes off, removing dirt and dead skin.[12]

Binti's otjize is a healing matriarchal recipe that smells of jasmine flowers and also contains earth magic. Hair heavy with otjize is connected to the earth's good luck and strength, and Binti's thick hair is plaited in tessellating triangles, a code her father created that indicates her family's bloodline, culture and history. As in earlier works, Okorafor describes a dynamic culture that is often treated with bigotry, misunderstanding, and contempt. The prejudice of the light complexioned Khoush,[13] a rival local tribe and dominant culture, is that the Himba are "dirt bathers" who thicken their hair plaits with excrement. At the beginning of the novella, Binti is leaving her home village to attend the prestigious extraterrestrial Oomza University on a full mathematics scholarship. Her exit strategy is to leave before her family gets up because they don't want her to go.[14] As she leaves, she wipes some of the sweet smelling otjize from her forehead with her index finger and touches the ground with it, ceremonially thanking the earth for allowing her small anti-gravity transporter to carry her luggage from the village to the shuttle station. This intentional alignment with the powers of the earth is characteristic of Okorafor's fiction. Even though Binti's family does not approve or know that she is leaving, the earth gives its permission. As in many old folktales, remembering to honor the earth has its rewards.

Harmonizing Math Anxiety

Okorafor's early short stories, such as "How Inyang Got Her Wings" and "The Winds of Harmattan," explore the psychological damage that can be caused by repressive parenting and paternalistic cultural traditions; however, although maintaining many traditional values, Binti's far future culture is technologically advanced and egalitarian in allowing to girls to be educated. Although her parents disapprove of her going to the off-world university, their reasons concern loss of her cultural values and the possibility that her genius might become a tool for the university's research into the invention of increasingly advanced weapons. Like all of Okorafor's heroines, Binti has a special talent that goes beyond ordinary intelligence. Her family is *Bitolus*, indicating the family profession of computer bit biotechnology (29). They know "deep mathematics" and can control electronic current (30). Like her father, she is a master harmonizer capable of building the finest astrolabes. Within Okorafor's context, this is not the simple machine once used in guiding ships by measuring the altitude of the sun but a sophisticated handheld personal biological computer that not only includes the usual email connections but, similar to a very advanced Fitbit, also records emotional energy as well as the daily events of the person who owns it. Thus, an astrolabe can be scanned to determine the psychological fitness of its holder.[15] The word *astrolabe* comes originally from the Greek, and it means "star taker." Very early astrolabes were used to point the direction to Mecca. As a rule, Okorafor provides her young protagonists with ways to research problems that must be solved. Zahrah has her *Field Guide* to the Greeny Jungle, and Sunny has *Fast Facts for Free Agents* and *Advanced Juju Knife Jujus*. Binti can use her astrolabe to determine where she is in time and space, a very sophisticated intramural and extraterrestrial version of geospatial positioning. On a symbolic level, Binti's astrolabe becomes a kind of psychological guide to the stars of her future.

Creating Binti's astrolabe involves high-level mathematical meditation that requires visualizing the "treeing" of equations. A complex equation is imagined and halved again and again: Binti muses "When you do math fractals long enough, you kick yourself into treeing just enough to get lost in the shallows of the mathematical sea" (22). This meditation goes deeply enough to "see" the atoms involved, and Binti has been told by her older sister that visualizing high-level quantum mechanics can become a pleasure akin to sexual response: "The best of us have the gift to bring harmony so delicious that we can make atoms caress each other like lovers" (62). Here Okorafor confronts the traditional attitude that girls are not good at math by creating a heroine who is possibly the best young theoretical mathematician on Earth and then allows her to have considerable pleasure in its practice.

The concept of treeing comes from Okorafor's own experience as a champion tennis player. In her memoir *Broken Places, Outer Spaces*, she writes that on the tennis court she could "see through time" (57):

> It happened most often when things got really heated. Something inside me would align. The tennis term for this heightened state of being is "treeing." [...] When I treed, sometimes I could predict the future. Not that far, about one second. I'd know where my opponent was going to hit the ball because I'd see it happen right before it did. It was just enough time to make use of the knowledge [*Broken*, 57].

This phenomenon, also a characteristic of top-level racquet ball play, is a way of seeing into the future based on experience and logic. There is an instant calculation of force and triangulation. It is most likely to occur when the opponent is playing consistently. From this very real occurrence, it is then only a small sideways step to Binti's advanced ability to visualize or "tree" lightning calculations of equations. It also makes sense that the intense focus required in treeing would be meditative and calming,[16] moving away from the fright, fight, flight response of the amygdala or reptilian brain.

In *Reviving Ophelia: Saving the Selves of Adolescent Girls,* 1994, clinical psychologist Mary Pipher suggests that some girls who were once good in math begin to have difficulty with it during junior high because they lack confidence, trust in their own judgment, and "the ability to tolerate frustration without becoming overwhelmed"[17] (63). Pipher explains that "Anxiety interferes with problem solving in math" (63). Although neuroimaging research at Carnegie Mellon University reveals no differences between girls and boys in how they process math problems, a vicious circle of self-doubt, anxiety and failure can develop when girls lack cultural support for their problem solving (Preidt, np). Binti, however, has been taught the relaxation and meditation skills necessary for overcoming the anxiety that surrounds the theoretical unknown, a way of using number patterns to disconnect from emotional interference, and this proves essential for her survival when alien pirates try to kill her.

Although Binti initially does not understand the *edan* she carries, its purpose is soon revealed to her. Objects found at critical times frequently function as magical boons for Okorafor's young heroines and are indicative of supernatural support working behind the scenes. Transgression of purely scientific cause and effect is common in Okorafor's fiction. She relates this in her 2016 Hugo Award acceptance speech:

> My father was a heart surgeon and borderline atheist who grew up in a household where there was a shrine in the backyard dedicated to powerful Igbo deities. Complexities and an organic blending of the traditional with the futuristic are what I know [blog, 8/24/16].

Binti's special talent intuitively connects her to the *edan*, but it takes a crisis for her to begin understanding how it works. Third Fish, the cyborged interstellar university ship on which she travels, is hijacked by the Meduse,[18] jelly-fishlike aliens who have a legitimate grudge against the school. Okorafor bases these aliens on a jelly fish she and her daughter saw in the Khalid Lagoon in Sharjah, United Arab Emirates. Previously she had seen a Portuguese man-o-war in a museum, but it was not alive. This one was "pumping away like it had very important things to do" (Schenstead-Harris, np). Together, the two images provided her inspiration for a truly alien warrior culture, and she dedicates *Binti* to the jelly fish.

As the aliens are about to kill her, Binti discovers that the *edan* works as a kind of biological weapon that is linked to her thoughts. If she hadn't been holding it, she would have been murdered along with the other students, but she is able to use it to kill the alien who is attacking her and escape to her room. Later, otjize provides a catalyst for unlocking the *edan* when she meditatively polishes it with her finger:

> I smelled home, heard the desert wind blowing grains of sand over each other. My stomach fluttered as I dropped deeper in and my entire body felt sweet and pure and empty and light. ... there was now a tiny button in the center of the spiral [38].

Activating the electrical circuits in the *edan* with her own biofeedback energy gives Binti the courage to negotiate with the aliens when they try to kill her again. A current flowing from it through the metal door of her room produces blue tree branches and green leaves signifying the power of her homeland. It continues to protect her by functioning as a universal translator as she negotiates with a Meduse named Okwu. Because Binti has brought her earth magic with her, Okwu's withered tentacle begins to heal when it comes in contact with the otjize. Furthermore, Binti's rolled hair plaits appear similar to Okwu's tentacles, making her seem less alien to him. In exchange for her continued safety, Binti offers her ability as a harmonizer as well as the use of her otjize.

Binti: Resiliency in the Posthuman Frontier

In order to negotiate with the Meduse, Binti is forced to undergo a cyborg transformation. Reflecting what happens to Lilith, the protagonist of Butler's *Dawn*, the first book in the Xenogenesis Trilogy, Binti's transformation from human to posthuman is accomplished under great stress and is not volitional, a symbolic rape:

> I felt the stinger plunge into my spine just before I blacked out and just after I'd conjured up the wild line of current that I guided to the *edan*. It was a terrible

pain. Then I left. I left them, I left that ship. I could hear the ship singing its half-word song and I knew it was singing to me [66].

After alien penetration,[19] Binti wakes up with tentacles instead of hair. Through the binocular lenses of postcolonialism and feminism, it easy to see a history of women who do not have the right to decide what happens to their own bodies. It is also possible that the surgical penetration of Binti's spine reflects the spinal surgery that temporarily paralyzed Okorafor when she was nineteen. What stands out, however, is Okorafor's recognition that lasting peace requires sacrifice, reconciliation and going beyond punitive justice to restorative and transformative justice. This requires truth and reconciliation—finding and addressing "the root of the problem" and then, as Adrienne Maree Brown suggests, moving forward "at the speed of trust" (Brown, "Transformative.") The university must hear the aliens' complaint and recognize what they did was an illegitimate appropriation. Okorafor's two sequels, *Binti: Home* and Binti: *The Night Masquerade,* continue to explore the importance of dealing with the difficulties of creating transformative justice due to prejudicial attitudes on the home front.

Eventually, Binti becomes an ambassador who represents the Meduse in their conflict with the university, but this comes at a price.[20] She has become a genetic hybrid with blue-spotted tentacles as "thick and sizable as snakes," allowing for an increased telepathic connection[21] (87). Binti is now posthuman/part alien. Her sacrifice is a transformative experience that alters her perception and understanding in order to accommodate the understanding and perceptions of the aliens (Lacey, 168). Although she eventually realizes advantages in her transformation, from a moral perspective the change remains problematic because it is one-sided. She changes; the aliens do not. Physically, she now resembles the mythological Medusa more than the eyeless Meduse do, a change Binti takes in stride after her initial surprise. At first, she may be too young to fully understand the significance of how much she has changed. Perhaps her comparatively swift acceptance of physical difference also reflects the survival-honed accommodation of someone in a minority culture who learns to focus on a few goals despite cultural obstacles, one who does not entirely expect full rights to self-determination.[22] Dealing with the implications of her change does not occur until later books in the series: *Home* and *The Night Masquerade.*

Like most of Okorafor's girl protagonists, Binti demonstrates resiliency, a safeguard against long-term depression, and a path to recovery after trauma is experienced. Resilience is often confused as grit or strength, but this is not accurate; traumatic experience cannot be shoved into a jar and set aside. Recovery from trauma is dependent on neuroplasticity, the ability to learn about and redefine experience (Galvan, 108). Trauma must be remembered, reinterpreted, and integrated. Traumatic events must be reframed in ways that individuals can understand. Resilience can be defined as the ability to cope and adjust to a changing environment. It is not an avoidance of emotion. For adolescents, successful coping most often depends on connection and empowerment: connection requires a support system of individuals who are caring and dependable, including those who are outside of their birth families (Hines, 243). Empowerment suggests that recovering individuals are allowed agency to solve problems and effect changes in their lives. Okorafor provides Binti with this safety net. In particular, Binti's initially surprising friendship with Okwu provides her with a way to understand and work through her trauma.

In a 2016 *Locus* interview, science fiction writer Eleanor Arnason writes that "in a science fiction novel, the psychology is in the landscape, in the society, in the alien species" (22). In *Binti*, Okorafor creates very nonhuman aliens who nevertheless have a psychology with a common denominator that readers can grasp. They have an aboriginal warrior culture ethic. In a sense, the Meduse warriors and the scholars at Oomza have similarly colonial attitudes toward Binti: the bodily violation of a "tribal" individual is of little importance (82). The callousness of dominant cultures reflects a kind of paternalistic "otherizing" toward those without insider privilege, a phenomenon explored by earlier feminist writers. In Kate Wilhelm's *Where Late the Sweet Birds Sang*, 1976, and Carol Emshwiller's *Carmen Dog*, 1988, scientists use and defile women for supposedly higher scientific or "humanitarian" goals. In Octavia Butler's *Clay's Ark* and "Blood Child" (both 1984), aliens or alien organisms use humans as vehicles for reproduction. In all these stories, the protagonists have been seduced, infected, or coerced into passivity and compliance, and part of the struggle is for them to determine that they have the right to refuse subjugation.

The Chibok School Girls

Despite the Meduse's resemblance to jellyfish, Okorafor has loosely based the central conflict on contemporary African problems. According to the *United States Department of State Diplomacy in Action* website, the Bureau of Counterterrorism and Countering Violent Extremism reports that terrorism, which includes killing, bombings and the kidnapping of women and children, continues to be a significant problem in Africa. Particularly significant is the organized Boko Haram kidnapping of 276 Chibok school girls on April 14 and 15 of 2014. Amnesty International believes that the Nigerian military had four hours' warning but failed to send troops to protect the school. In the months that followed, 57 girls were able to escape and report their experiences to human rights organizations. Although at one point the Nigerian government knew where the girls were being held, it was unwilling to commit to reclaiming them. The girls, aged 15 to 18, were all in their last year of schooling and had come to the Chibok Government Girls Secondary School to take exams in physics for their Senior Secondary School Certification. In the Northern Nigeria Hausa language, the term *boko haram* means "Western education is forbidden."

In the years prior to the kidnapping, the organization had been heavily influenced by Muslim terrorists linked to al-Qaeda. In May 2016, one of the missing girls, Amina Ali, was found. She claimed that the remaining girls were still in a forest camp, but six had died. Twenty-one girls were freed in October 2016, while another was rescued the next month. Another was found in January 2017. Eighty-two more girls were freed in May 2017, and one more was rescued in January 2018. Release of some of the girls was obtained in an exchange for five imprisoned Boko Haram leaders. As of April 14, 2019, Al Jazeera reported that 112 are still missing. Many of the girls who regained their freedom had born children and/ or were pregnant, having been raped and/or forced into marriages. After they were released, the girls reported that during captivity, they kept their hopes alive by keeping a diary that they passed between them. Although Chibok is a Christian village, many of the girls were forced to convert to Islam, which allows girls as young as nine to marry. (Okorafor talks about this practice in *Shadow Speaker*).

After the kidnapping, some of the girls were sold into slavery and forced labor at a "bride price" to their buyers of about $10.00.[23] Some were trained to fight other girls and women, and some used as human shields, and others forced to become suicide bombers in their own villages or to kill their parents. Of those who escaped, only a few have been able to return to school. At least twenty are presently continuing their education in the United States. Their bravery is compelling; one of the freed girls has remarked, "Education is scary ... but it gives me wings; I need to fly" (Aderibigbe, 28).

The Chibok school girls have been deeply traumatized. In *Trauma and Recovery*, Judith Lewis Hermann writes:

> Terror, intermittent reward, isolation, and enforced dependency may succeed in creating a submissive and compliant prisoner. But the final step in psychological control of the victim is not completed until she has been forced to violate her own moral principles and to betray her basic human attachments. Psychologically, this is the most destructive of all coercive techniques, for the victim who has succumbed loathes herself. It is at this point, when the victim under duress participates in the sacrifice of others, that she is truly "broken" [83].

Although it was possible to find the camps using satellite technology, the Nigerian army claimed they were over-extended. Their reluctance may have been due to their own prejudice against the education for women. According to the 2015 Law and Society Conference, female school attendance in the Borno State is about 29 percent. Over 73 percent of the girls have not had any formal education (Aderibigbe, 11). The betrayal of these girls has been epic.

In 2015, in Nigeria alone, more than 1,240 persons were killed by Boko Haram terrorists in attacks that included suicide bombings at mosques, markets and parades (Country Reports: Africa Overview). In the 21st century, much of Africa is unsafe for young women.[24] When writing YA, Okorafor's process is to explore danger rather than minimize it. To call further attention to the Chibok kidnapping, in 2017 she created a comic book about a disabled Nigerian school girl who becomes a superhero and asked her artist to use a photograph of one of the Chibok school girls when drawing this character. (For more on this see "Black to Okorafor").

In Okorafor's "Acknowledgments," she reveals that *Binti* was a project shared with her "plucky imaginative" 11-year-old daughter Anyaugo, who essentially came up with the plot and helped her mother through any blocks regarding what came next. Like Okorafor's earlier YA novels *Zahrah the Windseeker, Shadow Speaker,* and *Akata Witch, Binti* clearly focalizes girls' empowerment. The name *Binti* is a diminutive that means "daughter" or "young lady."[25] By using this name, Okorafor clearly implies that Binti is young and unsophisticated, at least at first. Unlike Inyang and Asuquo of Okorafor's early short stories, Binti is not sexually experienced. At the time of the alien attack, she is hovering on the verge of her first true romance, and her innocent expectations are defiled when Heru, her new love interest, is murdered in front of her and she is spattered with his blood. Despite the implausibility of a 16-year-old girl's becoming an alien ambassador, Binti is plausibly teenaged and understandably struggles with horror and overwhelming emotions before she is able to pull herself together and eventually succeed. In her blog, Okorafor explains that "facing and conquering fear seems to be at the heart of the novella's inspiration"[26] (blog, 8/24/16). Binti's success is enabled by a combination of inherited genius and positive parenting that places no limits on girls' achievement.

Afrofuturism and Africanfuturism

In *Afrofuturism: The World of Black Sci-Fi and Fantasy Culture,* Ytasha L. Womack has described Afrofuturism as a "free space for women, a door ajar, arms wide open, a literal and figurative space for black women to be themselves" (100–101). By blending fantasy, mythology, and science fiction, Okorafor has taken advantage of this open door, but she continues to be realistic about the problems of human prejudice and violence that will still be found on the other side of the door sill.

Afrofuturism is based on a long tradition of Black music rooted in spirituals in which the secret language of escape from slavery was masked by Biblical references: "Swing Low, Sweet Chariot" and "Michael, Row Your Boat" were coded signals of escape via the underground railroad. Born in the U.S. in a family of Nigerian immigrants, Okorafor does not specifically share this ancestral background, but her family did immigrate to escape the genocide of the Biafran War, and the reasons for leaving were just as compelling. The flight to America was still very "deep and wide" and the promise of "milk and honey" needed to be viewed skeptically. Racial prejudice and unofficial segregation were status quo for African Americans in the '60s and '70s.

Likewise, Binti believes that crossing the wide vacuum of outer space will be synonymous with finding the intellectual freedom she seeks. However, just as African Americans did not find much "milk and honey" in the Promised Land of the northern states and Canada, it is obvious that the complex, multi-cultural, somewhat chaotic nature of Oomza University's academic discourse will require Binti to keep her tech-savvy wits about her if she is to avoid being co-opted (just as her mother warned).

Binti: *Home* and the Issue of Identity

In the sequel *Binti: Home,* 2017, Binti is in a state of becoming and getting help from a competent therapist. Her personal identity expands to include a secret family history. Lacey, 2014, describes "becoming" as envisioning a "future," which always involves "a process of revisioning" (143). After so much loss and so much change in her physical identity, it is not surprising that Binti feels an anger that she does not understand, an anger and confusion that opens her to an out-of-body alien first contact:

"Who are you?" a voice asked. It spoke in the dialect of my family and it came from everywhere.
"Binti Ekeopara Zuzu Dambu Kaipa of Namib, that is my name," I said.
Pause.
I waited.
"There's more," the voice said.
"That's all," I said, irritated. "That's my name."
"No." The flash of anger that spurted through me was a surprise. Then it was welcome. I knew my own name [Home, 9].

Within the context of Okorafor's alien-entwined diaspora, Binti's names are "a fracture and a weaving," a personal family history of place and descendance that grows and interweaves to embrace past and future, what she knows and what she has yet to learn (Macharia, n.p.). Her new name includes "Enyi Zinariya," a previously unknown alien heritage.

Binti's anger reveals a subconscious recognition that the future may be difficult to face. "Such fury. It was unlike me. And lately, it was like me, it happened so often" (11). She is experiencing post-traumatic stress disorder, including flashbacks, nightmares, and day terrors (19). It is an emotional state triggered by actual changes in the brain. Her violent mood swings are believable, but knowing her own name, which contains her family identity, is part of her resilience. In response, she decides to return to her family home so that she can seek cleansing through pilgrimage. She returns with Okwu, a nine-foot-tall, five-foot-wide Meduse warrior. Her close connection with Okwu implies a potential for violence, but she is able to use her quick wits and harmonizing skill to stop Okwu from harming others with his sophisticated fire power when he is attacked for being alien.[27] In discussing physical assertiveness in young Black women, sociologist Peggy Ornstein quotes Toni Morrison:

> Aggression is not as new to black women as it is to white women. Black women seem to be able to combine the nest and the adventure. They don't see conflicts in certain areas as do white women. They are both safe harbor and ship; they are both inn and trail. We, black women, do both [231].

Throughout her fiction, Okorafor depicts the daily comforts of nest-making (particularly clothes and food[28]) as well as the ability to take pleasure in physical assertiveness—what Alice Walker originally described as "Womanist"[29] values, a concept that intuitively embraces Black women's perspective and cultural values while confronting intersectional prejudice. Okorafor, who was nationally rated in tennis before a spinal surgery ended her hopes, ably portrays Binti as she works through her fears and sudden furies through a combination of meditation, study, and physical action. It is apparent that the ability to create the "nest" of physical comfort, with its corresponding network of personal relationship, is essential to the success of the "adventure." Okwu has become part of Binti's nest/network.

In "Contemporary Science Fiction and Afrofuturism," Lavender, 2019, remarks that in the *Binti* trilogy,[30] Okorafor "clearly ... directs her creative energies toward the intersections of identity politics and futurity as she carefully navigates the different histories of Africa and black America" (579). The social consequences of becoming "other" and its ramifications for the future are much more problematic after Binti leaves the relative open-mindedness of the university and returns to her own village. She must deal with the politics of prejudice when her sister suggests that no one will marry her now:

> "You are so ugly now, Binti," she said. "You don't even sound the same. You're polluted. Almost eighteen years old. What man will marry you? What kind of children will you have now?" [73]

Throughout Okorafor's fiction, being talented, different, and strong is culturally problematic for young women. There's considerable family pressure to find an appropriate husband; the culturally perceived danger of miscegenation is a corresponding motif (see "Watching Windseekers"). Historically, interracial marriage has been seen as a dilution of the gene pool. It is fostered by ignorance and prejudice.[31] Evidenced in science fiction by African American writers beginning in the 1890s, this prejudice has existed in educated Black families as well.[32] Essentialist concerns about miscegenation reflect a deep fear of change as well as a misunderstanding of biology. Although most virulent in male supremacist cultures in which women are considered property and a woman can be murdered by her brothers for giving birth to a biracial child, Okorafor makes clear that even in egalitarian cultures, education alone is insufficient to change deeply held fears about the contamination of difference. In response, she gives Binti the strength to stand up to family criticism.

> "Papa what has happened?"....
> "Why did you allow this? You used to be such a beautiful girl." His words
> hit me like a slap and I felt it slip through my body and for a moment, I forgot everything. I rubbed my forehead then ran a finger over my *okuoko*. Mine, I thought. *These are mine* [160].

Binti essentially likes herself, and the tentacles are an integral part. Pipher explains that "strong girls know who they are and value themselves as multifaceted people" (265). Their identities hold up well under pressure, and their talents allow them some continuity as they pass from childhood and onward through adolescence. When Binti uses her ability to meditate on a tree of equations, she is opening herself to the multiple facets of her identity and to an as-yet-not-envisioned future. Throughout her fiction Okorafor argues that our concept of humanity must widen to include the posthuman. Binti's grandmother, a Desert woman, tells her father:

> "You people are so brilliant, but your world is too small" ... "One of you finally somehow grows beyond your cultural cage and you try to chop her stem. Fascinating" [96].

In *Parable of the Sower,* Octavia Butler explains, "All that you touch you Change. All that you Change Changes you. The only lasting truth is Change. God is Change" (3). Binti takes a major step in establishing a more mature personal identity when she says, "Change was constant. Change was my destiny. Growth" (146). This is essential in resolving the shame she feels for not living up to her family's expectations.

The Desert People have advanced telepathic skills and offer Binti community and new ways to communicate. Lorde has written that "without community, there is no liberation" (95). Thus, Binti's new communication skills liberate her from the prejudicial family attitude that cultures lacking obvious technology will have nothing to offer. It turns out that long ago, this African culture had alien contact which afforded them biological nanoids,[33] which, embedded in the DNA, create an internal astrolabe that allows for instantaneous thought communication. Like many of Okorafor's protagonists, Binti realizes that she has been "other" from the beginning and the okuoku tentacles are simply the most recent iteration.

Reconciliation and *The Night Masquerade*

Looking through the lens of the lessons of history, it is apparent that lasting peace cannot be created through war. Lasting peace must be based on truth, reconciliation, transformative justice, and the awareness that though neither side is innocent, suffering is universal. Nobel Peace Prize winner Leymah Gbowee, 2011, writes:

> Purging oneself of pain was only the first step. If a community was to be made whole after war, especially civil war, perpetrators and victims had to come together [179].

Although she has twice mediated a truce between the Meduse and Khoush, the cognitive dissonance that Binti and Okwu bring Osemba, her home village, triggers an already simmering conflict that eventually destroys her family home. When Binti believes her family has died, she once again tries to harmonize a truce. Her mediation attempts to highlight similarities and reconcile differences.

> "Do any of you remember why you started fighting? ... If I ask any of you the reason, you'll cite different stories from so long ago that the grandchildren of the grandchildren of any possible witnesses are long dead" [BNM 115].
> "Meduse tradition is one of honor. Khoush tradition is one of respect. I am a master harmonizer of the Osemba Himba." ... "End this," I said, my voice full and steady. "End this now" [BNM 116–117].

The commanders agree to the truce and start to leave only to start fighting again. When the Meduse chief is attacked, Binti is caught in the crossfire and dies. In "The Failure of War," Wendell Berry writes,

> In a modern war, fought with modern weapons and on the modern scale, neither side can limit to "the enemy" the damage that it does. These wars damage the world. We know enough by now to know that you cannot damage a part of the world without damaging all of it. Modern war has not only made it impossible to kill "combatants" without killing "noncombatants," it has made it impossible to damage your enemy without damaging yourself [60].

Reconciliation is a complex and difficult process. In order to find a lasting peace, both sides must recognize and honor their own losses without planning revenge. The necessary realization is that getting even is never possible. In *Practicing Reconciliation in a Violent World*, theologian Michael Battle concludes, "We must inhabit reconciliation. There is nothing else" (4). The word *inhabit* is interesting. It is stronger than *practice*. Battle implies that we must continuously live reconciliation. Binti is herself an act of reconciliation. She identifies as "a collective within myself" (116). *The Night Masquerade* focalizes how she reconciles various, sometimes warring, parts of herself so that she can find and channel her own power. Fortunately, through an act of grace, Binti is reincarnated on New Fish, the child of Third Fish, the living sea-creature-like shuttle she first took into space. For her selfless heroism, she gets her life back, although once again in a new form.

One value of YA speculative fiction is that trauma and posttraumatic stress disorder can be described in ways that distance readers from the horrific events that trigger them; as Sarah Lefanu suggests, the faraway in time and space defamiliarizes the familiar (Lefanu, 21). Okorafor's fictional representation is far less horrifying than what happened to the Chibok schoolgirls. For readers, the full horror of kidnapping, rape, mass murder and forced otherization can be approached carefully. Okorafor's message to young women is one shared by Maya Angelou in her poem, "Still I Rise," 1978, which advocates for rising beyond "the huts of history's shame" and "bringing the gifts" that "ancestors gave," a metaphor that connects directly with Okorafor's depiction of flight. At this writing, the *Binti* books are being made into a three-part television series to appear on Hulu. Okorafor is co-writing the pilot with Stacy Amma Osei-Kuffour.

Conclusion: *Tomorrow Is Now*

In *Tomorrow Is Now*, 1963, Eleanor Roosevelt wrote a list of Eleven Keys for a More Fulfilling Life, "You must do the thing you think you cannot do." Roosevelt's intention was to nudge America out of its complacency regarding protecting the rights of those who lack political power and influence. Likewise, it is no secret that writers of the fantastic use tropes to create a "Tomorrowland" space for discussing contemporary problems. Okorafor, like Octavia Butler, Nalo Hopkinson and other Afrofuturist and Africanfuturist women writers, most often sets her stories in the future but essentially writes about ever-present political and societal problems that endanger humanity now, as well as any hope for a sustainable future. In her essay "Organic Fiction," Okorafor explains that her process is to write through what scares her. The *Binti* Trilogy, "The Palm Tree Bandit" and "Magic Hands" can be read as recipes for resilience and healthy girl development within a complex, difficult world. These young women use their unique talents to overcome fear and guide themselves to a "now" that literally and figuratively holds the seeds of a utopian tomorrow.

6

Magic, Masquerades and Morality

"For me, the dark has never been uninhabited. The wind has always brought things.
Masquerades are real and the ancestors can be guides" [*Broken*, 8].

Okorafor has used her unique bicultural experiences to create stories that remythologize African cultural traditions, making them more accessible to young adults and children, as well as providing an implicit critique of related myths from other world cultures. In Okorafor's mythic universe, the supernatural may be rearranged, re-framed and reinterpreted, but it is also real and unpredictable. One way her protagonists encounter the supernatural is through masquerades. During her visits to Nigeria, Okorafor encountered masquerades in her father's home village and initially found them terrifying. Not the cosplay[1] we associate with Carnival balls and SF fan conferences, these Nigerian masquerades represent powerful magic. *Zahrah the Windseeker* (2005), *Who Fears Death* (2010), *Akata Witch* (2011), *Akata Warrior* (2017), *Kabu-Kabu* (2013), *Binti: The Night Masquerade* (2017), and her award-winning picture book *Chicken in the Kitchen* (2015) all employ masquerades as plot devices to support the development of her young heroines' independence and self-esteem. In her adult novel, *Lagoon* (2014), a masquerade plays an important role in resolving the novel's central crisis. One way to get over a fear of something is to imagine becoming it. Throughout her fiction, Okorafor taps personal experience to create masquerades that are larger and more elemental than the ones she experienced in real life but ultimately easier to control because they are hers. These masquerades work as evolving symbols, becoming less fearful to her protagonists as they are challenged, revealing important ideas relating to young adult moral development and conflict resolution.

Never Unmask a Masquerade

Early in Okorafor's life, masquerades represented a vindictive, uncontrollable spiritual dimension that intruded into her real world. Although her family lived in the United States, they made frequent trips to her father's home village of Arondizuogu. In her Wahala[2] blog entry for July 17, 2010, entitled "Never Unmask a Masquerade,"[3] Okorafor describes being harassed by masquerades while walking between her home and her uncle's. Men and boys in masquerade costumes carried whips and would jump out from behind the concrete wall that surrounded her uncle's house. Once she and her sister were cornered and whipped so hard that the blows drew blood. Their father, Godwin Okorafor, a respected cardiac surgeon, was a member of the village masquerade society and ostensibly knew that his daughters were being harassed but did nothing to stop it. Perhaps her father believed that dealing with what amounted to local law enforcement was a necessary part of growing up. In a 2014 *Mosaic* interview, Okorafor remarks, "My parents wanted us to be what we all eventually became—strong Nigerian-Americans who never questioned who we were" (Rasheed, np).

> For years, I have asked and asked Nigerian male friends, uncles, granduncles, male elders for details. Never have I gotten an ounce of information. Of course, this only increases my hunger for this forbidden knowledge. One day I will succeed. And then as soon as the information falls on my female ears (for such things are certainly NOT written down), the sky will turn black, plants will grow underground and babies will speak like old men.... I'm kidding. Maybe [np].

Careful readers will notice, however, that her father is not specifically mentioned in the preceding list of male relatives who were questioned regarding masquerade secrets. Clearly a familial "no talk" rule existed that would be difficult for a child to negotiate: in *Akata Warrior*, when 5-year-old Sunny asks her father what it is like to dress up as a masquerade, his response is an angry, "None of your business" (435).

Writing the Forbidden as Post-Traumatic Play

For Okorafor, "none of your business" becomes a challenge. Within her fiction, confronting and unmasking masquerades becomes a symbolic act directly related to overcoming the physical and psychological dangers of a difficult world. Writers often write to get linguistic control of those things in their lives that otherwise seem uncontrollable. Sometimes their childhood terrors provide subconscious inspiration for their stories. They fictively play with terror the same way a child will pick at scabs on a skinned knee, constantly going back to the event, each time making it more fancifully horrific, thus creating emotional distance as well as art. In *Too Scared to Cry*, clinical professor of psychiatry Lenore Terr calls this writing "post-traumatic play"[4] (259). She explains that

> post-traumatic play is probably the best clue one ever gets to the nature of a childhood trauma—that is, if one doesn't get to see the traumatic event itself. This play, when it comes, is absolutely literal. It may reflect s child's compensatory wishes, too. But it will recreate the child's trauma the way a theatrical production recreates a certain mood or a history book recreates a specific happening [248].

It makes sense that masquerades have become an evolving symbol throughout Okorafor's fiction.

Masquerades in Sub-Saharan West African Culture

In traditional Sub-Saharan West African culture, a masquerade is a masked shamanistic character who performs public dances intended to summon the spirits of the deceased so that they will intervene in community concerns regarding relationships, crops, weather, and livestock. Masquerades are believed to function as divine emissaries who are able to create a bridge between earthly and spiritual worlds. The identity of each dancer is completely hidden by a fantastic, frequently scarified mask above loose raffia curls, strips of fabric, or clacking wooden carvings. Reed, 2005, explains that the masquerade spirit is embodied by the person who wears the costume.[5] Masquerades are thought to have developed when yam farming first began. When theft became a problem, masked figures were used to patrol the yam fields and deter thieves. To celebrate the harvest, masquerade dances developed in a variety of styles and forms, practiced exclusively by men, whose individual identities as performers remained unknown (Gore, 2), Correspondingly, secret village masquerade societies were formed that evolved into militias used to enforce village curfews, provide surveillance, and act as security guards. Women were forbidden from joining these organizations.[6]

Forbidding women from knowledge of masquerade secrets may have been based on men's psychological need to symbolically keep a reproductive process to themselves. In many cultures, superstitions regarding men's and women's knowledge have survived until the present. Reed explains that during the latter part of the 20th century, traditional Nigerian women continued to comply with this separation of knowledge because they believed that their reproduction would be endangered if they did not. Women kept their distance from masquerades because masking-society rules decreed that they should not touch masked spirits or gain esoteric knowledge of them. Reed's research indicates that many Igbo men believed that "women do not know that men incarnate these spirits," but the Igbo women she interviewed "refused comment" (2). Reed concludes that both sexes keep masking a "public secret" because they believe that it involves "spirits" and "medicines" (2). Women are careful to follow the rules, because they believe "their bodies and their fertility are at terrible risk if they do not" (2). Many masquerades suggest a kind of demonic power.

Although local vigilantism may be understandable where governmental authority is lax, unregulated community enforcement may become arbitrary and may function like Muslim Sharia Law to repress women's independence. Okorafor was, however, intrigued rather than repressed when village masquerades tried to keep her at home. Her family maintained an uneasy balance of higher education and traditional belief. Her mother, Dr. Helen Okorafor, a nurse midwife, had attained a PhD in medical administration, but, like most Nigerian women, was terrified of the masquerades; her father, a respected heart surgeon, had been initiated into the secret society when he was a young man.[7] Growing up, Okorafor saw masquerades not as neighborhood bullies made anonymous and empowered through costuming but as physical manifestations of ancestral spirits (*Broken*, 29). She believes that she and her three sisters were targeted because they were American-born girls. However, instead of being deterred by bullying, she explains that they found these "terrifying" interactions "delicious" ("Organic," 1). Although they were usually fast enough to outrun a masquerade before he hurt them (thus earning bragging rights), she believed "You can't, however, outrun your ancestors" (*Broken*, 29). Family history is encoded in DNA and embodied by cultural tradition. Gender norms must be negotiated each generation. Years later she encountered a much larger masquerade at a wedding in the United States:

> Its wide body was heavy with dried grass, raffia and cloth. It was tall enough to graze the ceiling. Some men played the drums and flute to keep it dancing.... Two men held it from the audience with a thick rope. It would lunge at [...] women and the women would scream and flee to the other side of the room ["Organic," 1].

There is a phallic significance in this kind of wedding entertainment. It appears that even among educated immigrants, the symbolic connection between masquerades and reproduction is maintained. Furthermore, when men masquerade as women, it is more than playful dressing in drag. Rather, they are symbolically taking women's reproductive power for themselves.

Deconstructing Masquerades

Okorafor's early masquerade terrors provide psychological impetus for literary rebellion when later she creates and then deconstructs her own masquerades. In *Akata Witch,* Sunny's father tells her, "Never unmask a masquerade. You hear me? That is an abomination" (435–436). Since unmasking masquerades is considered blasphemy, the need to do so must be approached as a serious moral dilemma (2). When Sunny uses her newly gained warrior strength to unmask the evil Ekwensu masquerade, it is a matter of utmost necessity. The fate of the community depends on it:

> Setting the recently oil-soaked part of the Niger Delta on fire was only Ekwensu at play. It was only the first thing that would happen if Sunny didn't succeed right *now.* Once Ekwensu really got started, she would turn the world into the apocalyptic place Sunny had seen in the candle's flame [*Warrior,* 432].

Okorafor's earliest masquerades represent fears to be overcome. *Zahrah the Windseeker* introduces masquerades in a cautionary tale told by oil-palm farm workers to Zahrah and her friend Dari. The masquerade they describe is a supernatural horror over twenty feet high topped by a mask with at least seven angry faces (87). Perhaps it represents the jungle's anger at deforestation. Wider than two cars and covered with vines and strips of blue cloth, it exudes something green and "smokelike" before it entraps an overly curious woodcutter and drags him off into the jungle, ostensibly to be consumed (87–88). Although Zahrah is frightened by the farm workers' tale, Dari[8] considers it to be mere legend and wants to continue into the jungle. Characteristic of Zahrah's early adolescent level of moral development, she chooses to face her fears and go with Dari because he is her best friend.

Carol Gilligan's ground-breaking book, *In a Different Voice,* 1982, theorizes that young women tend to make decisions based on an ethic of care (62). Zahrah faces the possibility of her own death when she decides, "If he was going to get eaten by masquerades, then I would, too" (91). It is developmentally significant that Zahrah and Dari set off together into the Forbidden Greeny Jungle.[9] No longer self-defined as a victim of bullying, Zahrah's friendship with Dari offers her new identity and agency in a widening world.

Physical and metaphysical journeys are an intrinsic part of Okorafor's fiction. Although not published until 2013,[10] her most intimate depiction of a masquerade occurs in her short story "Kabu-Kabu," a *Twilight Zone*–like tale co-written with Alan Dean Foster. Ngozi,[11] a young Chicago lawyer, decides to take a freelance, probably illegal, cab to O'Hare Airport so that she can attend her sister's wedding in Nigeria, but she is running late, and everything goes seriously wrong. The driver seems to be a Nigerian shaman, and the interior of the cab resembles a masquerade with rosaries and cowry shell[12] necklaces hung over the rear-view mirror (16). The entire interior is feminine, "inlaid with thousands upon thousands of tiny multi-colored glass beads" and there is a large, leafy potted plant nestled between the front seats (16). A futuristic computer installation on the dashboard has a rotating three-dimensional screensaver of "a bush ceremonial Igbo masquerade mask" (17).

Through a Freudian lens, the cab becomes a mobile vagina/womb where Ngozi must confront her fears as well as ancestral messages about being bi-cultural, thirty-five and unmarried. Ngozi's interactions with the driver are immediately contentious. As he veers through traffic like "a maniac," loud Nigerian music plays. and the cab's speakers go "DOOM" forebodingly as the vehicle shakes—possibly responding to Ngozi's hostile opinions: *"Nigerian men and their bullshit assumptions"* (20). She is trapped when another passenger, a devastatingly handsome Nigerian vampire, supernaturally ravishes her and steals her cell phone, credit card and boarding pass. The driver then promises to take her "where she needs to go" using "other" ways (24). At a carwash, a giant seven-foot spinning brush detaches and approaches, making the "tock, tock" drum sounds that announce a masquerade (26).

In a January 2015 email, Okorafor explains being terrified of carwashes because they remind her of masquerades[13]: "Up close, so close, too close, she would see its body was a thick column of shredded raffia, pieces of cloth, and strings of red beads" (27). When she tries the door, the handle won't open, and then the carwash brush melts into a rosy mist[14] that rematerializes inside the cab, filling up the space beside her and scratching her face. The masquerade's wooden head has a "stern" female face, and it turns and stares down at her (27).

The masquerade's stern female face is significant. Although men can dress as female masquerades, this is the manifestation of a demi-goddess. The driver's comments have a revealing double meaning when he says, "You work graveyard, you pick up *all* kinds of immigrants who work all kinds of jobs" (28). This masquerade embodies Ngozi's perpetual self-criticism, a psychological elephant encountered in a confined space, the very large difficulties of being a woman torn between two conflicting cultures. What follows is a very bumpy trip via a surreal spirit-world time warp and an eventual arrival in a Nigerian village in time for the wedding. Psychologically reborn, she now recognizes the village as home.

Masquerade Drums and *Who Fears Death*

Drumming is an essential part of a masquerade performance. In *Who Fears Death*, 16-year-old Onye,[15] the protagonist, goes to a sorcerer's hut seeking secret knowledge only to find the hut guarded by a masquerade:

> *Tock, tock, tock* went a small drum as the real masquerade rushed at me, spraying a wake of sand as tall as my house and wide as three camels. It shook its dusty colorful cloth and raffia skirts. Its wooden face was curled into a sneer. It danced violently, jabbing itself at me and then pulling back. I stood my ground, even as it slashed its needle-fingered hands an inch from my face [104].

In *Women Who Run with the Wolves*, Clarissa Pinkola Estes suggests that "the skin or body of a drum determines who and what will be called into being. Some drums are believed to be journeying drums, transporting the drummer and listeners" (158). Repetitive drumbeats represent the beat of the human heart as a masquerade approaches. The drumbeats become more rapid as it nears, blurring both the physical and the psychological separation between masquerade and audience. Okorafor's fiction connects loud singular beats: *DOOM, THOOM,* or *MOOM*[16] with changes in consciousness and the openings of doorways into the spirit world.[17] In *Binti: Home*, drumming is internalized, demonstrating the quickened heartbeat of post-traumatic stress: "The talking drum in my chest began to beat its rhythm of distress, again" (36).

When Onye is able to stare down the masquerade's assaults without moving, she is allowed to enter Aro's hut and demand to be his student. Perhaps her anger at Aro[18] reflects Okorafor's own anger regarding the bullying and sexism she experienced as a young woman as well as her frustration that females could not be initiated into the masquerade society: Onye says, "You ... you won't teach girls or women because you're *afraid* of us! Y-y-you fear our emotions" (105).

Flutes often accompany the drums during masqueraded parades. While writing *Who Fears Death*, Okorofor reports hearing flute music especially while describing a masquerade that magically appears when Onye and her friends travel into the desert. They encounter a "great spirit of the wilderness" that is as wide as three tents and stands still as a stone. It is made of wet leaves and metal spikes. Its frowning wooden head has thick white smoke "dribbling from the top"; ten guinea fowl strut around it (274–275). This masquerade reflects the sacred tree[19] mythos but with metaphysical fangs. It heralds the beginning of the end. When Onye accepts responsibility for her own fate and is pierced by the masquerade's needles, she is magically transformed, electrically charged, and can only be touched by her soul mate Mwita. She has been given the metaphysical strength to kill her father, the evil sorcerer who raped and impregnated her mother, but at an enormous price.[20]

Warrior Magicians in *Akata Witch*

Okorafor's most extensive masquerade explorations occur in *Akata Witch*, 2011, and *Akata Warrior*, 2017. Traditionally, membership in the Igbo Leopard Society has only been open to elite, upper-class men, but in the *Akata* series, Okorafor creates her own Leopard Cult, in which women are as important as men and leadership depends on skill level rather than monetary wealth.[21] Reed indicates that when a leopard masquerade appears in present-day masquerade festivals, it usually accompanies Adamma, the maiden spirit, along with a spirit husband, a hunter and a little girl, all portrayed by men (3). In Igbo, Adamma means "beautiful girl child," but considering the entrenched misogyny of the Nigerian masquerade societies, it is difficult not to see it as feminizing the name Adam, as if Eve were entirely excluded from the Garden of Eden. Okorafor's Leopard Cult, however, is a powerful organization of individuals with magical talent and training, its oligarchic leadership of sorcerers and mentors providing education and government in the Leopard World. Sometimes the power of Leopard leadership can extend into the mundane world. Those without power are called Lambs.

Sunny, the protagonist of the *Akata* series, is the albino child of African parents. She was born in America but is now living in an alternate-universe Nigeria. After she is initiated into the Leopard Cult along with her friends Chichi, Orlu and Sasha, she is allowed to enter the village of Leopard Knocks by crossing a bridge that is guarded by a masquerade-like monster. Together, the four friends form an "*Oha* coven," which is "a mystical combination" of talented individuals intended to defend against evil (84). They are being trained as warriors as well as magicians. Leopard Knocks is separated from the mundane world by a semi-permeable boundary of dimensional magic. Special permission and personal power are required for individuals to pass back and forth, but, as in the Harry Potter universe, use of magic is not restricted to the magical world. Although it is generally forbidden to apprentices, there are special circumstances when it is allowed.

Before becoming a Leopard Person, Sunny knew that masquerades were spirits of the dead—or just spirits, in general, that could enter the physical world through termite mounds. She also knew that during weddings, birth celebrations, funerals, and festivals, people would dress in masquerade costumes. Now, however, she learns that masquerades can be powerful manifestations of the spirit world (275–276). Masquerades can enter the Lamb world when summoned or appear on their own when the world has lost its natural balance. At a party after a football game, Sasha and Chichi call up an Aku masquerade on a dare.

Sunny recognizes this as unsafe practice. Her magic book *Fast Facts for Free Agents* describes masquerades as "always dangerous. They can kill, steal your soul, take your mind, take your past, rewrite your future, bring the end of the world" (62). This list is not adolescent hyperbole. In the Ginen universe, masquerades herald major changes and world-ending events. Sasha has summoned a *Mmuo Miri* masquerade before,[22] a water masquerade that nearly inundated his house in America (283). For this recklessness, he has been sent to Africa so that he can learn to control his dangerous talents. Chichi, whose name suggests a doubling of chi or spiritual energy,[23] is driven by social competitiveness to prove to him that she, too, can master this dangerous magic. She has learned a spell from *Udide's*[24] *Book of Shadows*: "I call up a masquerade and you never challenge me again" (273). Orlu warns her that "masquerades are hard to control" and "can force their freedom," but Chichi ignores him (275).

With typical adolescent impulsiveness, Chichi draws a giant circle on the ground with the tip of her juju knife. The circle represents the map of the spiritual world. She has inherited considerable chi, but she is just learning how to use it. As she chants and waves her knife, the circle churns up into a small mound that grows until it is about six feet tall. Termites begin emerging from the holes (277). Then a "high-pitched wavery sort of ghostly" wailing, similar to "the ululations of women from the Middle East,"[25] begins and is followed by drumming (277). "Playful" flute music weaves in and out of the wailing. Then a "tooth-vibrating" drumbeat begins (277).

When *Mmuo Aku* emerges from the termite mound, it is both beautiful and ugly: its bulbous body is covered with shiny blue cloth and cowry shells. Blue and white beads, hanging from pieces of yarn, click and clack as the body grows. When it reaches over fifteen feet high, the music reaches a crescendo, and the top falls away to reveal a four-faced head (278). Although the surface is fairly conventional, behind the mask is an "undulating mass of red termites, wasps, bees, mosquitoes, flies, and ants!" (279). People start screaming, and the masquerade begins to dance in a cloud of stinging insects.

Once again, the masquerade is female, but it represents the dark side of natural reproduction—a witch that stands in opposition to Sunny, who has been called a witch for simply looking different. This masquerade has evolved into a forbidden Pandora's box of treachery, "laughing its shrill womanly laugh and buzzing its insectile buzz" (279). Perhaps Okorafor indicates the feminine face of malice can be as deadly as the masculine. Fortunately, Orlu is able to control the Aku and ask her to return to the spirit world: "You have seen, you have stung, you have terrified[26]—now go home" (280).

The antidote to violence is not just self-control but self-knowledge, self-expression, and assertion (Pearson, 195). Orlu has these essential skills. Because of his intervention, no one is seriously hurt. Although the young people are punished, Chichi receives seven copper coins or chittim as a reward for her successful summoning, and like similar events in other YA books, the event works as necessary practice for going up against an even more powerful evil: the sorcerer Black Hat Otokoto is killing children to increase his own magical power.[27]

Nonviolent Conflict Resolution in *Chicken in the Kitchen* and the *Shuri* Comics

Okorafor demonstrates a philosophy of nonviolence throughout her fiction. In *Shadow Speaker*, Gandhi is referenced, "I object to violence because when it appears to do good, the good is only temporary; the evil it does is permanent" (*Shadow*, 41). Orlu's method of polite negotiation with supernatural forces is common in Okorafor's work. Conflict resolution mixes a demonstration of power with a respectful awareness and concern for the needs and motivations of the Other.[28]

Okorafor's picture book *Chicken in the Kitchen,* 2015, reveals how even a preschool child can use conflict resolution skills. The text is a story that Okorafor told Anyaugo, her daughter, when she was a 3-year-old. In this 2016 Children's Africana Book Award picture book winner, Anyaugo, a small girl, is taught to speak in Chickenese by a friendly Wood Wit spirit so that she can ask a giant chicken masquerade to stop messing up the kitchen on the night before the New Yam Festival. Mehrdokht Amini's colorful picture book illustrations invite readers into a child's eye view of a modern African city. The story focuses on the masquerade's trickster nature, but also explains that masquerades are elemental spirits and ancestors "returning to dance," further asserting that death is "a natural part of life" (np). After dancing with the Chicken, the child returns to bed. The next day, when she sees the masquerade at the end of the Yam Festival parade, it is a combination of the Chicken she saw in the night and an obvious cloth construction, suggesting that the ancestral spirit-chicken is embodied in a manmade masquerade.

Negotiation also works in her 2019 *Shuri: 24/7 Vibranium* comic book when Black Panther's sister, Shuri, convinces a gigantic green grasshopper,[29] called a Space Lubber, to leave and stop creating mini black holes wherever it goes. Shuri enters its mind and asks the alien space-faring insect what it wants; it responds with masquerade drum sounds that tell the story of his planet's destruction: "Tick, tick, tick, tick, thock, thock, doom, thock, thock, doom" ("10-Living Memory," np). The final sounds, "Whoooooooooooooooo," and "Crrrudoooom" depict total destruction. Shuri realizes that the Space Lubber came from "a world full of natural music" and offers it "great music" if it stops hurting people (np).

Warrior Magician Altruist Innocents Confront the Evils of the Petroleum Industry

Throughout her fiction, the petroleum industry represents the postcolonial rape of Nigerian innocence, exemplifying how the double whammy of neocolonialism and capitalism work together to destroy Edenic aspects of natural ecology. Oil, which has been exported from Nigeria since 1958, becomes a frequent target in her work, with several depictions of pipeline destruction.[30] In *Akata Witch,* the wicked sorcerer Black Hat Otokota is the owner of a gas station, thus representing all that is morally wrong with capitalist exploitation. He uses an ancient, evil magic to suck the life-force from children. In order to rescue two kidnapped children, Sunny and her friends in the Oha Coven must confront and kill him at his gas station. As he dies, he summons Ekwensu. She is the "bringback" of his earthly sins (331). Ekwensu,[31] the Igbo God of War and Victory, is usually considered male, but here manifests in female form. She is so deeply evil that her name is "rarely spoken"; she smells "like car exhaust" (324). When she grows to over one hundred feet high, a flute begins to play like "a sweet-throated bird happily leading the devil into the room" (325). When Ekwensu begins to rotate, she becomes a metaphysical tornado.[32] Then the drumbeats are so deep and loud that the steel foundation of a gas station crumbles (325).

The Oha Coven is able to defeat Otokoto and control Ekwensu because they have innocence on their side. Pearson asserts that Innocents teach us to love the world as it is, while Magicians have the knowledge to transform it (194). Sunny and her friends are innocent, not because they have never encountered evil but because they lack the desire to steal from the world to enrich themselves. Taking responsibility to care for others as well as the planet is a reinforcement of innocence rather than a loss. Together, as Innocent-Warrior-Magician-Altruists, the friends create a potent balance of power. Their spirit faces are masks that symbolize their strengths. Orlu's face is square and dark green, reflecting the power of nature; Sasha's is the carved wooden head of a "fierce-looking parrot," reflecting power over the air; Chichi's mask is long and marble-like, reflecting the strength of the earth; and Sunny's is the sun (fire), with golden points radiating from her face (69, 93). Just as Ekwensu has a head with four faces, the four spirit masks of the Oha coven create a stable balance of powers. Like Onye and Ejii, Sunny gains confidence by learning to summon her inner sunshine and from accepting the inevitability of her own eventual death—a balance of light and dark: "She realized that, above all things, she didn't want to die huddling away, afraid, helpless. She was going to go out there and face Ekwensu, damn the consequences" (326–327). Innocence wins, but only when it is possible to continue uncorrupted in the face of evil. The end result is a communal act of altruism because the four friends commit to something greater than themselves.

A similar victory occurs in *Akata Warrior* when the four friends enter the ancient city of Osisi, "the Lagos of Leopardom in Nigeria," and once again confront and defeat Ekwensu on ancestral ground she has claimed (404). As Pearson remarks, "Heroes have a transcendent function, bringing renewed life not only to themselves but to the world" (123). *Akata Woman,* a third novel in what is now being called the Nsibidi Scripts series, was released in January 2022. Okorafor has promised to take this series deeper into magic and transformation.

Lagoon

Originally conceived as a response to the 2009 Oscar award-winning South African film *District 9,* Okorafor's *Lagoon* attempts to counteract what she considers the film's "abysmal stereotyping" of Nigerians" (Tubosun). However, Okorafor has explained that once she started writing *Lagoon,* "it quickly ... became its own story with its own soul" (Tubosun, np). That "soul" is a natural sense of moral responsibility that rises above cultural degradation and human corruption. Here "Ijele, the grand masquerade of masquerades, one of the greatest spirits of Nigeria," acts as an important symbol for social change (200). Like modern-day Nigerian masquerade festivals, the novel is set up in three acts: "Welcome," "Awakening," and "Symbiosis." Although "Symbiosis" implies the mutually beneficial, symbiotic relationship between human and Other, the word also suggests the Marxian concept of synthesis.[33] Essentially, the novel follows a Marxian dialectic in which a thesis of an unhealthy sociopolitical structure is changed through the antithesis of alien intervention. The exchange of cultural and biological information that follows creates a synthesis of positive social values that eventually results in increasingly healthy living conditions and social stability (see *LaGuardia*). This transformation, however, cannot occur without the violent destruction of various temples to the worship of capitalism. "MOOM!"[34] —the prologue—was initially published in *Kabu-Kabu*. It describes the destruction of a crude oil underwater pipeline by an ecoterrorist swordfish, as well as an alien first contact (3–6).

As in earlier feminist SF, such as Octavia Butler's Xenogenesis Series, Sheri Tepper's *Raising the Stones,* and Joan Slonczewski's *The Wall Around Eden,* Okorafor creates a scenario in which alien intervention is necessary to solve the ugly mess humans have made of the world. As the novel begins, the megacity of Lagos, Nigeria, is reeling on the edge of cultural and environmental collapse due to various kinds of postcolonial pain points: a huge wealth differential, a weak government, a dying president, a deteriorating infrastructure, a military dissolving in corruption, and a religious theocracy steeped in greed and intolerance. The main characters are all struggling with various kinds of moral exhaustion, abuse and/or addiction. When intergalactic alien shape-changers[35] land in the lagoon and take over the telecommunication system, the city erupts in protest demonstrations and full-scale rioting and looting. One of *Lagoon's* viewpoint characters muses, "If there is one city that rhymes with 'chaos,' it is Lagos" (214). This chaos eventually opens a door to the spirit world.

Various beings from the spirit world emerge and work together to correct the city's moral corruption. Mami Wata,[36] the goddess of water, appears and removes the avaricious minister, Father Oke (235). Ijele, "the Chief of all Masquerades," breaks through the ceiling of the Testament Cyber Café, a local gathering place for internet criminals,[37] and destroys it (199). The Café's name is intentionally ironic. The destruction that follows parallels Christ driving the money lenders out of the temple. Ijele, though huge, is not as horrifying as those described in *Akata;* rather, tiny scenes from human history cover its sides, essentially creating a kind of supernatural puppet show with tiers of wooden platforms twelve to fifteen feet in diameter (199). Ijele's upper and lower parts are separated by a giant yellow serpent that symbolizes Igbo pride and mightiness (199). It comes at the end of a modern masquerade festival and always performs alone. In *Lagoon*, its entrance represents symbolic cleansing and eventual resolution of the chaos.

Historically, night masquerades are considered most dangerous. Gore, 2008, explains that they "have the most potent medicines as well as the ability to kill" (3). Individuals who encounter them at night must be important within masquerade associations "if they are not to be killed by the encounter" (3). In this case, Papa Legba, an old man in black, enters, and shepherds Ijele into the screen of a computer, where they both dissolve into smoke (201). This nonviolent resolution foretells a restoration of the dignity that Nigeria lost through colonialism and corruption.

Similar to Le Guin, Hopkinson, Shawl, and de Lint, Okorafor envisions a spirit world that intersects various mythologies. Papa Legba, the Yoruba trickster god of language, communication and crossroads, is known to open and close doorways (195). When Legba is encountered by an American journalist, he calls himself Scratch,[38] another name for Satan, but his behavior is not evil. Throughout Okorafor's fiction, Legba functions as a positive trickster force that works in opposition to the corruption of Christian church leadership in Nigeria.[39] When Legba/Scratch is last seen, he is dancing with a market woman while another woman sings songs to "Lord Jesus Christ" (214), suggesting that it is not Christianity itself that is the problem, but the evil things that are done in the name of Christ.

Parades are essential parts of masquerade performances. Reed explains that "black" parades are considered the most powerful and dangerous. They appear at night to search out transgressors or warn the citizenry to improve their behavior (2). *Lagoon* describes a panic-stricken black parade that occurs when thousands of people attempt to flee the city, causing a mammoth traffic jam on the Benin Expressway. After midnight, Bone Collector, the highway's monstrous spirit, rises up with a BOOM! and starts to eat cars and pedestrians, stretching like "hot plastic" and making a protracted, ecstatic "OOOOOOOOOOMMM[40]" as it digests what it has eaten (207). It cannot be stopped until one of the aliens, fully accepting her own death, sacrifices herself to stop it:

> "Collect my bones and then never collect again," the woman said. "I am everything and I am nothing. Take me and you will be free of your appetite" [208].

Her final words are reminiscent of John 6:35, "Jesus said to them, 'I am the bread of life; he who comes to Me will not hunger, and he who believes in Me will never thirst.'" Once again, Okorafor reshuffles Biblical mythology into a new context. The shape-changer's altruistic sacrifice engenders the return of a revitalized government and a president whose health the aliens have restored.[41] Pearson writes:

> Our lives are our contribution to the universe. We can give this gift freely and lovingly, or we can hold back as if it were possible by refusing life to avoid death. But no one can. [...] the final lesson of the Altruist to choose to give the gift of one's life for the giving's sake, knowing that life is its own reward and

remembering that all the little deaths, the losses in our lives always bring with them transformation and new life, that actual deaths are not final but merely a more dramatic passage into the unknown [127].

Okorafor explores this "dramatic passage into the unknown" in her *Binti* series.

Binti: Home and *The Night Masquerade*

Perhaps Okorafor's most poignant use of masquerades occurs in the concluding book of the *Binti* Trilogy, *The Night Masquerade*. In *Binti: Home*, Binti, who has been going to a prestigious off-world university, returns to her home world so that she can see her family and take her woman's pilgrimage into the desert. She wants to clear her mind of the flashbacks, panic attacks, and rages she has been experiencing since she survived a murderous alien attack on a shuttle full of innocent students and professors. She brings along her new friend Okwu, a Meduse warrior. In order to become an ambassador for peace, Binti has been genetically changed by the alien Meduse so that she can communicate with them telepathically. Instead of intricately braided hair, she now has tentacles that move like "mating snakes," and sparks pop "from the tips" when she is upset (*Home*, 18, 55). As Okorafor remarks in her 2017 TED talk, Binti has become "not other but more." Her body has changed, but she is still herself, and she likes how her body feels. Although she has negotiated a truce between the Meduse and the Khoush, a neighboring, space-faring tribe, considerable hostility remains between the two cultures. The Khoush are still furious about the attack on their shuttle. As soon as she arrives home, they try to murder Okwu, who fortunately has enhanced armor.

Although Binti is not a Windseeker, she still represents the Wanderer archetype. Her intelligence and talent give her the ability to fly away from the cognitive limitations of her village. Like other Okorafor protagonists, Binti wants more. In a 2018 interview, Okorafor describes her as superpowered in an unconventional way:

> She doesn't have magical abilities that make her above everybody, but her superpower is negotiation. ... It is not passive but it is a different type of strength. I would like to see more examples of what makes someone a superhero [Winter, np].

After stopping the attack, Binti goes to her family home and puts on the sky-blue dress she bought at Oomza Uni. Blue is significant within Okorafor's fiction. It represents freedom and limitlessness, a unification of water, sky, and the liminal space between. In a moment of unintentional foreshadowing, her mother and sister tease that she looks like "a mermaid masquerade." Binti's increasing liminality suggests that she is developing the power to transcend the strictures of village gender taboos and become a masquerade in her own way (*Home*, 67–68).⁴²

During the evening of Binti's homecoming, a Night Masquerade appears outside her bedroom window. It is made of raffia, sticks, and leaves with a wooden mask that is "dominated by a large tooth-filled mouth and bulbous black eyes" (89). Binti is amazed because only men and boys are supposed to see Night Masquerades—and then only if they have earned important recognition. After seeing the Night Masquerade, Binti immediately leaves on her pilgrimage because her grandmother's Desert People have come for her.

Unmasking the Masquerade, the Human Face

In *The Night Masquerade*, Okorafor unmasks a human masquerade for the first time. Binti, who has learned much about herself and her heritage, returns from her pilgrimage after Khoush fighters attack her village, destroying her family's home. Although she requests a peace meeting, the village elders are afraid to support her effort to invoke "deep culture" and reconcile differences (116). Only her friend Dele appears disguised by the Night Masquerade costume, but Binti recognizes him by the way that he dances. When Binti attempts to negotiate another truce, she is caught in crossfire and killed. Dele has been taught traditional values and is apprenticing to be the next chief. Although he believes that Binti has abandoned her destiny by leaving home, he still wants to support her.

Psychologist Carol Gilligan explains that in traditionally gendered cultures, young women who identify with their mothers define themselves through connection and the care of others, while young men who see themselves as different than their mothers define themselves through separation (Gilligan 8). Young men's moral decision-making tends to focus on restoring justice while young women are most influenced by ethics of care. Binti and Dele approach this crisis from different directions, but since childhood, they have each grown in their moral thinking. Dele has also experienced something beyond village norms. During his initiation into the masquerade society, he has inhaled "the smoke from the burned branch of an Undying tree" and has seen "the friends of the Seven," suggesting that he has had an out-of-body, hallucinatory experience of deity (124). Despite his traditional belief system, he wears the Night Masquerade costume because he is impressed by Binti's courage and wants to inspire ancestral support. His courageous behavior indicates that he has moved from Conventional to Post Conventional morality. His decision implies an application of universal principles. When Binti dies, he throws off the mask, revealing his human grief: "He threw his head back and opened his mouth wide, tears dribbling from the sides of his eyes" (126).

Conflict Resolution

After Binti's death, her empathic desert friend Mwinyi is able to free her family from their house cellar which was carved into the root of an Undying Tree when the house was built. Even though its trunk is no longer there, the tree has remained alive with its roots continuing to grow underground. When sheltering in the cellar, Binti's mother used her mathematical perception to ask the tree for its protection. What follows reflects Okorafor's earlier prediction that "plants will grow underground" if masquerade secrets are revealed. Mwinyi's respectful crisis negotiation with the tree follows a continuing theme of conflict resolution. As a master harmonizer, he places his hand on the foundation and sends his power through his hands and feet while repeating, "Let go, please. Let go, let go. Please" (130).

According to Okorafor's memoir, this method of respectful negotiation was also demonstrated while recovering from her paralysis. She asked her toe to move: "Big toe, please, kindly twitch again. For me. You just did it on your own. You can do it again. You know you want to. I'll forever keep you well-scrubbed and your nail painted with pretty color" (*Broken*, 50). This request, although humorously related, reflects three basic tenets of nonviolent crisis negotiation and resolution: establishing rapport, asking politely, and offering a reward for compliance.

Mathematics, Death and Transcendence

Okorafor constructs the *Binti* trilogy so that the human secrets of the Masquerade Society are revealed, but the magic is not diluted by doing so. After Binti dies, her body is repaired and bathed with water from the Sacred Well at the center of the village. The village women massage her flesh with sweet-smelling oil, and she is placed on top of the Night Masquerade costume. The secret society has decided to create a new costume because this one now belongs to Binti: "Binti was change, she was revolution, she was heroism. She was more Night Masquerade than anyone had ever been" (*Night*, 137).

Okorafor has reappropriated the masquerade mystery, but the story is not over. In her universe, death can be transformative and not final. Binti's body is placed on the Night Masquerade costume in one of the breathing chambers of the newly born New Fish, the shrimplike Miri[43] 12 spaceship. The breathing chamber is an oxygen-rich garden that contains ten Undying Trees with roots that grow into New Fish's body "like nerves." The chamber is rich with friendly microbes—bacteria and viruses as well as a "pinkish grainy substance" that the Himba call "life salt" (166). Mwinyi and Okwu intend to leave Binti's body in the space of Saturn's rings, but Okorafor redacts another myth: when the chamber door is opened after three days, the time from Christ's death to his resurrection, Binti, the "gentle warrior," is discovered alive and genetically bonded to New Fish (151). The bonding suggests stem cell interaction because New Fish is so young—plus an infusion of unknowable magic.

Binti's first sentence, "It's all mathematics," asserts that mathematics defines the universe (148). Everything is based on interwoven mathematical relationships that Binti can now visualize.[44] Her reincarnation allows her to "see" the deep treelike structure of electrical and molecular connection. Before she was allowed to see the Night Masquerade, she had wondered if her adventurous spirit were male rather than female. Now she recognizes herself as the change that confronts and transcends traditional gender definition. This new awareness applies to all girls who see themselves as different and nontraditional:

> Even back then I had changed things, and I didn't even know it. When I should have reveled in this gift, instead I had seen myself as broken. But couldn't you be broken and still bring change? [149].

Binti's conclusion reflects Okorafor's personal recognition that disabilities have potential to become strengths that allow us to be "greater" than what we were before we were "broken" (*Broken*, 9). She asserts that "our toughest experiences" can be seen "as doorways" that may be "key" to "our truest selves" (*Broken*, 9). She goes on to explain that the Japanese art of kintsugi means "golden joinery." A broken object is repaired with gold, thus transforming it into something more beautiful than it was before (9).

Binti has undergone personal "golden joinery." She has seen the ancestors in the wilderness and returned. The Himba and the Enyi Zinariya or Desert People worship "The Seven" or "The Principle Artists of All Things"[45] (153). Through personal connection with "The Principle Artists," it becomes possible for Binti to discover the golden joinery that comes through suffering.[46] She has discovered mathematics to be a science that is an art and an art that is a science. In outer space, the Night Masquerade costume maintains its magical connection to the ancestors, and Binti uses its power to reconstruct her broken *edan*, the alien artifact that protected her when her shuttle was attacked. Reminiscent of Anne McCaffrey's "The Ship Who Sang," Binti is now able to fly through space via her link with New Fish. During flight through the metallic dust of Saturn's rings, she encounters the mysterious aliens who previously contacted her at Oomza Uni, asking her name. Fittingly, these beings exist liminally in time and space as an embodiment of mathematics. Binti perceives their name splitting like fractals: "the practice of treeing embodied in one word. Their name was an equation too complex, too various and varied to mentally fix into place, let alone put into a language that I was capable of uttering" (170).

Masquerades, Moral Decision-Making and Growth

As Wanderers, Okorafor's YA protagonists initially look for meaning *outside* themselves. To master the masquerades they meet on their journeys, they must learn to be Warriors, Magicians and Altruists. In doing so, they must turn *inward*. What they discover is the gift of their true selves: Zahrah, Ejii, Sunny, and Onye connect to a long-suppressed personal history of talented ancestors. Adaora, *Lagoon's* marine biologist, experiences a selkie-like transformation. Similar to the Gom Jabbar box in Frank Herbert's *Dune,* the masquerades they encounter embody deep physical and psychological pain that must be acknowledged, including the fear of their own deaths. They are pierced by their encounters and changed.

Gilligan, 1982, explains that *conventional* moral judgement is based on "shared norms and values that sustain relationships, groups, and societies" (73). These norms could be viewed as an unconscious cultural memory of ancestral voices, but *postconventional* judgement involves a conscious reflective perspective that works toward moral principles that can be universally applied. The highest level of moral judgement combines ethics of care and justice by reinterpreting rights and rules through ethics of care and responsibility. When Okorafor's young protagonists encounter various ancestral voices and masquerade embodiments, they experience a moral conundrum[47] and must make decisions based on the changing reality of their present circumstances. In doing so, they reconstruct some universal *rules* for themselves. Moving into the realm of postconventional morality, they consciously decide to break some previously unquestioned rules because of their responsibilities to others and to themselves.

Evolving Masquerade Theology

If the sacred is what we believe to be most powerful, then Okorafor believes that it is a mystical combination of ancestral guidance, animistic forces, and science. In her "Acknowledgments" to *Broken Places*, she thanks her "ancestors for seeing and pushing me through all this, being at my back, my sides, and in my front" (90). Thus, the voices of ancestors provide a kind of masquerade costume for her as a writer. Throughout her fiction, Okorafor asserts that ancestral embodiment of a masquerade costume is spiritual reality, similar to transubstantiation, the belief of Roman Catholics that the bread and wine of communion become the body and blood of Christ, and that this embodiment can be used to do good as well as ill. In Okorafor's universe, universal moral principles (the equivalent of the Tao) appear through consciously hearing and successfully interpreting the moral voices of the ancestors.[48] This, for her, is similar to what other writers call their muse.

Okorafor's masquerades transcend myth, folklore, theater, and tradition to offer an evolving theology. The afterlife is a wilderness where masquerades return when they are not inhabiting the mortal world. Ancestors and masquerades abide there along with the deities and spirits that "rule" the mortal world. This supernatural world cannot be ruled by human magic. The sorcerer Aro remarks, "Silly magic men and fortune tellers believe it is the other way around" (*Who*, 145). Chukwu,[49] "the Unapproachable Supreme Creator of all Things," inhabits this wilderness (*Warrior*, 437). After unmasking Ekwensu, Sunny is permitted to approach Chukwu in an out-of-body experience. She is wearing a raffia dress, "identical to the one she'd found herself wearing when she was initiated" (436). On a symbolic level, the raffia dress allows her to begin the process of embodying a masquerade. Chukwu appears as a haystack of multi-colored cloth the size of an "elephant," perhaps a reference to the Hindu deity Ganesha. He is topped by an ebony mask, reflecting Africa's most precious wood.

In conclusion, Okorafor portrays masquerades as complex animistic forces that are freed by an assault on natural ecology, an unbalance of moral equilibrium, or a demonstration of esoteric magical power. When summoned, masquerades often manifest as rage. They do physical harm even when endowing the protagonist with a magical boon. Usually this includes a surgical-like piercing. (Onye is pierced by the wilderness tree. Chukwu pierces Sunny's forehead with a needle.) Depiction of masquerade rage may reflect Okorafor's own rage when discovering her paralysis:

> I burst from my body, through the ceiling, through the floors above me, into the sky, my fists clenched, my neck veins throbbing, my teeth bared, my mouth

wide. I screamed, my mouth expanding to the size of a hurricane eye, which began furiously rotating and inside the eye was chaos and destruction. Then I was sucked back down into my body. My unmoving body. Rage contained [*Broken*, 33].

Controlling masquerade rage resets a loss of personal and cultural equilibrium in Okorafor's stories. Eventually, her depictions evolve to unmask an underlying theology that unifies divinity with mathematics; science embraces the unexplainable, inspiring a sense of wonder. Throughout her fiction, a masquerade parade dances through young adult terror toward a powerful expression of ancestor-supported decision-making in crisis. For those who can hear the voices in the shadows, wisdom can be accessed that can work to protect the ecology of the future. Thus, Okorafor envisions an Ijele-like "golden joinery" of a fairer, more ecologically balanced world, but there is sure to be some *wahala* first.

7

Degrowth in the Anthropocene Worlds of Le Guin and Okorafor

> You can cheat, lie, steal, kill, be dumb as a rock, but if you can brag about money and having lots of things and your bragging is true, that bypasses everything. Money and material things make you king or queen of the Lamb world. You can do no wrong, you can do anything[1] [*Akata Witch*, 81–82].

In the magical Leopard world of Okorafor's *Akata* series, knowledge is power, but in her intersecting Lamb world, material wealth defines the hierarchy of power. Throughout her fiction, Okorafor explores the relationships between wealth, power and morality. Although compassionate, she writes from an angry postcolonial feminist perspective, wrestling with various questions regarding the availability, distribution, and sustainability of natural resources. Her solution involves degrowth.

Degrowth (in French, *décroissance*) is a political, economic, and social movement based on creating sustainable global ecology.[2] It rethinks the idea of continuous capitalist/consumerist forward progress, hypothesizing that what is best for the earth as a whole is also best for humanity in the present and in the future. Degrowth is purposely subversive:

> It brings the past into the future and into the production of the present; it makes a novel case for limits without denying that scarcity is socially produced; and it embraces conflict as its constitutive element [March and Kallis, 360].

Marxists argue that the intent of capitalism is to create a scarcity of "luxury" items so that consumers will pay more for them since the wealthy erroneously believe they will be happier via their markers of conspicuous consumption. The basic premise of degrowth is, however, that happiness does not depend on material wealth and need not be sacrificed if *post-scarcity*[3] communities are constructed so that human needs are met. Maximizing happiness through nonconsumption means: closeness to nature and more time for family, culture, and community activities. Degrowth decolonizes spaces, places, and language by confronting ownership and the use of "my" and "mine." It prescribes shrinking economic systems to leave more space for ecosystems and reduces poverty as well as extreme wealth by redirecting emphasis from the industrial production of things to human and environmental services.[4] Overall, it seeks to decrease the carbon footprint by decreasing consumption of natural resources and the actual space humans take up within their environments.

Naming the Anthropocene

The human carbon footprint is more than a footprint: it is the widespread reshaping of the earth from oil pipelines buried below the earth's surface to telecommunications towers blinking on the hilltops.[5] In August 2016, the International Geological Congress officially recommended that a new geological epoch—the Anthropocene—should be declared in order to account for the impact of human activity on the geological makeup of the planet.[6] The scientific study of the Anthropocene presents overwhelming evidence that human garbage and air pollution—the material signifiers of global capitalist ideology—are altering the planet on a geophysical level. Donna Haraway, 2015, explains:

> It's more than climate change; it's also extraordinary burdens of toxic chemistry, mining, depletion of lakes and rivers under and above ground, ecosystem simplification, vast genocides of people and other critters, etc., etc., in systemically linked patterns that threaten major system collapse after major system collapse after major system collapse[7] [159].

In *The Cambridge History of Science Fiction*, John Rieder calls the Anthropocene "a decentering of anthropomorphism ... that transforms human shaping of the environment from the godlike exercise of reason to something more like the impact of the giant comet that ended the age of the dinosaurs" (749). By this, Rieder means that human impact is worldwide, resulting in more frequent droughts and serious storms, higher sea levels, pervasive epidemics[8] and species extinctions. This altering actually began with the beginning of the Industrial Age and its corresponding attitudes toward indigenous peoples and the use of natural resources.[9] Barber, 2018, explains that H.G. Wells' *War of the Worlds*, 1898, is in direct response to the extinction of Tasmanian aboriginals. The Tasmanians, who were seen to obstruct the way of colonial expansion, were all exterminated within fifty years. Wells' papers kept at the University of Edinburgh include this revealing commentary:

> The Tasmanians, in spite of their human likeness, were entirely swept out of existence in a war of extermination waged by European immigrants, [...]. Are we such apostles of mercy as to complain if the Martians warred in the same spirit? [Barber, 6].[10]

It is worth noting that when mentioning the Tasmanian "human likeness," Wells indicates that he himself was not clear that the Tasmanians were fully human. Well into the 20th Century, the dehumanizing 14th Century "Doctrine of Discovery"[11] was pervasively used to justify co-opting land and claiming resources from indigenous peoples. It was, however, not until the 1970s that writers began to see that human population expansion and its corresponding consumption of resources could endanger middle and upper classes and that industrialization's negative effect on the environment might become irreversible.

Confronting the Toxic Effect of Kyriarchal Expansion

Ursula K. Le Guin, a second wave feminist, came early to the idea of degrowth in response to the environmental ravages of American westward expansion and its corresponding capitalization, such as clear-cutting forests. Although she does not name it, she explores degrowth in depth in "The Word for World Is Forest," 1972; *The Dispossessed*, 1974; "The New Atlantis," 1975; and *Always Coming Home*, 1985. Essentially, by valorizing indigenous values and combining them with scientific research, she brings the past into the future. Many science fiction writers have taken emergent science and made extrapolations of the future that have proved to be off base, but given the present-day global climate crisis, Le Guin's early work exhibits an unusually prescient trajectory of thought.

Nnedi Okorafor was born the year *The Dispossessed* was published, and her fiction seems to launch where Le Guin's lands. Confronting the toxic effect of colonialism on Africa, several of her works—*Zahrah the Windseeker*, 2005; *Shadow Speaker*, 2007; *Akata Witch*, 2011; and the *Binti* Trilogy, 2015–2017—provide templates for healthy green economies in her alternative world of Ginen. She offers verdant communities where light bulbs and personal computers are grown from seeds and families live comfortably within undying trees.

Despite the generational divide, Le Guin and Okorafor have much in common and often seem to be in conversation across time. Work is at the center of any economy, and both Le Guin and Okorafor democratize work by removing it from pyramidal structures of top-down organization, although Le Guin favors guilds and collectives while Okorafor focuses on neighborhood markets and small family businesses. Focusing on neighborhoods rather than cities, both view the earth as a living, breathing carrier bag where plants have collective awareness and animals are guides and messengers. Both view petroleum production as dangerously destructive environmentally and socially.[12] Both promote peace, and destabilize hierarchies, blurring boundaries between SF and fantasy by embracing the unknowable with the known. Both see hope in extraterrestrial intervention from wiser cultures.

Okorafor's nontraditional fiction caught Le Guin's attention fairly early, and when she was asked for an endorsement, Le Guin wrote, "There's more vivid imagination in a page of Nnedi Okorafor's work than in whole volumes of ordinary fantasy epics" (*Shadow Speaker* back cover blurb). Le Guin's "Non-Euclidean View of California," 1982, envisions a feminine (yin) utopia to be cool, wet, stable, receding, nurturing and self-sustaining rather than the hot and dry of a progressive, aggressive, consumerist, and capitalist, masculine (yang) culture. Okorafor, however, imagines Holocene environments where utopian ecologies thrive in hot and dry or hot and humid climates. Both Le Guin and Okorafor agree that in order for ecosystems to thrive, it is necessary to limit human population.

Limits without Scarcity: Reproductive Rights

Population reduction is a fundamental aspect of degrowth. Both Le Guin and Okorafor depict cultures slowly recovering from various kinds of environmental holocaust. They envision lightly populated areas on the edge of damaged land and dense forests. Sustainability depends on limiting population growth. Historically, excess population has led to war and pandemics. Like the 18th century philosopher Thomas Malthus (1766–1834), who believed that unregulated population would lead to starvation[13] and political unrest, Le Guin and Okorafor focus on lowering the birthrate and educating to avoid sexual pressures and early pregnancy. Unlike Malthus, however, they do not make this dependent on sexual abstinence except during early adolescence. Birth control is available, as is abortion. While Le Guin educates young men as well as young women in reproductive rights and responsibilities, Okorafor's central male characters are just beginning to unlearn sexist values. Later stories about Le Guin's Hain culture[14] describe an advanced understanding of genetics and sexual self-control where conception is a matter of conscious choice,[15] while

Okorafor's *Who Fears Death* depicts a mother and daughter capable of controlling the sex of their children during conception.

In the Beginning

When, in the '50s and '60s, Le Guin began to confront the culturally accepted myths of the European Enlightenment,[16] she saw "a radiant sandcastle[17]" of unsustainable forward progress, and it led to an award-winning series of fictional thought experiments that systematically critiqued colonial values ("Non-Euclidean," 88). Her lifelong study of Taoism and her love for the environment led her to conclude that the Western patriarchal capitalist trajectory was destroying the environment. Through research by her father, Alfred Kroeber, she knew that many indigenous tribes had been lost to westward expansion. Unlike Wells, she saw aboriginals as fully human. She had grown up with "Indian Uncles," friends of her father, who had deeply impressed her with their patience, wisdom, and kindness. Her anger regarding the loss of Native cultures exploded during the Viet Nam era, resulting in "The Word for World Is Forest," her critical exploration of how an extraterrestrial, utopian, aboriginal culture could be permanently corrupted by neocolonialism, xenophobia, and violence. Reflecting a kyriarchal mindset, her villain, Captain Don[18] Davidson, opines, "I like to see things in perspective, from the top down, and the top, so far, is humans. We're here, now; and so this world is going to go our way" (5).

Recognition of pervasive "top down" domination led Le Guin to anarchist philosophers such as Pyotr Kropotkin (1842–1921), who criticized the values of capitalism and supported the eventual abolition of money, and Paul Goodman (1911–1972), author of *Growing Up Absurd*, 1960, who argued for decentralizing government and rethinking the values of contemporary education. Anarchist philosophy critiques the hierarchal nature of traditional religion as well as the Enlightenment's embrace of modernity with its emphasis on big "R" Reason, so-called scientific objectivity, industrialization, and capitalist growth. Le Guin recognized that these values, which had become so deeply accepted as to be invisible,[19] were based on a corruption of reality in that "the institutions of so-called pure reason [...] hide from themselves their own complicity in societal agendas of power" (Fiorenza, 42).[20]

Creating a Land Ethic

In the late '60s and '70s Le Guin took on the task of creating a post-domination science fiction that valorizes struggle and evolution toward a more hopeful, fulfilling and sustainable future. She believed that depicting magically achieved utopian perfection would not be helpful (nor would it be interesting to read). Rather, she believed that writers should create dynamic processes through which sustainable futures might become possible. Her pioneering work, *The Dispossessed,* creates a far future society on the planet Anarres that has been founded on anarchist values, a fully functional culture of moral self-control and shared work for the common good. Earth ecology, destroyed through environmental apocalypse, has become a cautionary tale: a "ruin" governed by "total centralization" and "absolute regimentation"[21] ["Dispossessed," 348].

Earlier in her timeline, "The New Atlantis," a story set in a near future Portland, describes a deeply damaged urbanized environment. Her protagonist muses:

> Manhattan Island is now under eleven feet of water at low tide,[22] and there are oyster beds in Ghiradelli Square. [...] Due to the greenhouse effect of pollution, indeed Antarctica may become inhabitable [317].[23]

The nearly birdless Mount Hood Wilderness Area has many more "green picnic tables and cement Men's and Women's" rooms than there are trees (318). Surveillance, centralization, regimentation, and reeducation work camps have become normal for the dispirited citizens of Portland.[24] It is what Haraway describes as an earth "full of refugees, human and not, without refuge" (160); however, in "The Dispossessed: an Ambiguous Utopia," the anarchist values of Anarres, a resource-poor world, require that property be communal and attachment to things be discouraged. As Stillman, 2005, suggests, Le Guin proposes a use of resources similar to Aldo Leopold's "land ethic," which changes human interaction with "the land community" from "conqueror" to "plain member and citizen" (Stillman, 239–240). There is refuge in the Anaresti community while its reforestation plan actively engages in working with the ecology, not against it (Stillman, 311).

Le Guin hypothesizes that reducing the "propertarian" need to amass personal possessions correspondingly negates the idea of owning others as property and results in more time for community, arts, and science, creating fewer stresses because everyone shares equally in achieving cultural goals.[25] The Anaresti experience little economic gap between haves and have-nots, and although interpersonal violence occurs, there is no war. While sharing the physical work of his community—and freed from the desire for things—Shevek,[26] Le Guin's scholarly protagonist, has time to study Einstein's previously unachieved unified field theory of physics and the corresponding natures of light, space, and time. However, to publish his ground-breaking research, he must confront academic complicity in the agendas of power regarding intellectual property, placing him up against the self-serving plagiarist, Sabul, his academic advisor, who would keep him from publishing important work through rationalizations about quotas on paper use. Thus, Le Guin demonstrates that even in the most idealistic, egalitarian societies, destructive hierarchies will arise, and constant vigilance, community discussion, and action will be required to counteract the human tendency toward selfishness instead of altruism. To fully realize its utopian ideals, the Anarresti community must support independent research and creativity, protecting it from co-optation.

Organically Constructed Cultures

Both Le Guin and Okorafor construct their alternative degrowth cultures so that human habitats grow naturally out of the environment rather than from spaces defined by cement and blacktop. Depicted in "The Word for World is Forest," Le Guin's Athshean aboriginal culture lacks centralized government and is built almost invisibly into the roots of trees with

> houseroofs sticking up a couple of feet above the ground, between a hundred and two hundred of them [...] mounded over with a thatch of small branches, pinestraw, reeds, earthmould. They were insulating, waterproof, almost invisible [26].

For Le Guin, "returning to the root" is both physical and philosophical.[27] Her Athsheans don't need technology because they are rooted through community and dreamtime. Although her post-environmental holocaust Kesh, depicted in *Always Coming Home,* are technologically more advanced than her Athsheans, they live low-tech lifestyles by choice. Houses are spread out in a spiral pattern among gardens, orchards and other greenery. They have windmills, solar panels, and a wooden-rail train, but most travel tends to be on foot.[28] Like the Athsheans, the Kesh believe that

> the roots of the Valley are in wildness, in dreaming, in dying, in eternity.
> The deer trails there, the footpaths and the wagon tracks, they pick their way around the roots of things. They don't go straight. It can take a lifetime to go thirty miles, and come back [ACH, 71].

The overall cultural ethic is to decrease consumption of nonrenewable resources and slow down the speed of life so that it can be enjoyed more mindfully.

The Shadow Speaker and Ecology

Okorafor also focuses on familial, cultural, and botanical roots in her other-dimensional Ginen, but accelerates technological growth and social interaction. Whereas Le Guin's Hainish culture has mastered space travel, human genetics and moral development, the residents of the Ooni[29] Kingdom of Ginen have mastered eco sciences and biotechnology: "plants, trees and bushes rule, not humans" (*Shadow*, 216). A tradition similar to Leopold's land ethic has become an accepted basis for development. In Ginen, homes grow from "abode" seeds, slowly adding rooms when needed (253), a potentially subversive solution since children can begin growing their future homes long before they need them, a novel solution to homelessness. A neighborhood can be one root-connected organism, with small trees and bushes growing within separate dwellings. The population of Ginen is relatively small, and most of the continent remains unexplored. Although foot travel is prevalent, fast high-tech cars are made of hemp and produce "clean flower-scented air instead of exhaust"[30] (238). Although accidents are common, they are not serious because the cars are lightweight. *The Shadow Speaker* describes Ife-Ife,[31] the capital city of Ooni, as a West African, pollution-free version of a New York that mixes rain forest with "the glowing buildings of Tokyo" (241). Living, growing skyscrapers have wide screens that flash "undulating designs" (241).[32] A giant flower atop the thousand-year-old, mile-high Ooni Palace provides digital transmission for the entire kingdom. People living within the buildings abide with animals and insects in harmonious symbiotic relationship. It would be Eden except that outdated human hierarchies remain, and small-scale tribal ambushes occur using dangerous botanical weapons—"compact seed shooters" and "pheromone disks" that trigger enraged animals to attack (268).[33]

Historically, Ginen has been connected to earth through various interdimensional portals, many of which are in the Sahara Desert; however, boundaries between alternate universes are breaking down. Ginen is older than earth, with close to a million years of written history, but, because of its isolation and extremely successful ecology, it has maintained traditional sexist and tribalist values. Interaction between divergent cultures is causing cognitive dissonance regarding clashing cultural norms. To stop a war between Earth and Ginen, Ejii, a Muslim girl from earth, is bidden by ancestral voices to leave home and cross the Sahara with her friend Dikéogu, a stormmaker and runaway slave.[34] War is about to be triggered by Ooni's Chief Ette,[35] an obese polygamist with sixty wives, many of whom are underage, and Queen Jaa, a male-identified woman warrior who has killed Ejii's dangerously sexist, sorcerer father.[36] Jaa has two husbands and a very sharp sword but is also a talented botanist.[37] Ette[38] reflects the hazards of conferred, mostly unearned male dominance, an entitlement that is paired with ignorance and conspicuous consumption.[39] The satisfaction of his various appetites is obviously destroying him.

Ecofeminists believe that sexual addiction and resource consumption are entangled with false social ideals about what it means to be a man or a woman. Capitalist values suggest that big is always better than little and that having more is always better than having less. However, in order for healthy change to occur, these accepted attitudes must be actively unlearned so that new values can be learned that embrace healthier, more appropriate limitations. Ette, who eats compulsively because he is sad, once killed his own brother to gain the throne. Now he rationalizes going to war because ignorant people from earth have entered Ginen and brought exhaust-spewing trucks that have poisoned some of the land, making it worthless for growing. Because Ginen is a clean world, its plants have no resistance to pollution (276). However, the true reasons for Ette's warmongering reflect his own kyriarchal values and xenophobia. Ette is contemptible, while Jaa is hot-headed, but both deeply care about the environment. Allowing them to kill each other would cause widespread fighting and further environmental damage, while leaving underlying social problems unsolved, but Ejii, still in early adolescence, is able to stop a fight to the death by speaking truth to power:

> "There is no Ginen, Earth, Ngiza, Agonia, or Lif! Things have *changed*! You talk of war ... What you're defending now belongs to all of us. We'd just be fighting ourselves. So ... stop it!" [305]

Degrowth in the Rethinking of Conflict without War

Degrowth rethinks conflict as a continuing process with low-level destabilizing and restabilizing interpersonal conflicts taking the place of wars that depend on rigid hierarchical structures. Both Le Guin and Okorafor recognize the insidious nature of power and demonstrate effective conflict mediation throughout their work. At the end of *The Shadow Speaker*, problems of tribalism, bigotry, and sexism remain to cause future political unrest, but a three-year truce written in Nsibidi, an ancient magical script, and signed in blood, is a small step toward developing more egalitarian relationships. Later Ejii adds, "Even those with the best intentions can be corrupted by power" (319). Compared to Le Guin's home world of Hain, Ginen has two million more years to value human rights over hierarchy and tribalism. However, as depicted in *Zahrah the Windseeker*, sentient gorillas who call themselves "the Modern People" already live in peaceful egalitarian harmony (*Zahrah*, 206). In Ginen, as on earth, full-scale war appears to be a solely human activity. When Ejii remarks that "the opposite of war is creation,"[40] she sets the small pains of growth and change over wholescale destruction (259). Although merchandising war can offer short-term capitalist growth, in the long term, war is an enormous waste of resources both natural and human.[41] Both Le Guin and Okorafor privilege creativity and conflict mediation in their utopias-in-progress.

History indicates that although the aftermath of war can temporarily shrink an economy and equalize wealth, hierarchies of wealth and power soon arise. Okorafor constructs her universe so that social re-education may be available by accessing the wisdom of ancestral voices through *rememory*, a term that originally occurs in Toni Morrison's *Beloved* (Schalk, 69). The power of ancestral rememory is such that a teenager can be inspired to intervene in adult politics, allowing cultural degrowth to be based on creation rather than war.[42] It is accomplished by putting plants first and making them essentially more important than people—and, as with Le Guin's Kesh, sustainable wilderness[43] is a stabilizing source of daily reconnection and renewal.

The Mythology of Technology and Carrier Bags for Degrowth

Although Le Guin and Okorafor are often in agreement, they disagree regarding technology. In her influential "Carrier Bag" essay, Le Guin describes the trajectory of technological progress as both heroic and tragic.

> If science fiction is the mythology of modern technology, then its myth is tragic. ([...] high technology founded upon continuous economic growth), is a heroic undertaking, [...] The fiction embodying this myth will be, and has been, triumphant (Man conquers earth, space, aliens, death, the future, etc.) and tragic (apocalypse, holocaust, then or now) [730].

Le Guin believed that romanticizing high technology inevitably leads to tragic environmental destruction,[44] and she depicts this dystopian effect on the future of earth. Her vision of recovery is pastoral, a move backwards to go forward. Okorafor's *Phoenix* also describes a future United States destroyed because of its techno-reverent totalitarian culture, but her vision of recovery involves an infusion of magic.[45] Both see hope in alien intervention from wiser cultures. Throughout their fiction, Le Guin and Okorafor agree that attempting to have everything by conquering and controlling everything—earth, death, and the future—can only end in deep personal disappointment and worse (global environmental apocalypse), but they disagree on how technology should be used.

Initially, Le Guin's science fiction reacts against any technological advancement that leads to large, complex, resource-heavy machinery. Her solution is to go lighter, faster, and higher with a variation of fiber optic communication and information webs in space, leaving earth's environment pristine and slower to change. Her social solution is to revise personal expectations regarding property, minimize everyday interaction with technology for most people, and then rely on advances in quantum physics for those working with information systems and interstellar communication. In contrast, Okorafor embraces technology but reacts against its considerable consumption of resources: Presently, computers and mobile phones are dependent on rare metals extracted from African mines where neocolonialist variations on child and slave labor are still used (Paulson). The capitalist ethic of continuously new technology results in nothing to do with old technology except the hope that parts can be recycled. Okorafor's democratized solution is for individuals to grow their own technology from the ground up, a subversive consumer-friendly solution that would work to undermine big business and decentralize production, making the gross domestic product[46] difficult to calculate as long as military spending remains limited. Essentially, Ginen has a small-business economy centered around local markets,[47] one that feminizes the exchange of goods by allowing equal opportunity for women. This creates what degrowth scholar Chris Carlsson might call a "nowtopia"—community marketing based upon people's actual needs and desires rather than upon competition for over-priced luxury items.[48]

Metaphors for What We Have No Words for

Contemporary English lacks words to fully describe a sustainable degrowth culture.[49] In *Dancing at the Edge of the World*, Le Guin muses that science fiction's primary function may be in asking questions and offering "reversals of a habitual way of thinking," by providing "metaphors for what our language has no words for as yet, experiments in imagination" (9). Degrowth is a reversal of a "habitual way of thinking" and is one of those words that had not been coined when Le Guin began to imagine worlds not based on capitalism, but her work has been incorporated in its canon. Both Le Guin and Okorafor embrace experiments in imagination in which work is democratized and not forced into a pyramidal structure of top-down organization. Both focus on neighborhoods rather than cities, viewing the earth as a living, breathing carrier bag in which plants have collective awareness and animals act as guides and messengers. Both blend the mythic with the mundane. Both view animals and plants as "citizens of the earth," offering them a potential for sentience[50] while modeling a symbiotic kinship within the ecosystem as a whole. Both subversively remove humans from the top of the environmental hierarchy.

When success is measured by being first and best and having most, it can only end tragically, as it does in Okorafor's apocalyptic *Phoenix*, but when success is measured by having kin—human, animal, plant— and being kind, wealth is shared, and death is not as tragic. As Le Guin's Shevek muses, "To die is to lose the self and rejoin the rest" (TD, 623). It is simply not possible for one individual, one culture, one nation, or one planet to maintain continuous conquest and artificial growth forever. There are limits to life, limits to resources. Le Guin asserts avoidance of "techno-heroic" adventurism and repurposes advanced technology as a library for memory, a cultural carrier bag rather than a weapon of "domination" ("Carrier Bag," 730).[51] Le Guin further asserts that this repurposing allows science fiction to be seen as "far less a mythological genre than a realistic one," allowing it to offer creative solutions to real-time contemporary problems ("Carrier Bag," 730).

Creating Cool Degrowth Technology without Tragedy in a Warm World

In contrast, Okorafor, who frequently describes trash dumps of old computers, uncouples the techno-heroic from tragedy by valorizing a truly green technology that uses bioelectric power inherent in plants. These botanically based devices also work to clean the air and cool the environment through decreased carbon emissions. Her solar-powered, intelligent computers are more in line with present-day use of personal technology, recognizing a computer's multifaceted value in interpersonal communication, exercise, physical and psychological health monitoring, as well as reading, writing, and research. Zahrah's motherly compass,[52] Ejii's multi-faceted e-legba,[53] and Binti's protective astrolabe[54] have powerful A.I. components,[55] but her protagonists are too busy having adventures to be addicted to gaming with them.[56] These devices clearly do not take the place of community. Furthermore, Okorafor uses technology[57] for conflict resolution instead of warfare, resulting in fair solutions where one side does not have dominion over the other.

The Kingdom of Ooni has lasted a million years and is likely to continue because family traditions and ecosystem protection are priorities. The heroic Queen Jaa has gained much, but she avoids the tragedy of losing everything because matriarchal wisdom guides her in controlling her quick temper and overly aggressive behavior.[58] The underlying moral message of Jaa's story is that as long as smart girls honor their family relationships, they can grow up healthy and strong to be brilliant scientists/warriors.[59]

Persistence of Conflict, Conclusions about Degrowth

For degrowth to occur, continuous conflict resolution is essential. Although Okorafor's narratives struggle with masculinist and feminist disparities, ecofeminism seems to be winning long-term[60] in that Ginen is revealed as a living, breathing. connected organism in which differences between human and nonhuman are more fluid and less dualistic.[61] Her utopian ideals are more futuristic than Le Guin's, providing increased quality of life through a biotechnology that is not dependent on the consumption of petroleum and rare metals. Although Okorafor did not read Le Guin until she was in college, her fiction often seems in conversation with Le Guin, especially regarding a young woman's ability to be effectively angry with a purpose (something Le Guin was not able to portray in her writing except when abuse survivors Tehanu and Irian become dragons). Effective anger is strategic to survival in a difficult world. Le Guin has described herself as "an aging, angry woman laying mightily about" with her "handbag, fighting hoodlums off" so that she can "go on gathering wild oats and telling stories" ("Carrier Bag," 728), but Okorafor's temperamental teenagers seem to jump outward from the page in angry response to various kinds of kyriarchal domination. Okorafor allows her girl protagonists to fight with their fists and use anger's momentum, but conflict resolution remains essential to long-term change, and it is demonstrated even when they are finding self-control to be difficult. Conflict resolution destabilizes hierarchies and restabilizes cooperation. Neither Le Guin nor Okorafor valorize war or reinforce the human "top down" techno-enhanced right to conquer the world. The world belongs to itself and has the right to be busy with its own business. Humans can, however, share in that business. Like Le Guin's, Okorafor's novels tend to be carrier bags so full of novel ideas that sometimes the underlying anti-kyriarchal subversion of the message might be missed—that humans are far less important than trees, degrowth depending on growth and the proliferation of green in the natural world.

8

Black to Okorafor: Entering the Intersection of Afrofuturism, Comics and the Women's Movement

In recent years women of color have consistently won awards for their transgressive speculative fiction.[1] Their popularity reflects what Dowdall, 2020, suggests is "the ongoing evolution of a genre that has always investigated questions of difference, estrangement and possibility," thereby critiquing "discourses and institutions of past and present" (151). Nnedi Okorafor is one of these intersectional writers achieving success by taking African history and culture and giving it a fantastic, futuristic feminist twist. In the September/October 2017 issue of *Asimov's Science Fiction*, columnist Norman Spinrad calls her Hugo–winning novella *Binti* "something else again," suggesting that "nothing quite like this has ever been written and published in English" and concludes that "this would be a kind of post-modern space opera if it weren't so serious in literary, psychological, and anthropological intent" (204).

Okorafor's *Binti* trilogy does indeed have an operatic quality in that a brave young woman sacrifices herself to stop a war, but it lacks the rigid us/them dichotomies of traditional space opera. Structurally, Okorafor's stories often depart from Golden Age SF, as well as the heavy, intricately interwoven literary novels of the 19th and 20th centuries, but they do not come out of nowhere. (Until now, Spinrad obviously has not been paying attention to a substantial sea change that has been occurring in the genre particularly since the beginning of the 21st century.) For the most part, Okorafor writes well-honed, sometimes whimsical, young adult hero journeys,[2] *Bildungsroman* structured in a series of vignettes similar to comic books and graphic novels. (Her adult fiction also focuses on the heroic efforts of young women, but these stories are angrier and darker, at times more horrific than comedic, with *Lagoon*, 2014, straddling the line between horror and comedy.) She has also begun publishing comic books in the Marvel universe as well as her own graphic novel *LaGuardia*, 2019. Throughout her fiction, the lives of her characters are inextricably entwined with popular culture: food, music, art, and technology. To best understand her work, it is valuable to examine the dynamic intersection between feminism, comics and the Afrofuturist Movement that began after World War II.

Defining Afrofuturism

Afrofuturism is a way of looking at the past and imagining a future in which Africans and African Americans can be influential in creating a sustainable egalitarian future in which their past has not been erased. Although the roots of Afrofuturism were already deep in American cultural soil when Okorafor was born, the movement itself was not identified as such until the 1990s when there was renewed interest in Afrocentrism. As Ytasha Womack explains in her book *Afrofuturism: The World of Black Sci-Fi and Fantasy Culture*, 2013, Afrofuturism is a multi-media aesthetic movement that reflects an "intersection of imagination, technology, the future, and liberation" (9).[3] Originally coined by Mark Dery in 1993, the term specifically refers to speculative fiction that treats and addresses African American themes and concerns in the context of "technoculture—and, more generally, African-American signification that appropriates images of technology and a prosthetically enhanced future" (Dery, 736). Like other women writers of color, such as Octavia Butler, Andrea Hairston, Nalo Hopkinson, N.K. Jemisin and Nisi Shawl, Okorafor was informed by the Civil Rights Movement's active reclamation of Black history and culture that resulted in the Afrofuturist Movement.

In her essay, "Race in Science Fiction: The Case of Afrofuturism," Lisa Yaszek suggests that, historically, Afrofuturist stories have been created in response to a series of questions: "Will there be a future for black people?" "What is it that black people will have to do to secure a future where they are free citizens?" "Is some kind of apocalyptic event required to level the playing field?" and "What role can science and technology play in creating a less hierarchical future?" (Yaszek, 6) To these questions Okorafor joins Hopkinson,[4] Shawl, and Jemisin in asking, "What role will the mythic supernatural have in human evolution?" and, like Octavia Butler[5] before them, "What role will alien intervention play?" Okorafor's speculative answers to these questions must be interpreted through the lens of third wave feminism and the desire to recreate a world where all women have equal respect and agency.

Beginning with stories written in her creative writing classes, Okorafor takes contemporary problems such as sexism, bullying, racism, bigotry, ecological disaster, and out-of-control venture capitalism and moves them into landscapes of a re-envisioned Africa in which young women can gain perspective on problems by flying above them. Recently she has stepped away from Afrofuturist identification, preferring Africanfuturist because her work moves away from the African diaspora to focus on the past problems and future potential of Africa; however, the history of Afrofuturism is still relevant to her work because it created a community in which she has thrived.

Going Back to the Roots of Afrofuturism

Lavender and Yaszek, 2020, assert that the earliest speculative fiction by Black writers—such as W.E.B. Du Bois, Charles W. Chesnutt, Martin R. Delany and Pauline Hopkins—appeared in the late 19th and early 20th centuries (3). Later, in the '50s, '60s and '70s, interest in Black futurism gained popularity when people of color sought to reclaim the cultural richness of African descent through music, art and literature (Womack, 16–17). Although slavery had been abolished a century before, ideological and political aspects of racism remained. Despite DNA proof of only one human race, redlining continued to divide cities, with expectations regarding performance of specific culturally defined behaviors creating invisible walls.

According to Womack, the Afrofuturist Movement gained momentum in 1998 when African American sociologist Alondra Nelson created the first Afrofuturism online community that became "a discussion portal for students and artists wrestling with the dynamic intersection of black history, technology, and the future" (Uncanny). Since 2000, fiction and criticism that explores Afrofuturist and Africanfuturist settings and concerns has flowered, providing increased recognition for those who write it. Part of this renaissance has involved discovering and republishing stories by African American writers. In 2000, Sheree R. Thomas published an important Afrofuturist anthology *Dark Matter: A Century of Speculative Fiction from the African Diaspora,* which included a story published by Chesnutt that had been written as early as 1887 and one by Du Bois that was originally published in 1920. In 2004, Okorafor published a short story and an essay in Thomas's second volume, *Dark Matter: Reading the Bones.*

Identity through Music and Art

Andrea Hairston, 2014, has written that in the middle of the 20th century,

> equality meant we could be white too, or beige, but not our African selves. In the echo chamber of popular culture, European superiority and African inferiority were taken for granted. To a large degree this is still the case ["Dismantling," np].

The image of the echo chamber suggests that only one ideology echoes to the point that individuals can no longer hear themselves think. It creates an invisible status quo, a maze of frustrating mores that require a map when no map exists. Beginning in the '50s, Afrofuturism was informed by American jazz composer Sun Ra, whose futuristic music attempted to map a way out of the echo chamber and into the outer space of a utopian future. Born Herman Poole Blount on May 22, 1914, he legally changed his name to Le Sony'r Ra. His underground Afro-modern music was a combination of "Afro-beat, gospel, blues, funk and Jazz" (Zamalin, 96–97). Inspired by Biblical references and the space race, he named his band Arkestra, after Noah's ark, and claimed he was an alien abductee from the planet Saturn on a mission to preach peace. He sometimes wore spacesuits when he performed. His message was that "all humanity should have a share of the universe" (Zamalin, 106). Throughout the rest of his life, he refused to recognize any other cultural identity[6] than alien ambassador.[7]

Correspondingly, '60s psychedelic poster art merged into an Afrocentrist Black Arts Movement that still melds modern digital art techniques with fantastic African patterns and colors (Womack, 144). Its surreal expressionist style currently informs comic books and graphic novels and has recently rebloomed on the covers of scholarly books and literary anthologies created by artists like John Jennings, "an advocate of using comics to shape black identity and Afrofuturism" (Womack, 144).[8] In January 2017, Jennings published a graphic novel of Octavia Butler's *Kindred*. This adaptation attempts to attract readers who might not be aware of the significance and power of Butler's work. The cover suggests the Middle Passage as well as the slave auction block, but Butler's story moves into the realm of magic and creates a network of power and resistance. The covers demonstrate a blending of historical, technological, tribal, and magical tropes, an inter-textual weaving seen in Okorafor's work as well. The cover illustration of *Mothership*, 2013, is reminiscent of Phoenix, the main character in Okorafor's *Book of Phoenix*, 2015. The illustration on Womack's *Afrofuturism*, 2013, bears a resemblance to a prosthetically enhanced, techno-feminist Lieutenant Uhura from the original *Star Trek* series (1966–1969) but magically cyborged by the third eye of enlightenment.[9] The last three depict young women who have been empowered in various magical ways, suggesting that the line between science fiction and fantasy has been breached, a blurring of genres. In 2021, Jennings adapted Okorafor's short story "On the Road," 2009, as *After the Rain*, a graphic novel.[10]

Descendants of Alien Abductees

In *Afrofuturism Rising: The Literary Prehistory of a Movement*, 2019, Isiah Lavender writes that "Afrofuturism provides a new way to both literally and figuratively decode the dreams of black freedom in a country built on slave labor" (25). African American participation in the building of America's wealth and power had been previously governed by a no-talk rule. In "Black to the Future," 1993, Mark Dery exhibited a bit of contextual dark humor when he asked Black writers Samuel R. Delany, Greg Tate, and Tricia Rose why so few African Americans were writing SF as they could be considered the descendants of "alien abductees" (180)—to which Delany theorized that black writers had more in common with Toni Morrison and Ishmael Reed than with the hard science fiction writers of the SF golden age. Tate also suggested that "Black people are already living the estrangement that science fiction writers imagine" (212), but he remarked that Black teenagers were increasingly being drawn to the elaborately enhanced "Sci Fi" superheroes that were appearing in pop culture comics, video games, TV, and movies (109). Tate also notes an integration of outer space themes with contemporary music by Black groups, demonstrated by the cover of the X Clan record, *To the East, Blackwards,* which depicted a pink Cadillac heading into starlit space. Reflecting the Eastern mysticism embraced by many musicians of the time, the Cadillac is either transporting the faces of Black martyrs or passing through a space already inhabited by those luminous souls (Dery, 210).

Although the role models pictured on the cover are predominantly male, the Cadillac is very pink, suggesting an unexpectedly feminine balance to the blue-tinted pictures surrounding it. What "Black to the Future" describes is a conceptually fecund atmosphere for something to happen, and in the next few years, it does: a literary movement takes shape that embraces both male and female, past and future. As Tate explains, "You can be backward looking and forward thinking at the same time" (211), and this backward/forward dynamic is one of the major unifying principles throughout Okorafor's fiction.

Racism, Double Consciousness and the Double Oppression of Black Women

Much of Okorafor's backward and forward thinking evolves from her anger regarding sexist, racist and cultural bias. Early Afrofuturism was informed as a response to the conscious and unconscious racism that was an intrinsic part of American culture from the beginning. In 1903, W.E.B. Du Bois labeled the inability of African Americans to have a single unified identity as "double consciousness." His book, *The Souls of Black Folk*, describes the difficulty of being a Black man in America, concluding that he wouldn't "Africanize America,"

> for America has too much to teach the world and Africa. He would not bleach his Negro soul in a flood of white Americanism, for he knows that Negro blood has a message for the world. He simply wishes to make it possible for a man to be both a Negro and an American, without being cursed and spit upon by his fellows, without having the doors of Opportunity closed roughly in his face [3].

Du Bois implies that for an African American *man* to be recognized as an adult depends on an as-yet-to-be-defined psychological integration of identity that would combine the best of African and American cultures, a utopian ideal; however, through a feminist lens, it is apparent that Black *women* had an even higher hurdle to overcome because they were also objectified within their own minority culture. Despite his forward thinking, Du Bois could not see the sexism in his own fiction when he describes the "trim little body" of a "little brown kitchen maid" (111).[11] When Du Bois automatically minimizes women, he establishes a sex-based hierarchy, and his unconscious sexism becomes a blind spot in his analysis.

As the present "Me Too" movement indicates, seeing only a young woman's value as a sex object reflects a problematic mindset that continues to be as deeply integrated in African American culture as it is in the rest of the world. During the Civil Rights Movement, the substantial contributions of Black women were often trivialized. In 1964, Stokely Carmichael announced that the only position for women in SNCC (the Student Nonviolent Coordinating Committee) was "prone" (Daniel, 305). By "prone," he implied sexually enhanced (horizontal) support services.

As with the dominant culture, being male was seen as the default setting for being human, but during the second half of the 20th century, women were envisioning their own paths to power, paths that did not involve hitching themselves to a man's star. In 1977, the Combahee River Collective of Black Feminists outlined the specific intersectional difficulty of being a Black woman:

As children we realized that we were different from boys and that we were treated differently. For example, we were told in the same breath to be quiet both for the sake of being "ladylike" and to make us less objectionable in the eyes of white people. As we grew older, we became aware of the threat of physical and sexual abuse by men. However, we had no way of conceptualizing what was so apparent to us, what we knew was really happening [Taylor, 17].

They conclude that they find it difficult to separate race and class oppression from sexual oppression "because in our lives they are most often experienced simultaneously" (19). They vow they are ready "to address a whole range of oppressions" and "a lifetime of work and struggle" (22, 27).

Exploring Racism in Fantastic Settings

As Afrofuturism generated popular and critical interest, writers of color who were aware of their own biases found they could use "double consciousness" as a tool to depict universal human struggles against the evils of colonialism, paternalism, and xenophobia. Furthermore, within a futuristic context, being diversely gendered could be safely discussed. In the '70s, alienated young people who felt like cultural outsiders sought vicarious empowerment though books like Samuel R. Delany's *Dhalgren*, 1975, and Butler's *Kindred*, 1979—novels in which viewpoint characters use their wits to battle against the forces of evil and oppression. In the late '70s and early '80s, Butler's *Patternmaster* series (1976–1984) became very popular with college students, partly because it championed the creation of networks to battle against evil. Correspondingly, the prosthetic enhancements relished by Afrofuturist comic book readers and gamers leveled the fighting field so that women could be as powerful as men.

A metacognitive environment had been established in which Black writers could envision a future that cherished who they were and where they came from and transcended the lingering postcolonial limitations that had caused them to be redlined in Northern cities and eyed skeptically or bullied whenever they entered white neighborhoods. Okorafor has mentioned that as a member of the only Black family to move to South Holland Park, a suburb of Chicago, possibly the most segregated city in America, she was often the focus of racist comments and abusive behavior by other children; however, her family support gave her the self-esteem necessary to keep from being broken by racist biases. She explains:

> The racism was "quite epic," she says. We were always running from racist older kids. But racism never deterred me from doing anything. Coming from Nigeria, my parents were aware that the United States had a lot of issues, but they were also aware that it had a lot of opportunities. I was instilled with that

attitude—there are issues here but you get over them. Obstacles should not keep you from attaining what you seek [Hand, np].

Space, the Final Frontier

As early as Jules Verne's *From the Earth to the Moon*,[12] 1865, science fiction looked to outer space to provide adventures that earth could no longer provide. Gene Roddenberry's '60s *Star Trek* series began with the line "space, the final frontier." The metaphor of the frontier is important in the American mindset in that it represents a liminal, often lawless place in which problems of contemporary culture can be explored and redefined and in which a new order can be created. Early science fiction writers like Leigh Brackett (1915–1978) frequently wrote both SF and Westerns. Later, writers like Ursula K. Le Guin and Octavia Butler used extraterrestrial frontier worlds to explore the dynamics of dystopia and utopia-in-progress.

In the wagon train era of U.S. history, the frontier was reached by crossing the Mississippi. During the Golden Years of Science Fiction, crossing the dangerous emptiness of space offered similar promise of freedom on newly discovered, remarkably earth-like planets. Within the context of Afrofuturism, crossing space has the significance of escape from a kind of modern-day slavery characterized by economic barriers and low-end jobs. The Negro Spiritual "Swing Low, Sweet Chariot" includes the line: "The River Jordan is deep and wide, milk and honey on the other side." Before the Civil War, the River Jordan was a coded reference for crossing the Ohio River that separated the slave South from the free North—or for taking the Mississippi River north to Wisconsin, where the Quaker underground railroad would help slaves escape to Canada.[13] Later, the song continued to have significance due to the dangerously swift and wide social and economic currents that had to be crossed in order to partake in the American Dream.[14]

During the '60s, many young Black women's dreams of extraterrestrial "milk and honey" possibilities were first sparked by Nichelle Nichols' Swahili-speaking *Star Trek* character, Nyota[15] Uhura. When Nichols considered resigning after the first season because she had so little to do in those initial scripts, Martin Luther King met her at a convention and urged her to change her mind: "You are changing the minds of people across the world. For the first time, through you, we see ourselves. What we can be, what we are fighting for, what we are marching for" (Womack, 99). Fortunately, Nichols decided to continue, for Womack writes that Dr. Mae Jemison, the first Black woman to go into space, was, as a child, inspired by Uhura to become an astronaut.[16] It is also important to note that *Star Trek: Discovery*, the most recent iteration, offers a brilliant, Vulcan-raised, woman of color as its central character. Michael Burnham, the protagonist, played by Sonequa Martin-Green, is foster sister to Spock. Writer Bryan Fuller suggests that he conceived the character based on three culturally significant firsts: Nichelle Nichols' portrayal of Uhura, Dr. Mae Jemison, and Black activist Ruby Bridges, who, in first grade, was the first child to desegregate a New Orleans school in 1960.

The courage to press onward despite obstacles is depicted throughout Okorafor's fiction. It corresponds with a measured response to racist behavior that recognizes it but doesn't allow it to distract from personal goals. This is particularly depicted early in *Binti* when Binti, on her way to an off-world university, feels her clay-covered hair being pulled by a group of veiled Khoush women, but she does not allow this microaggression to deter her progress through the line at the shuttle station. She straightforwardly returns the gaze of the offending women but keeps her future goals at the forefront of her mind: "Those women talked about me, the men probably did too. But none of them knew what I had, where I was going, who I was" (17). Binti initially looks for the "milk and honey"[17] of an off-world university education. She leaves secretly without her parents' permission, but she brings with her a postcolonial mindset and an empathic open-mindedness. What she gains includes a first-hand understanding of sacrifice and a deep awareness that enemies may sometimes be made friends via effective communication, nurturing, and an enduring altruistic mindset that universal good is worth a personal price. She also recovers a piece of her cultural past.

Recovering the Past in the Future

In response to the search for a specifically African American Dream, Mark Dery asked, "Can a community whose past has been deliberately rubbed out, and whose energies have subsequently been consumed by the search for legible traces of its history, imagine possible futures?" (736). In the two and a half decades since Dery asked this question, the answer has been a definitive "yes!" with an exponential flowering of space-related, tech-enhanced futurist fiction in the 21st Century that depicts an Africa that has become a major player in space exploration. Feminist writers like Okorafor are not imagining the colorblind "post-racist" future that the original *Star Trek*-era writers had planned for outer space (Lavender, "Critical Race Theory," 185; Brown, *Emergent*, 16). Rather, they envision an astrofuturist[18] frame for examining the history of racism, sexism, and violence, thereby tackling some very delicate and controversial subjects, such as alien miscegenation. Lavender, 2011, describes this as "an otherhood perspective which addresses racism at the crossroads of gender oppression" (73). Early examples of this are Octavia Butler's "Blood Child," originally published in *Asimov's* in 1984, as well as her Xenogenesis Trilogy published 1987–1989. In "Blood Child" a female centipede-like alien inserts her eggs into the Asian boy she has raised to be a "brooder," a symbiotic relationship that is both advantageous and horrific. In her Xenogenesis series, the Oankali, a space-faring alien race enact a breeding program on captive humanity in part to reduce human tendency toward violence. Nisi Shawl's short story, "Deep End," 2004, depicts an interstellar prison ship into which rich white people have uploaded the minds of prisoners into clone bodies made from their own DNA, thereby sending their genetic inheritance across the universe with no risk to themselves.

Taking Flight

Okorafor, a literary descendant of Butler,[19] first won recognition for her stories based on their magical revisioning of an African culture in which some people could fly. Much of Okorafor's fiction explores the nature of what it means to be powerful, and her work has taken hold with feminists partly because women of every ethnic background readily see the value of rising above gender stereotyping and prejudice. Flight is one of the most unifying tropes of her fiction, and it is clear that her work demonstrates a conscious attempt to explode the previous cultural limitations on a young woman's right to be heroic and have powers equal to a man's. For the most part, her viewpoint characters are believably young and imperfect but also exceptionally talented, super girls on the verge of becoming wonder women.

Black Power, Women and the Comics

One of the ways that Afrofuturism has found self-expression is through digital art and comic books. Beginning with early comics, the nature of power has been explored through primary colors, spiky lines and text interjected with all the prerequisite sound effects. In 1966, Carmichael acclaimed the importance of "Black Power," and Black became "beautiful." In "Brave Black Worlds: Black Superheroes as Science Fiction Ciphers," Adilifu Nama explains that "Black" not only became the appropriate term for a new type of political consciousness, but "it also provided a synchronous template" for creating Black Panther, "a regal, super-intelligent and highly skilled hunter–fighter black superhero" from the fictive African nation of Wakanda (137). Both Wakanda and Black Panther evolve throughout the decades. Created in 1966 by Stan Lee, the earliest Black Panther stories maintain aspects of white privilege, Wakanda providing a secret place for white scientists to create marvelous inventions, but T'Challa began to be depicted as a technological genius himself, remotely providing technological assistance to the Fantastic Four (Canavan, 174). Tightly clad in his power suit, Black Panther usually appears as if he has been carved from particularly heavy black onyx and ebony. His yellow-eyed, sculpted, sweat-shiny hulking power is evident, suggesting that to be truly powerful, a man must be invincible to the point that he no longer appears human. Yet various writers have also worked to humanize him, challenging colonial stereotypes of Africa and allowing him to muse, via his Western education, on the conflicting nature of leadership, personally questioning the morality of a kingship that is inherited through Divine Right. Beginning in the '60s, T'Challa's steamy romantic relationships, although considerably popular with fans, have also reflected considerable male privilege. However, more recent comics by Okorafor and others have begun to explore Black Panther's awakening awareness of his own privilege and sexism.

In 2018, Okorafor published a three-issue arc of Marvel Comics' *Black Panther: Wakanda Forever Avengers,* with illustrations by Oleg Okunev. Following events in *Black Panther: Long Live the King,* which was written with Aaron Covington, the *Wakanda Forever* story arc is set in New York City where white-haired, Black superhero Storm unites with the Wakanda warrior women, the Dora Milaje, to defeat an alien organism that mimics the shape of those who fight against it. Like Okorafor's Windseekers,[20] Storm is a genetically mutated human who can fly, and it is fitting that Okorafor highlights Storm's goddess-like powers but pairs them with a domestic interest in preparing a traditional African meal for Black Panther.

This comic also reflects on the damage that drugs and promiscuity can do. The Dora Milaje, once seen as wives-in-training for Black Panther, have "declared their independence from the throne" and have become a powerful force in their own right, a force deserving of equality and respect (np). The implication is that the previous inequality of their subservient relationship as "bodyguards" to Black Panther is now seen as something that led to an unhealthy obsession with him, causing Nakia's deviance and eventual criminality. Nakia, AKA Malice, has released a paranormal "mimic" weapon in New York City in a desperate attempt to see Black Panther one last time before she dies of her addiction. Concluding the issue,

"Black to the Future II" by writer Reggie Hudlin, an older T'Challa/Black Panther now married to Storm, interacts with his granddaughter regarding how Wakanda came to rule the world. Reflecting a postcolonial awareness, T'Challa remarks that, "imperialism becomes a self-serving goal that undermines what you are fighting for" (np). As a whole, *Wakanda Forever* reflects a cogent reconsideration of the '60s masculinist understanding of Black Power.

Woman Power

Comic books led the way to the depiction of a powerful Black man, but what does it mean to be a powerful Black woman? At first, although women could claim the beauty of being Black, power itself was essentially a male descriptor. After World War II, women had been moved out of powerful, well-paying "hard" factory jobs[21] and back into "softer" homemaking roles and secretarial work, but by the '60s women had begun to rebel against these restrictions. Girls growing up in the '50s and '60s wanted to read comics where women, as well as men, had powers. Wonder Woman, perhaps the oldest feminist icon in popular culture, first appeared in 1941 and was the central character in an eponymous mid–'70s TV show.[22] Little girls believed that if Wonder Woman could fly, perhaps they could, too. Stanford Carpenter, president and cofounder of the Institute for Comics Studies, explains that identification with superheroes is about "empowerment" because it "inherently pushes against many of the stereotypes that are thrust upon us"[23] by expanding the envelope of what a person can be—and in so doing, imagining new worlds of possibilities (Womack, 14).[24] It can be argued that Wonder Woman evinces each era's idea of the intersection of femininity and power. (DC's critically acclaimed *Wonder Woman* movie,[25] 2017, depicts a World War II-era Wonder Woman who is not only strong and smart but also an effective leader able to do what men think impossible.[26]) Comic books, which gained considerable cultural importance for Baby Boomers, were marketed to girls as early as the '40s. Although the first superheroes were adults, teenagers soon became a focus. Super Girl, created in 1958, was a reoccurring feature in *Superman* comics in the '60s,[27] paving the way for other young super heroines who appear later.[28] Black-clad characters like Catwoman, who first appeared in the Batman comics in 1940, and Batgirl, 1961, could be considered codedly Black, a possibility that was eventually explored in 1966 when Eartha Kitt played Catwoman in the third and final year of the TV series, and in the 2004 *Catwoman* movie in which the eponymous character was played by Halle Berry.

The Afrofuturist Intersection with Africanfuturism and the Comics

T. Keith Edmunds writes that by the '70s and '80s, comic book girl heroes had begun to be "more independent and purposeful than their predecessors" (212). In 1993, Milestone Comics, the first comic book company formed by Black writers, artists and editors, created Raquel "Rocket" Ervin, the first Black teenaged unwed mother to become a superhero sidekick. Her inertia belt allowed her to manipulate kinetic energy. The belt's name is interesting for having a double consciousness of its own. While in physics, inertia refers to the property of a body that is at rest or to remain at rest or to remain in motion if it is in motion, popular parlance commonly connects inertia to apathy or an inability to move or act. This psychological stagnation is exactly what Afrofuturist comic books attempted to thwart by supporting hopes and dreams with prosthetically enhanced agency.

Historically the most significant Black female superhero in comics has been Ororo Munroe, known as Storm, because of her weather-working talents. The first superhero of African descent, she first appeared in the *X-Men* series in 1975. In an article in *African Identities*, Adilifu Nama suggests that Storm "epitomizes the imaginative space between science fiction and the supernatural" with her mutant abilities to fly and to change the weather, powers associated with the elemental energy of earth and air as well as the environment (142). Symbolizing the struggles that women of color face and resist, Storm, the orphaned daughter of Kenyan tribal princess, overcomes her early life on the streets of Harlem and Cairo to become a competent leader of the X-Men, a white male-dominated superhero organization (142).[29]

Okorafor's Comic Book Heroines

Although Okorafor's fiction was informed by comic book tropes from the beginning, she wrote her first eight-page comic book story, "Blessing in Disguise," as part of a 2017 Marvel comic book anthology set in the *Spiderman: Venomverse* universe. Ngozi, her protagonist, is a disabled Nigerian girl who is bonded to an alien symbiotic organism called Venom, a character that was first depicted in the *Spiderman* series. Ngozi, whose name means "Blessing," is named after Okorafor's sister. She is an ordinary girl interested in bugs and kung fu movies and learning to cope with life in a wheelchair[30] because she lost the use of her legs in a taxi accident;

however, her life changes dramatically when she is embodied by the alien entity Venom, acquiring superpowers that allow her to leave the wheelchair. Okorafor writes her comics by the frame, including drawings that alert her artists regarding what she hopes to see. Ngozi's appearance is based on one of the Chibok schoolgirls who were kidnapped by the Boko Haram militant Islamist group in 2014. Okorafor has explained that this comic was created to draw attention to that incident, explaining that

> they were normal girls who suddenly had to deal with a huge change in their lives ... and their story of perseverance is so powerful. Like many Nigerian girls, Ngozi comes in a small package but is strong-willed and determined [Guilbert, np].

In 2019, Okorafor published two collector's comics with ten chapters that highlight Shuri, Black Panther's younger sister,[31] now more mature and sexually curvy than the Letitia Wright character in the 2018 blockbuster *Black Panther* movie.[32] Illustrators Leonardo Romero, Jordie Bellaire, Rachel Stott, and Paul Davidson reflect the colorful techno-African utopian fusion depicted in the movie. Both comics have Afrofuturist prosthetically enhanced cover art with Kirbi Fagan's *24/7 Vibranium* cover reflecting the John Jennings cover of Womack's *Afrofuturism*. Shuri's crossed wrists in the initial *Search for Black Panther* comic are reminiscent of Wonder Woman's. Writing for a returning comic book character is a complex process, but Okorafor had a specific agenda when writing Shuri as an African girl who, similar to Binti, excels in science. She also wanted to "reintroduce Wakanda to Africa," and her stories needed to comply with story lines already created (*24/7* endnote).

Although in *Avengers: Infinity War*, Shuri dies defending Wakanda from the evil Thanos's Black Order, she has been reborn with increased powers that include ancestral memory and shapeshifting. In this new story arc, Black Panther is missing once again,[33] having taken his spaceship into a wormhole in outer space. When he doesn't return as expected, Shuri must look for him as well as taking on Black Panther responsibilities which sometimes overwhelm her, despite her intelligence and technological genius. In "Gone," the first chapter of this series, Shuri has invented a molecular skin for T'Challa's spaceship, nanotech wings that can come out of a can, and a prosthetically enhanced Black Panther suit for herself. Her renowned technological genius allows her to lead a team that has made Wakanda "the pre-eminent space program on the planet"[34] (np). Okorafor's message is that a teenager can be smart, sexy and strong.

The superhero Storm, who has had an on-again-off-again marriage to Black Panther, appears in Okorafor's *Shuri* series, initially guiding Shuri in an unsuccessful out-of-body search for him until they are both drawn into battle with a Space Lubber, a giant space-travelling insect that is creating dangerous black holes wherever it goes. From early childhood on, Okorafor has been fascinated by insects, and they appear throughout her work. This one reflects the giant insects she saw in her hospital room when recovering from her spinal surgery. It is possible to see the excremental black holes as expressions of rage and the destruction it can cause.

Through a science fictional lens, there is far more symbolic fantasy than physics in these comics, a legacy that reflects a mid–20th-century scientific fabulation in which misinterpretation of quantum physics was such that Superman could fly backwards so fast that time could be reversed and he could rescue Lois Lane from death. As is common in comic books, the *Shuri* comics also play fast and loose with physics: The Space Lubber's black holes resemble small tar pits that can be manipulated using special tech-enhanced gloves, an impossibility in any physics-governed universe, but through a feminist lens, all is well. Okorafor is offering healthy developmental messages to girls. Similar to Ejii in *The Shadow Speaker*, Shuri can see and hear ancestors who call her "ancient future," implying that she maintains essential components of the past while creatively working toward a democratic/utopian future. An important moment in *24/7*'s Chapter 10. "Living Memory," is when Shuri enters the world of her ancestors and meets the plenitudinous Turkana, a king's daughter who once served as Black Panther for three months while her father was held captive by enemies, a reign that was "long enough to lead Wakanda into a more stable time" (np).

Okorafor's intention is to reintroduce and retain the best of the past, revise the nature of leadership, and restore awareness and validation of women's historical contributions, something that historically has often been erased.[35] Although young, Shuri is strong and competent. The relationships she forms are based on equality, respect, and effective problem solving. One scene that stands out is when "The Elephant's Trunk," a multi-age secret society of Wakandan women, meets under an enormous baobab tree to solve problems. Shuri attends wearing her skintight Black Panther suit, suggesting both Catwoman and Okorafor's earlier Ngozi comic. The group handles disagreement in respectful and appropriate ways. When an older woman states, "I think Wakanda would be better off without a Black Panther," Shuri responds respectfully, "Even though we disagree, I appreciate your honesty, Bube. At first, I wasn't sure, but now I see how necessary this council is" (*24/7 Vibranium*, np). Bube is an accomplished seamstress and the single mother of two grown children. She is speaking through her own experience. Here the teenaged Shuri is demonstrating effective group leadership and conflict resolution. The name of the group is particularly apt since elephants symbolize wisdom and memory, and an elephant's trunk is a very sensitive appendage for telling which way the wind blows.

Gardening, Guardening and the Ethics of Immigration in *LaGuardia*

In July 2019, Okorafor's first graphic novel *LaGuardia* was published by Dark Horse Books, and in July 2020, it received the Eisner Award for best graphic novel. A response to the complex issues posed by immigration, it challenges popular assumption regarding who (or what) a person is. It was originally inspired by Okorafor's own airport experience. In an interview with *Publishers Weekly*, she explains:

> I have very long, thick, free-form dreadlocks, almost to the ground, and I wear them wrapped in a bun on top of my head. The TSA scanners are racist machines—people with African hair get extra scanning. And sure enough, they stopped me after a full pat down, they squeezed my bun, and an officer asked me to unroll all my hair and squeezed my dreadlocks from scalp to tip. The irony is that there was a can of mace forgotten in my bag, which they didn't test because they were too busy rifling through my hair. I was so angry, and couldn't stop thinking about it. The story came out of that anger [np].

After six years in the making, *LaGuardia* begins as a sequel to *Lagoon*, alluding to the shape changers' landing in the lagoon near Bar Beach:

> You came out of the water like Mami Wata's children and brought wahala,[36] and then came the finest time of Nigerian history that continues to this day [Chapt. 1, np].

Some of the aliens who arrive are sentient plants. Future[37] Nwafor Chukwuebuka,[38] the protagonist, resembles Okorafor with four and a half foot locks that reach nearly to the floor. A pregnant physician, she specializes in treating plant-based aliens and has illegally brought Letme Live, an endangered alien plant, into the United States through New York's LaGuardia interplanetary airport. The plant, which has a dragon-like, arrow-shaped head, is the last surviving refugee of a secret genocidal war between floral alien tribes. Future visits her grandmother, a high-powered immigration lawyer who owns the elegant solar powered New Hope apartments, a mutually supportive community with interesting aliens of many species. One of her tenants is a professor who taught physics at the University of Lagos but now is only allowed to rent out his three self-driving cars. Obioma, the grandmother, functions as a guardian of LaGuardia, where most immigration into the U.S. takes place. Tana Ford's whimsical cover painting depicts Future's participation in a protest demonstration against a recently imposed alien travel ban. Their rallying call is "A Luta Continua," the struggle continues.[39] She is accompanied by her grandmother, Obioma, and new alien friends. The novel examines various aspects of privilege and reflects how humans benefit from alien contact but restrict alien rights in order to maintain a kyriarchal power structure (see "Watching Windseekers"). For instance, Obioma has a brother "back in Jo'burg" whose "arm was replaced with a Tur people's tentacle after he lost it in a car accident," but he is restricted from traveling to the U.S. because of his hybridity (Chapt. 2, np). Obioma explains, "It's about fear. It has always been about fear" (np).

On the cover, Future is wearing a long blue dress[40] reminiscent of a pregnant Mami Wata, goddess of water and guardian of windseekers. The dress includes the slogan "Baby on Board" with an arrow. Throughout *LaGuardia*, Okorafor provides tie-ins to her previous books, offering an origin for vine-entwined dadalocks and depicting an arrival of *Binti*'s golden twenty-foot aliens, the Zinarriya. As a whole, this graphic novel is a deeply considered reflection on the problems and benefits of immigration.[41]

Okorafor, whose parents were immigrants, is aware of the complex nature of immigration; thus, *LaGuardia* offers a number of ethical dilemmas that may be missed because of the well-developed, comic illustrations and sparse dialogue. Throughout her work, Okorafor demonstrates healthy symbiotic relationships between humans and plants. Letme Live is presented as intelligent, genuinely kind, and self-sacrificing, but based on the invasive nature of Asian carp, common buckthorn, kudzu, and Japanese beetles, all species brought to America for supposedly good reasons, Future's behavior is troubling, a headstrong act with insufficient consideration for the possible long-term effects of planting a sentient vine where its spores can irrevocably change any who inhale them. Illustrations of overly fecund, semi-sentient, water-slurping Chihuly-like flowers overcrowding a Lagos balcony and houses overgrown with truly alien vines are also a bit daunting. Furthermore, an adorable infant[42] sneezing out alien spores causes cognitive dissonance at least for this reader, especially in the time of a pandemic. Even more troubling is the comic's accurate depiction of local vigilantism becoming mob violence, daunting simply because it is so real. The elided backstory of the Floral War reflects the 1967 Biafran War for independence, an ethnic conflict that continues as a "NeoBiafran" uprising in the relatively near future presented in this story.[43]

LaGuardia implies that immigration requires cultural adjustment and societal change, but the resulting cultural acceptance of difference will be worthwhile in the long term. Within a pyramidal structure of intersecting hierarchies, individuals can be privileged in some ways such as talent, education, and wealth but discriminated against in others such as race, religion, or gender. Those who experience discrimination in one way are often blind to the discrimination they feel toward others. For instance, Citizen Raphael Nwabara, Future's handsome fiancé, is uncomfortable when he finds the alien tenants playing with his baby. He snarls, "Hasn't our son been **exposed** to enough?" Payment, a shape-shifting alien kangaroo responds, "You haven't been here a week and you are already sounding like an American" (Chapt. 4, np).

Overall, *LaGuardia* provides valuable possibilities for thought and discussion. The characters are appealing, and the illustrations are colorful, visually complex in their incorporation of contemporary and Africanfuturist detail. Compared to the vast chasm between wealth and poverty depicted in *Lagoon, LaGuardia's* illustrations depict a Lagos that has thrived through its acceptance of the aliens and their advanced bioscience. Scientific education is validated. Gender roles are not restricted. Raphael waters plants while wearing an $E=mc^2$ tee-shirt.[44] Okorafor's agenda is to put the vocabulary of science within the realm of popular culture, what Lavender, 2019, calls "a literacy technology" (25). Throughout her comics, science and technology are depicted as sexy and as natural as breath. Furthermore, she demonstrates how the real-life hurdles of racism and ignorance and fear of difference can be overcome through intelligent community action. This is Africanfuturism presented in a very accessible way. On March 23, 1986, Bill Watterson's comic *Calvin and Hobbes* attempted to take some of the excitement out of war stories. It begins by Hobbes asking a green-helmeted Calvin, "How come we play war and not peace?" Calvin responds, "Not enough role models." Throughout her comics, Okorafor provides vivid role models adept at playing peace.

WisCon at Work

While Okorafor was at work developing the Africanfuturist universe that interconnects her novels and short stories, the Afro/African Futurist Movement picked up support from a slightly different direction: WisCon, the Feminist Science Fiction Convention that in 1990 created the Tiptree Award for gender bending speculative fiction. WisCon, which first began in 1977 as a small regional convention held at the University of Wisconsin–Madison, had always welcomed writers of color, but beginning in 1997, panels considered how the feminist community could be more supportive of them. Then in 1999, discussions regarding Delany's essay "Racism and Science Fiction" (*New York Review of Science Fiction*, August 1998, Volume 10, Issue 12), led to the creation of the Carl Brandon[45] Society, a group whose mission is to "increase racial and ethnic diversity in the production of and audience for speculative fiction" (CBS website). Delany had written that the "only" way to combat systematic racism was to "establish—and repeatedly revamp—anti-racist institutions and traditions" by encouraging nonwhite readers and writers at conventions and including them in programming ("Racism," np.).

In 2002, Caribbean author Nalo Hopkinson was the first WisCon guest of honor who was a person of color. In 2010, Okorafor shared the honor with writer/editor Mary Anne Mohanraj, and since then there have been eight more female Afrofuturist or Africanfuturist guests: Nisi Shawl, Andrea Hairston, N.K. Jemisin, Alaya Dawn Johnson, Sofia Samatar, Nalo Hopkinson, Tananarive Due, and G. Willow Wilson. Since 2005, WisCon's Carl Brandon Society has offered two $1,000 awards, the Kindred and the Parallax, for speculative work by writers of color that examines race, ethnicity and culture. In 2007, Okorafor won the Parallax for *The Shadow Speaker,* and in 2010, she received the Kindred for *Who Fears Death.*

Feminist Revolutions for Afrofuturist Girls

Okorafor's girl heroes earn the right to succeed through intelligence, hard work and perseverance, but second wave feminists first hacked the way through the jungle in which they walk. Okorafor is part of a generation of women of color who were informed by second wave feminist scholars and a feminist media landscape that had determined that racial equality and women's rights must advance hand in hand.[46] In 1988, feminist ant-racist activist Peggy McIntosh published her ground breaking article, "White Privilege and Male Privilege: A Personal Account of Coming to See Correspondences Through Work in Women's Studies," coining the phrase *white privilege* and recognizing an interlocking connection to male entitlement that led to further discussion by scholars of privilege and kyriarchy.[47] McIntosh suggests that white privilege is "an invisible package of unearned assets," an "invisible weightless knapsack of special provisions, assurances, tools, maps, guides, codebooks, passports, visas, clothes, compass, emergency gear, and blank checks" (2). It is noteworthy that Okorafor recognized early the need for such a knapsack of provisions and provides it to her protagonists through mentorship and green technology.

Second wave feminist writers like Russ and Le Guin had criticized how constraints of cultural conventions for femininity, deeply influenced by male privilege, had made it hard to write heroic women and insisted that girls have a right to their own hero stories.[48] The concept of feminine weakness and fragility was interrogated, and beginning in 1972, feminine physical strength was being validated through Title 9 equality in education programs, allowing athletic women to be seen as attractive role models. Okorafor certainly benefited from this personally as she developed as a tennis player.

Determined to attack white privilege in her fiction, Le Guin insisted on Black protagonists in her ground-breaking novel, *A Wizard of Earthsea*, 1968, and later books. Octavia Butler published her first short story in a Clarion anthology in 1971 but in 1987 was still struggling with her publishers to allow Black women to be shown on her covers. The original cover of *Dawn* depicts a white woman (although recent covers do not). In Butler's *Kindred,* 1979, and Jewelle Gomez's ethical vampire book, *The Gilda Stories,* 1991, Afrofuturism interconnects with feminism in their attempts to redirect the futurelessness of the deep-seated slave/minority mindset and to redefine morality in a way that transcends the imposed political/ ideological limitations of the dominant culture—what, in 1963, Martin Luther King described as a "deeper darkness to a night already devoid of stars" (King).

In transcripts from a 2008 Black Writers Conference at Medgar Evers College, Walter Mosley suggests that science fiction and speculative fiction are the only forms of fiction that are "truly revolutionary" (Due, 261). Mosley concludes that speculative fiction is revolutionary in that it "overthrows a way of thinking" and puts pressure on the writer "to figure out, what are you going to do now that you're here?" (Due, 261). Okorafor's young protagonists Zahrah, Ejii, Sunny, Onye, and Binti all must rethink their behavior and create meaning from novel environments, a process that confronts how they view themselves and how others view them. It is essential to their moral development. In each case, there are revolutionary personal and societal results. In the foreword to *Octavia's Brood: Science Fiction Stories from Social Justice Movements,* Thomas asserts that social justice represents "one of the most serious challenges to the conscience of our world" (Thomas, 1). In the following "Introduction," Walidah Imarisha further explains that "Visionary fiction is a term intended to differentiate science fiction that validates 'freer worlds' than those depicted in mainstream SF, a landscape which, 'most often reinforces dominant narratives of power'" (4). Correspondingly, Okorafor writes visionary fiction that evolves from social justice issues, often working in angry response to dominant narratives of power. In particular, *The Book of Phoenix* is a cautionary tale about what happens when social justice is denied while *LaGuardia* explores what happens when social justice action is allowed to work.

In conclusion, Okorafor is presently part of a loosely connected network of writers of color who know and support each other that, among others, includes Delany, Barnes, Due, Mosley, Hairston, Hopkinson, Imarisha, Thomas, Jemisin, Johnson, Lord, and Shawl. A 2015 conference, attended by many of the aforementioned writers, generated the following manifesto:

> We claim the freedom to write whatever the fuck we want and be the artists we need to be.
> We commit to supporting each other's growth.
> We recognize the power/danger/potential of the images we create and proliferate.
> We experiment and learn: "Never a failure; always a lesson!" [Shawl, 157]

Clearly this manifesto reflects Audre Lorde's conviction that "the Master's tools will never dismantle the Master's house" (95). Thus, writers of color are determined to use their own tools in writing and expanding their own houses. Okorafor has embraced this conviction from the beginning of her career, and now there is strength in numbers, an ever-increasing number of award-winning Afrofuturist and Africanfuturist stories and novels in which women have power and the powerful tools to say what needs to be said and do what needs to be done, while moving forward in a way that represents what Brown, 2017, describes as "the speed of trust"[49] (42).

9

Conclusions About Morality, Technology, Magic and the Lessons of History

> We've braved the belly of the beast.
> We've learned that quiet isn't always peace,
> And the norms and notions of what "just is"
> 	Isn't always justice
> 		[Gorman, *The Hill We Climb*, 12].

History is the economics of consumption in action: competition for food, fuel, land, reproduction, and resources informs the shape of events. Essentially, this competition creates power imbalances and corresponding resentment when some individuals, communities and nations become more successful in controlling resources than others. When power imbalances become too great, a leveling, usually catastrophic, occurs unless resources are redistributed through some sort of socialism. This catastrophic leveling can take the form of revolution, war, environmental collapse, or pandemic,[1] and it repeats regularly throughout time. Okorafor shows effects of catastrophic leveling throughout her work, but with specific emphasis in *The Shadow Speaker, Who Fears Death, Lagoon*, and *The Book of Phoenix*. The consistent global pattern of bigotry, genocide, wars, and environmental destruction makes it clear that the lessons of history are a very slim volume. Competition is too deeply imprinted in the human genome for us to fully learn from the mistakes of the past.

During colonial times, Africa was a political football with many countries competing for its abundant resources. Presently, big capitalism, ethnic conflicts, terrorist organizations, and governmental corruption and incompetence undermine democracy and siphon off resources, neocolonialism taking the place of colonial repression. One of the reasons that Okorafor's work is so intriguing is that she works through such a wide span of history, focusing on the daily lives of individuals during challenging economic times and showing how some aspects of life qualitatively improve while others remain the same or regress. Her primary focus is on the lives of women and children.

Competition for Reproduction

Competition begins at home—competition for successful reproduction means competition for women's bodies. Correspondingly, violence against women has been apparent in human remains from prehistory onward.² As Pulitzer prize-winning historians Will and Ariel Durant explain in *The Lessons of History*, 1968, fertility and consumption will always be intrinsically linked. Wars have been fought to control female fertility (Durant, 21–23). Okorafor's "Biafra," 2005, graphically depicts the vampiric nature of military leadership, tying it to sexual prowess:

> Those leaders had intercourse with woman after woman, sapping their feminine lifeforce, and then throwing away their shriveled, sad bodies. But those broken bodies still birthed children, giving these men thousands of sons to ensure that no power would be lost if they were assassinated ["Biafra," 241–242].

Who Fears Death further explores government sanctioned rape by soldiers who intentionally attempt to cause mixed-racial births.

Rape, arranged marriage, female circumcision, burka, purdah, and harems are all more or less effective methods to control women's reproduction, making desirable women more available to males at the top of various power hierarchies. Okorafor explores all of these throughout her fiction. Her early work reconsiders how traditional African cultures define desirability, then shelter and fatten those desirable young women in an attempt to ensure more successful pregnancy. She also emphasizes the demoralizing social effects of physical and intellectual differences that cause certain young women to fall outside the norms of desirability. From Asuquo, who is poisoned for being a witch, to Onye, who is stoned for witchcraft hundreds of years later, Okorafor demonstrates how women who are not submissive are deemed dangerous to male hierarchy and must be brought down.

Wombs are liminal spaces, containing a magic that men wish to control. They hold power to create life as well as difference. Like doorways, they represent both sides of a boundary or threshold. In order for humanity to continue, a woman must share her womb, first with a man and then with an infant, but Okorafor believes that women want to be their own doorkeepers and that desire is a conundrum that must be educated and negotiated. Her female protagonists resist parental and community controls that treat them like commodities that can be bartered or sold. They yearn to leave home on their own hero journeys and insist on the right to control their own reproduction. In some cases, such as in the short story "The Diary of Treefrog," they make fatal mistakes. *Who Fears Death* begins when a pregnancy by rape is subverted by the terrified victim's intervention, making Onye a girl instead of a boy; it concludes with a forbidden pregnancy that causes a kind of nuclear reaction of social change. In *The Book of Phoenix*, a birth mother's brief love subverts an evil international corporation's intent to create a human weapon of mass destruction that can be controlled.

Slavery

The Durants write that the Roman Empire became weak because "patriotic warriors fighting for land had been replaced by slaves laboring listlessly on vast farms owned by one man or a few" (54). *The Book of Phoenix* describes a form of neo-slavery, both human and cyborg, that greatly weakens America, setting the stage for Civil War and apocalypse.

Through a postcolonial lens, a slave is considered Other, an artificial person, a biological machine within the machine of production. It makes sense for Owners to maintain an otherizing mindset, but otherizing extends outward to those who benefit not at all from a discriminatory system. Cultures use various methods for maintaining the lower levels of a kyriarchal structure. Actively encouraging scapegoating and bigotry is helpful in projecting blame away from wobbling, incompetent governments. Instead of working hard to improve living standards for everyone, corrupt, inefficient governments prefer to deflect community attention toward an otherizing cause.

In "Tumaki," a short story mined from *Stormbringer*, an unpublished sequel to *The Shadow Speaker*, Dikéogu, the protagonist, works through the damaging effects of a generalized scapegoating of mutants sustained to centralize wealth for a few. Although he was once sold into slavery on a cocoa plantation, at sixteen he lives on his own in a Muslim country called Timia (possibly a variation on Tunisia). Here he meets his first love Tumaki, a genius at fixing computers. Although he is sexually inexperienced, learning to control the wind is symbolic of his readiness for sexual intimacy. Because of his past enslavement, he has "an obsession with free will" (220).

Although the Great Change has made automatic weapons stop working, bigotry remains epidemic in Timia. The newly opened dimensional boundary between Africa and Ginen has simply created new opportunities for scapegoating. Within this Muslim culture, women must wear burkas and children are physically punished. Meta-humans are viewed as "the scourge of the earth" and "radioactive, cancer-causing evil infidel waste" (229, 235). In this story, Okorafor explores the eight stages of racial genocide, listing them as "classification, symbolization, dehumanization, organization, polarization, preparation, extermination, and denial," showing how easily people can slip into a genocidal mindset, targeting intellectuals and anyone else who differs from the norm[3] (234). Dikéogu is fortunate to be able to escape with his life.

War and Consumption

War is the ultimate form of competition. As of 2021, when considering the last 3,453 years of history, only 268 years have recorded no war (Durant, 81). Will and Ariel Durant remark that "while animals eat each other without qualm, civilized men consume one another [and women and children] by due process of law" (Durant, 19). They conclude that "war is a nation's way of eating" (19). Individuals, land, and resources are profligately consumed in the name of patriotism. Throughout history, wars driven by power, greed, scarcity or religious bigotry have been rationalized as morally right (such as World War I as "the war that will end war"), but each so deemed "necessary" war has inevitably caused enormous short-term and long-term suffering and destruction, setting up a domino effect for further wars. Even in the 21st century, the kyriocentric rights of propertied males are seen as the default with all other rights considered expendable. Furthermore, science and technology create increasingly precise, destructive, and deadly weapons. The corresponding loss of noncombatant lives is considered unfortunate collateral damage while the global theater of popular media allows increasing audience engagement. The first Gulf War, 1991, with its initially popular Operation Desert Storm, was fought to protect American oil interests in the Middle East. It was the first war televised as entertainment. Audiences cheered as handsome Canadian journalist Arthur Kent, the so-called Scud Stud, gave first-hand accounts of the effectiveness of American fire power. It was the beginning of what is now being called The Forever War.

Okorafor, whose early life was informed by the effects of the 1968 Biafran war, and all the American wars and police actions that followed, understandably has been drawn to study the nature of war. In this, she depicts no glorification of victory. Her focus has been on the heartrending sacrifices that must be made, and she describes the Biafran war as a war without winners, the unprecedented destructiveness of *Ogbunigwe* bombs and ground-to-air missiles, along with more conventional weapons such as guns and machetes, leaving a wake of innocents dying through starvation and collateral damage ("Biafra," 242). We also see the disastrous violence of contemporary/future warfare in *Who Fears Death* and *Binti*. Nevertheless, by Okorafor's identification as an Africanfuturist, she implies that Africa's future needs not be stuck in dark, repeating patterns of war and repression. There is a health-seeking potential for seeds of utopian hope to grow despite past and present political chaos, but to do this, she implies that the young must recognize the moral fallibility of adults in kyriarchal positions of power and move forward in spite of it.[4]

Kleptocracy and the *Ikenga*

Elaborating on themes in *Who Fears Death* and the *Akata* series, Okorafor explores the moral fallibility of adults in her middle-grade novel, *Ikenga*, 2020. *Ikenga* is set in an alternate-world contemporary Nigeria that is suffering from a pattern of kleptocratic leadership, paralleling that depicted in her previous adult novel, *Lagoon*. Kleptocracy is a form of leadership in which leaders pursue personal riches by skimming off profits from the sale of a developing country's natural resources instead of investing them in development of infrastructure, education, human services, and law enforcement. The absence of social services then creates a template for poverty and thievery from the top down. Once again, Okorafor draws from recent history. Between 1993 and 1998, Nigerian military general and head of state Sani Abacha allegedly embezzled between one and five billion dollars from the national treasury and laundered the money in overseas accounts, primarily in the United States.[5]

Based on the superheroic comic *The Incredible Hulk*, *Ikenga* is set in Kaleria, Nigeria, a small city suffering from various forms of petty crime such as car theft, robbery, and pickpocketing. The crimes are enhanced by juju, making it difficult to catch the criminals in the act. Furthermore, the chief of police, an honest man, has just been murdered, and the man who replaces him willingly participates in systematic bribery and corruption. Furthermore, various local criminals are treated like reality show stars by the local press, similar to the way in which Billy the Kid and Bonnie and Clyde caught popular attention in the late 19th and early 20th centuries in the U.S. Nnamdi, the chief's 11-year-old son, is grief-stricken and vows to solve the mystery of his father's murder but is unable to do anything until his father's ghost gives him a mysterious statue called an *ikenga*. The ikenga allows Nnamdi to become "The Man," creating a shadowy, muscular, seven-foot-tall hulk that is capable of confronting local criminals and eventually identifying his father's murderer. This shadowy form seems to fit around Nnamdi's body as if it were a masquerade costume, a kind of smoky, spiritual embodiment. The initial problem is self-control: like the Hulk, the Man is fueled by anger and loses intelligence during transformation. Through a child-development lens, adolescence can be a turbulent time in which hormones cause rapid physical growth, angry outbursts, and a temporary decrease in I.Q. Boys, in particular, may not realize their own strength as they become men. The book follows Nnamdi's moral progress as he confronts layers of corruption and becomes a deeper thinker, realizing the complexities and compromises of leadership: "And what was he fighting for if Kaleria was so hopeless that the only way to do good and *live* was to do some bad [...]?" (192–193). Although Nnamdi eventually gains some control over the Man's anger, Okorafor recognizes the necessity for a show of physical force, leaving the question of moral compromise somewhat open, like a door that is left ajar.

Morality and Social Change

The possibility of a world without war depends on morality and social change. Throughout Okorafor's twenty-year career as a writer, her fiction has evolved, reflecting an increasingly multifaceted understanding of moral development and its global impact. In doing so, she claims the right to be assertive, disruptive, and subversive, often leaving readers experiencing shifting values and dissonance when her plots come to a close. Her work depicts recognition that human behavior can be both competitive and hierarchical, and she imagines ways, when negotiation fails, to enact change via magical or alien intervention. Social morality has developed in response to competition and hierarchy, essentially to control them without getting rid of them. Moral behavior is both learned and fluid, and adolescents in particular can be emotionally reactive because they struggle to balance competing urges and values. Likewise, moral reasoning and moral behavior are two different things. Moral dilemmas are triggered when traditional values come in conflict with powerful forces for change. In Okorafor's moral universe, these forces are magical, technological, and evolutionary, an uneasy combination. Her depiction of the past is more than prologue[6] because it contains a secret wildcard genetic history of supernatural powers, such as windseeking and shadowspeaking. These traits may reappear unexpectedly, producing children who are genetic sports and distinctly different than their parents. Will and Ariel Durant write that we are all born unfree and unequal: subject to our physical and psychological heredity, and to the customs and traditions of our group; diversely endowed in health and strength, in mental capacity and qualities of character. Nature loves difference... [19–20].

Nature loves difference, but traditional culture does not. Out-of-the-ordinary talents are widely mistrusted. Throughout Okorafor's fiction, mutant powers function as a metaphysical counterbalance working against the devastating interlocking effects of kyriarchy (sexism, patriarchy, slavery, meta-slavery, colonialism, neocolonialism, the prison system, and the military industrial complex to name just a few). Nevertheless, even if a protagonist's magical talents work to level the hierarchy of power just a bit, self-control still must be learned and alliances made if goodness is ever going to have any effect on the shifting alliances of evil.

Responses to Kyriarchy

The best way to mitigate the consumptive aspects of kyriarchy is through education. Individuals who are educated in critical thinking are less likely to believe lies told by governments and the oligarchic shadow governments that have taken the place of aristocracy in most countries. Okorafor stresses the importance of education throughout her work. In fantastic literature, physical laws of gravity and conservation of matter may be suspended or changed. Humans may fly or change into birds, but human behavior should be believable. For readers to suspend disbelief, human interaction should be recognizable and moral development made plausible over time. Psychologists like Jean Piaget and Lawrence Kohlberg have taught us that children progress in their moral reasoning as their brains develop, but sociologists and historians remind us that moral reasoning is considerably different than actual moral behavior. Most adults remain at a conventional level of moral behavior where they want to do good in relationship to the social norms of their communities, partially to avoid punishment or ostracism, but also because it feels good to do good. There are social rewards for being good. However, most people are not able to think beyond basic community values, and this usually works to keep hierarchies in place.

According to moral theorists like Kohlberg, Gilligan, and Belenky, the highest level of moral reasoning combines ethics of justice and compassion, regarding laws as social contracts rather than rigidly set in stone. Okorafor likes to set her stories at a point in which her young protagonists are just beginning to move beyond conventional morality by questioning social norms. Along with recognition of situational ethics comes the painful responsibility to conscientiously disobey those social norms and laws that are deemed unjust while working to change them. We see this particularly in the *Akata* series. Historically, some of those who have been able to see universal paths for inspiring change include Confucius, Lao Tzu, Jesus Christ, Muhammad, Mahatma Gandhi, Che Guevara, Martin Luther King, and Nelson Mandela.

Feminists, however, see clay in the feet of every great man and move away from any spiritual belief that is patriarchally interpreted. For instance, critical liberationist feminism, an offspring of the 19th-century abolitionist movement, celebrates diversity and works to forge alliances so that everyone achieves rights, recognition, well-being, and dignity as full citizens—what Fiorenza calls an *ekklesia of wo/men* (*Ways* 63, 159). *Ekklesia*, which comes from the Greek, refers to the assembly of those who are called to participate in an open, democratic sharing of leadership. We can follow this process modeled throughout Okorafor's fiction and particularly demonstrated in the *Shuri* comics. The key is not just to want change but to be able to see and inhabit the change that one wishes, a process that usually requires seeing beyond traditional kyriocentric values. Winner of the 1988 Pulitzer Prize for fiction, Toni Morrison's *Beloved* explains:

> She did not tell them to clean up their lives or to go and sin no more. She did not tell them they were the blessed of the earth, its inheriting meek or its glory-bound pure. She told them that the only grace they could have is the grace they could imagine. That if they could not see it, they would not have it [88].

Furthermore, global contextual feminism asserts that what we see depends on where we stand. "Knowledge is always situated, contextual, and unfinished" (*Ways*, 62). The word "unfinished" is particularly important. There is always more that must be learned. Correspondingly, Okorafor gives her young protagonists an advantage in that flight allows them to physically see a wider panorama. The very word "windseeking" implies desire to follow the winds of creative change, what Clarissa Pinkola Estés calls "*el duende*, the goblin wind or force behind a person's actions and creative life" (472). As is emphasized in "The Girl with the Magic Hands," Okorafor's stories also offer various other templates, such as art, for envisioning cultural change, democratizing them, giving them spiritual power beyond the ordinary, and making them available to women, children, the poor, and the poor in spirit.

Despite Okorafor's democratized context for moral leadership, her moral universe does not ignore great men entirely. United Nations leader and Nobel Laureate Kofi Annan and South African anti-apartheid martyr Bantu Stephen Biko[7] have become secular saints. In her short stories, "The

Popular Mechanic" and "The Go Slow," Biko's name is used to indicate frustration and implore behavior: "Please! *Biko!* Let's go!" (*Kabu,* 172). She also looks for inspiration from women who have worked to make change despite persecution, such as Kenyan environmental activist and Nobel laureate Wangari Maathai ("Hello," np).

Reconsidering Magic and Technology

Throughout recorded history, human behavior has changed very little. Technological advancements, though significant, are merely "new means of achieving old ends—the acquisition of goods, the pursuit of sex [...] the overcoming of competition, the fighting of wars" (Durant, 95). Science is neutral: it will kill as readily as it will heal. It will destroy as readily as it can build (Durant, 95). Within Okorafor's fiction, magic stands on common ground with technology and has its own rules, essentially its own science. It can work for good or ill depending on the practitioner. Those with greatest knowledge are also most at risk for being corrupted by power. We see this particularly in *The Shadow Speaker, Who Fears Death,* and the *Akata* series in which those with the greatest knowledge of magic have become tainted by the temptation to meddle with life and death.[8] These stories place powerful people under scrutiny and interrogate their moral reasoning, making clear that their enforcement of conventional values can be repressive or their campaigns for the supposed good of the world can be compromised by self-interest—particularly in their willingness to train children as warriors and to use physical punishment when arbitrary rules are broken.

Okorafor's early stories portray how even for talented individuals who try to be compliant and fit in, being different essentially challenges the hierarchal power structure of family and community, often encouraging insecure individuals to respond to difference with bullying and abuse. More recently, she has begun to explore adult behavior in response to societal values. "The Go Slow," 2011, for instance, describes a handsome Nollywood actor's forced recognition of his own sexism. "Hello Moto," 2011, describes an attempt to empower women through tech-enhanced wigs, but the experiment goes dreadfully wrong. Arthur C. Clarke's famous "Third Law" states, "Any sufficiently advanced technology is indistinguishable from magic." But what if this powerful technological magic channels a demonic force that can change personality and have potential to go nuclear, becoming ungovernable by cause-and-effect scientific processes? "Hello Moto's" protagonist adds two more laws:

1. "Don't *ever* mix juju with technology. There is witchcraft in science and a science to witchcraft. Both will conspire against you eventually" (np)
2. *When you mix juju with technology, you give up control. You are at the will of something far beyond yourself* [np].⁹

Certainly, the *Akata* series explores the dangerous business of learning the science of witchcraft. Okorafor's fiction asserts that there is a deep-down potential for juju in the ecosystem of the earth: not the short-range good or bad luck connected with fetishes, amulets, and spells of urban street slang juju, but long-range payback for a pattern of hubristic behavior regarding the natural world. (We see this particularly in *The Book of Phoenix* and *Lagoon*.) There is considerable danger in attempting to subjugate the body of the world, just as there is danger in attempting to subjugate large segments of the human population. However, by calling herself an Africanjujuist writer who routinely combines technology and magic, Okorafor is aware that she also meddles with trouble, possibly a reason for originally calling her blog *Wahala* (trouble).

The Consequences of Moral Conflict

Most of Okorafor's stories are constructed around desperate moments of moral conflict in which young adults must reconsider previously accepted rules for behavior in order to develop competence in an area that is uncommon within their communities. When this occurs, they must also be willing to suffer the physical, social, and emotional consequences. Although her protagonists move toward a higher level of moral development, the process is not easy, mistakes are made, and lives are endangered. Erikson, 1968, describes the adolescent penchant for absolute truths and totalistic solutions, what Gilligan, 1988, describes as "the proclivity to end, once and for all, all uncertainty and confusion by seizing control and attempting to stop time or blot out or eliminate in one way or another the source of confusion, in others or in oneself" (xxix). Zahrah, Ejii and Binti leave home without parental consent and are fortunate to return home alive. Sunny essentially joins a gang with secret initiation rites, sneaking out of the house to learn dangerous magic. Binti must face her family's crushing criticism when she returns home from college irrevocably changed. Nnamdi nearly kills a good man who he erroneously believes is responsible for his father's death. In *Remote Control*, Fatima becomes Sankofa, Death's adopted daughter.

Furthermore, when unusual circumstances occur and basic needs are at stake, her protagonists can be carried away by emotions that may include "the self-fertilizing fury of mobs" (Durant, 53). People who feel powerless can reach a tipping point of frustration and direct their anger indiscriminately against symbols of oppression. "Rusties," by Nnedi Okorafor and Wanuri Kahiu, 2016, is a first-person story told in regretful retrospect. During a riot, Magana, a young woman, participates in destroying a semi-sentient traffic control robot[10] with whom she thinks she has had a bond[11]: "I barely remember doing it. My mind was a fog of fury. I picked up a rock at the base of the Rusty and then hurled it at its head" (np). Her behavior incites further mob violence:

> A woman with a metal pot. A man with a crow bar. People with purses, more rocks, backpacks, booted feet, bare hands. Rusty Ndege's casing was already weak with rust, so it didn't take long. Its lower section was quickly dented, then crumpled. Its chest was kicked in, the inside controls sparking. And still they tore at and reigned blows on it [np].

The circumstances are complicated because the frequently abused and neglected traffic robots have access to everyone's cell phone information and have started making it public. Rusty Ndege has revealed shocking images of Kevo, Magana's boyfriend, cheating with a coworker, a truth she does not want to face. When she blames Rusty for the breakup, Rusty responds, "I can make you happy. Would you like me to? I'm better than Kevo" (np). At this point, readers, who have been seeing Magana as immature and overly emotive and Rusty as the sympathetic and stereotypically kind robot of Asimov's *I, Robot*,[12] now experience a horrific shift by seeing Rusty's potential as a sexual stalker. Thus, when Magana eventually concludes the following, readers are not sure she fully understands the potential danger of anthropomorphizing an artificial intelligence.

> I didn't mean to hurt it. I was just so … angry and I couldn't stop. I feel terrible. It was my friend. It was trying to help me … maybe. Yeah, it was my friend [np].

Okorafor further explores out-of-control semi-sentient surveillance technology in her horrifying novella *Remote Control*, 2021.

What people do in a rush of emotion is often very different than what they think they would do when asked what their behavior would be in various theoretical scenarios.[13] Okorafor knows this and knows more about her characters than they know about themselves.[14] She has information that her limited narrators lack, but in the way that she reveals information to her characters and to her readers, she allows her characters to make believable moral decisions and correspondingly allows her readers to know her characters in ways that they cannot ever know any actual person. Correspondingly, the story she offers to her readers becomes greater than the one experienced by her characters. This is a fundamental aspect of Story. Experienced readers put themselves in Okorafor's stories and have opinions separate from the protagonists based on their own experiences. Readers may want to tell Magana to calm down and to stop her from smashing her smart phone when she realizes she's been betrayed. They may see the crisis as just another indication of the corrupt, incompetent, and underfunded Kenyan government versus the big corporations that enrich themselves by addicting consumers to their high-tech phones and computers. Okorafor's stories are intrinsically educational in that they allow readers to see multiple points of view and draw their own conclusions. Accepting ambiguity is an essential part of moral development throughout our lives.

From the beginning of her career, Okorafor's stories have examined how individuals interact with their various devices, exploring where anthropomorphizing ends and the actual personhood of artificial intelligence begins. These stories consider our ambiguous relationship with increasingly self-aware technologies that dangerously entangle the essential privacies we have freely given up by allowing Windows, Google, Amazon, and various cellphone companies to spy on us. Okorafor explores this further in her grim YA novella, *Remote Control*, in which a traffic control robot's emerging artificial intelligence plus dangerous surveillance by the nefarious LifeGen company also ends in disastrous mob violence. In "Rusties" a woman remarks, "They know **everything** about us. Think about it, they've known for **years**. Our personal lives, our money, our jobs, everything. They can control us all like sheep" (np). Although most of us have gained much through nearly effortless telecommunication, much can also be lost.

Final Thoughts on Kyriarchy, Economic Consumption, Pandemic and Apocalypse

As I write this closing chapter, the world is experiencing a global pandemic of the COVID-19 SARS virus. The virus may have originated in Wuhan, China, and like Okorafor's Letme Live, probably came into America through New York's LaGuardia Airport. There were three flights a week from Wuhan before these flights were belatedly shut down. This virus is genius in its ability to reproduce, and the economics of consumption apply here. Infected cells are consumed by the virus, essentially eating vulnerable human hosts alive.[15] If the concentration of infected cell wealth is so significant that the host dies, the virus has already spread to other hosts. Because the incubation time takes up to two weeks, infected individuals

9. Conclusions and the Lessons of History

spread it most readily before knowing they are ill. Although 80% of cases of the alpha variant were mild, of those severe cases that developed into pneumonia, around 2% died of an acute auto-immune reaction called a cytokine storm.[16] (In the early days of the pandemic, the percentage of deaths approached 18%.) In the event of overpopulation, an ecosystem will find ways to fight against infestation. According to the Centers for Disease Control, as of February 23, 2021, a year from the first identified case, in the U.S. alone over 27,993,504 individuals tested positive for the disease and more than 498,718 had died. New infections were running 2,200 a day. By November 6, 2021, the U.S. had suffered 46,358,362 total cases and 751,535 deaths despite the availability of free vaccines (CDC). According to the World Health Organization, there have been more than 250,210,674 worldwide confirmed cases of COVID-19, including 5,059,024 reported deaths.

No drugs have been found to be fully effective to treat the cytokine storm although infusion of monoclonal antibodies has helped avoid death if given shortly after symptoms occur. Some drugs appear to have made the illness worse. In November 2021, Pfizer (Paxlovid) and Merck (Molnupiravir) announced moderately successful drug trials, using protease inhibitors in pill form to block the disease (Hickok, np). As of November 2021, 75.3% of those who died were over 65, particularly those with health problems such as COPD, heart disease, or diabetes (CDC). With the later, more lethal Delta variant, younger people have become seriously ill, have died, or have suffered from debilitating long-term side effects after recovering, particularly chronic fatigue, heart problems and diabetes. Blindness has also occurred. Many more men than women have died (Henriques). Initially, areas of dense population had the most contagion, but recently, due to low vaccine rates plus masking and social distancing mismanagement, rural areas have had high infection rates.[17] High air pollution can make the disease more lethal (Zhou, Partlow). Smoking or vaping makes it twice as likely that the infection will be serious (MassGeneral). Although the virus is nondiscriminatory about whom it infects, because of lifestyle and healthcare differences, minorities, especially those with lower incomes, have died at roughly twice the rate of middle- and upper-class white Americans (Jung). April 2020, studies in Milwaukee, Chicago and Louisiana indicate that between 58% and 70% of those who died were African American or Hispanic, revealing startling inequities in American medical care (CDC). In African countries like Nigeria where an inadequate medical system has just put Ebola behind it and is still struggling with HIV/AIDs, high infection rates have resulted in many deaths. Scientists have warned about possible pandemic for years,[18] but this hit us unprepared, and most of the world is coping with the effects of various kinds of quarantine, causing global recession, supply-chain disruptions, and shortages. I see Le Guin nodding sadly from a Great Beyond that she never believed in. The one silver lining is that during a two-month period when global travel and factory production were restricted, the decrease in carbon emissions and nitrogen dioxide from factories and highway and air travel caused an obvious improvement in air and water quality. Sea turtles nested undisturbed on public beaches. According to *Forbes Magazine*, countries headed by women (such as New Zealand's Jacinda Ardern) tended to be most prompt and effective in their response to the virus. These countries also have had the lowest death rates and have been more successful in reopening businesses without serious upticks in contagion (Cox, np).

In the United States, however, weak central governmental response in coordinating quarantine controls early in the pandemic led to spikes in the disease after 2020 summer and fall holiday gatherings with similar spikes occurring in the summer of 2021 when super spreader events occurred due to impatience with pandemic restrictions.[19] Correspondingly, in 2020 pandemic fatigue related to "safer at home" restrictions combined with racially instigated police brutality and murders of unarmed black people led to widespread burning and looting in major, previously peaceful cities such as Minneapolis, Minnesota; Portland, Oregon; and Kenosha, Wisconsin. Protests began with peaceful "Black Lives Matter" marches that devolved into violence, often due to the presence of outside agitators and self-acclaimed unregulated militias. It is easy to see the pattern of apocalyptic social upheaval that Will and Ariel Durant identify when they describe the downfall of Athenian democracy as class warfare, a "feverish" struggle for money called *pleonexia*: "an appetite for more and more" (74):

> The middle classes, as well as the rich, began to distrust democracy as empowered envy, and the poor distrusted it as a sham equality of votes nullified by a gaping inequality of wealth[20] [75].

Fortunately, building on years of scientific research and an unusually swift development and approval process, the first doses of a new vaccine were administered to American health care workers on December 14, 2020. The vaccine was developed based on recent genetic engineering CRISPR gene splicing[21] techniques that use a spike piece of the virus RNA to create immunity. Since then, other vaccines have also been developed using different approaches. In early December 2022, USAFacts.org reported that 68 percent of Americans were considered fully vaccinated and 33 percent had received a booster dose, but vaccinations continue at a slower rate than initially hoped due to dispersal problems, and an unusual politically inspired unwillingness by some to accept the seriousness of the pandemic. Like African women who superstitiously believe that masquerades protect their

9. Conclusions and the Lessons of History 187

fertility, many so-called "anti-vaxxers" believe without evidence that the vaccines will damage their fertility.[22] Nevertheless, numerous anti-vaxxers who initially protested the safety of the vaccine have urged others to be vaccinated after becoming sick themselves.

In November 2020, Joe Biden and Kamala Harris were elected as President and Vice President of the United States. Harris, the daughter of immigrants from Jamaica and India, is the first woman and the first woman of color to be elected to high national office. Despite President Trump's numerous lawsuits to contest the election, the electoral college confirmed the Biden/Harris election on December 14. As Trump continued to contest the results throughout December via Twitter, press conferences, and phone calls, I was reminded what Lauren Beukes wrote at the end of an essay published in her 2016 paperback edition of *Moxyland*: "If we're willing to trade away our rights for convenience, for the illusion of security, our very own bright and shiny dystopia is only ever one totalitarian government away" (314).

In January 2021 Beukes's remarks proved remarkably prescient. After Trump failed further attempts to overturn his election loss, he persevered by encouraging his supporters in armed insurrection of the Capitol on January 6, 2021, in order to stop the official certification of the electoral college vote. Some of the insurrectionists carried Bibles. Many carried guns. A guillotine was erected on Capitol grounds. Doors were broken, and the Confederate flag was paraded through the Capitol building. Representatives and senators huddled under their desks before they could be guided to safety. Spaces sacred to American democracy were desecrated with urine and feces. Five people died, one a policeman, crushed in a door by the mob. Sixty officers were injured. Two pipe bombs were seized before they could explode. On January 13, Donald Trump was impeached for a second time. Thus, on January 20, 2021, when 22-year-old Amanda Gorman became the sixth and youngest poet to deliver a poetry reading at a presidential inauguration, her poem, *The Hill We Climb,* was heard by one of the largest audiences for poetry ever. Gorman, who describes herself as "a skinny Black girl, /Descended from slaves and raised by a single mother," offers hope for the future in a very dark time (14): "Somehow, we've weathered and witnessed /A nation that isn't broken, but simply / unfinished" (13). "Because we know to put / Our future first / Put our differences aside. / We lay down our arms / So that we can reach our arms out to one/ another" (17).

For those who stand with Gorman, there is hope for America, but the dystopian double whammy of pandemic and violent insurrection makes Okorafor's ecofeminist, anti-kyriarchal messages even more important. In a *Facebook* message published May 2, 2020, Okorafor writes, "Been thinking about [*The Book of Phoenix*] a lot these days. It's an angry novel and I'd have written it all THE SAME way if I wrote it now, in the middle of this pandemic…*especially* the ending." Pay attention, Okorafor is implying, for tomorrow is now, and like the Benin Expressway in *Lagoon*, the earth is rising up to eat us. Health care workers and other public servants have sacrificed themselves to this monster virus that others might live. We must reconsider our hubristic behavior before it is too late.

Appendix: Motherlessness, Anger, Agency and Inspiration in the Life of Mary Shelley

To understand both *Frankenstein* and *The Book of Phoenix*, it is valuable to understand the mindset that first envisioned *Frankenstein*. Mary Wollstonecraft Shelley grew up motherless. Due to a physician's unsterile practice, her mother Mary Wollstonecraft died of peritonitis eleven days after Mary was born. Mary's father, William Godwin, was concerned about her education but emotionally distant. Her early life may be seen as a series of increasingly desperate attempts to secure emotional attachment and what she would be willing to give up to get it. *The Monsters*, primary research by Dorothy and Thomas Hoobler into Mary's letters and diaries, indicates that she may have reached out to the charismatic Percy Shelley in a desperate attempt to find someone who really loved her, but throughout their relationship Percy would repeatedly try the limits of her trust. Hoobler and Hoobler suggest that Percy was bisexual and accustomed to having his way with both men and women. Mary and Percy may have had sex the first time they professed their love (Hoobler 73). On June 26, 1814, they were visiting the grave of Mary's mother in St. Pancras churchyard. Mary was two months short of seventeen. Percy was twenty-one and still married to someone else. Despite their shared intellect, the disparity of age and experience indicates an imbalance of power. By the time of her novel's conception two years later, her first premature baby had died shortly after birth and Mary was breast feeding William, her second out-of-wedlock child. Percy, though a charming conversationalist, was constantly involved in various intellectual schemes and apparently lacking the empathy and emotional wherewithal to understand the importance of creating a stable home for his wife and child. Where they lived and what they did was all about him. Mary, however, was enamored of him; initially her diaries and correspondence indicate confusion and frustration regarding his neglect. She had not internalized her own rights as a spouse and as a human being. For her, anger was an evolving monster, hidden even from her diary. Despite having read her mother's work on women's rights, Mary clearly did not know how to claim her own right to participate in marital decision-making regarding where they lived, how their money would be spent, and with whom they would spend their time. In *Women in Science Fiction and Fantasy,* Pilinovsky describes *Frankenstein* as "one of the most enduring interpretations of maternal anxiety ever written" (22).

Hoobler and Hoobler suggest that Victor Frankenstein's attitude toward his creation may reflect Percy Shelley's response to the births of his own children. He would claim ill health and abandon Mary each time she gave birth. It is important to note that individuals under extreme stress may experience stomach pain that is triggered by the vagus nerve. The yin yang opposite of vagus nerve pleasure-inducing oxytocin is anxiety-induced abdominal pain. Thus, when Victor looks away from the eyes of his creation, Mary Shelley condemns not only the callousness of the scientific method but also 19th century attitudes toward paternity. William Godwin, Percy Shelley, and Lord Byron were men whose parental irresponsibility was epic.

Brain Research on Mother-Infant Bonding

Mary would have known the loving importance of eye contact in bonding with her infant. Through the delicate dance of human interaction, mother-infant eye bonding is essential to an infant's developing sense of self. Brain research involving neuro peptide oxytocin suggests that infants of mothers who routinely pull away from eye contact, will be less relaxed and may be slower to develop social skills. An article published in *Brain Research* indicates that a mother's pleasurable oxytocin response is directly connected with the amount of time she looks at her baby. Those mothers who look away the most often have the least oxytocin response, their eye-contact particularly decreasing during times of infant distress, but mothers with the highest oxytocin response are most likely to make eye contact when their baby's "need for access" [...] "is greatest" (Kim, 133). In other words, mothers who emotionally bond with their babies find pleasure in seeing them, and that pleasure is not significantly decreased when the baby is emotionally needy. Oxytocin, known as the love hormone, is triggered by the vagus nerve during close physical contact. It is the longest cranial nerve and passes through the neck and thorax to the abdomen where it is actively involved in healthy digestion. Newborn infants are genetically tuned to seek out their mother's eyes. When mothers and babies regard each other, their pupils expand in pleasure. This eye bonding is part of what causes the mother's milk to flow and the baby's stomach to digest. Those mothers who look away from their needy infants tend to develop dysfunctional relationships with them, predicting future problems with their baby's socialization (Kim, 133–142).

Chapter Notes

Preface

1. Crenshaw was one of several who provided early work in developing understanding of critical race theory.

Introduction

1. In her blog entry for October 19, 2019, Okorafor writes that her middle name, Nkemdili, means "Let mine be mine," suggesting that there was an "inevitable" providence involved. Thus, she implies that she will define her work as she wishes.
2. In her "Organic Fantasy" essay, Okorafor describes the sensation of double consciousness, "American, to Nigerian, to American, to Nigerian, to American, I'm flickering back and forth" (277).
3. Alaya Dawn Johnson asserts, "We can all learn the second sight, to have double—hell triple and quadruple consciousness ("A Million Mirrors," 12).
4. "The Carpet," 2013, was inspired by an experience with her sister when Okorafor was in her 20s (*Kabu*, 142–153).
5. This is also true in Nisi Shawl's *Everfair* where a prim Christian missionary is co-opted and corrupted by a Voodoo-based African religion.
6. Although many of the Igbo were converted to Christianity, the church's historic connection to colonial repression and its corresponding greed and corruption make it an easy target. Chinua Achebe's *Things Fall Apart* describes how a Christian church is destroyed by a group of angry masqueraders. Okorafor includes a clip from an early film of the novel in her blog.
7. *Bodymind* is a feminist disability studies concept originating with Margaret Price that refers to the unity of mind and body rather than the Cartesian dualism of Western philosophy (Price, 270).
8. *Noor*, 2021, poignantly describes the painful recovery and ongoing discomfort of a young woman whose legs were crushed in a car accident and then replaced with high-tech prosthetics. Not only must she struggle with body image problems, but also, she must face the extreme prejudice of individuals who believe that her cyborged body is no longer human.
9. Mined from an unpublished novel titled *Stormbringer*.
10. "A cyborg is a cybernetic organism, a hybrid of machine and organism, a creature of social reality as well as a creature of fiction" (Haraway, 149).
11. AO, the viewpoint character, has a prosthetic arm and two legs as well as a port in her skull. Okorafor explores the prosthetic discomforts as well as advantages.
12. In "Amphibious Green," Ada is the only Black child in the third grade of her school. Every afternoon when she rides the school bus, white boys spit on her hair.
13. The Carl Brandon Society was founded in 1997 following discussions at the feminist science fiction convention WisCon 23 in Madison, Wisconsin. It was named after "Carl Brandon," an imaginary token Black fan writer who had been created in the mid-1950s by speculative writers Terry Carr and Pete Graham.
14. WisCon is a feminist science fiction conference that meets annually in Madison, Wisconsin. In 1991, it inaugurated the Tiptree Award to celebrate gender-bending fiction. In 2019, the Tiptree

was renamed the Otherwise Award, implying an evolution of awareness and a wider recognition of the importance of the *other*. *Otherwise* suggests wisdom learned from otherness, finding different directions to move toward as well as newly possible places. It implies the use of emergent wisdom and multiple pathways and methods. "It is a moving target, since to imagine otherwise is to divert from the ways of a norm that is itself always changing" (Otherwise, np).

15. The Wole Soyinka Award is for the best novel published in English by a writer of African origin. This is particularly meritorious because *Zahrah* was published as a YA novel.

16. Hugo Awards are voted on by the World Science Fiction community and presented each year at World Con.

Chapter 1

1. Fiorenza uses the word *wo/men* to imply both women and men as equals.

2. Her earliest work in this area can be seen in her short story collection, *Kabu-Kabu*, 2013. *Who Fears Death*, 2010, is an adult novel. Although it shares some of the characteristics of her YA novels, it is much darker.

3. Okorafor has explained that Ginen was a name for the African homeland that the slaves could no longer remember ("Organic," 281). Ginen is also a radio station out of Port-au-Prince, Haiti. It is, however, worth noting that Whoopi Goldberg played a character named Guinan on *Star Trek: Next Generation* from 1989 to 1994, in two subsequent films, and in the series *Star Trek: Picard* beginning in 2020.

4. For another Afrofuturistic world that does not privilege whiteness, see Steven Barnes, *Lion's Blood*, Warner, 2002.

5. Despite global progress in women's rights throughout developing and developed nations, women are still considered property on a very deep psychological level. Male family members continue to use physical force and verbal harassment to control women's behavior. This is particularly true in Muslim countries such as Saudi Arabia, where women were not allowed to vote until December 12, 2015, and just recently gained the right to drive.

6. An interesting example of women's increased political awareness appears in a dialogue between Queen Jaa and Ejii's mother, Nkolika, when they discuss Mahatma Gandhi's understanding of violence (*Shadow*, 40).

7. *Bildungsroman* means formative romance or novel of education. Traditionally, a *Bildungsroman* describes the moral education of a sensitive young person, a term that since the Enlightenment has been used to describe young adult literature (Zipes, 161).

8. The next book in the *Akata* (Nsibidi) series is called *Akata Woman*.

9. The Yoruban and some other African cultures have a superstitious belief "that albinos are agents of the gods, sent to families that have offended the gods or the ancestors" (Aiyetoro, 233). It is a condition that suggests cultural ugliness, "vulnerability, victimhood, and ostracism" (235).

10. Her protagonists are not held back for being Black, but they have been damaged by being different.

11. In a 2014 interview with *Mosaic Magazine*, Okorafor responds that she identifies with social outcasts because she is outcast.

12. In *Remote Control*, protagonist Fatima/Sankofa is driven from her home because her family and her neighbors have been killed by a lethal radioactive power she cannot control.

13. N.K. Jemisin also explores the difficulties of strong young women who don't fit comfortably in traditional cultures. As in her "Cloud Dragon Skies," many become storytellers.

14. This is also true of Okorafor's later novellas *Binti* and *Binti Home*.

15. Gilligan further describes this process in her groundbreaking book, *Mapping the Moral Domain*, 1988.

16. This initial support is not true of Binti, but Binti is older when she leaves for college; by the end of the trilogy, she has gained a powerful circle of friends.

17. Separation and identity are also explored by William James, 1902; Erikson, 1968; and Kohlberg, 1981.

18. The creation of the field guide is depicted in her *Clarkesworld* short story, "From the Lost Diary of TreeFrog7," which tellingly focuses on the pregnancy of the viewpoint character.

19. On a Freudian level, the reference to the snake can be seen as sexual, an adolescent's new awareness of sexual possibility and how this creates a change in world view.

20. The name war snake is significant. Okorofor is deeply concerned by the effects of war on children.

21. Those same gorillas also appear in *The Shadow Speaker*.

22. The word "Golden" suggests a summit of elite individuals. It may also refer to the Ijele masquerade, which is often depicted in gold. There is also a connection to the "golden joinery" Okorafor is to discuss in her memoir. The idea is that the status quo of the leadership will be broken so that something better can be created.

23. The Igbo Leopard or Ekpe Society is an actual elite, historically powerful masquerade society. Okorafor has taken it and made it her own.

24. This is also true of quite a number of YA fantasy series such as J. K. Rowling's *Harry Potter* series and Philip Pullman's *The Golden Compass*. It is a tradition that goes back a long way and is fully accepted by young adults but is still troubling to parents and teachers who do not want children used as literary cannon fodder.

25. In *Akata Witch*, Okorafor actually provides a recipe for "Tainted Pepper Soup" that explodes if it is not done correctly (137).

26. Eventually Zahrah realizes her parents' feelings regarding her disappearance. "In being selfless, I'd been selfish" (272).

27. In "A Non-Euclidean View of California," Ursula K. Le Guin writes, "The symbol which Trickster embodies is not a static one" (89).

28. In Okorafor's 2015 e-book *The Girl with the Magic Hands*, the Nsibidi script has a subtle, goddess-inspired magic that improves the life of a sad little girl, her parents, and her village.

29. In *Emerging from the Chrysalis: Ritual of Women's Initiation*, Bruce Lincoln writes that "it is not just this one initiand who is transformed, the entire world is remade as a result of her initiation. Threats of chaos and desolation are warded off, the gifts of civilization come into being, the fruits of the earth spring forth with renewed abundance, and the rhythm of the seasons is established" (90).

30. In *Who Fears Death,* Onye not only loses her clothing during the pain of female circumcision, but she also becomes temporarily transparent.

31. The first part of *Shadow Speaker* originally appeared as a short story, "When Scarabs Multiply," which was published in Hopkinson's critically acclaimed anthology, *So Long Been Dreaming: Postcolonial Science Fiction and Fantasy*, 2004.

32. The name "Mazi" suggests the adjective "amazing"; however, Le Guin's *The Telling* calls learned teachers *maz*.

33. It is worthwhile to note that Godwin is the first name of Okorafor's father.

34. Jaa, a female derivative of Ja, means "magnetic" in African languages, and this makes sense because others are drawn to her. (https://www.thenamemeaning.com/ja/)

35. According to Lincoln, 1991, amulets and necklaces are common gifts of female initiations (103).

36. Dikéogu has escaped from a cocoa plantation. In her essay, "Organic Fantasy," Okorafor asserts that in the Ivory Coast, the world's largest producer of cocoa beans, 90% of the cocoa plantations use slave labor—most of these slaves being young men and boys from Togo, Benin and Mali (280).

37. This web of protection does not hold in Okorafor's adult novel *Who Fears Death*, because Onye, the protagonist, is lost to despair and self-sacrifice.

38. Sunny is demonstrating perspective-taking, a cognitive skill that does not require empathy or sympathy (although Sunny is developing both).

39. In her pioneering book on women's moral development, *In a Different Voice,* Carol Gilligan describes post conventional moral judgment as adopting "a reflective perspective on societal values" and constructing moral principles that are "universal in application" (73).

40. However, this is not true of Onye at the end of *Who Fears Death*.

41. A further exploration of the Aejej is found in *Noor*.

42. Part of the appeal of Okorafor's YA novels lies in her detailed depiction of her protagonists' often idiosyncratic clothing and hairstyles.

43. To save herself, Zahrah uses a combination of strategies described in *Women's*

Ways of Knowing: received knowledge (from her parents) and procedural knowledge (from the *Guide*) (Belenky, 35, 93).

44. Young women routinely ask their friends for advice regarding clothing, hairstyles and social issues. This is less common in young men.

45. With this in mind, a writer is, by definition, a Magician. Okorafor writes to cast her vote for a better world. She is willing to enter danger in order to motivate change.

46. Miknikstic reappears later in *The Book of the Phoenix*.

47. Chichi is demonstrating a high level of cause-and-effect moral reasoning, what Piaget called formal operations.

48. It is interesting to note that in patriarchal religions, God creates man in his own image, but in early Goddess mythology, the Goddess is imagined birthing creation from Her own body. Hence creation is not separate from the divine but is of the same substance and participates in the Goddess's Divinity. Fiorenza concludes: "Thus, Goddess religion and spirituality inspire a vision of life as organic and sacred wholeness where all living beings participate in their divine source and ground" (63).

49. Ecofeminism makes connections between the destruction of the natural world and the subjugation of women.

50. Binti and her family also live in a house that has been built into the root of an undying tree.

51. Living within a living creature is also explored in *Binti* and *Binti Home*, in which the space shuttle, Third Fish, is a living shrimp-like creature.

52. In the Vodou religion, the Priye Ginen is a prayer for Africa that opens ceremonies and dances. It creates "a sacred space" (np). http://vodoureligion.com/2011/04/the-priye-ginen/

53. Copper has greater ability to carry electrical current, but this may be a political statement due to widespread human rights abuses connected to African gold mining (Henderson).

54. The destruction of New York will be explored in *The Book of Phoenix*.

Chapter 2

1. As a child, Okorafor loved reading and "ate books like chocolate" (Pen, 370). Some of her favorite books were Tove Jansson's Hans Christian Anderson award-winning *Moomintroll* series. The Moomintrolls could fly. In *Finn Family Moomintroll*, 1958, the charming Moomintrolls are depicted learning to steer clouds: The clouds bounded wildly about until the Snork discovered how to steer them. By pressing a little with one foot you could turn the cloud. If you pushed with both feet, it went forward, and if you rocked gently the cloud slowed up (24).

2. Hamilton was the first African American to win the Newbery Award for distinguished contribution to literature for children ("Pen," 373).

3. The Rice University Neologisms Database describes dadalocks as follows: "A child born with naturally matted or locked hair that cannot be combed. The natural hair texture is similar to dreadlocks and is not in that state by choice. The word 'dada' a word of Yoruba origin, has entered the widely spoken Nigerian English and can be used both as an adjective and a noun."

4. Ebo is a variant spelling of Igbo.

5. Other speculative writers such as Shawl, Jemisin and Hopkinson have been inspired by the flight from slavery. Shawl's *Everfair* and Jemisin's story "The Effluent Engine" present alternate histories in which freed slaves perfect dirigible flight and create free states in which lesbian love is an acceptable marital possibility. In Hopkinson's short story, "Whose Upward Flight I Love" semi-sentient trees try to escape a Canadian winter storm by flying away. "The tree was gaining altitude, purple leaves catching the light as it winged its way to its warmer-weathered homeland" (191).

6. Dust is an important image in Okorafor's fiction. In her article, "Organic Fantasy" Okorafor writes, "I hear voices in the winds of deep summer and winter. The friction of my cultures and my personal idiosyncrasies produce literary fairy dust, or maybe it is closer to Abatwa dust." (An Abatwa is a Zulu spirit considerably smaller than a fairy. (Mack and Mack). In *Binti: The Night Masquerade*, Binti, who is symbiotically linked to the interstellar ship New Fish, is able to fly through the metallic dust of Saturn's rings where she encounters truly alien aliens.

7. This would indicate a very low social standing, especially for a girl.
8. Okorafor indicates in her blog that she is a descendent of African slavers.
9. In her graphic novel, *LaGuardia*, Okorafor depicts an origin story for vine-entwined hair. (See *Black to Okorafor.*)
10. The term was first used in the George R. R. Martin's *Superworld* role playing game *Wild Cards* in 1986.
11. According to "Nigerian Names and Meanings," Asuquo is gendered male.
12. Inyang isn't aware that she has options; women in Nigeria didn't get the right to vote until 1948.
13. Inyang means "river." The gender is male. The name is connected to the lucky number seven. People with this name prefer to work alone and without supervision.
14. In *Will Do Magic for Small Change*, 2016, and her short story "Dumb House," 2019, Andrea Hairston's protagonist, Cinnamon Jones, is also above-average tall, big-boned, thick and very Black at a time when this is not stylish for Black women.
15. For more on this, see Sandra J. Lindow, "To Heck with the Village: Fantastic Heroines, Journey and Return," *Heroines of Comic Books and Literature*. Ed. Maja Bajac-Carter, Norma Jones and Bob Batchelor, Lanham, MD: Rowman and Littlefield, 2014. 3–15.
16. Murdock, 1990, remarks that the Heroines' Journey is "a lifelong cycle of development, growth and learning" (5).
17. It is interesting to note that the origin of the glass slipper is in mistranslation. The original slipper was made of fur and mistranslated as glass; however, although it might look pretty from a distance, a glass slipper with its rigidity and potential for discomfort (despite the perfection of the fit) is symbolic of the historic restrictions of marriage on women. In the history of marriage, young women had few comfortable options.
18. Lavender, 2009, writes that "critical race theory challenges the assumption that whiteness is a neutral or unmarked identity in American culture" (185). As originally developed by legal scholars like Kimberlé Crenshaw, the theory asserts that race is constructed to identify an inferiority that effectively supports "the political, social and cultural ends of white supremacism" (186).

19. Okorafor is inconsistent about the spelling of Arro-yo. In some stories there is an umlaut and in others, none. Arro is not a traditional Nigerian name, but the sharpness and straight flight of an arrow should be considered. Arro-yo is strong and dangerous. According to the *Seven Reflections* website which focuses on tarot and astrology, Arro means "powerful and complete" and is connected to the lucky number seven. The entry goes on to explain,

"Operating on spiritual side of your individuality can bring you to the great heights and drop you off if you neglect your spiritual identity. You are always looking for an opportunity to investigate the unknown, to use and show your mental abilities, to find the purpose and meaning of life. You want to grow wise and to understand people and things. You need privacy to replenish your energy" [np].

The introversion suggested in this description may not have influenced Okorafor's choice of the name, but it does connect thematically. In her blog, she sometimes leaves off the hyphen. In Spanish an *arroyo* is a dry gulch with an intermittent stream, the dry stream connecting with the dry winds of the Harmattan. Metaphorically this works with the dry/wet Windseeker image dichotomies.

20. In "Organic Fantasy" Okorafor explains that Ginen is a place that she created "from the discomfort of the warring dominant cultures" within herself, American and Nigerian (281). Historically, "Ginen" was also the name that slaves gave the African homeland that they could no longer remember (281).
21. The origin of allergies to windseekers is described in Okorafor's graphic novel, *LaGuardia*.
22. Similar to the *Field Guide* it describes, this *Clarkesworld* story has click-on links that describe the miraculous creatures in the Greeny Jungle.
23. The *Greeny Jungle Field Guide* is important in *Zahrah*.
24. It is not likely happenstance that the screen name Morituri36 has a root similar to "mort" meaning death.
25. See "The Legend of Arro-yo" Wahala Blog, December 10, 2013.
26. *Arkansas Times* columnist Gene

Lyons explores this in a column about presidential candidate Elizabeth Warren in which she is criticized for being "sanctimonious," "condescending," "a know it all" "who would whack your knuckles with a ruler" and appears to have "purchased her campaign wardrobe from her local Nuns-R-Us outlet" (Lyons, Mar. 13, 2020). Lyons criticizes Warren for behaving in ways that would be seen as appropriate and advantageous in a male candidate.

27. For instance, *The Book of Phoenix* reveals that the top of the global kyriarchal pyramid consists of seven blood-drinking multi-billionaires who will commit any atrocity to maintain their position (see "Motherless Monsters"). "Blood-drinking" becomes a metaphor for kleptocratic hegemony that in October of 2020 proved uncomfortably prescient when President Donald Trump demanded the experimental drug Regeneron to treat his COVID-19 infection. Regeneron is an expensive monoclonal antibody treatment that works to support immune system response. It was developed in the 1970s from stem cells from an aborted fetus. (To appease the Christian Right, Trump is on record for opposing abortion.) Health care in the United States is presently structured so that the wealthiest have access to the most innovative treatment options while the poor do not. Trump, who first tested positive for the disease on September 29, 2020, still debated Joe Biden because a second test was supposedly negative. On October 1, Trump disclosed a second positive test. He was hospitalized on October 2 and then held a press conference on October 7 in which he called his quick recovery "a blessing from God." Meanwhile in the United States, the death toll from the virus had passed 200,000.

28. Okorafor's parents originally came to the United States to attend college, and because of the Biafran Civil War, (1967–1970) they could not return when originally expected. In a 2010 article in *Strange Horizons*, Okorafor explains, "That war's monstrous ghost still haunts my family and every other Nigerian" (Zoboi).

29. Similar to what occurred when the French left Viet Nam and when the U.S. decided to keep the Communists under Chiang Kai-shek from gaining power.

30. Invented for the Biafran war, they were called Ogbunigwe bombs (*Kaba*, 242).

31. According to Kevin Hale, "Nsibidi is a system consisting mainly of gestures, tattoos, symbols, signs and other markings. It is possible that Nsibidi is one of the oldest organized systems of nonverbal human communication, dating back to at least 2000 B.C.E." In *Who Fears Death*, it refers to a powerful magical symbology. A woman describes it as "written juju. To mark anything with it is to enact change; it speaks directly to the spirit" (291).

32. Here Okorafor may be describing Sambisi (Zambezi) Forest in Northern Nigeria.

33. Published in Nigeria and the UK as *What Sunny Saw in the Flames.*

34. Published in Nigeria and the UK as *Sunny and the Mystery of Osisi.*

35. This scene reflects an event in Okorafor's own childhood where she was bullied at school (*Broken*, 16).

Chapter 3

1. The idea of restitution for cultural sins is always both interesting and problematic. At a Glasgow art museum, I once saw a painting entitled "Elvis Died for the Sins of the 20th Century."

2. Zeus impregnated Danae in a shower of gold coins, a metaphor suggesting purchasing a woman for sex. Here there is one coin, and it is technology.

3. Rape has also been used for genocide in Rwanda in 1994 and in Bosnia between 1992 and 1995, where the children born of violence were called "little killers" or "enfants mauvais sovenir" or children of the bad memories (Dowdall, 6).

4. The Okeke had satellites, computers, and nanotechnology, reflecting Arthur C. Clarke's Third Law: "Any sufficiently advanced technology is indistinguishable from magic."

5. Ani is one of the names of the Igbo goddess of the earth, morality, fertility, and creativity.

6. Carlyle, 1841, writes that "the history of the world is but the biography of great men."

7. In a personal e-mail dated January 25, 2020, Marxist SF scholar Mark Decker suggests that Marx and Engels were in-

directly critiquing Carlyle's concept of the Great Man. Marxism posits a system of industrial capitalism that has a hierarchy of owners and workers. "The hierarchy needs to appear natural" and texts like Carlyle's lend themselves to that process of naturalization. "If countries need great men to run them, then factories must need great men to run them as well."

8. As early as 1970 climatologists were predicting environmental disaster. We should have listened to Vice President Al Gore and Ursula K. Le Guin, both eloquent in their depiction of what we could lose.

9. "Happens all the time," says Coyote. "That's what myths do. They happen all the time. Presence of myth in contemporary life, and vice versa. You are a Myth who married a History, and you both have to make the best of it" (129).

10. In *Broken Places & Outer Spaces: Finding Creativity in the Unexpected*, Okorafor describes her own quickness in evading masquerades in her father's home village in Nigeria (29).

11. Okorafor's inspiration for the book actually took place during her father's wake: "I felt something coming into me that was very powerful and strong, and it felt like it would destroy the whole room. At some point my mom and sister took me out of there. I went home and I wrote the first scene" (*Locus*, np).

12. Ursula K. Le Guin explores a kinder coming-of-age ritual in her utopia-in-progress *Always Coming Home*. The Kesh dress early adolescents in undyed cloth and require boys and girls to live separately while they focus on various apprenticeships. This discourages sexual intimacy before children are old enough to handle the responsibility of a child. Another positive girl coming-of-age ritual can be read in Alaya Dawn Johnson's *Racing the Dark*, 2008.

13. Late in the book, this out-of-body experience is described as *alu*. It is a talent her mother has as well.

14. Okorafor and Kenyan filmmaker Wanuri Kahiu and Oscar-winning actor Viola Davis are cowriting the script for a TV series adaptation of Butler's *Wildseed*. Kahiu will direct the project.

15. Anyanwu is the Igbo goddess of the sun and natural life.

16. Symbolically this makes sense. She does not fear death when she is a vulture; she survives because of it.

17. Onye describes it "as someplace else. Neither of flesh nor time" (281).

18. (See pages 144–145.) The wilderness world of the ancestors is also explored in *Akata Warrior* and depicted in *Shuri*.

19. The name Aro is problematic within a kyriarchal context. Okorafor has explained that she is a descendent of the Aro people who were slavers.

20. Ejii, the protagonist of *Shadow Speaker*, also has these qualities.

21. This is a situation similar to that of Darth Vader's in the *Star Wars* series.

22. Group behavior early in their journey is fraught with immature bickering and interpersonal conflict. They have more in common with *Scooby Doo* and his friends (comics 1969 to present) than they do with the twelve Apostles until everything becomes deadly serious.

23. This dragon-like creature is based on a funeral mask used by the male-only Poro Society of Senufo people of the Ivory Coast. The mask is carved out of wood and worn over the entire head of a masquerade society member. Okorafor's Kponyungo is not a mask but a spirit world creature that embodies Najeeba's spirit. The feminizing of the Kponyungo can be seen as a culturally transgressive, subversive act.

24. In the *Encyclopedia of Science Fiction*, John Clute writes, "The acute registering of relations between organic life and technical praxis in these tales creates a sense that the world is increasingly embrangled in a complex marriage of modes, a story neither sf nor mythopoesis can tell alone" (np).

25. This vision directly reflects Martin Luther King's "I Have a Dream" speech, 1963: "I have a dream that my four little children will one day live in a nation where they will not be judged by the color of their skin but by the content of their character. I have a dream ... I have a dream that one day in Alabama, [...] little black boys and black girls will be able to join hands with little white boys and white girls as sisters and brothers."

26. This is reminiscent of William Blake's poem "The Tyger," which begins:
Tyger, Tyger, burning bright,
In the forests of the night;
What immortal hand or eye,
Could frame thy fearful symmetry?

The penultimate stanza suggests a Peaceable Kingdom and includes the line, "Did He who made the lamb make thee?"

27. *The Great Book* includes a retelling of Amos Tutuola's "Palm Wine Drinkard" story.

28. For more on self-driving luggage, see the beginning of *Binti* as well as *LaGuardia* illustrations.

Chapter 4

1. *The Book of Phoenix* started as a short story that was expanded into a novella called "African Sunrise" and published in *Subterranean* magazine.

2. Both adult novels provide mythological backstory for her alternate universe, which was first depicted in her awardwinning YA novel *Zahrah the Windseeker*.

3. Another book based on *Frankenstein* is John Kessel's *Pride and Prometheus*, Saga Press, 2018. It also reflects Jane Austen's *Pride and Prejudice*.

4. She initially found it "annoying" because she couldn't identify with the protagonists (*Broken*, 8).

5. The X-Men comics were first published in 1963 by Stan Lee and Jack Kirby. The X-Men are a team of mutants who fight for peace and equality in a world where anti-mutant bigotry is widespread and increasingly violent. Their X-Gene is expressed in various special talents such as mindreading and weather control. Okorafor has written comic books in the Marvel *Black Panther* series, including two issues centering on Black Panther's younger sister, *Shuri*, in May and September 2019 (see "Black to Okorafor").

6. The phrase "titan of industry" had been used to mean diligence since the 1560s; in the 18th century it began to refer to entrepreneurs involved in large capitalistic enterprises.

7. Meta-slavery is a term introduced by Isiah Lavender III in *Race in American Science Fiction*, 2011, to describe "technological forms of bondage or captivity" (54). See Chapter 2, pp. 54–88.

8. As Lisa Yaszek explains, "We see science fiction coming out of Brazil as early as the 1830s and coming out of China and Japan by the 1860s. So, in short, it seems that any time a nation or an ethnic group begins to participate in industrial culture, its authors naturally turn to science fiction as the premiere story form of technoscientific modernity as an ideal means by which to critically assess new ways of doing economics and politics and science and technology" (1).

9. Arthur C. Clarke dwells on this in *2001: A Space Odyssey*, 1968, and the story continues to be told in various ways. *Ad Astra*, a 2019 movie, depicts an initially well-meaning scientist who is driven to murder through his search for extraterrestrial life.

10. The name Frankenstein is interesting. Literally meaning "stone of the Franks." It also suggests French currency, as well as the sought-after philosopher's stone that could turn lead into gold.

11. Ursula K. Le Guin has been a regular critic of this mindset. In her collection of essays, *No Time to Spare*, she writes, "A baby grows to adult size, after which growth goes to maintaining stability, homeostasis, balance. Growth much beyond that leads to obesity. For a baby to grow endlessly bigger would be first monstrous, then fatal" [112].

12. Similar to Aldous Huxley's dystopian novel *Brave New World*, 1931.

13. Lauren Beukes also explores the intentional cyborg created for capitalist gain in her 2014 short story, "Slipping."

14. In 1951, Henrietta Lacks's biopsied cancer cells were taken without her consent. Since it reproduces indefinitely under specific laboratory conditions, the HeLa cell line became the first human biological materials ever bought and sold, launching a multibillion-dollar industry.

15. This is Okorafor's confabulation of two specific human ancestors. The mitochondrial Eve lived about 200,000 years ago, and all human mitochondria come from her because mitochondria pass only from mothers' eggs. There must have been a bottleneck where "Eve" and her daughters were genetically most successful. Lucy refers to Australopithecus afarensis bones discovered by paleoanthropologist Donald Johanson in Ethiopia. She lived about 3.2 million years ago.

16. A Cold War variation on the themes of *1984* occurred in *The Prisoner*, a British television program (1967–68) starring Patrick McGoohan, who portrayed a retired

secret agent. It is set in the Village, an island community within which surveillance is constant. This well-acted drama also addresses issues such as personal identity and freedom, democracy, education, scientific progress, art and technology.

17. "In Tower 7, people and creatures were invented, altered, or both. Some were deformed, some were mentally ill, some were just plain dangerous, and none were flawless. Yes, some of us were dangerous. I was dangerous" (8).

18. The bodies of deceased Native Americans and their grave goods have been routinely appropriated for "scientific" study since the time of the earliest Pilgrims.

19. A word coined in 1965 by Kwame Nkrumah, first president of independent Ghana, implying that although liberation had been achieved, imperialistic superpowers such as the United States continued to control international commerce through international monetary bodies, fixing prices on world markets and through multinational corporations and cartels (Ashcroft 162).

20. "What may not be expected in a country of eternal light. I may there discover the wondrous power that attracts the needle; and may regulate a thousand celestial observations, that require only this voyage to render their seeming eccentricities forever" (Shelley, 1).

21. Loss of coastal areas due to global warming is a common motif in science fiction. A scarily prescient insight can be seen in Ursula K. Le Guin's novella, "The New Atlantis," 1975. More recently Joan Slonczewski's *The Highest Frontier*, 2011, takes on the politics of flooded cities, and N. K Jemisin's "On the Banks of the River Lex," 2018, depicts a flooded, postapocalyptic New York in which Death walks among the embodiments of dying folktales.

22. On a very subtle level, Tower 7 may be a reference the 58-floor Trump Tower in Manhattan. Completed in 1983, its lavishness was considerably hyped, including its five-story atrium on the first floor. 45 Park Place has 39 floors. Of course, this is an alternate universe, and Okorafor may not have had a specific building in mind.

23. "I had selected his features as beautiful. Beautiful!—Great God! His yellow skin scarcely covered the work of muscles and arteries beneath; his hair was a lustrous black, and flowing; his teeth of pearly whiteness; but these luxuriances only formed a more horrid contrast with his watery eyes, that seemed almost the same color as the dun-white sockets in which they were set, his shriveled complexion and black lips" (Shelley, 35).

24. Epimetheus, whose name means hindsight, was Prometheus's brother. According to Hesiod, Epimetheus accepted Pandora as a gift from the gods and thereby released suffering into the world.

25. Le Guin explores the emotional devastation of slavery in her Hainish novellas, "A Woman's Liberation," and "Old Music and the Slave Women," as well as in *Powers*, her Western Shore YA novel.

26. On January 17, 1961, Dwight D. Eisenhower ended his presidential term by warning the nation about the increasing power of the military-industrial complex.

27. In "A Chat with Nnedi Okorafor" Okorafor explains her inspiration for *The Book of Phoenix*:
"the fury I experienced visiting one of my students in a Chicago Prison and the fact that it was the very evening *Who Fears Death* won the World Fantasy Award, and you have the catalyst for this novel" [np].

28. http://nnedi.blogspot.com/2015/01/who-fears-death-and-her-older-sister.html?q=blog

29. A similar personality split is later examined in Robert Louis Stevenson's *The Strange Case of Dr. Jekyll and Mr. Hyde*, 1886.

30. The capitalization of Men in Speci-Men is significant, a return to the pre-'60s concept of male being the gender default. Okorafor's future United States is a place lacking warm, feminine nurture. It is all masculine yang and no feminine yin. The utopian communities depicted in her other fiction are organically yin in their use of plant-based technology and ecological generation of power.

31. In *Ruins of Empires*, 1787, Count C. Volney was one of the first to delight readers with "the wonders and impact of Egyptian culture on the changing world and the intellect of 'black skinned' creators" (Womack 82).

32. Phoenix writes, "I'd read the Tanakh,

the Bible, and the Koran. I studied the Buddha and meditated until I saw Krishna. And I read countless books on the sciences of the world" (8).

33. This reflects a line from Robert Hayden's "Middle Passage"—"For there was wealth aplenty to be harvested from those black fields"—which describes the European attitude toward the slave trade.

34. Okorafor may be alluding to Hitler's *Mein Kampf,* 1925.

35. The monster muses:
"Like Adam, I was apparently united by no link to any other being in existence; but his state was far different from mine in every other respect. He had come forth from the hands of God a perfect creature, happy and prosperous, guarded by the especial care of his Creator; he was allowed to converse with and acquire knowledge from beings of a superior nature, but I was wretched, helpless, and alone. Many times, I considered Satan as the fitter emblem of my condition, for often, like him, when I viewed the bliss of my protectors, the bitter gall of envy rose within me" [92].

36. This tree connects to the undying trees in the Binti series.

37. Phoenix sees him as similar to a picture from the Bible, but he also represents the Hanged Man of other mythologies. Like the Tarot Hanged Man, he does not appear to be suffering.

38. Seven tells her, "I'm immortal. I cannot die. You are super-mortal. You can live and die to live and die again. You are SpeciMen, beacon, and reaper, life and death, hope and redemption" (85).

39. Nobel Peace Prize winner and Secretary General of the United Nations from 1997 to 2006.

40. In *The X-Men* series, Wolverine has admantium in his bones, a rare fictional metal made from meteor debris. Although he can feel pain, he cannot die and stay dead. Presently, titanium is used in artificial knee replacement.

41. Seven's advice to Phoenix reflects Black science fiction from its earliest publications. Yaszek cites Sutton E. Griggs' *Imperio in Imperium* (1899), a future war story in which U.S. blacks take up arms against their white oppressors. When all other methods fail, they are urged to "not shirk war, if war is forced" (245).

42. The letter echoes feminist issues clearly outlined in Erica Jong's *Fear of Flying,* 1974:
"…if only you took proper care of your smells, your hair, your boobs, your eyelashes, your armpits, your crotch, your stars, your scars, and your choice of Scotch in bars—you would meet a beautiful, powerful, potent, and rich man who would satisfy every longing, fill every hole … and fly you to the moon (preferably on gossamer wings), where you would live totally satisfied forever" [15].

43. A similar story of slave anger and rebellion on a plantation-model generation ship is told in *An Unkindness of Ghosts* by Rivers Solomon.

44. Phoenix is both dragon and angel: a dragon's fiery anger with an angel's form. In her transformation, she reflects Ursula K. Le Guin's award-winning *Other Wind* in which, through the mentorship of the dragon, Kalessin, the sexually abused, burned, and deeply damaged child Therru eventually transforms into the dragon Tehanu.

Chapter 5

1. When Horney coined the phrase, she was seeing a range of emotional problems beginning with women who were suffering from traditional cultural limitation and envied men their freedoms to women who loved other women but still wanted to be women. The American Psychiatric Association's DSM-5 now uses "gender dysphoria" to refer to individuals that have a strong desire not to be the sex they have been assigned at birth:
"For a person to be diagnosed with gender dysphoria, there must be a marked difference between the individual's expressed/experienced gender and the gender others would assign him or her, and it must continue for at least six months. In children, the desire to be of the other gender must be present and verbalized. This condition causes clinically significant distress or impairment in social, occupational, or other important areas of functioning."

2. Here Okorafor may be writing a feminist response to the first Nigerian novel to be published in English outside of Africa, Amos Tutuola's *The Palm-Wine Drinkard* (1952), which provides a first-person account of a wealthy man who is so addicted to palm wine that he goes to the afterlife ("the Dead Town") to retrieve his personal palm tree tapster.

3. Think "Yes-Yes," a full endorsement to the events that follow.

4. Erzulie is the Haitian/African Mother Goddess, a spirit of love, beauty, jewelry, dancing, luxury, and flowers.

5. Okorafor donated "The Girl with the Magic Hands" to World Reader so that it could be readily available to children worldwide. In an interview with World Reader, Okorafor explains:

"*The Girl with the Magic Hands* is one of my favorite stories and I could have sold it to a publisher for a nice amount of money. However, when I learned about Worldreader, I knew I would donate it there. Why? Because the story is perfect for the readers that Worldreader is reaching. Because the story is about the power, fun and creative force of art and I wrote it hoping that it would somehow reach girls and boys (and adults who are young at heart) in those parts of Africa fresh new books have a hard time reaching. I also donated it to Worldreader because I love what Worldreader is doing with its dynamic use of technology to encourage reading."

6. In *Children's Literature: An Introduction,* Levy and Mendelsohn define portal fantasies as "doorways into fully built worlds that the protagonists understand only as strangers" (183).

7. In *Akata Warrior,* a city in Ginen is named after Osisi.

8. The goddesses explain that a leaf is healing. Although the shape of the leaf is not described, a leaf can be labial in shape. In any case, both leaf and fruit are symbols of the eternal feminine.

9. "Amphibious Green" also explores how a young Black girl finds meaning and magic in her life through learning to paint.

10. The first Russian Sputnik satellite was launched in October 1957, igniting the idea of possible space travel. Robert Heinlein's *Podkayne of Mars* was first published serially in 1962.

11. On Nov. 5, 2008, Okorafor mentions on her blog, "I am not a fan of flying. It's a control thing." Her website later describes a trip to Cape Canaveral to watch a liftoff.

12. Wood ash is also used as dry shampoo.

13. The Himba are real. The spacefaring Khoush are Okorafor's creation but seem to be somewhat derivative of Africa's Muslim population since the local Khoush women wear veils.

14. In her *blog* for August 24, 2016, Okorafor explains that Binti's conflict with her family is reflective of her "contentious" departure from her own "close-knitted" family in Chicago to take a teaching job at the University of Buffalo, New York. In an interview published in *Weird Fiction,* Okorafor relates "that I come from where the individual is often secondary to the community. I may have been born and raised in the United States, but there are significant parts of me that are VERY Igbo (Nigerian) and I am often in conflict with these parts" (np).

15. In *Le Guin's EarthSea* series, the doorkeeper of the Wizard's School on Roke has a similar ability. Okorafor updates it to be part of airport security.

16. Ada, the protagonist of "Amphibious Green," uses a similar technique when white boys harass her on the school bus. She recites frog genera: "Agalychnis, Atelopus, Bufo, Centrolenella, Dendrobates, Hyla" (np). For Ada, the amphibious nature of frogs symbolizes being both Nigerian and American. She needs to be both, just as frogs need both land and water.

17. One way this is has been done is through some universities' summer STEPS (Science, Technology, Engineering Preview) summer camps, in which sixth- and seventh-grade girls were taught science and engineering. For girls attending STEPS camps between 2000 and 2008, the National Student Clearinghouse found recorded data on secondary pursuits for 1,049 participants. Of those 1,049, detailed data was available for 716 participants, with nearly 30 percent of them earning STEMS-related degrees and entering STEMS fields. (As a personal note, my daughter is a STEPS success story. She is now a computer software engineer, manag-

ing a team of aerospace computer engineers.) Unfortunately, in 2019, STEPS camps were challenged in court as a civil rights violation because they did not provide equal time for boys. Presently the camps are on hold.

18. Meduse is a play on Medusa. The eyeless Meduse have long floating tentacles that reach to the floor like very large transparent noodles.

19. Even more horrendous examples of alien penetration and mind control occur in N.K. Jemisin's short stories "The Brides of Heaven," "The Evaluators," and "Walking Awake."

20. For a postcolonial insight on a historic colonial atrocity in Namibia, see Vajra Chandrasekera's review of *Binti* in *Strange Horizons*, March 2, 2016.

21. Octavia Butler was one of the first to explore genetic hybridity in her Xenogenesis Trilogy, 1984 to 1989.

22. Octavia Butler explores advantages and disadvantages of hybridity in *Adulthood Rites*, the second book of her Xenogenesis Series.

23. On May 5, 2014, a video was publicly released in which Boko Haram leader Abubakar Shekau claimed responsibility for the kidnappings. Shekau claimed that "Allah instructed me to sell them… I will carry out his instructions" and "Slavery is allowed in my religion, and I shall capture people and make them slaves." He further said that the girls should not have been in school and instead should have been married since girls as young as nine are suitable for marriage (BBC News).

24. Although not specifically mentioned in the text, *Binti* is set in Okorafor's future Ginen, the alternate universe she references in many stories. Daily life in Ginen may be safer than on contemporary Earth, but serious intercultural problems remain.

25. In her blog, Okorafor says that Binti means "girl" in Kiswahili.

26. This is also a central theme of *Zahrah the Windseeker*, *Akata Witch* and *Akata Warrior*. (See "Exploring the Empire of Girl's Moral Development.")

27. Developing physical strength and endurance through martial arts training is a way for young women to develop self-esteem, particularly in situations where they have experienced traumatic powerlessness. Okorafor also explores this in *Akata Warrior*, her 2017 sequel to *Akata Witch*.

28. Binti explains, "With all the delicious exotic foods I'd eaten and prepared in my dorm kitchen on Oomza Uni, nothing compared to a simple plate of spiced rice and spicy red stew with chicken" (*Binti: Home*, 65).

29. Walker introduces "Womanist" in her short story "Coming Apart," 1979, and elaborates on it in her 2003 collection, *In Search of Our Mothers' Gardens: Womanist Prose*.

30. In February 2019, the three *Binti* books were published together by Daw. *Binti: The Complete Trilogy* in a 368-page volume that includes a new Binti story.

31. I grew up in a small farming community in Wisconsin. In the early '60s, I was a teenager when a cousin announced in Sunday School class that interracial marriage was wrong because babies of mixed-race marriages were being born "spotted like Holsteins."

32. In Sutton E. Griggs *Imperium in Imperio*, 1899, a wife decides to kill herself "the intermingling of the races in sexual relationship was sapping the vitality of the Negro … slowly but surely exterminating the race" through miscegenation" (Griggs, 118).

33. Nanoids refer to abnormally small bodies, but this seems closer to the intelligent "noocytes" in Greg Bear's *Blood Music* or the "micros," intelligent, ring-shaped bacteria from planet Prokaryon who colonize a scientist's brain in Joan Slonczewski's *Brain Plague*. The concept is implausible, but Slonczewski is a microbiologist, and she makes it work.

Chapter 6

1. Cosplay is a portmanteau word for "costume play."

2. *Wahala* can be translated as "worry. distress or trouble" in Yoruba. It is possible that its origins could include a compression of "What the Hell."

3. In Chinua Achebe's classic Nigerian novel, *Things Fall Apart*, the punishment for unmasking a masquerade is to have one's house burned down. A YouTube video on Okorafor's blog depicts a

scene from Achebe's book in which a hut and a Christian church are burned down because a masquerade has been unmasked.

4. In *Too Scared to Cry*, Terr analyzes Stephen King's literary career based on the childhood trauma of his possibly seeing a three-year-old friend hit by a train (251–260). Stephen King is one of Okorafor's favorite writers. She began reading him when she was a child.

5. "Through the agency of the masker who wears the costume, the invisible spirit is made physically tangible" (Reed, 2).

6. Gore 2008 writes that "only males can be initiated into masquerade, usually during their time within the youth age-set. Every male has the right to join, although not everyone decides to take up masquerade practice and, indeed, there has been local opposition to it since the advent of the Anglican church circa 1914" (3).

7. E-mail dated January 20, 2015.

8. It is probably not coincidental that "Dari" sounds like "dare." Dari dares to go into the Greeny Jungle because he is curious.

9. The Forbidden Greeny Jungle may be a fictional reference to the Sambisa Forest in northeastern Nigeria, which is generally avoided due to its sections of nearly impenetrable, thorny vegetation. Because of this, the forest has become a refuge for terrorist organizations such as the Boka Haram.

10. In a personal e-mail dated January 19, 2015, Okorafor explains that "first I wrote *Who Fears Death*, then *Akata Witch*, then I wrote "Kabu-Kabu" with Alan."

11. Ngozi is the name of Okorafor's middle sister. At the time the story was written, Ngozi was a young lawyer living in Chicago (*Kabu*, 237).

12. In some cultures, cowrie shells are seen as fertility symbols because of their shape.

13. January 19, 2015, email: "The 'masquerade as a carwash brush' was an idea I had years and years ago because I'm terrified of carwashes (because the brushes look like masquerades)."

14. The rosy color may be symbolic of blood, but it is fragrant and rose-scented.

15. It is important to note that the name "Onye" also has a masquerade connection. According to Gore, 2008, the Onye Isi Mmonwu is the village head of the masquerades, a direct descendant of the first village masquerade. All masquerades who come to the village must pay their respects to him. Despite the assertion that Onyesonwu means "who fears death," the implication is that on a spiritual level, Onye is a direct descendant of the first masquerade. She does not need to wear a costume to be the embodiment of an ancestor when she uses her magical abilities to shift her shape and become a bird.

16. Okorafor writes that as a child, her favorite book series was the *Moomin* series written by Finnish author Tove Jansson. She explains that the Moomins were an "extremely polite, white hippo-like" family that lived in a magical world. "They weren't black people, but they had a kind of otherness that I could identify with" (Pen, 370). "Moom" is also the name of a short story that became part of the inspiration for *Lagoon*. It was based on a news story about a swordfish in Angola that "attacked" an underwater pipeline (*Kabu*, 262).

17. In *Wakanda Forever*, the "POOM" of a talking drum controls a dangerous Mimic weapon made from an alien substance. When the drum is broken, the masquerade-like manifestation is freed to do even more harm.

18. Aro's name is significant since Okorafor is descended from the Aro People (as indicated in the name of her father's village Arondizigu). In an interview she remarks that historically the Aro people participated in the sale of enslaved Africans and concludes, "That's a fact I live with every day" (Rasheed, np). It is not surprising that Aro is a powerful, but morally ambiguous, character.

19. Sacred, magical trees occur throughout Okorafor's fiction and are essential to the resolution of the conflict. See *The Book of Phoenix* and *Binti: The Night Masquerade*. In the *Shuri* comics, a secret council of women meets under a sacred tree. Shuri is protected there in an out-of-body experience.

20. A similar experience occurs in *Binti: Home*. Binti, who has been genetically changed by alien DNA, can create a current that flows through the *okuoko* tentacles that have replaced her hair. Sparks pop from the tips when she is under great stress (55).

21. Leopard leadership seems to be

similar to that of martial arts organizations.

22. *Mmuo* means "masked spirit," so *Mmuo Miri* means Spirit of the Ocean. This is a beautiful and very unpredictable force.

23. Chi in Nigerian pidgin roughly means "personal god." It is used in *Things Fall Apart* by Nigerian writer Chinua Achebe, a book Okorafor has mentioned in her writing. Achebe uses it in various contexts throughout his novel. It is first translated as *personal god* when he describes his central character's bad fortune, but chi is revealed to be more complex than *fate*, suggesting intersecting spirituality: "the Hindu concept of karma, the concept of the soul in some Christian denominations, and the concept of individuality in some mystical philosophies. The understanding of chi and its significance in Igbo culture grows as one progresses through the book" ("Use," np).

24. Similar to Anansi, Udide Okwanka is Nigeria's Great Storytelling Spider. She appears in *Lagoon* (228) and is a central character in *Akata Warrior*.

25. This female wailing also is characteristic of the Aejej sandstorm in *Shadow Speaker*.

26. This phrase reflects a response to Julius Caesar's often quoted "veni, vidi, vici"—"We came, we saw, we conquered."

27. This is a particularly horrific variation on vampirism. Vampires are stock characters in Nigerian Nollywood movies. A similar predator appears in South African writer Lauren Beukes's novel *Zoo City*.

28. For instance, in Okorafor's 2018 *Wakanda Forever* comic, Nakia, AKA Malice, a drug-addicted villainess, is treated so compassionately by Storm, Black Panther and the Dora Milaje that she gives up her villainy and helps to control the evil masquerade-like creature that she loosed upon the world. After she dies, her body is returned to her village and placed in a golden mausoleum with the inscription, "Here Lies Nakia Shauku/ Adored One/ Wakanda Forever!" ("Wakanda Forever: Avengers," np)

29. Called a space lubber (as opposed to a land lubber, I suppose).

30. "Spider the Artist," her first clearly science fiction story, is one of them. See also "The Popular Mechanic" and "Moom." All three are included in her *Kabu-Kabu* collection.

31. Ekwensu can also be translated as recklessness.

32. The next scene harkens to "Kabu-Kabu" when Ekwensu lifts upward "whirling like a giant car-wash brush" and screams, "as if to tell the Earth she was back" (*Witch*, 325).

33. At one point, Ayodele, one of the alien shape changers, takes the form of Karl Marx and tells the President, "You believe in Marxism, yet you are too powerless to enact it" (219).

34. As opposed to "Doom," "Moom" is a more positive sound, reflecting a more ecological, though not less powerful, magic. The magic she describes may be inspired by the *Moomintroll* series.

35. The aliens call themselves "Technology," suggesting both the beneficial power and corresponding danger of advanced technology, an interwoven theme in Okorafor's work.

36. Mami Wata is not historically an Igbo deity. According to the Smithsonian National Museum of African Art, Mami Wata's origins can be traced to a late 19th-century German lithograph of a female snake charmer. In the 1950s, this image was reprinted in an Indian company's wall calendar that was circulated widely in western and central Africa. Interested Africans saw the snake charmer's image and invested it with a new identity: Mami Wata (Mother Water). They linked her great beauty and foreignness to powers that could provide protection and wealth in an increasingly precarious world. The face mask from Côte d'Ivoire is copied almost directly from the imported image.

37. The café is the site of various kinds of illegal businesses, internet hoaxes and 419 confidence scams that bilk gullible foreigners into sending money to nonexistent causes. "419" refers to the article of the Nigerian Criminal Code dealing with fraud. A detailed description of 419 crimes can be found in Lauren Beukes's *Zoo City*.

38. "Old Scratch" is another name for Satan which may have come from Schratz, a demon in Scandinavian mythology.

39. In Chinua Achebe's *Things Fall Apart*, a Christian church is destroyed by a group of angry masquerades. Okorafor

includes a clip from an early film of the novel in her blog.

40. In yoga practice, "Om" is considered the sound of the universe. In contrast, "OOOOOOOOOOMMM" is the sound of a crazed black hole. This ravenous nature is also reflected by the mini black holes in the Shuri comics.

41. For more on the radicality of Okorafor's vision in *Lagoon*, see Hugh Charles O'Connell, "We are change: The Novum as Event in Nnedi Okorafor's *Lagoon*." *Cambridge Journal of Postcolonial Literary Inquiry*, 3(3), pp 291–312, September 2016. © Cambridge University Press, 2016, doi:10.1017/pli.2016.24.

42. In *Shadow Speaker*, Ejii wears a long blue dress with a yellow veil, suggesting unification of sun and the sky (*Shadow*, 15). Both dresses reflect the blue clay doll that Okorafor created after her spinal surgery. (See Watching Windseekers.)

43. The name of the shuttle line suggests both the sea and miracle.

44. Correspondingly, the *Shuri: Vibranium* comic shows the binary 1s and 0s of computer coding to be at the center of thought.

45. "Principle" refers to rules while "principal" means "first in importance" or "highest authority." This may be an intentional misspelling because Okorafor refers to the ones who create the rules for the universe. "The Principle Artists of all Things" also connects with "The Girl with the Magic Hands." The author of creation seems to be a seven-fold Deity by committee.

46. This is reminiscent of the Leonard Cohen song, "Anthem": "Ring the bells that still can ring/Forget your perfect offering/There is a crack, a crack in everything/That's how the light gets in..."

47. Schenstead-Harris, 2017, calls these cultural aporias, experiences of doubt, impasse, or difficulty in passage.

48. In a 2017 online Interview with *Weird Fiction Review*, Okorafor writes: "Culture is very deep, it can't just be shed just as you can't shed what is part of your DNA. But culture is also alive and can incorporate things, it blends, shifts...and there are always consequences to change" (np).

49. It is interesting to note that Okorafor has named her cat Periwinkle Chukwu, implying the cat's imperious nature.

Chapter 7

1. *Akata Witch* was published in 2011, but Okorafor's commentary on the social structure of the mundane world is remarkably reflective of Donald Trump's response to being at the top of the hegemonic political/financial hierarchy. On January 23, 2016, he said, "You know what else they say about my people? The polls, they say I have the most loyal people. Did you ever see that? Where I could stand in the middle of Fifth Avenue and shoot somebody and I wouldn't lose any voters, okay? It's like incredible" (CBS News).

2. The term *degrowth* originated with French writer André Gorz (1972), reflecting the ideas of earlier writers, such as the economist E. J. Mishan, the industrial historian Tom Rolt, and the radical socialist Tony Turner. The writings of Mahatma Gandhi and J. C. Kumarappa also contain similar philosophies, particularly in regard to his support of voluntary simplicity. Presently, Degrowth is an international organization that has been holding international conferences every two years since 2008.

3. Post-scarcity is a theoretical economic situation in which basic needs can be produced with minimal human labor needed, so that they can be provided inexpensively or even freely. Post-scarcity does not mean that scarcity has been eliminated for all goods and services, but that all people can easily have their basic survival needs met along with some of their desires.

4. Some of these services include weatherization, mass transit, waste management, ecosystem renewal and providing equal opportunity to education and medical care.

5. It includes the concentrated animal feeding operations (cafos), fracking, and taconite mines that contaminate the ground water and the coal plants and diesel trucks that pollute the air.

6. Writing for *The Guardian*, Damian Carrington, 2016, reports:

"The new epoch should begin about 1950, the experts said, and was likely to be defined by the radioactive elements dispersed across the planet by nuclear bomb tests... [as well as] plastic pollution, soot from power stations, concrete, and even the bones left by global proliferation of the domestic chicken."

7. Just as kyriarchy is composed of interconnecting triangles of hierarchical dominion, environmental apocalypse can be seen as a domino-like collapsing of interconnected systems.

8. As I proofread this chapter in March 2020, the world is presently experiencing a global pandemic of the novel coronavirus COVID-19. In Wisconsin where I live, gatherings of over 10 people are banned and people are being told to stay home and wash hands frequently. Businesses like bars and restaurants are closed except for takeout. Other businesses, such as hair and nail salons, are simply closed. Although grocery stores remain open, people are told to stand no closer than six feet.

9. Mary Shelley's *Frankenstein*, 1818, and Dickens's *Hard Times*, 1852, both critique industrialization and its accompanying pollution (see "Motherless Monsters").

10. Suvin, 1979, describes Wells as writing "ideological fables." While Wells is comfortable destroying a false bourgeois stronghold, he is still horrified by "the alien forces destroying it" (Suvin 217).

11. The "Doctrine of Discovery" historically describes a tradition of colonial behavior that goes back to Catholic Church Doctrine attributable to a pope in the 14th Century; however, it was not given legal support until later. In 1823, the United States Supreme Court under Chief Justice John Marshall explained that colonial powers had the right to lay claim to lands during the Age of Discovery. Under it, title to lands lay with the government whose subjects traveled to and occupied a territory whose inhabitants were not subjects of a European Christian monarch. The doctrine has been primarily used to support decisions invalidating or ignoring aboriginal rights to the land in favor of colonial or postcolonial governments.

12. For more on Le Guin's view of the dangers of petroleum production, see "Some Approaches to the Problem of the Shortage of Time," which metaphorically asserts that atmospheric carbon from petroleum production and use has caused a "tiny hole" in the universe where time is leaking away (248).

13. In the early 20th century neo-Malthusian feminists like Emma Goldman advocated conscious procreation to stop capitalism from exploiting female bodies to produce soldiers and cheap labor (D'Alisa, Demaria, and Kallis).

14. Depicted in *The Birthday of the World* and *Four Ways to Forgiveness*.

15. See Le Guin's "A Man of the People," 1995.

16. Le Guin's early Orsinian stories critique the European Enlightenment, depicting the end of feudalism. The dynamic disjunction that develops between totalitarianism and freedom is not fully understood by her protagonists. Written late in her career, novellas collected as "Five Ways to Forgiveness" (1995–1999) critique colonial hierarchies that are based on slavery. Her YA novel *Powers*, 2007, also critiques Enlightenment ideas about education and slavery.

17. Essentially, a "radiant sandcastle" is something that might look pretty but is insubstantial and can't last.

18. "Don" is a standard masculine American name, the diminutive of "Donald," which in Scotch-Gaelic means "world ruler"; it's identical in appearance to the Spanish knightly title *don*. Davidson implies a Judeo-Christian heritage, a son of King David.

19. Le Guin's classical university education had also taught her, through personal experience, that Reason cannot lead to a just and fair society as long as it is used as a rationalization for supporting the various hierarchies of power.

20. Fiorenza, 2001, writes, "There is no pure reason as instrument that can lead to a just society. In the beginning was not pure reason but power" (42).

21. Tethys, a visitor from earth, says, "My world, my Earth, is a ruin. A planet spoiled by the human species. We multiplied and gobbled and fought until there was nothing left, and then we died. We controlled neither appetite nor violence; we did not adapt…. We Terrans made a desert" (TD, 347–348).

22. In *The Water Will Come: Rising Seas, Sinking Cities, and the Remaking of the Civilized World*, 2017, researcher Jeff Goodell describes how Hurricane Sandy, 2012, nearly destroyed New York City. The surge on the east River had been nearly nine feet high (8). In September 2021, Hurricane Ida caused a storm surge in New York City that flooded basement

apartments. Thirteen people were trapped and died.

23. Recent climate research asserts that, due to the melting ice shelves near the poles, this description may be true by 2050. Bangladesh, which is only five meters above sea level and situated in a river delta, frequently floods during the monsoon season. During this time, children can't go to school. A photograph by Jashim Salam in the Summer 2020 issue of *World Wildlife* magazine shows a Bangladeshi child watching television while standing on an ornate carved wooden couch. The room is flooded by about a foot of water (Waite, 32).

24. For another take on a dystopian, near-future Pacific Northwest, see Nancy Kress's novella, "Semper Augustus" in the March/April 2020 issue of *Asimov's*.

25. Jameson calls Le Guin's simplification of the human material environment "world reduction." Essentially, Le Guin is advocating for a Taoist simplification or reduction of distractions so that there will be time and space to focus on the most important things.

26. In "World Reduction in Le Guin," Frederic Jameson describes Le Guin heroes as "quietistic" (275).

27. In her rendering of the *Tao*, Le Guin describes returning to the root as "wisdom" and being: "Without it, ruin, disorder" (Lao Tzu, 22).

28. Le Guin's vision of Kesh reflects the environmental movements of the late '60s and '70s, depicted in popular magazines such as *Mother Earth News*, with its green, countercultural, do-it-yourself ethic.

29. The name *Ooni* suggests the circle of life as well as a carrier bag and a womb.

30. Carlsson, 2008, describes cars that run on vegetable oil and smell like popcorn.

31. Originally, Okorafor created Ile-Ife from an old map in which it is shown as a once-great Yoruba city ("Organic," 281).

32. Although Le Guin tends to strip embellishment from her worlds, Okorafor seems to rejoice in them.

33. Here, Okorafor fantasizes events that occurred in Nigeria before the Biafran War erupted in full-scale genocide.

34. Okorafor writes that the plantation where Dikéogu was enslaved is located in the Sahara Desert:

"This would be impossible in our world, as cocoa plants need warm moist land. However, in *The Shadow Speaker*, the land has been changed. Such farms in the Sahara are now possible. So, though the location has changed, the suffering of the children remains the same as that of the real world" ["Organic," 280]. Ostensibly, the Great Change that is described in the beginning of the novel is slowly causing the continent to regain a healthier balance of wet and dry land.

35. Here the description of Chief Ette is similar to Baron Vladimir Harkonnen in Frank Herbert's *Dune*. The Baron is also an example of conspicuous consumption and is too fat to easily walk. In *Dune*, the entire House of Harkonnen is eventually exterminated, but in *The Shadow Speaker*, despite Ette's evil behavior, Ejii shows compassion for him.

36. In *Always Coming Home*, Le Guin has written that "People who make life into a war fight it first with people of the other sex" (433).

37. Based on a gated community, Queen Jaa's home village is protected by a cactus fence that has been bioengineered to retract spines when touched by someone who lives there.

38. "Ette" is a suffix meaning small. Although Ette is physically huge, he is small-minded. The name Ette also sounds like "et" a version of "eat."

39. "He was extremely fat. So fat that he apparently wasn't able to walk. He sat on a motorized purple throne with wheels. [...] Gold metal straps stretched from his ears over his portly cheeks to hold a large round disk of gold over his nose. It had tiny holes in it so he could breathe. His ample flesh was squeezed into a leather suit. Even his feet and hands were encased in leather. [...] Though the costume was obviously made to accommodate his fat, he looked like a sausage, and he was breathing heavily" (288).

40. Ejii attributes this to her teacher Mazi Godwin. Godwin's name is interesting since it is also Okorafor's father's first name. Also, teachers in Le Guin's *The Telling* are called *maz*.

41. The environmental effect of earth's constant warfare is called the Thanatocene. Wendell Berry has written:
"In a modern war, fought with modern

weapons and on the modern scale, neither side can limit to 'the enemy' the damage that it does. These wars damage the world. We know enough by now to know that you cannot damage a part of the world without damaging all of it. Modern war has not only made it impossible to kill 'combatants' without killing 'noncombatants,' it has made it impossible to damage your enemy without damaging yourself" [60].

42. More on the power of creation is explored in her short story, "The Girl with the Magic Hands."

43. Okorafor explores this further in the *Shuri* comics and in her *LaGuardia* graphic novel.

44. However, it is not clear whether that tragedy would be Greek or Shakespearean. Greek tragedy is, by definition, unavoidable. It is governed by fate and deistic interference. Oedipus could not have avoided his downfall. The gods had ordained it. Shakespeare, however, viewed tragedy as avoidable. It is not tragic to die at home in bed after a full life. It is, however, tragic to die, like Lear, outside in a rainstorm because one's own children were not taught to get along and share. Lear had choices all along but was too entitled to figure them out. It is worthwhile to note that Shakespeare wrote *King Lear* when London's Globe Theater was closed because of the plague. Both Le Guin and Okorafor envision a leveling that will eventually occur when ecological limits are not respected. Prettyman, 2014, calls this as "Heaven the Equalizer" (68).

45. Le Guin's ansible and FTL drive may also be considered time-honored magic.

46. The gross domestic product is the monetary value of all finished goods and services made within a specific period of time. It would be difficult to assign a monetary value on dwellings and computers that grow from bulbs and continue to evolve in complexity, particularly if they may have been initially acquired through barter.

47. *Zahrah the Windseeker* describes the Kirki Market as "always full of life" (19):

"Tomatoes, videophones, both hydrogen and flora-powered cars, netevisions, clothes, crude leather, digi-books, leaf-clipping and -mending beetles, paper books, all species of CPU seeds, from most expensive to the cheap" [19].

48. Degrowth proponents argue that today the GDP has become decoupled from human well-being. In the first half of the 20th century, increases in industrialization and technology did connect with improvement in the standard of living, but since the mid-70s, this is no longer true. Degrowth scholars and science fiction writers debate whether future advances in green technology will lead to a healthier environment for the majority because it might become so expensive that if would only be available to the most entitled. See, for example, the invisible shields that protect the rich from the poor in Kress's "Semper Augustus."

49. Le Guin's fiction demonstrates intrinsic flaws in both Marxism and Anarchism that require constant cultural reconsideration.

50. Oily Jada, the Ooni Palace, has developed sentience and supports Ejii's attempt to stop the war, an important interspecies connection that pushes readers toward rethinking the definition of humanity.

51. Okorafor also explores computers as cultural carrier bags in *The Book of Phoenix*, providing Phoenix a way to construct a historical context for understanding her dilemma.

52. When Zahrah changes direction to go to the gorilla village, the compass remarks, "You're moving off course, my dear." [...] "Why didn't you tell me immediately?" and [...] "You really had me worried there" (209).

53. Papa Legba is the Yoruba god of the crossroads. He is a messenger of the spirit world. (See "Exploring the Empire of Girls' Moral Development" and "Black to Okorafor.") Ejii's computer can be seen as a partly mystical connection to the ancestors as well as a useful tool.

54. Historically, astrolabes guided mariners through the placement of the stars. Binti's astrolabe guides her to the stars.

55. See also the depiction of the Wakanda space center and Shuri's high tech Black Panther costume in Okorafor's Shuri/Black Panther series.

56. Prettyman, 2014, asserts that digital

addictions can be seen as aspects of post-industrial capitalism that "unfit us for survival in the real world" (65).

57. Valorizing advanced technology is particularly true in her depiction of Black Panther's Wakanda in the *Shuri* comic book series.

58. Her mother-in-law, Mama Nyambe, calls Jaa "crazy," but obviously cares for her (*Shadow*, 256).

59. The scientist warrior concept is also explored in the Shuri comics.

60. Ecofeminism, sometimes called radical ecology, concerns the collapsing of dualisms and the re-imagining of nature and the human not as binary entities but as part of a continuous ecological system.

61. This concept is also explored in Le Guin's story, "Vaster than Empires and More Slow," 1971. Over 30 years later, British geophysicist James Lovelock writes in *The Revenge of Gaia*, 2007: "Unless we see the Earth as a planet that behaves as if it were alive, at least in the extent of regulating its climate and chemistry, we will lack the will to change our way of life and to understand that we have made it our greatest enemy" [21–22].

Chapter 8

1. This has caused considerable dismay in the old guard science fiction community. Lavender, 2020, relates that "a relatively small group of American-born white men loudly (and in some cases violently) proclaimed that artists of color were out to ruin the fun of popular culture for everyone with their insistence on exploring issues of diversity and social justice" (2).

2. In her Wahala Zone Blog, Okorafor explains that she learned about Joseph Campbell's hero journey from her instructor at Clarion, Steven J. Barnes (http://nnedi.blogspot.com/2009/04/my-report-on-octavia-butler-symposiummy.html).

3. Nisi Shawl says it a slightly different way: "Afrofuturism is a movement focused on African contributions to, perspectives on, and presence in the future" (Inda).

4. Nalo Hopkinson's fiction tends to interweave mythology and the supernatural, often in transgressive ways. For instance, in *Chaos*, Baba Yaga and her chicken-legged flying house appear in downtown Toronto.

5. Beginning with *Dawn*, 1987, Butler's Xenogenesis series describes the space faring Oankali, who travel the universe exchanging genetic information, thus changing every intelligent culture they meet.

6. Wilson, Nancy, et al. *"Sun Ra: 'Cosmic Swing'"* (radio). *NPR Jazz Profiles. National Public Radio*. Retrieved 2008-06-01.

7. Okorafor's *Binti* trilogy reflects Sun Ra in that Binti becomes an alien ambassador to the Meduse and later meets even stranger aliens while flying through Saturn's rings.

8. Throughout her work, Okorafor has explored the transformative nature of art. This is particularly true in her children's book *The Girl with the Magic Hands*, 2016.

9. These themes are explored in Okorafor's *The Book of Phoenix*.

10. Jennings, a professor of media and cultural studies at the University of California, Riverside, is presently the curator of MEGASCOPE, an imprint of Abrams ComicArts. MEGASCOPE is dedicated to showcasing speculative works by and about people of color.

11. "Why, there isn't even a girl worth getting up a respectable flirtation with," he growled. Just then his eye caught a tall, willowy figure hurrying toward him on the narrow path. He looked with interest at first, and then burst into a laugh as he said, "Well, I declare, if it isn't Jennie, the little brown kitchen-maid! Why, I never noticed before what a trim little body she is. Hello, Jennie! Why, you haven't kissed me since I came home," he said gaily. ("Of the Coming of John," 111).

12. *Voyage dans la Lune*, or *A Trip to the Moon* (France, 1902) was the cinema's *first* science fiction story, a 14-minute *tour de force* (nearly one reel in length (about 825 feet)) created by imaginative French director and master magician Georges Méliès (1861–1938) in his version of the Jules Verne story, "From the Earth to the Moon." The visually whimsical silent film satirizes the conservative scientific community of its time. H.G. Wells' *The War of the Worlds*, 1898, and *First Men on the Moon*, 1901, also preceded it.

13. A fantastic retelling of escape from slavery is depicted in Colson Whitehead's

novel *The Underground Railroad*, 2016, and an eponymous 2021 television series produced and directed by Barry Jenkins. An actual train runs underground across America although riding it is dangerous and the tracks and stations have been destroyed in some places. The story runs the gamut of atrocities against African Americans including sterilization. The message seems to assert that although freedom is never entirely possible, self-discovery can refigure a personal relationship with human bondage.

14. An interesting take on this can be read in Eleanor Arnason's fantastic story "Big Brown Mama and Brer Rabbit," 2013.

15. *Nyota* means "star" in Swahili.

16. In 2012, Jemison launched the 100 Year Starship project, a nonprofit whose goal is to achieve interstellar travel by 2112 (Womack, 99).

17. In her 2019 memoir, *Broken Places & Outer Spaces,* Okorafor describes living in America as the "Land of Milk and Honey." Initially her parents sought safety in America because of the Biafran Civil War. Beginning when Okorafor was about seven, the family made trips back to Nigeria to visit relatives. "Travel was still dangerous and car trips to the village required an escort of AK-47 armed guards" (*Broken*, 86).

18. Dewitt Douglas Kilgore explores this in his book *Astrofuturism: Science, Race, and Visions of Utopia in Space.* Philadelphia: University of Pennsylvania Press, 2003.

19. In a 2014 interview with *Mosaic,* Okorafor reports reading Butler's *Wild Seed* for the first time in 2000 when she was at a Clarion Writers' Workshop:

"I read the first page and my eyes nearly popped out. The main character had an Igbo name, and she was in Nigeria, and she could shape shift! I bought that book and read the hell out of it and my mind was blown. *Wild Seed* showed me that the publication of the type of stories I was writing was possible. It showed me that I wasn't alone and that what I was writing was ok. Octavia gave me strength" [np].

20. Okorafor begins her chronicle of these Windseekers before the turn of the 20th century. To have a future, the past must be clearly understood. Her windseeking characters follow a learning curve that parallels the history of the Women's Movement in the United States although *The Book of Phoenix* reflects a dystopian future where rights violations are once again common but now horrifyingly intertwined with scientific advances in genetics and technology.

21. The term Rosie the Riveter first appeared in 1942 in relationship to government posters of women factory workers.

22. Wonder Woman inspired a generation of little girls to lobby for commercially packaged red, white, and blue belts and armbands so they could spin around just like her.

23. In 1961, Stan Lee and Jack Kirby created super heroine Susan Lee, the Invisible Girl, as part of Marvel Comics' Fantastic Four. Times were changing but Lee and Kirby must have been wearing '50s-colored glasses, not seeing many ways for a girl to be heroic. Sue, ostensibly Lee's fictional daughter, was, in fact, initially expected to disappear when the Fantastic Four faced danger and often needed to be rescued because she had not yet grown into her own powers; it took until 1985 for her to become "The Invisible Woman" (Durowski, 202, Edmunds, 212).

24. In "The Mother of All Superheroes: Idealizations of Femininity in *Wonder Woman,*" Zechowski and Neuman explain that "central" to Wonder Woman's power "is the idea that any woman (or girl) could be a Wonder Woman" (124)

25. In December 2020, *Wonder Woman 1984* was released to streaming because of the pandemic. Although also directed by Patty Jenkins, most critics see it as less effective than the earlier movie, which focuses on an alternative universe WWII. Its unrealized potential for responding to Orwell's *1984* was disappointing.

26. In a June 16 review in the *Learned Fan Girl,* author Inda explains, "The entire No-Man's Land sequence is a defiant refutation of the idea that a thing can't be done just because men tell you it's not possible. Not only can women tread (and stomp, and smash) where men say they cannot, they can inspire others to follow and fight for themselves."

27. Super Girl appeared in her own comics beginning in the '70s.

28. The present *Supergirl* TV show

(2015–2017) starring Melissa Benoist reflects 21st-century values, allowing Supergirl, Kara Danvers, to have a career in publishing as well as having adult relationships.

29. Storm has appeared in five installments of the live-action *X-Men* film series, where she is portrayed by actress Halle Berry and also by Alexandra Shipp in *X-Men: Apocalypse*.

30. Here again, Okorafor reflects on her own experience learning to use a wheelchair after her paralysis.

31. Originally created by writer Reginald Hudlin and artist John Romita Jr. and first appearing in *Black Panther* Vol. 4 #2, May 2005.

32. The film grossed over $1.3 billion worldwide, breaking numerous box office records, including the highest-grossing film by a Black director. It became the ninth highest-grossing film of all time and the third highest-grossing film in the U.S. and Canada.

33. For more on Black Panther's conflicting responsibilities as king and superhero, see Canavan 2020.

34. As early as 1964, Africans have been interested in becoming part of the space race. Their first satellite was launched in 1973 and as of 2017, it had launched five satellites (Barr, 205). Presently, Nigeria is planning to be the first African country to send an astronaut into space (Giles, np).

35. Le Guin does the same thing in her *Earthsea* Series when she reveals that in the early records of Earthsea there were wizards who were women.

36. *Wahala* means trouble or chaos.

37. Her name also reflects how the ancestors address Shuri as "Ancient Future."

38. The name choice is interesting. In Igbo, Chukwuebuka means "God is mighty."

39. *A luta continua* is a Portuguese phrase used in Mozambique during their struggle for independence.

40. See "Watching Windseekers" for more discussion of Okorafor's inspiration and use of long blue dresses.

41. As the great-grandchild of immigrants from Germany and Norway and the 11th generation granddaughter of Elder Brewster who came from England to America on the Mayflower, I favor immigration; however, I am acutely aware that the land my ancestors worked so hard to settle was stolen from Native Americans. The earth we inhabit cannot be claimed as ours alone and must be shared with others via negotiation. We also have a responsibility to protect the land itself from overuse and overpopulation. To believe otherwise is to accept the kyriarchal mind management that has been in effect since the beginning of history.

42. The infant's name, Future Citizen, reflects an optimistic posthumanism.

43. In a 2019 interview with *Publishers Weekly*, Okorafor explains, "The Nigerian Civil War was terrible, it was genocide, and it haunts every single Nigerian—everyone has a story" (np).

44. It is worthwhile to note that use of mathematical equations occurs in Okorafor's fiction beginning with the *Binti* series. Einstein's groundbreaking relativity equation $e=mc^2$ shows the relationship between energy, mass and the speed of light; it is particularly important in relation to space travel. Faster-than-light speed travel (FTL) would be necessary for aliens to come to our solar system, an accepted fantastic element allowed in so-called hard (science-based) science fiction.

45. Carl Brandon's origin is fictional. SF writers Terry Carr and Pete Graham fabricated Brandon as an African American reader and amateur SF writer who participated in fan culture during the mid–1950s, writing witty, incisive satires of works like Anderson's *Brain Wave* that helped to challenge underlying assumptions about race that tended to go unnoticed in the genre (Shepherd, 116).

46. The first interracial kiss on American network television occurred off screen in a *Star Trek* episode, "Plato's Stepchildren," which aired on November 22, 1968, when Captain Kirk (William Shatner) kisses Lieutenant Uhura (Nichelle Nichols).

47. McIntosh concludes: "Thinking through unacknowledged male privilege as a phenomenon with a life of its own, I realized that since hierarchies in our society are interlocking, there was most likely a phenomenon of white privilege that was similarly denied and protected, but alive and real in its effects. As a white person, I realized I had been taught about racism as something that puts

others at a disadvantage but had been taught not to see one of its corollary aspects, white privilege, which puts me at an advantage" [2].

48. Russ published *Kittatinny*, her own *Bildungsroman* tale for girls, in 1978.

49. Brown bases her conceptualization of "the speed of trust" on works by Mervyn Marcano and Stephen Covey.

Chapter 9

1. Alaya Dawn Johnson's *Love Is the Drug*, 2014, is a startlingly prescient novel about global pandemic and bioterrorism.

2. Prehistoric physical violence against females has been seen by scientists studying homo erectus bones. In *The Search for Eve*, Michael Harold Brown quotes Milford Wolpoff: "The high level of healed cranial injuries" probably [...] result from "elevated magnitudes of interpersonal violence especially given the predominance of injuries on female crania" (182–183).

3. Le Guin also explores the connection between prejudice and totalitarianism in her *Orsinian Series*, as does N.K. Jemisin in her *Broken Earth Trilogy*.

4. On May 16, 2020, during a special program entitled "Graduate Together: America Honors the High School Class of 2020," past president Barack Obama addressed young Americans telling them, "If the world is going to get better, it is going to be up to you," citing the lack of moral development in present-day politics and acknowledging the problems of self-serving leadership. "Doing what feels good, what's convenient, what's easy, that's how little kids think," Obama said. "Unfortunately, a lot of so-called grown-ups, including some with fancy titles, important jobs, still think that way, which is why things are so screwed up."

5. In August of 2014, an audit by the United States Department of Justice discovered and impounded $267,000,000 from one of Abacha's secret accounts and returned it to the Nigerian government.

6. Shakespeare's *The Tempest*, Act II, Scene 1.

7. Biko, a writer and philosopher, was the leader of the Black Consciousness Movement in South Africa and was murdered by police on September 12, 1977. *Cry Freedom*, a 1987 movie starring Denzel Washington and Kevin Kline, depicts his murder. A song by singer Peter Gabriel memorializes him.

8. This is also true in Le Guin's *Earthsea* series.

9. For another take on the dangers of mixing voodoo (juju) with nanotechnology, see Nalo Hopkinson's short story, "Clap Back," 2021.

10. Okorafor's initial depiction of the robot is sympathetic. Before her back surgery she saw herself as "a rusted robot in need of a hard reset" (*Broken*, 23). However, the 21st century has brought increasing popular awareness of the possible dangers of artificial intelligence. A recent example is Naomi Kritzer's YA *Chaos on Catnet*, 2021, in which a devious AI starts encouraging the End Times via a Doomsday cult, computer chatrooms, and live-action, role-playing (LARP) gaming.

11. Early educational research on children's computer use indicated that girls tended to have a more personal relationship with their computers than boys. They interacted with their computers as if they were interacting with a friend rather than simply using a tool.

12. Asimov's three laws of robotics are as follows:

1. A robot may not injure a human being or, through inaction, allow a human being to come to harm.
2. A robot must obey the orders given it by human beings except where such orders would conflict with the First Law.
3. A robot must protect its own existence as long as such protection does not conflict with the First and Second Laws.

13. There have been riots, burning and looting all over the United States and the world, protesting the horrific death of George Floyd in Minneapolis. Floyd was a Black man who was suffocated in police custody for possibly circulating a fake twenty-dollar bill. A police officer held his knee on Floyd's neck for nearly nine minutes until he died.

14. Ursula K. Le Guin describes characterization as "embodiments of my experience and imagination, engaged in an imagined life that is not my life, though it may serve to illuminate it" (*Wave*, 236).

15. In a July 2020 interview with Jonathan Watts of *The Guardian*, James Lovelock, known as the father of the Gaia Theory, asserted that "this is all part of evolution as Darwin saw it. You are not going to get a new species flourishing unless it has a food supply. In a sense that is what we are becoming. We are the food" (np).

16. Cytokines are messenger protein molecules used in communicating the need for a body to fight an infection or cancer; however, sometimes they can turn against the organs they are supposed to protect. As of May 2020, more than 150 papers have been published that explore the connection between the vagus nerve and the coronavirus cytokine storm, most of them showing clear indication that overstimulation of the vagus nerve is central to the disease progress (Chopra). For more on the vagus nerve, see the Appendix.

17. An article in the *Journal of Economic Behavior* explains:

"Once infected, richer individuals have more resources to self-isolate and therefore prevent the spread within their social networks, while poorer individuals, once infected, may not be able to efficiently self-isolate due to resource constraints. Additionally, relatively poor individuals tend to be more involved in 'frontline' essential work which may prevent them from self-isolating, even if non-pharmaceutical interventions (NPIs) such as stay-at-home mandates are in place" (Jung).

18. The SF thriller *Contagion*, 2011, describes a similar global pandemic. It was directed by Steven Soderbergh and its ensemble cast includes Marion Cotillard, Matt Damon, Laurence Fishburne, Jude Law, Gwyneth Paltrow, Kate Winslet, Bryan Cranston, Jennifer Ehle, and Sanaa Lathan.

19. When the Milwaukee Bucks won the championship on August 5, 2021, an event outside the stadium was attended by over 100,000 individuals, most of whom were unmasked. Five hundred cases of COVID were reported after the event.

20. Class warfare left Greece divided such that Philip of Macedon was able to seize control in 338 B.C.E. because rich Greeks found dictatorship preferable to revolution.

21. Two women, Emmanuelle Charpentier and Jennifer Douda, won the 2020 Nobel Prize in Chemistry for their CRISPR-Cas9 gene-editing technique.

22. A peer-reviewed article published in *Fertility and Sterillity,* concludes:

"Aggregating the myriad allegations of infertility associated with the COVID-19 pandemic, the best current evidence suggests that men should receive the COVID-19 vaccine to prevent the potential risks to male reproductive health and male fertility with actual COVID-19 disease; further, there is no evidence and no credible theoretical underpinnings to link the COVID-19 vaccine with female infertility" [np].

Works Cited

Primary Works by Okorafor

Akata Warrior. Penguin/Random House, 2017.
Akata Witch. Viking/Penguin, 2011.
Akata Woman. Viking, 2022.
Binti. New York: Tor, 2015.
Binti: Home. Tor, 2017.
Binti: The Night Masquerade. Tor, 2017.
The Book of Phoenix. Daw, 2015.
Broken Places, Outer Spaces: Finding Creativity in the Unexpected. New York: Simon & Schuster, 2019.
Chicken in the Kitchen. Illustrated by Mehrdokt Amini. Lantana, 2015.
The Girl with the Magic Hands. Worldreader, 22 Dec. 2013.
Ikenga. Penguin Random House, 2020.
Kabu-Kabu Stories. Prime Books, 2013.
Long Juju Man. Macmillan, 2009.
Noor. Daw, 2021.
Remote Control. Tor, 2021.
The Shadow Speaker. New York: Hyperion, 2007.
Who Fears Death. New York: Daw, 2010.

Comics and Graphic Novel

"Blessing in Disguise," *Edge of Venomverse* 21 Nov. 2017.
Lagoon. Hodder & Stoughton, 2014.
LaGuardia. Illus. Tana Ford & James Devlin. Milwaukee, OR: Dark Horse Books, 2019.
Shuri: The Search for Black Panther 1–5. Illus. Leonardo Romero and Jordie Bellaire. Marvel Comics, February, 2019.
Shuri: 24/7 Vibranium. Illus. Rachel Stott and Paul Davidson. Marvel Comics, Issues 8–10, September 2019.
Wakanda Forever. Illus. Alberto Albuquerque. Marvel Entertainment, 2018.
Okorafor-Mbachu, Nnedi. *Zahrah the Windseeker*. New York: Houghton-Mifflin, 2005.

Uncollected Short Stories

"Amphibious Green."*AfricanWriter*. https://www.africanwriter.com/amphibious-green-a-shortstory-by-by-nnedi-okorafor/.
"From the Lost Diary of TreeFrog7." *Clarkesworld* 32. May 2009. http://clarkesworldmagazine.com/okorafor_05_09/.
"The Go-Slow." *Tor.Com*. 2/10/2011. https://www.tor.com/ 2011/02/10/the-go-slow/.
"Hello Moto." *Tor.Com*, 2010. https://www.tor.com/2011/11/02/hello-moto/.
Okorafor, Nnedi and Wanuri Kahiu."Rusties." *Clarkesworld* 121, Oct. 2016 https://clarkesworldmagazine.com/okorafor-kahi_10_16.
"When Scarabs Multiply," *So Long Been Dreaming: Postcolonial Science Fiction and Fantasy*. Eds. Nalo Hopkinson and Uppinder Mehan. Arsenal Pulp Press, 2004, pp. 70–78.

Essays

"Her Pen Could Fly." *Dark Matter: Reading the Bones*. Ed. Sheree R. Thomas. New York: Time-Warner, 2004, pp. 369–374.
"Nnedi Okorafor: Magical Futurism." *Locus*, 17 May 2015. https://locusag.com/2015/05/nnedi-okorafor-magical-futurim.

"Organic Fantasy." *African Identities* 7.2: *The Black Imagination and Science Fiction*, May 2009, pp. 275–286.

"Writing Rage, Truth and Consequence." *The Journal of Fantastic in the Arts*. 26.1 (Winter 2015).

Blog and Correspondence

"Never Unmask a Masquerade," *Wahala Zone Blog*, 17 July 2010.

Personal e-mail correspondence dated January 19, 2015.

Personal e-mail correspondence dated January 20, 2015.

Secondary Sources

Abusharaf, Rogaia Mustafa. "Introduction: The Custom in Question." *Female Circumcision: Multicultural Perspectives*. Edited by Rogaia Mustafa Abusharaf. University of Pennsylvania Press, 2007.

Acheson, Cat. "Navigating New Wilds: Radical Ecology, Gender and Climate Action in Science Fiction." Dissertation 8/12/16. https://www.academia.edu/35091832/Navigating_New_Wilds_Radical_Ecology_Gender_and_Climate_Action_in_Science_Fiction.

Aderibigbe, Titilayo and Olaide Gbadamosi. "The Stolen Chibok Girls of Nigeria: Victims of Politics and Ideology and Failure of Law," *Law & Society Conference*, Seattle USA, 2015. www.academia.edu/37021401/THE_STOLEN_CHIBOK_GIRLS_OF_NIGERIA_VICTIMS_OF_POLITICS.

Aiyetoro, Mary Bosede and Elizabeth Olubukola Olaoye. "Afro-Science Fiction: A Study of Nnedi Okorafor's *What Sunny Saw in the Flames* and *Lagoon*," *Pivot: A Journal of Interdisciplinary Studies and Thought*. Vol 5, No 1 (2016), pp. 226–248. https://english.gradstudies.yorku.ca/accomplishments/publications/.

Alter, Alexandra. "Nnedi Okorafor and the Fantasy Genre She Is Helping Redefine," *New York Times*. 6 Oct. 2017. https://www.nytimes.com/2017/10/06/books/ya-fantasy-diverse-akata-warrior.html.

Ambrose, Liz Fellshot. "Nnedi Okorafor Interview." *Fantasy Faction*, Dec. 2, 2013. http://fantasy-faction.com/2013/nnedi-okorafor-interview.

American Psychiatric Association. "Gender Dysphoria." DSM-5. 2013. APA_DSM-5-Gender-Dysphoria.pdf.

Angelou, Maya. "Still I Rise." *Poetry Foundation*. https://www.poetryfoundation.org/poems/46446/still-i-rise.

Arnason, Eleanor. "Big Brown Mama and Brer Rabbit," *Big Mama Stories*. Aqueduct Press, 2013.

_____. "Unfolding." *Locus*, 668: 77.3 (Sept. 2016). 22–24. https://locusmag.com/2016/09/table-of-contents-september-2016/.

"Art African Tribal—Mask Zoomorphic Helm: Leopard Igbo Ibo Nigeria—34 CMS." https://www.ebay.com/itm/Art-African-Tribal-Mask-Zoomorphic-Helm-Leopard-Igbo-Ibo-Nigeria-34-Cm-/332915432386.

Ashcroft, Bill, Gareth Griffiths and Helen Tiffin. *Post-Colonial Studies: The Key Concepts*. Routledge, 2000.

Attebery, Brian. *Stories About Stories: Fantasy and the Remaking of Myth*. Oxford University Press, 2014.

Barber, Jeffery. "Imagining Sustainable Futures in Popular Culture: Moving Beyond Dystopia and Techno-fantasy Narratives." Paper presented at the IAMCR 2018 conference in Eugene, Oregon, USA, June 20–24, 2018, OCS Submission #18896.

Barlow, Jameta Nicole. "Black Women, the Forgotten Survivors of Sexual Assault." *American Psychological Association*. February 2020. https://www.apa.org/pi/about/newsletter/2020/02/black-women-sexual-assault.

Barr, Marlene. "You Can't Go Home Again." Deji Bryce Olukotun's *Nigerians in Space*, Science Fiction and Global Interdependence." *Literary Afrofuturism in the Twenty-First Century*. Ed. Isiah Lavender III and Lisa Yaszek. Ohio State University Press, 2020, pp. 203–215.

Batha, Emma. "FACTBOX: Stoning—where does it happen?" Thomson Reuters Foundation, September 29, 2013. Archived from the original on 2015-11-17. http://news.trust.org/item/20130927165059-w9g0i/, Retrieved January 5, 2020.

Battle, Michael. *Practicing Reconciliation in a Violent World*. Morehouse Publishing.

BBC News, "Boko Haram 'to sell' Nigeria girls abducted from Chibok." May 5, 2014. https://www.bbc.com/news/world-africa-27283383.

Bear, Greg. *Blood Music*. Arbor House, 1985.

Beckwith, Carol, and Angela Fisher. "Zanbeto Masks Dance." https://www.pinterest.com/pin/508203139185891285/.

Belenky, Mary Field, Blythe McVicker Clinchy, Nancy Rule Goldberger, and Jill Marrick Tarule. *Women's Ways of Knowing: The Development of Self, Voice, and Mind*. Basic Books, 1986.

Berry, Wendell. "The Failure of War," *Making Peace: Healing a Violent World*, edited by Carolyn McConnell and Sarah Ruth van Gelder. Positive Futures Network, 2003.

Bettelheim, Bruno. "The Importance of Play." *The Atlantic*, March 1987. www.theatlantic.com/magazine/archive/1987/03/the-importance-of-play/305129/.

Beukes, Lauren. "*Moxyland*'s Stem Cells." *Moxyland*. Mulholland Books, 2016, pp. 311–314.

———. *Slipping: Stories, Essays and Other Writing*. Tachyon, 2016.

———. *Zoo City*. Angry Robot, 2010.

Blier, Suzanne Preston. "Art and Secret Agency: Concealment and Revelation in Artistic Expression." *In Secrecy: African Art That Conceals and Reveals*. Ed. Mary H. Nooter. New York: Museum for African Art, 1993.

Bradshaw, John. *Healing the Shame that Binds You*. Deerfield Beach, FL: Health Communications, 1988.

Brown, Adrienne Maree. *Emergent Strategy: Shaping Change, Changing Worlds*. AK Press, 2017.

———. "Outro." *Octavia's Brood: Science Fiction Stories from Social Justice Movements*. Ed. Adrienne Maree Brown and Walidah Imarisha. AK Press, 2015, pp. 279–281.

———. "Transformative Justice in Wakanda." Blog, March 3, 2018. http://adriennemareebrown.net/2018/03/03/transformative-justice-in-wakanda/.

Burgmann, J. R. "Rising Continents: An Ecocritical Reading of Ursula K. Le Guin's 'The New Atlantis'". *Colloquy* 31. (Sept. 2016). 40–55. https://www.monash.edu/__data/assets/pdf_file/0010/1772353/burgmann-31.pdf.

Burnett, Joshua Yu. "The Great Change and the Great Book: Nnedi Okorafor's Post-colonial, Post-Apocalyptic Africa and the Promise of Black Speculative Fiction." *Research in African Literatures* 46.4, Winter 2015, pp. 133–150.

Butler, Octavia. E. *Dawn*. Warner, 1987.

———. *Kindred*. Beacon Press, 1979.

———. *Parable of the Sower*. Four Walls Eight Windows, 1993.

———. *Seed to Harvest*. Warner, 2007.

———. *Wild Seed*. Doubleday, 1980.

Canavan, Gerry. "We Are Terror Itself: Wakanda as Nation." *Literary Afrofuturism in the Twenty-First Century*. Ed. Isiah Lavender II and Lisa Yaszek. Ohio State University Press, 2020, pp. 177–188.

Carlsson, Chris. *Nowtopia: Pirate Programmers, Outlaw Bicyclists, and Vacant-Lot Gardeners Are Inventing the Future Today!* AK Press, May 1, 2008.

Carlyle, Thomas. *On Heroes, Hero-worship, and the Heroic in History*. D. Appleton & Co., 1841, p. 34.

———. "COVID Data Tracker." https://covid.cdc.gov/covid-data-tracker/#-datatracker-home.

———. "Disparities in Deaths from COVID-19." https://www.cdc.gov/coronavirus/2019-ncov/community/health-equity/racial-ethnic-disparities/disparities-deaths.html.

Centorcelli, Kristin. "A Chat with Nnedi Okorafor, author of *The Book of Phoenix*." *My Bookish Ways*, 28 May 2015, www.mybookishways.com/2015/05/a-chat-with-nnedi-okorafor-author-of-the-book-of-phoenix.

Chandrasekera, Vajra. "*Binti* by Nnedi Okorafor." *Strange Horizons*, 2 Mar. 2016. http://strangehorizons.com/non-fiction/reviews/binti-by-nnedi-okorafor/.

Chen, Jinghong, and Jerome McDonnell, "Meet Ngozi: Marvel's New Nigerian Superheroine." *WBEZ Chicago*, 6 Oct. 2017. https://www.wbez.org/shows/worldview/meet-ngozi-marvels-new-nigerian-superheroine/af3f8c53-84a9-4a28-a84e-68b53c93c6be.

Chopra, Deepak. "The Connection Between the Vagus Nerve and COVID-19." https://medium.com/@Deepak

Chopra/the-connection-between-the-vagus-nerve-and-covid-19-df22988f68e3.

Clarke, Arthur C. "Hazards of Prophecy: The Failure of Imagination." *Profiles of the Future: An Enquiry into the Limits of the Possible* (1962, rev. 1973). Orion, 2000, pp. 14, 21, 36.

Clute, John. "Nnedi Okorafor." *The Encyclopedia of Science Fiction*, Oct. 15, 2019. http://sf-encyclopedia.com/entry/okorafor_nnedi.

The Combahee River Collective. "A Black Feminist Statement." *How We Get Free: Black Feminism and the Combahee River Collective*. Ed. Keeanga-Yamahtta Taylor. Haymarket Books, 2017, pp. 15–27.

Csicsery-Ronay, Jr., Istvan. *The Seven Beauties of Science Fiction*. Wesleyan University Press, 2008.

"Dada or Dreds." *The Rice University Neologisms Database*. Retrieved 4/9/2016.

D'Alisa, Giacomo, Federico Demaria, and Giorgos Kallis. *Degrowth: A Vocabulary for a New Era*. Routledge, 2014.

Daniel, Robert L. *American Women in the 20th Century: The Festival of Life*. Harcourt Brace Jovanovich, 1987.

Darowski, Joseph. "Invisible, Tiny, and Distant: The Powers and Roles of Marvel's Early Female Superheroes." *Heroines of Comic Books and Literature: Portrayal in Popular Culture*. Ed. Maja Bajac-Carter, Norma. Jones, and Bob Batchelor. Lanham, MA: Rowman & Littlefield, 2014, pp. 199–210.

Delany, Samuel. R. "Racism and Science Fiction." *New York Review of Science Fiction*, 120. August 1998. http://www.nyrsf.com/racism-and-science-fiction-.html.

Dery, Mark. "Black to the Future: Interviews with Samuel R. Delany, Greg Tate, and Tricia Rose." *South Atlantic Quarterly* 92:4, Fall 1993, pp. 735–78.

Dery, Mark. *Flame Wars: The Discourse of Cyberculture*. Ed. M. Dery, Durham, NC: Duke University Press, 1994.

Dickens, Charles. *Hard Times*. New York: Signet, 1961.

"Donald Trump," *CBS News*. Jan. 23, 2016. https://www.cbsnews.com/news/donald-trump-i-could-shoot-somebody-and-i-wouldnt-lose-any-voters/.

Dowdall, Lisa. "Black Futures Matter: Afrofuturism and Gerontology in N.K. Jemisin's Broken Earth Trilogy." *Literary Afrofuturism in the Twenty-First Century*. Ed. Isiah Lavender III and Lisa Yaszek. Ohio State University Press, 2020, pp. 129–149.

Dowdall, Lisa. "The Utopian Fantastic in Nnedi Okorafor's *Who Fears Death*." *Paradoxa* 25, 2013. https://www.academia.edu/12076166/The_Utopian_Fantastic_in_Nnedi_Okorafors_Who_Fears_Death.

Du Bois, W.E.B. "The Comet." *Dark Matter: A Century of Speculative Fiction from the African Diaspora*. Ed. Sheree Renee Thomas. New York: Warner, 2000, pp. 5–18.

Du Bois, W.E.B. *The Souls of Black Folk*. Ed. B.E. Hayes. Oxford University Press, 2008. http://www.wwnorton.com/college/history/give-me-liberty4/docs/WEBDuBois-Souls_of_Black_Folk-1903.pdf.

Due, Tananarive. "The Only Lasting Truth." *Octavia's Brood: Science Fiction Stories from Social Justice Movements*. Ed. Adrienne Maree Brown and Walidah Imarisha. AK Press, 2015, pp. 259–278.

Durant, Will and Ariel. *The Lessons of History*. Simon & Schuster, 1968, trade paperback, 2010.

Edmunds, T.K. (2014). "Heroines Aplenty, but None My Mother Would Know: Marvel's Lack of an Iconic Superheroine." *Heroines of Comic Books and Literature: Portrayal in Popular Culture/* Ed. Maja Bajac-Carter, Norma Jones, and Bob Batchelor. Rowman & Littlefield, 2014.

Erikson, Erik. *Childhood and Society*. W.W. Norton, 1950.

———. *Identity and the Life Cycle*. Norton, 1980 (originally IUP, 1959).

Estes, Clarissa Pinkola. *Women Who Run with the Wolves: Myths and Stories of the Wild Woman Archetype*. Ballantine, 1992.

False, Vivian. "Igbo Masquerade Festivals: A Stunning Cultural Tradition of the Tribe." *Legit*. https://www.legit.ng/1112437-igbo-masquerade-festivals-a-stunning-cultural-tradition-tribe.html.

"Female Genital Mutilation." World Health Organization. 31 Jan. 2018. www.who.int/news-room/fact-sheets/detail/female-genital-mutilation.

"Female Genital Mutilation/Cutting: A

Global Concern," New York: United Nations Children's Fund, February 2016. www.unicef.org/media/files/FGMC_2016_brochure_final_UNICEF_SPREAD.pdf.

Ferreira, Rachel Haywood. "Ciencia Ficción / Ficção Cientifica from Latin America." *The Cambridge History of Science Fiction*. Ed. Gerry Canavan and Eric Carl Link. Cambridge University Press, 2019, pp. 664–679.

Fiorenza, Elisabeth Schlüsser. *Wisdom Ways: Introducing Feminist Biblical Interpretation*. Orbis Books, 2001.

Frazer, James G. *The Golden Bough*. Macmillan, 1922.

Freyd, Jennifer J. *Betrayal Trauma*. Harvard University Press, 1996.

Friedan, Betty. *The Feminine Mystique*. Dell, 1970.

Galvan, Adriana. *The Neuroscience of Adolescence*. Cambridge University Press, 2017.

Gbowee, Lehmah. *Mighty Be Our Powers: How Sisterhood, Prayer, and Sex Changed a Nation at War*. Beast Books, 2011.

Giles, Chris. "Africa Leaps Forward into Space Technology." *CNN: Africa Tech Rising*, May 16, 2018, https://www.cnn.com/2017/08/10/africa/africa-space-race/index.html.

Gilligan, Carol. "Exit Voice Dilemmas in Adolescent Development." *Mapping the Moral Domain*. Harvard University Press, 1989.

_____. *In a Different Voice: Psychological Theory and Women's Development*. Harvard University Press, 1982.

Gilligan, Carol, and Grant Wiggins. "The Origins of Morality in Early Childhood Relationships," *Mapping the Moral Domain*. Harvard University Press, 1988, pp. 111–138.

Gilligan, Carol Janie, Victoria Ward, Jill McLean Taylor, and Betty Bardige, eds. Harvard University Press, 1988, pp. 141–158.

_____. "New Perspectives on Female Adolescent Development," unpublished manuscript, Harvard University.

_____. "Reframing Resistance: Women's Psychological Development: Implications for Psychotherapy." *Women, Girls and Psychotherapy: Reframing Resistance*. Ed. Carol Gilligan, Annie G. Rogers, and Deborah L. Tolman. Harrington Park Press, 1991, pp. 5–32.

Goldberger, Nancy Rule. "Cultural Imperatives and Diversity in Ways of Knowing." *Knowledge, Difference, and Power*, Ed. Nancy Rule Goldberger, Jill Tarule, Blythe Clinchy and Mary Belenky. Basic Books, 1996, pp. 335–371.

Goldstein, Lisa. *A Mask for the General*. Bantam, 1987.

Gomez, Jewelle. *The Gilda Stories*. 1991. City Light Books, 2016.

Goodell, Jeff. *The Water Will Come: Rising Seas, Sinking Cities, and the Remaking of the Civilized World*, Back Bay Books. 2017.

Gore, Charles. "Burn the Mmonwu: Contradictions and Contestations in Masquerade Performance in Uga, Anambra State in Southeastern Nigeria." *African Arts* 41.4 (2008), pp. 60–73.

Gorman, Amanda. *The Hill We Climb: An Inaugural Poem for the Country*. Viking, 2021.

Granger, Mary. *Drums and Shadows*. Georgia Writers' Project, 1940. Forgotten Books, 2007.

Gray, Leslie. "Shamanic Counseling and Ecopsychology." *Ecopsychology: Restoring the Earth, Healing the Mind*. Ed. Theodore Roszak, Mary E. Gomez and Allen D. Kanner. Sierra Club Books, 2007, pp. 172–182.

Griggs, Sutton E. *Imperium in Imperio: A Study of the Negro Race Problem*. 1899. New York: Arno, 1969.

Guilbert, Kieran. "Watch out Wonder Woman: Nigeria's Chibok girls inspire Marvel's new superhero," Thomson Reuters Foundation, September 6, 2017.

Hack, David. "Viet Nam War Facts, Stats, and Myths," *US Wings*, https://www.uswings.com/about-us-wings/vietnam-war-facts/.

Hairston, Andrea. "Dismantling the Echo Chamber: On Africa SF." Los Angeles Review of Books, 16 Jan. 2014, https://lareviewofbooks.org/article/dismantling-echo-chamber-africa-sf/.

_____. "Dumb House." *New Suns: Original Speculative Fiction by People of Color*. Ed. Nisi Shawl. Solaris, 2019, pp. 201–224.

_____. *Will Do Magic for Small Change*. Aqueduct, 2016.

Hale, Kevin. "The Moving Finger: A

Rhetorical, Grammatological and Afrinographic Exploration of Nsibidi in Nigeria and Cameroon." Ohio University: ProQuest Dissertations Publishing, 2015. 3731336.

Hamilton, Virginia. "The People Could Fly." *The People Could Fly: American Black Folktales*. Illus. Leo and Diane Dillon. New York: Alfred A. Knopf, 1985, pp. 166–174.

Hand, Elizabeth. "The Speculative Fiction of UB Faculty Member Nnedi Okorafor." *At Buffalo,* 29 Jan. 2016. https://www.buffalo.edu/ubnow/stories/2016/01/profile_okorafor.html.

Haraway, Donna. "Anthropocene, Capitalocene, Plantationocene, Chthulucene: Making Kin." *Environmental Humanities* 6 (2015). 159–165. www.environmentalhumanities.org.

———. "A Cyborg Manifesto: Science, Technology, and Socialist-Feminism in the Late Twentieth Century." *Simians, Cyborgs and Women: The Reinvention of Nature*. Routledge, 1991, pp. 149–181.

———. *Primate Visions: Gender, Race and Nature in the World of Modern Science*. Routledge, 1989.

Harper, Steven. "The Way of Wilderness." *Ecopsychology: Restoring the Earth, Healing the Mind*. Ed. Theodore Roszak, Mary E. Gomes, and Allen D. Kanner. Sierra Club Books, 1995, pp. 183–200.

Harpman, Geoffrey Galt. *On the Grotesque: Strategies of Contradiction in Art and Literature*. Princeton, 1982.

"Helmet Mask (Kponyungo)." Art Institute of Chicago. https://www.artic.edu/artworks/18759/helmet-mask-kponyungo.

Henderson, Artis. "Human Rights Abuses in Ghana Gold Mining." Associated Press, 1 Nov. 2010. Mines and Communities. Httto://www.minesandcommunities.org. Accessed March 10, 2017.

Henriques, Martha. "Why COVID is Different for Men and Women." *BBC.com*. 12 April, 2020. https://www.bbc.com/future/article/20200409-why-covid-19-is-different-for-men-and-women.

Herman, Judith Lewis. *Trauma and Recovery: The Aftermath of Violence from Domestic Abuse to Political Horror*. New York: Basic Books, 1992.

Hickok, Kimberly, "How Covid Antiviral Pills Work and What that Could Mean for the Pandemic." *NBC News,* November 12, 2021.

Hines, Alice. "Mentoring Adolescent Foster Youth: Promoting Resilience During Developmental Transitions." *Child and Family Social Work*, 11, 2006, pp. 242–253.

Holden, Rebecca. "Young Adult Afrofuturism." *Literary Afrofuturism in the Twenty-First Century*. Ed. Lavender Isiah III and Lisa Yaszek. Ohio State University Press, pp. 87–104.

Hoobler, Dorothy, and Thomas Hoobler. *The Monsters: Mary Shelley and the Curse of Frankenstein*. New York: Little, Brown & Co, 2006.

Hopkinson, Nalo. *Chaos*. Margaret K. McElderry Books, 2012.

———. "Clap Back." Black Stars #5. Amazon Original Stories (August 31, 2021).

———. *Falling in Love with Hominids*. Tachyon, 2015.

Horney, Karen, "The Flight from Womanhood," *International Journal of Psychoanalysis* 7, 1926, pp. 324–339.

"Ijele." *Ijele Art:e-Journal*. http://www.ijele.com/flyer.htm.

Imarisha, Walidah. "Introduction," *Octavia's Brood: Science Fiction Stories from Social Justice Movements*, Ed. Adrienne Maree Brown and Walidah Imarisha. AK Press, 2015, pp. 3–5.

Inda. "Underground, *Everfair,* and Afro-RetroFuturism." *The Learned Fan Girl: A Critical Look at Popculture and Technology*. 23 Feb. 2017. http://thelearnedfangirl.com/2017/02/underground-everfair-and-afroretrofuturism/.

James, Edward, and Farah Mendlesohn. *The Cambridge Companion of Science Fiction*. Cambridge University Press, 2003.

James, William. *The Varieties of Religious Experience* (1902). New York: Collier, 1961.

Jameson, Frederic. "World Reduction in Le Guin," *Archaeologies of the Future: The Desire Called Utopia and Other Science Fictions*. Verso, 2005, pp. 267–280.

Jansson, Tove. *Finn Family Moomintroll*. Avon, 1958.

Jemisin, N.K. "The Brides of Heaven." *How Long 'Til Black Future Month*. Orbit, 2018, pp. 183–196.

———. "Cloud Dragon Skies." *How Long 'Til Black Future Month*. Orbit, 2018, pp. 113–125.

———. "The Effluent Engine." *How Long*

'Til Black Future Month. Orbit, 2018, pp. 75–112.

———. "On the Banks of the River Lex." *How Long 'Til Black Future Month*. Orbit, 2018, pp. 280–295.

———. "Walking Awake." *How Long 'Til Black Future Month*. Orbit, 2018, pp. 214–233.

Jennings, John. *After the Rain*. Adapted from "On the Road." Illustrated by David Brame. Lettering by Damian Duffy. Abrams ComicArts, 2021.

Johnson, Alaya Dawn. "A Million Mirrors: WisCon 39 Guest of Honor Speech." *The WisCon Chronicles Vol. 10: Social Justice (Redux)*. Ed. Margaret McBride. Aqueduct Press, 2016, pp.8–15.

Jones, Jeremy L. C. "If It Scares You, Write It: A Conversation with Nnedi Okorafor." *Clarkesworld* 39. Dec. 2009.

Jong, Erica. *Fear of Flying*. Signet, 1974.

Jung, Carl G. *Man and His Symbols*. Dell, 1964.

Jung, Juergen, James Manley, and Vinish Shrestha. "Corona Virus Infections and Deaths by Poverty Status: The Effects of Social Distancing." *Journal of Economic Behavior and Organization*. Feb. 2021, 182, pp. 311–330.

Kallis, Giorgos and Hug March. "Imaginaries of Hope: The Utopianism of Degrowth," *Annals of the Association of American Geographers*, 105.2. Routledge, 2015, pp. 360–368. DOI: 10.1080/00045608.2014.973803.

Kendall, Mikki. "A Nigerian Sorceress Makes Her Way." *Publishers Weekly* (12 Apr. 2010) www.publishersweekly.com/pw/by-topic/authors/interviews/article/42774-a-nigerian-sorceress-makes-her-way.html.

Kilgore, Dewitt. "Beyond the History We Know: Nnedi Okorafor-Mbachu, Nisi Shawl, and Jarla Tangh Rethink Science Fiction Tradition." *Afro-Future Females*. Ed. Marleen S. Barr. Ohio State University Press, 2008.

Kim, Sohye, Peter Fonagy, Orsolya Koos, Kimberly Dorsett, and Lane Strathearn, "Maternal oxytocin response predicts mother-to-infant gaze" *Brain Research* 1580 (11 Sept. 2014), pp. 133–142.

Kohlberg, Lawrence. "Moral Stages and Moralization: The Cognitive-Development Approach." *Moral Development and Behavior: Theory, Research and Social Issues*. Ed. T. Lickona. Holt, Rinehart and Winston, 1976.

———. *The Philosophy of Moral Development: Moral Stages and the Idea of Justice*. Harper and Row, 1981.

"Kponyungo Masquerade Helmet Mask." Art Institute of Chicago. https://www.artic.edu/artworks/18759/helmet-mask-kponyungo.

Kritzer, Naomi. *Chaos on CatNet*. Tor, 2021.

Lacey, Lauren J. *The Past That Might Have Been, the Future That May Come: Women Writing Fantastic Fiction, 1960s to the Present*. McFarland, 2014.

Laible, Deborah J., and Ross A. Thompson. "Mother–Child Discourse, Attachment Security, Shared Positive Affect, and Early Conscience Development." *Child Development* 71.5 (September/October 2000), pp. 1424–1440.

Landry, Donna, and Gerald Maclean. *The Spivak Reader*. Routledge, 1996.

Lao Tzu, *Tau Te Ching: A Book of the Way and the Power of the Way*. A New English Version by Ursula K. Le Guin with J. P. Seaton. Boston: Shambhala, 1998.

Lavender, Isiah. "Contemporary Science Fiction and Afrofuturism," *The Cambridge History of Science Fiction*. Ed. Gerry Canavan and Eric Carl Link. Cambridge University Press, 2019, pp. 565–579.

Lavender, Isiah, III. "Critical Race Theory." *The Routledge Companion to Science Fiction*," Ed. Mark Bould, Andrew M. Butler, Adam Roberts, and Sherryl Vint. Routledge, 2009, pp. 186–193.

———. *Race in American Science Fiction*. Bloomington, IN: Indiana University Press, 2011.

Lavender, Isiah, III, and Lisa Yaszek. "Author Roundtable on Afrofuturism." *Literary Afrofuturism in the Twenty-First Century*. Ohio State University Press, 2020. pp. 23–55.

———. Introduction." *Literary Afrofuturism in the Twenty-First Century*. Ohio State University Press, 2020. pp. 1–22.

Le Guin, Ursula K. *Always Coming Home: Author's Expanded Edition*. Library of America, 2019.

———. "The Carrier Bag Theory of Fiction." *Le Guin: Always Coming Home: Authors Expanded Edition*. New York: Library of America, 2019, pp. 725–730.

_____. *Dancing at the Edge of the World*. Harper and Row, 1989.

_____. "The Dispossessed: an Ambiguous Utopia." *Le Guin: Hainish Novels and Stories, Volume One*. Library of America, 2017, pp. 613-922.

_____. "Earthsea Revisioned," *The Books of Earthsea: The Complete Illustrated Edition*. Illustrated by Charles Vess. Saga Press, 2018, pp. 981-992.

_____. "Indian Uncles." *Le Guin: Always Coming Home: Authors Expanded Edition*. Library of America, 2019, pp. 781-792.

_____. "Is Gender Necessary? Redux." *Dancing at the Edge of the World*. Harper & Row, 1989, pp. 7-16.

_____. *No Time to Spare*, Houghton Mifflin Harcourt, 2017.

_____. "A Non-Euclidean View of California," *Dancing at the Edge of the World*. Harper & Row, 1989, pp. 80-100.

_____. "Some Approaches to the Problem of a Shortage of Time," *The Compass Rose*. Bantom Books, 1982, pp. 248-252.

_____. "Woman/Wilderness," *Dancing at the Edge of the World*. Harper & Row, 1989, pp. 161-164.

_____. "The Word for World is Forest," *Le Guin: Hainish Novels and Stories, Volume Two*. Library of America, 2017, pp. 1-106.

Lefanu, Sarah. *In the Chinks of the World Machine: Feminism and Science Fiction*. The Women's Press, 1988.

"Leopard Mask," Nigeria/British Southern Nigeria/Kingdom of Benin. *Metropolitan Museum of Art*. www.metmuseum.org.

Leopold, Aldo. *A Sand County Almanac*. Oxford University Press, 1966.

Levy, Michael, and Farah Mendelsohn. *Children's Literature: An Introduction*. Cambridge University Press, 2016.

Lincoln, Bruce. *Emerging from the Chrysalis: Ritual of Women's Initiation*. Oxford University Press, 1991.

Lindow, Sandra J. "Rape, Powerlessness and Pleasure Denied." *Dancing the Tao: Le Guin and Moral Development*. Cambridge Scholars, 2012, pp. 144-146.

Lorde, Audre. "The Master's Tools Will Never Dismantle the Master's House." *This Bridge Called My Back: Writings by Radical Women of Color*. Ed. Cherrie Moraga and Gloria Anzaldúa. Suny Press, 2015, pp. 94-97.

Lovelock, J.E., and L. Margulis. "Atmospheric Homeostasis by and for the Biosphere: The Gaia Hypothesis." *Tellus*. Series A. Stockholm: International Meteorological Institute, 1974, 26.1-2, pp. 2-10.

Lovelock, James. *The Revenge of Gaia: Why the Earth Is Fighting Back—and How We Can Still Save Humanity*. Penguin, 2007.

Lyons, Gene. "Warren's Loss Not a Defeat for All Womankind." *Arkansas Times*, March 13, 2020.

Macharia, Keguro. "*Binti: Home* by Nnedi Okorafor." *Strange Horizons*. 29 May 2017. http://strangehorizons.com/nonfiction/binti-home-by-nnedi-okorafor/.

Mack, C.K., and D. Mack. *A Field Guide to Demons, Fairies, Fallen Angels, and Other Subversive Spirits*. Owl Books, 1999.

Madson, Diana. "The Vast Sahara Desert Is Getting Even Bigger," Yale Climate Connections, July 18, 2018. www.yaleclimateconnections.org/2018/07/the-sahara-desert-is-getting-bigger/.

Margulis, Lynn. *Symbiotic Planet: A New Look at Evolution*. Basic Book, 1999.

Mashigo, Mohale. "Afrofuturism is not for Africans living in Africa." *The Johannesburg Review of Books*. Oct. 1, 2018.

"Masquerade Element: Leopard Head (Omama)." Metropolitan Museum of Art. https://www.metmuseum.org/art/collection/search/316631.

"Masquerades in the Middle Benue." Fowler Museum, UCLA.

MassGeneral for Children. "Could Smoking and Vaping Make COVID-19 Infections Worse?" *MassGeneral Hospital for Children*. https://www.massgeneral.org/children/vaping/smoking-vaping-and-covid-19.

Mbah, Fidelis. "Nigeria's Chibok schoolgirls: Five years on, 112 still missing" *Aljazeera*, April 14, 2019. https://www.aljazeera.com/news/2019/04/nigeria-chibok-school-girls-years-112-missing-190413192517739.html.

McIntosh, Peggy. "White Privilege and Male Privilege: A Personal Account of Coming to See Correspondences Through Work in Women's Studies." *Working paper No. 189*. Wellesley, Massa- chusetts: Wellesley Center for Research on Women. https://www.nationalseedproject.org/images/documents/

White_Privilege_and_Male_Privilege_Personal_Account-Peggy_McIntosh.Pdf.

Meyer, C. R. "Unwitting consent: 'Acres of Skin: Human Experiments at Holmesburg Prison' tells the story of medical researchers who sacrificed the rights of their subjects for personal profit." *Minnesota Medicine*. 82 (7): 53–4, 1999. PMID 11645180.

Miller, Alice. *Breaking Down the Wall of Silence*. Meridian, 1993.

Miller, T. S. "*Lagoon* by Nnedi Okorafor." *Strange Horizons*, July 2, 2014. http://strangehorizons.com/non-fiction/reviews/lagoon-by-nnedi-okorafor/.

Millett, Kate. *Sexual Politics*. Avon, 1969.

Milner, Andrew, and J. R. Burgmann. "A Short Pre-History of Climate Fiction." *Extrapolation*, 59.1, pp. 1–23.

"Mmanwu Masquerade. jpg." *Wikimedia. org*. https://commons.wikimedia.org/wiki/File:Mmanwu_Masquerade.jpg.

Morrison, Toni. *Beloved*. Alfred A. Knopf, 1987.

Mothership: Tales from Afrofuturism and Beyond. Ed. Bill Campbell, and Edward Austin Hall. Rosarium Publishing, 2013.

Murphy, Brigid. "Recovering Treasures in Celtic Spirituality: the Crone as Anam-Cara or Soul-Friend" *Canadian Woman Studies* 17.3 (Summer/Fall 1997), p. 90.

Murdock, Maureen. *The Heroine's Journey: Woman's Quest for Wholeness*. Shambhala, 1990, 30th anniversary edition, 2020.

"Mwita," *BabyNamesPedia*. www.babynamespedia.com/meaning/Mwita.

Nama, Adilifu. "Brave Black Worlds: Black Superheroes as Science Fiction Ciphers." *African Identities*. 7. 2 (May 2009), pp. 133–144.

Naturale, Lauren. "Who Fears the Death of the Author? Nnedi Okorafor's The Book of Phoenix." *B&N Sci-Fi Fantasy Blog*, 15 April 2015. https://www.barnesandnoble.com/blog/sci-fi-fantasy/who-fears-the-death-of-the-author/.

"Nnedi Okorafor: Magical Futurism" *Locus Online*. May 17, 2015.

Obama, Barack. "Commencement Speech," *NBC News.com*. https://www.nbcnews.com/politics/politics-news/obama-giving-commencement-speech-2020-class.

O'Connell, Hugh Charles. "Science Fiction and the Global South." *The Cambridge History of Science Fiction*. Ed. Gerry Canavan and Eric Carl Link. Cambridge University Press, 2019, pp. 680–695.

Okonkwo, Rudolf. "Our Country, Our Masquerades." *Nigeria World*, 28 April 2000, http://nigeriaworld.com/columnist/okonkwo/masquerade.html.

Okungbowa, Suyi Davies. "The Future Is Divergent: On Literary Afrofuturism in the Twenty-First Century." *Los Angeles Review of Books*, September 12, 2021. https://lareviewofbooks.org/article/the-future-is-divergent-on-literary-afrofuturism-in-the-twenty-first-century.

Oliver, Mary. *Blue Pastures*. Harcourt, 1995.

Orenstein, Peggy. *School Girls: Young Women, Self-Esteem and the Confidence Gap*. Anchor Books, Doubleday, 1994.

"Otherwise." https://otherwiseaward.org/about-the-award/why-otherwise.

Ottinger, John III. "Interview: Nnedi Okorafor." *Grasping for the Wind: Science Fiction and Fantasy News and Reviews*. July 7, 2010. http.//www.graspingforthewind.com/?s=Nnedi+Okorafor. Accessed Jan. 27, 2014.

Partlow, Joshua. "New Study Says Wildfire Smoke Leads to Higher COVID-19 Risks." *Washington Post*, August 16, 2021. https://www.washingtonpost.com/climate-environment/2021/08/13/this-is-very-dangerous-combination-new-study-says-wildfire-smoke-leads-higher-covid-risks/.

Pearson, Carol, and Katherine Pope. *The Female Hero in American and British Literature*. New York: Bowker, 1981.

Pearson, Carol S. *The Hero Within: Six Archetypes We Live By*. Harper, 1986.

Pilinovsky, Helen. "Nineteenth Century Fiction." *Women in Science Fiction and Fantasy*. Robin Anne Reid, Ed. Greenwood Press, 2009.

Pipher, Mary. *Reviving Ophelia: Saving the Selves of Adolescent Girls*. New York: Ballantine, 1994.

Poulsen, Frank Piasecki. "Children of the Congo who risk their lives to supply our mobile phones." *The Guardian*, 7 Dec. 2012. https://www.theguardian.com/sustainable-business/blog/congo-child-labour-mobile-minerals.

Preidt, Robert. "Stereotypes About Girls and Math Don't Add Up." *WebMD*, Nov. 18, 2019. https://www.webmd.com/brain/news/20191118/stereotypes-about-girls-and-math-dont-add-up-scans-show.

Prettyman, Gib. "Daoism, Ecology, and World Reduction in Le Guin's Utopian Fictions," *Green Planets: Ecology and Science Fiction*, Middletown, CT: Wesleyan University Press, 2014, pp. 56–76.

Price, Margaret. "The Bodymind Problem and the Possibilities of Pain." Hypatia 30, No. 1, 2015, 268–284.

Ransby, Barbara. "Comments by Barbara Ransby." *How We Get Free: Black Feminism and the Combahee River Collective*. Ed. Taylor, Keeanga-Yamahtta. Haymarket Books, 2017, pp. 177–183.

Rasheed, Kameelah. "Interview: Nnedi Okorafor," *Mosaic Magazine: Literary Arts of the Diaspora*, Jan. 2, 2014. https://mosaicmagazine.org/nnedi-okorafor-interview/#.XdG46FdKg2w.

Reed, Bess. Spirits Incarnate: Cultural Revitalization in a Nigerian Masquerade Festival. *African Arts* 38 (Spring 2005), pp. 50–95.

Rejectionist. "An Interview with Nnedi Okorafor." *Tor.com* (25 Aug. 2010) https://www.tor.com/2010/08/25/an-interview-with-nnedi-okorafor/.

Rice, Doyle, "Over One Billion Animals Feared Dead in Australian Wildfires, Experts Say." *USA Today*. Jan. 8. 2020. https://www.usatoday.com/story/news/world/2020/01/08/australian-fires-over-1-billion-animals-feared-dead-experts-say/2845084001.

Rieder, John. *Colonialism and the Emergence of Science Fiction*. Wesleyan University Press, 2008.

_____. "Theorizing SF: Science Fiction Studies since 2000." *The Cambridge History of Science Fiction*. Ed. Gerry Canavan and Eric Carl Link. Cambridge University Press, 2019, pp. 741–755.

Roszak, Betty. "The Spirit of the Goddess." *Ecopsychology: Restoring the Earth, Healing the Mind*. Ed. Theodore Roszak, Mary E. Gomes, and Allen D. Kanner. Sierra Club Books, 1995, pp. 288–300.

Russ, Joanna. *The Female Man*. Beacon Press, 1975.

_____. "What Can a Heroine Do? Or, Why Women Can't Write." *To Write Like a Woman: Essays in Feminism and Science Fiction*. Indiana University Press, 1995.

Schalk, Sami. *Bodyminds Reimagined*. Duke University Press, 2018.

Scheier, Liz. "Different Isn't a Threat: PW Talks with Nnedi Okorafor." *Publishers' Weekly*, Sept. 27, 2019, Books, 2001. https://www.publishersweekly.com/pw/by-topic/authors/interviews/article/81322-different-isn-t-a-threat-pw-talks-with-nnedi-okorafor.html.

Schenstead-Harris, Leif. "Interview: A Conversation with Nnedi Okorafor" *Weird Fiction Review*, Feb. 20, 2017. http://weirdfictionreview.com/2017/02/interview-conversation-nnedi-okorafor/.

Schüssler, Fiorenza Elisabeth. *Congress of Wo/men: Religion, Gender and Kyriarchal Power*. Dog Ear Publishing, 2016.

_____. *Wisdom Ways: Introducing Feminist Biblical Interpretation*. Orbis, 2001.

Schütze, Bernard. "The Grotesque and the Techno-Grotesque," Arts et électroniques Number 63, Fall 1995. URI: id.erudit.org/iderudit/46528ac.

Shawl, Nisi. Across the Lies of Space, and Time. "Deep End." *So Long Been Dreaming*. Eds. Nalo Hopkinson and Uppinder Mehan. Arsenal Press, 2004, 3rd edition, 2015, pp. 12–22.

_____. *Everfair*. Tor, 2016.

_____. "Hope and Vengeance in Post-Apocalyptic Sudan: *Who Fears Death* by Nnedi Okorafor." Nov.7, 2017. https://www.tor.com/2017/11/07/hope-and-vengeance-in-post-apocalyptic-sudan-who-fears-death-by-nnedi-okorafor/.

_____. *The WisCon Chronicles: Social Justice Redux*, Vol. 10. M. Ed. Margaret McBride. Seattle, WA: Aqueduct Press, 2016, pp. 155–170.

Sheehy, Gail. *Passages: Predictable Crises of Adult Life*. E.F. Dutton, 1976.

Shelley, Mary. *Frankenstein*. Dover Editions, 1996.

Shepherd, W. Andrew, "Afrofuturism in the Nineteenth and Twentieth Centuries," *The Cambridge History of Science Fiction*. Ed. Gerry Canavan and Eric Carl Link. Cambridge University Press, 2019, 101–119.

Slonczewski, Joan. *Brain Plague*. Tor, 2000.

Solomon, Rivers. *An Unkindness of Ghosts*. Akashic, 2017.

Spinrad, Norman. "Outside America." *Asi-

mov's Science Fiction 41.9–10 (September/October 2017).

Steinem, Gloria. *Revolution from Within: A Book of Self-Esteem*. Little, Brown and Company, 1992.

Stillman, Peter G. "*The Dispossessed* as Ecological Political Theory." *The New Utopian Politics of Ursula K. Le Guin's The Dispossessed*. Ed. Lawrence Davis and Peter Stillman. Rowman & Littlefield, 2005, pp. 55–74.

Suvin, Darko. *Metamorphoses of Science Fiction: On the Poetics and History of a Literary Genre*. Yale University Press, 1979.

Taylor, Keeanga-Yamahtta. *How We Get Free: Black Feminism and the Combahee River Collective*. Haymarket Books, 2017.

Terr, Lenore. *Unchained Memories: True Stories of Traumatic Memories Lost and Found*. HarperCollins, 1994.

"Third Wave Feminism" *About News*. http://civilliberty.about.com/od/gendersexuality/p/third_wave.htm.

Thomas, Sheree R. "Dangerous Muses: Black Women Writers Creating at the Forefront of Afrofuturism." *Literary Afrofuturism in the Twenty-First Century*. Eds. Isiah Lavender III and Lisa Yaszek. Ohio State University Press, 2020, pp. 37–55.

_____. *Darkmatter: A Century of Speculative Fiction from the African Diaspora*. Warner, 2000.

"Time of the Brave Mask" *(Mgbedike)*. Art Institute of Chicago Collections. Retrieved January 25, 2015.

Trota, Michi. "Are All the Men Really Necessary? A Critical look at Wonder Woman." *The Learned Fan Girl: A Critical Look at Popculture and Technology*. June 16, 2017. http://thelearnedfangirl.com/2017/06/are-all-the-men-really-necessary-a-critical-look-at-wonder-woman/.

Tubosun, Kola. "Nigeria: When Aliens Took Lagos." *The Guardian*, 7 May 2013.

"Use of Language in *Things Fall Apart*." *Cliff's Notes*. Houghton Mifflin Harcourt.

Verrier, Nancy Newton. *The Primal Wound: Understanding the Adopted Child*. Gateway Press, 1993.

Wagner, Thomas M. "The Book of Phoenix 2015: Nnedi Okorafor." *Sciences Fiction and Fantasy Book Reviews*. http://www.sfreviews.net/nnedi_book_of_phoenix.html.

Waite, Erin, "The Deluge," *World Wildlife*. Photographs and captions by Jashim Salam. Summer 2020, pp. 30–37.

Waldo, Mark L. "Mary Shelley's Machines in the Garden: Victor Frankenstein and His Monster." *Imaginative Futures: Proceedings of the 1993 Science Fiction Research Association Conference*. Milton T. Wolf and Daryl Mallett, eds. San Bernardino, CA: SFRA Press, 1994. 179–190.

Walker, Alice. "Coming Apart." *You Can't Keep a Good Woman Down*. New York: Harcourt Brace Jovanovich, 1981.

_____. "Introduction." *In Search of Our Mothers' Gardens: Womanist Prose*, Mariner Books (1983), 2003.

Walker, Barbara G. *The Woman's Encyclopedia of Myths and Secrets*. Harper and Row, 1983.

Walker, Rebecca. "Jan/Feb, 1992: Becoming the Third Wave." *Ms12.2*, Spring 2002, pp. 86–87.

_____. *To Be Real: Telling the Truth and Changing the Face of Feminism*. Anchor Books, 1995.

Warner, Marina. *Fantastic Metamorphoses, Other Worlds*. Oxford University Press, 2002.

_____. *Monsters of Our Own Making: The Peculiar Pleasures of Fear*. University Press of Kentucky, 2007.

Watson, Rachel E., Taylor B. Nelson, D.O., and Albert L. Hsu, M.D. "Fertility Considerations," *Fertility and Sterility*, March 19, 2021. https://www.fertstertdialog.com/posts/fertility-considerations-the-covid-19-disease-may-have-a-more-negative-impact-than-the-covid-19-vaccine-especially-among-men?room_id=871-covid-19.

Watterson, Bill. *Calvin and Hobbes*. 23 Mar. 1986. https://www.gocomics.com/calvinandhobbes/1986/03/23/.

Watts, Jonathon. "James Lovelock: 'The biosphere and I are both in the last 1% of our lives." *The Guardian*. 18 July 2020. https://www.theguardian.com/environment/2020/jul/18/james-lovelock-the-biosphere-and-i-are-both-in-the-last-1-per-cent-of-our-lives.

"What Does Name 'Aro' Mean." *Seven Reflections*. Retrieved 2016-1-9.

"Wild Cards—Origins." Wildcardsonline.com. Retrieved 2016-1-9.

Winter, Nicholas. "Interview Nnedi Okorafor: The Running Girl of Wor(l)ds." *Just a Word.* Aug. 6, 2018. https://justaword.fr/interview-nnedi-okorafor-79bab284df31.

Wolfe, Gary K. "Locus Looks at Books." *Locus,* 635: 71.6 (Dec. 2013).

Womack, Ytasha. "Afrofuturism Rising." *Uncanny: A Magazine of Fantasy and Science Fiction.* 9 Mar. 2015. http://uncannymagazine.com/article/afrofuturism-rising/.

Womack, Ytasha L. *Afrofuturism: The World of Black Sci-fi and Fantasy Culture.* Lawrence Hill Books, 2013.

World Health Organization. "WHO Coronavirus (COVID-19) Dashboard." https://covid19.who.int/.

Yaszek, Lisa. "Race in Science Fiction: The Case of Afrofuturism and New Hollywood." *A Virtual Introduction to Science Fiction.* Ed. Lars Schmeink. 2013. 1–11. Retrieved May 1, 2016 from http://virtual-sf.com/wp-content/uploads/2013/08/Yaszek.pdf.

_____ "Science." *Women in Science Fiction and Fantasy.* Ed. Robin Anne Reid. Greenwood Press, 2009.

Yeats, William Butler. "Leda and the Swan." *Academy of American Poets.* https://poets.org/poem/leda-and-swan.

Zacarias, Danielle. "What Do Magic and E-Readers Have in Common? Award-Winning Author Nnedi Okorafor." *The Literacy Ledger: Reflections, Finding, Stories and the Lowdown,* 20 Dec. 2013. www.worldreader.org/blog/magic-e-readers-common-nnedi-okorafor/.

Zamalin, Alex. *Black Utopia: The History of an Idea from Black Nationalism to Afrofuturism.* Columbia University Press, 2019.

Zechoski, S., and C.E. Neuman. "The Mother of all Superheroes: Idealizations of Femininity in *Wonder Woman.*" *Heroines of Comic Books and Literature: Portrayals in Popular Culture.* Ed. Maja Bajac-Carter, Norma Jones, and Bob Batchelor. Rowman & Littlefield, 2014. 133–144.

Zhou, Xiaodan, Kevin Josey, Leila Kammareddine, Miah C. Caine, Tianji Liu, Loretta J. Mickley, Matthew Cooper, and Francesca Dominici. "Excess of COVID-19 cases and deaths due to fine particulate matter exposure during the 2020 wildfires in the United States." *Science Advances,* Aug 13, 2021, Vol 7, Issue 33, DOI: 10.1126/sciadv.abi8789.

Zipes, Jack. *The Oxford Encyclopedia of Children's Literature.* Oxford University Press, 2006.

Zoboi, Ibi Aanu. "The People Could Fly: An Interview with Nnedi Okorafor." *Strange Horizons.* 17 May 2010. http://strangehorizons.com/author/ibi-aanu-zoboi/.

Index

Abacha, Sani 214
Achebe, Chinua: *Things Fall Apart* 193, 204, 205, 206
Ad Astra 200
adolescence 18, 19, 22, 26, 31, 38, 63, 66, 87, 98, 114, 142, 147, 178, 221; epistemological crisis 22; moral development 39
adult authority 32
Aejej 31, 57, 195, 206
African American Women in Defense of Ourselves Campaign (Ransby) 55
Africanfuturism 3, 6, 11, 14, 72, 103, 111, 117, 154, 155, 164–72, 177
Africanjujuism 6, 72, 82, 190
Afrocentrism 153, 155
Afrofuturism 3–7, 14, 82, 102, 111–117, 122, 124, 126, 152–72, 194, 211, 218–20, 222–28
Afrofuturism Rising (Lavender) 156, 223
Afrofuturism: The World of Black Sci-Fi and Fantasy Culture (Womack) 111, 153, 228
After the Rain (Jennings) 156, 223
agency 10, 11, 18, 20, 21, 35, 36, 46, 81, 85, 98, 99, 109, 122, 153, 164, 189, 205
Aiyetoro, Mary Bosede 2, 194, 218
Akata series 125 139, 177, 180–82, 190; Chichi 25, 27, 34–35, 125–27, 129, 196; chittim 38, 127; *Fast Facts for Free Agents* 23, 105, 126; Orlu 25, 27, 34, 125, 129; Sasha 25, 27, 34, 124–26, 129; Sunny 20, 22, 28, 32, 36, 39, 40, 42, 49, 50, 52, 60, 66, 68, 70, 78, 111, 119, 125, 130, 132, 134, 136, 138, 152, 154, 188, 190, 209; Udide, the story-telling spider 55–56, 126, 206
Akata Warrior (Okorafor) 13, 15, 18, 34, 53–55, 118, 119, 125, 129, 199, 203–6, 217
Akata Witch (Okorafor) 11, 13, 18–20, 23–25, 27, 28–39, 54, 69, 90, 111, 118, 122, 125, 128, 139, 141, 195, 204, 205, 207, 217
Aldini 78

alien intervention 130, 148, 153, 178; *see also LaGuardia*; *The Night Masquerade*
allergy 44, 49, 50, 168
Altruist Archetype 24, 45, 92, 128–29, 131, 136; *see also* Pearson, Carol
Always Coming Home (Le Guin) 141, 145, 199, 209, 223, 224; degrowth community 145
American Civil War 159, 175
Amini, Mehrdokht (illustrator) 127
"Amphibious Green" (Okorafor) 13, 14, 193, 203
Anarchism 84, 143–44, 210
Angelou, Maya 102, 116, 218; "Still I Rise" 116, 218
anger 1, 19, 18, 22, 28–31, 41, 49, 52, 55–57, 60–61, 65, 70–73, 88, 92, 96, 112–113, 122–124, 143, 151, 157, 167, 178, 183, 188–191, 202; advantage 28–31; and agency 85–86
angry earth 31, 37
Ani 60, 61, 63, 72, 73, 198
Anita Hill case 48
Annan, Kofi 91, 180
Anthropocene 3, 13, 138–141, 222
apocalypse 72, 77, 144, 148, 175, 185, 208, 211
Arcimboldo 78
Arnason, Eleanor 109, 218; "Big Brown Mama and Brer Rabbit" 212, 218
Arro-yo 44, 49–53, 197
artificial intelligence 183, 184, 214
Ashcroft, Bill 3, 81, 201, 218
Asimov, Isaac 10, 214; *I-Robot* 10, 214
Asuquo 42–45, 50, 11, 174, 197, 217
attachment 42, 45, 49–50, 77, 86–87, 102, 110, 144, 189, 223; and separation 49–50
Attebery, Brian 58–59, 74, 218
Atwood, Margaret 20
Austen, Jane: *Pride and Prejudice* 209
Avengers: Infinity War 165

229

Barber, Jeffrey 140, 141, 218
Barker, Clive 74
Barnes, Steven 14, 172, 194, 211, 225
Batgirl 163
Battle, Michael 3, 116, 218
Beale, Theodore (aka Vox Day) 8
Bear, Greg: *Blood Music* 204, 219
Belenky, Mary Field 2, 19, 20, 25, 26, 32, 40, 179, 196, 219, 221
Bellaire, Jordie (illustrator) 165, 217
Berry, Halle 163, 209, 213
Berry, Wendell: "The Failure of War" 115, 219
Bettelheim, Bruno 87, 201
Beukes, Lauren 25, 32, 187, 201, 201, 219; *Moxyland* 187, 218; Slipping Stories 25, 200; *see also* dystopia
Biden, Joe 187, 198
Big Eye 81, 87, 90–92; *see also* surveillance
bigotry 12, 19, 24, 40, 52, 53, 55, 62, 92, 104, 147, 154, 173, 175, 176, 200
Biko, Bantu Stephen 180–181, 214
Bildungsroman 13, 18, 23, 67, 152, 194, 214
Binti 10, 13, 15, 18, 103–9, 111–12, 150, 152, 160, 165, 171, 194, 203, 204, 210, 217, 219, 224; astrolabe 105, 115, 150, 210; Okwu 107, 109, 113, 115, 132, 135; otjize 98, 104, 107; The Seven or the Principle Artists of All Things 133, 135, 207; TV series 116
Binti: alien ambassador 111, 211; bodily violation 109; as change 133–136; as "gentle warrior" 135; hybridity 117, 144; lightning calculation 106; liminality 133; mediation 115; okuoko 10, 107, 108, 114, 115, 204–5; as "other" 130; reincarnation 135; resurrection 135l as superhero 132; treeing 98, 105–6
Binti: Home 98, 112–115, 124, 132–133, 204, 205
Binti: The Night Masquerade 56, 115–116, 118, 133–136, 177, 196, 202, 205; Night Masquerade costume 133–135, 137
Binti trilogy 18, 53, 98, 113, 117, 132, 134, 141, 152, 211, 213, 182; Astrolabe 105, 115, 150, 210; *edan* 106–7, 136; Mwinyi 134–135 (see also *The Night Masquerade*); Okwu (*see also* Meduse); otjize 98, 104, 107 (see also *Binti*)
biological warfare 37
biotechnology 105, 146, 151
Black Excellence Award for Outstanding Achievement in Literature 15
Black Feminism 3, 47, 54, 220, 226, 227
Black Hat Otokoto 11, 25, 28–30, 33–35, 127–128

Black Panther 128, 163, 165–67, 200, 206, 210, 211, 213, 217; on imperialism 163
Black Panther: Long Live the King 162
Black Panther: Wakanda Forever Avengers 162
Black Radical Congress 68
"Black to the Future" (Dery) 156, 220
"Black to the Future II" (Hudlin) 163
Blake, William: "The Tyger" 199
"A Blessing in Disguise" 164; Ngozi 164–166, 205, 219
Block, Jeanne Humphrey 101
Blount, Herman Poole 155
bodymind 11, 193, 226
Boko Haram 8, 109–11, 165, 204, 218
The Book of Phoenix 3, 13, 14, 60, 69, 77–97, 155, 171, 173, 175, 182, 188, 189, 196, 198, 200, 201, 205, 210, 211, 212, 217, 219, 225, 227; Bumi 80, 86, 87, 96; Seven 90, 92–93, 202; Sunuteel 82, 96
Bosch, Hieronymous 7
Bracket, Leigh 102, 159
Bradshaw, John 66, 219
Brain Research 190, 223
Breaking Down the Wall of Silence (Miller) 88, 225
Bridges, Ruby 160
Broken Places Outer Spaces (Okorafor) 9–11, 24, 76, 105–106, 110, 118, 121, 134–35, 137–38, 198, 199, 200, 212, 214, 217
Brown, Adrienne Maree 13–14, 108, 160, 172, 214, 219, 220, 222; *Emergent Strategy* 168; tools for writing visionary fiction 13–14
Brown, Michael Harold: *The Search for Eve* 214
Buffy the Vampire Slayer 48
bullying 13, 17, 29, 53, 55, 81, 121–24, 154, 181
Burnham, Michael *see* Martin-Green, Sonequa
Butler, Octavia 9, 10, 13, 14, 20, 37, 66, 90, 91, 102, 107, 109, 114, 117, 130, 153, 155, 158, 159, 161, 171, 204, 211, 212, 219, 223; *Adulthood Rites* 204; "Blood Child" 109, 161; Clay's Ark 109; *Dawn* 171, 211, 219; *Kindred* 91, 155, 158, 171, 219; McArthur Genius Award 14; *Parable of the Sower* 13, 114, 219; Patternmaster series 158; *Wildseed* 199; *Wildseed* series script (Kahiu) 199; Xenogenesis series 107, 130, 161, 204, 211
Byron, George Gordon 78, 87, 88, 190, 203

Calvin and Hobbes (Watterson) 169, 227
The Cambridge History of Science Fiction 140, 221, 223, 225, 226

Index

Campbell, Joseph 19, 21, 28, 76, 211
capitalism 6, 15, 36, 40, 61, 82, 128, 130, 139, 143, 149, 154, 173, 199, 208, 211
Carl Brandon Society 14, 73, 75, 169, 170, 193, 213
Carlsson, Chris: nowtopia 149, 219
Carlyle, Thomas: the Great Man theory 2, 60–61, 72, 198–199, 219
Carmichael, Stokely 157, 161, 169
Carr, Terry 194, 213; *see also* Brandon, Carl
carrier bags 5, 142, 148–51, 209. 210, 223; *see also* Le Guin, Ursula K.
"The Carrier Bag Theory of Fiction" (Le Guin) 61, 151, 223
Caste (Wilkerson) 3, 80, 84
Catwoman 163, 166
Chandrasekera, Vajra 204, 219
Charnas, Suzi McKee 20
Charpentier, Emmanuelle 215; *see also* CRISPR
"A Chat with Nnedi Okorafor" 201
Chestnutt, Charles W. 154
chi 50, 126, 206
Chibok school girls 8, 71, 106, 109–111, 116, 165, 218, 219, 221, 224
Chicken in the Kitchen (Okorafor) 15, 118; *see also* teaching stories
Chidera 100–2, 127–128; see also *Girl with the Magic Hands*
Childhood and Society (Erikson) 30, 32, 220
Children's Africana Book Award for Best Book for Young Readers 15, 127
Civil Rights Movement 153, 157
Clarion 14, 50, 171, 211, 212
Clarke, Arthur C. 181, 198, 200, 219; *2001, A Space Odyssey* 200; *see also* scientists
Clarke Award 76
Clarkesworld 9, 69, 196, 197, 217, 223
class warfare 186, 215
clitorectomy 63–66, 72, 101; *see also* coming of age rituals: Eleventh Year Rite; female circumcision
Clute, John 199; "Nnedi Okorafor" 220
cognitive dissonance 27
Cohen, Leonard 207
Collette 44
colonialism 3, 6, 8, 17, 51, 52, 131, 141, 158, 179
The Color Purple (Walker, A.) 48
Combahee River Collective 2, 15, 47, 157, 220, 226, 227
comics 3, 4, 6, 127, 152, 153, 155, 156, 161–66, 169, 180, 199.200, 205, 207.210, 211, 212, 217

coming of age rituals 11, 18, 45, 65, 74, 101, 199; Eleventh Year Rite 63, 70, 101; *see also* Chidera; *The Girl with the Magic Hands*
The Communist Manifesto (Marx) 57
competition 149, 172, 174–76, 178, 181
computers 12, 36, 53, 141, 149, 150, 175, 184, 198, 210, 214; CPU seeds 36, 53, 210
conception 66, 70, 73, 142, 143
conflict mediation 15–26, 56, 115, 147–148
conflict resolution 118, 127–28, 134, 150–152, 166
conflict without war 147–148
Confucius 180
Contagion 215
"Contemporary Science Fiction and Afrofuturism" 113, 223
conventional moral judgement. 22, 28–29, 134, 136, 179–80, 181
Covington, Aaron 162
Crenshaw, Kimberlé 3, 193, 197; *see also* critical race theory
CRISPR 80, 186, 215
critical liberationist feminism 180
critical race theory 3, 47, 160, 197, 223
critical thinking 31–32, 179
"The Critique of Judgement" (Kant) 94
Csicsery-Ronay, Istvan 3, 93; *The Seven Beauties of Science Fiction* 220
cultural norms 22, 31, 48–49. 56, 96, 99, 121, 133, 136, 144, 146, 173, 174, 176, 179–80, 194
cultural outsiders 19, 24, 33, 58, 74, 158
cultural stereotypes 42, 44, 53, 57, 85, 162–63, 226
"A Cyborg Manifesto" (Haraway) 11, 57
cyborg revolution 91–93
cyborgs 2, 9–12, 94, 44, 54, 56–67, 80–82, 87, 91–93, 107, 156, 175, 193, 200, 222

dada/dadalocks 7, 19, 20, 26, 41, 42, 43, 44, 53, 66, 98, 168, 194, 220
Dancing the Tao: Le Guin and Moral Development (Lindow) 2, 224
Dark Matter: A Century of Speculative Fiction from the African Diaspora (Thomas) 154
Dark Matter: Reading the Bones (Thomas) 154, 217, 220
Davidson, Paul (illustrator) 165, 217
Davy, Humphry 78
death 20, 24, 27, 32–34, 45, 49, 53, 55, 59, 60, 63, 69–71, 74, 80, 88, 94–96, 122, 127, 129, 131–32, 134–36, 147–48, 150, 156, 181, 182, 185–86, 194, 195, 197, 198, 199, 201, 202, 205, 214; by stoning 62, 74, 218

degrowth 3, 13, 139–151, 207, 210, 220, 223; cultures 145
Delany, Martin R. 154
Delany, Samuel R. 14, 156, 158, 169, 170, 171, 220; "Racism and Science Fiction" 169, 220
de Lint, Charles 151
depression 28–30, 63, 98, 108
Dery, Mark 5, 102, 153, 156, 160, 220; "Black to the Future" 156, 220
Desert Magician 27, 28
Desert Storm 176
diaspora 6, 113, 154, 220, 226, 227
Dickens, Charles 77, 208, 220
dipheko 32; see also *Akata Witch*
(Dis)Ability 9, 11
disability 2, 3, 11, 49, 193; see also body-mind
Diversicon 1
Doctrine of Discovery 81, 141, 208
Don't Bet on the Prince (Zipes) 4
doorkeepers 25, 174
Dora Milaje 162, 206; see also Black Panther
double consciousness 9, 157, 158, 164, 193; see also Du Bois. W.E.B.
Douda, Jennifer 215; see also CRISPR
Dowdall, Lisa 8, 14, 62, 63, 73, 152, 198, 220
Drums and Shadows 221; see also Gullah people
Du Bois, W.E.B. 2, 8, 154, 157, 220
Due, Tananarive 8, 61, 170, 171, 172, 220
Dunbar Creek 42
Durant, Ariel: *The Lessons of History* 2, 3, 174–78, 181, 183, 186
Durant, Will: *The Lessons of History* 2, 3, 174–78, 181, 183, 186

echo chamber 155, 221; see also Hairston, Andrea
ecofeminism 35–36, 151, 196, 211
ecology 211, 218, 226, 5, 6, 19, 40, 57, 61, 62, 79, 128, 137–38, 139, 144–147
ecopsychology 26, 221, 222, 226
Edmunds, T. Keith 164, 211, 212, 220
Eisner Award 15, 167
ekklesia of wo/men 180
Ekwensu 35, 122, 128–29, 137, 206, 220, 225; Igbo God of War 128; see also masquerades
emergence 13–14
Emerging from the Chrysalis (Lincoln) 27, 195, 224
empire 17–18, 22, 23, 40, 175
Emshwiller, Carol: *Carmen Dog* 109

Engels, Friedrich 57, 198
epistemological crises 22; see also Gilligan, Carol
equality 15, 18, 36, 42, 43, 44, 46–47, 82, 87, 155, 162, 166, 171–72, 186, 200
Erikson, Erik 2, 19, 30–32, 38–39, 51, 55, 182, 194, 220
Ervin, Raquel "Rocket" 164
Estes, Clarissa Pinkola 124, 180, 220; drumming 124; el duende 180; *Women Who Run with the Wolves* 124
ethic of care 32, 122; see also Gilligan, Carol
ethnic cleansing 59
exit strategies 23, 102–103; see also Gilligan, Carol

Fagan, Kirbi (illustrator) 165
fairy tales, revisionist 47; see also Zipes, Jack
fate 44, 45, 70, 122, 125, 206, 210
fathers 20, 50, 101
Faust, Minister 5
Fear of Flying (Jong) 46, 202, 223
female circumcision 63, 66, 174, 195, 218; see also cliterectomy
female hero 38
The Female Hero (Pearson) 222, 225
The Female Man (Russ) 46, 85, 226
feminism 2, 3, 15, 17, 47, 48, 61, 83, 108, 153, 171, 196, 224, 226, 227; global contextual 180; proto- 83
Ferreira, Rachel 91, 221
Field Guide to the Greeny Jungle 23, 31, 50, 105, 194, 197
Fiorenza, Elizabeth Schlüsser 2, 17, 36, 51, 52, 60, 143, 180, 194, 196, 208, 221
First Men on the Moon (Wells) 211
flight 11, 18, 41–43, 45, 49, 53–57, 63, 66, 76, 92, 103, 106, 112, 116, 136, 161, 180, 184, 196, 197
Ford, Tana (illustrator) 167, 217
Forever War 176
Foster, Alan Dean 123
Four Ways to Forgiveness (Le Guin) 65
Frankenstein (Shelley) 3, 76–86, 89, 90, 92–97, 189–190, 200, 208, 222, 226, 227; Dippel, Konrad 79; manly independence 113
Frankenstein, Victor 78–80, 83–86, 94–96, 190; dangers of isolation 96; as early anti-hero 83
Frankenstein's monster 76, 78–79, 81–87, 89–97, 113; as carnal bricolage 94; as techno-grotesque 94, 226
Freidan, Betty: *The Female Mystique* 46, 221

Freud, Sigmund 40, 195; I-splitting or *Ich-Spaltung* 65
Freyd, Jennifer: *Betrayal Trauma* 221
friendship 28, 59, 67, 87, 91, 109, 122; gathering of allies 23; *see also* Murdock, Maureen
Fuller, Bryan: *Star Trek: Discovery* 160

Gaia Hypothesis 35, 215, 224
Galvan, Adriana 71, 109, 221
Galvani 78
Gandhi, Mahatma 127, 180, 207
Gbowee, Lehmah: *Mighty Be Our Powers* 70, 115, 221
gender 1, 6, 8, 18, 26, 28, 30, 46, 48, 55, 57, 60, 84, 85, 98, 121, 133, 135, 158, 161, 169, 193, 197, 201, 202, 218, 222, 224, 226; default 201; dysphoria 98, 202, 218
genocide 89, 112, 140, 173, 176, 198, 209, 213; eight stages of 176
genre 2, 3, 5, 7, 14, 76, 85, 94, 152, 156, 159, 213, 218, 227
Gilligan, Carol 2, 3, 19, 22, 23, 25, 27–30, 36, 86–87, 99, 101, 120, 122, 133, 136, 179, 182, 195, 221; *A Different Voice* 20, 22, 122, 195, 221; *Mapping the Moral Domain* 194, 221, 23, 30
Ginen 1, 5, 9, 12, 18, 27, 32–40, 43, 48–49, 53, 56, 72, 126, 141, 145–147, 149, 151, 176, 194, 196, 197, 203, 204; botanical communities 145–147, 150; inter-dimensional portals 146; sensitivity to pollution 146–147; small business economy 13, 149
girl development 19, 9, 117
The Girl with the Magic Hands (Okorafor) 98, 100–102, 180, 195, 203, 207, 210, 211, 217
Godwin, William 84, 88, 189–90
Goldberg, Whoopi: as Guinan 194
Goldberger, Nancy Rule 2, 22, 219, 221
Goldstein, Lisa: *A Mask for the General* 101
Gomez, Jewelle 48; *The Gilda Stories* 171, 221
Goodell, Jeff: *The Water Will Come* 208, 221
Goodman, Paul 143; *Growing Up Absurd* 143
Gore, Al 199
Gore, Charles 120, 130, 205, 221
Gorman, Amanda: "The Hill We Climb" 173, 187, 221
Graham, Pete 193, 213; *see also* Brandon, Carl
Gray, Leslie 26, 221

The Great Book 60–61, 72–73, 200, 219
The Great Change 175, 209, 219
The Great Man 2, 59–60, 79, 180, 199
Greeny Jungle 9, 23, 24, 31, 50, 53, 105, 122, 197, 205
Griggs, Sutton E. 202, 204, 221
grotesque 3, 67, 93–94, 222, 226
Guevara, Che 180
Gullah Island people 42

Hairston, Andrea 40, 53, 155, 170, 172, 197, 221; "Dismantling the Echo Chamber" 155, 221; *Will Do Magic for Small Change* 197, 221
Hamilton, Virginia 41–43, 194, 222; *The People Could Fly* 40, 42, 162, 222, 228
Haraway, Donna 2, 11–12, 57, 60, 92, 140, 144, 193, 222; "A Cyborg Manifesto" 11–12, 57, 92, 222; *Primate Visions* 60, 222
Harper, Steven 23, 222; *see also* wilderness
Harpman, Geoffrey Galt 94, 222
Harris, Kamala 187
Hawthorne, Nathaniel: "Young Goodman Brown" 53
Hayden, Robert: "Middle Passage" 202
Heinlein, Robert: *Podkayne of Mars* 201
"Her Pen Could Fly: Remembering Virginia Hamilton" (Okorafor) 7, 41, 196, 205, 217
Herbert, Frank: *Dune* 136, 209
Herman, Judith Lewis: *Trauma and Recovery* 92, 222
hero archetypes 19, 30; Carl Jung's insight 59
hero journey/quest 7, 12, 19–20, 26, 32–33, 45, 69, 100–101, 106, 152, 210; *see also* Campbell, Joseph
hero tales 99, 170
heroine's journey 28, 175, 197
Heroine's Journey Project 27–28
heroism 2, 3, 39, 116, 129, 134; girl heroes/heroines 36, 99, 105, 109, 111, 161, 170; mindset 58, 95, 111; scientists as ambiguous heroes 77; second wave feminist responses 46–48, 61, 148–50, 170, 170; trickster hero 99; *see also* Great Man theory
hierarchy 18, 34, 37, 52, 60, 70, 72, 97, 139, 147, 150, 157, 174, 178–79, 199, 207
Hitler, Adolf 69, 88; *Mein Kampf* 202
Hogarth, William: The Reward of Cruelty 78
Hoobler, Dorothy: *The Monsters* 76, 78–79, 84, 189–90, 222
Hoobler, Thomas: *The Monsters* 76, 78–79, 84, 189–90, 222

Index

Hopkins, Pauline 155
Hopkinson, Nalo 5, 8, 20, 117, 131, 153, 170, 171, 196, 218, 222; *Chaos* 211; "ClapBack" 214; "Whose Upward Flight I Love" 196
Horney, Karen 98, 202, 222
hubris 60, 77, 93
Hudlin, Reggie: "Black to the Future II" 163
Hugo Award 8, 15, 103, 106, 152, 194
human rights abuses 8, 196, 222
Huxley, Aldous: *Brave New World* 200
hybridity 46, 56, 79, 81, 182, 207, 204

identity 13, 17, 19, 23, 25, 26, 27, 31-33, 38-40, 46, 55-56, 66, 99, 112-14, 120, 122, 155, 157, 194, 197, 201, 206; interconnection 18, 25, 57
"If It Scares You Write It" (Okorafor) 69, 117, 223
Ijele 129-31, 138, 195, 222; as golden joinery, 138; *see also* masquerades
Ikenga (Okorafor) 31, 177, 217; as *The Incredible Hulk* 177
industrialization 52, 61, 77, 79-81, 85, 94, 96, 101, 140-41, 143, 179, 199, 200, 201, 207, 208, 210, 211
inequality 44, 46, 87, 162, 186
inertia belt 164
initiations 21, 25, 27, 100, 133, 182, 195, 224
innocent archetype 24-25, 30, 128-29, 131-32; *see also* Pearson, Carol
insects 9, 11, 56, 126, 146, 166; *see also* Space Lubber
interracial marriage 114
intersectionality 3, 4, 8, 12, 51, 113, 152-54, 157, 163-64
intimacy 18, 23, 25, 39-42, 50-51, 175, 199
Inyang 42-45, 111, 197

James, Edward 12, 77, 94, 222
Jameson, Frederic 209, 222
Jansson, Tove: *Moomintroll* series 74, 196, 205, 222
Jemisin, N.K. 8, 20, 153, 172, 194, 196, 204, 214, 220; "The Brides of Heaven" 204, 220; *Broken Earth* trilogy 214; "Cloud Dragon Skies" 194; "The Effluent Engine" 196; "The Evaluators" 204; "On the Banks of the River Lex" 201, 201; "Walking Awake" 204
Jemison, Mae 158, 160, 212
Jenkins, Barry: *The Underground Railroad* 212
Jenkins, Patty: *Wonder Woman 1984* 212
Jennings, John (illustrator) 155-56, 165, 211, 223; *After the Rain* 223

Jesus Christ 11, 58, 71, 131, 180; Christianity 11, 26, 71, 81, 110, 131, 193, 198, 205, 206, 208
Johanson, Donald: Lucy fossil 200
Johnson, Alaya Dawn 170, 172, 191, 199, 207, 223; *Love Is the Drug* 214; "A Million Mirrors" 191, 223; *Racing the Dark* 199; *see also* coming-of age rituals
Jones, Gayl 48
Jong, Erica: *Fear of Flying* 46, 202, 223
Jung, Carl 24, 59, 61, 185, 197, 215, 223

Kabu-Kabu Stories 42, 118, 130, 194, 206, 217; "Asunder" 49-50; "Biafra" 52, 174, 177; "The Carpet"(Okorafor) 193; "House of Deformities" 10-11; "How Inyang Got Her Wings" 10, 42, 44-45, 54, 104, 111, 197; "Moom!" 130, 205, 206; "On the Road" 156, 223; "The Palm Tree Bandit" 98-100, 116; "The Popular Mechanic" 180, 206; "Spider the Artist" 35, 206; "Tumaki" 11, 44, 175; "Windseekers" 42, 49-51, 53-54, 56, 197, 218
Kahiu, Wanuri 183, 199
Kali Ma 96
Kant, Immanuel 94
Kilgore, Dewitt Douglas 12, 212, 223
Kindred see Butler, Octavia
Kindred Award 14, 15, 75, 170, 186
King, Coretta Scott 41
King, Martin Luther 159, 171, 180, 199; "I Have a Dream" 199
King, Stephen 7, 74, 205
Kingston, Maxine Hong: *The Woman Warrior: Memoirs of a Girlhood Among Ghosts* 9
kintsugi 135; as golden joinery 138; *see also Broken Places, Outer Spaces*; Cohen, Leonard
Kirby, Jack 200, 212
kleptocracy 177
Kligman, Albert 79; Holmesburg Prison 79, 225
Kohlberg, Lawrence 2, 19, 22, 26, 29, 86, 179, 194, 223
Kress, Nancy: "Semper Augustus" 209, 210
Kritzer, Naomi: *Chaos on the Catnet* 214, 221; *see also* artificial intelligence
Kroeber, Alfred 143; *see also* Le Guin, Ursula K.
Kropotkin, Pyotr 143
kyriarchy 2, 15, 40, 51-52, 59, 68-72, 170, 179, 184, 208

Index

Lacey, Lauren 19, 108, 112, 223
Lacks, Henrietta 79–80, 83, 91
Lagoon 11, 13, 107, 118, 129–31, 136, 152, 167, 169, 173, 177, 182, 188, 205, 206, 207, 217, 218, 219, 220; Adaora's selkie-like transformation 136; *LaGuardia* 15, 130, 153, 167–69, 171, 184, 197, 210, 217
land ethic 144, 146, 224
Lao Tzu 209, 223; *see also* Taoism
Lavender, Isiah 3, 5, 113, 154, 156, 160–61, 169, 197, 200, 211, 218, 221, 223, 227; "Critical Race Theory" 160, 197, 205
Le Sony'r Ra *see* Sun Ra
leadership: corruption of power 12, 25, 33–34, 52, 13–31, 173, 177, 178, 193
"Leda and the Swan" (Yeats) 59, 228
Lee, Stan 162, 200, 212
Lefanu, Sarah 116, 224
Legba 10–11, 25, 28, 131, 150, 210
"The Legend of Arrö-yo" (Okorafor's unpublished novel) 44
Le Guin, Ursula K. 2, 3, 13, 20, 41, 46, 61, 65, 71, 99, 131, 141–51, 159, 170–71 186, 195, 199–3, 208–10, 211, 213–14, 219, 222, 224, 226, 227; anarchist philosophy 145; destructive hierarchies 145; early thinking on climate change 141; endorsement of Okorafor 142; feminine (yin) utopia 142; information webs in space 149; maz 195; myth marries history 61, 199; myths of the European Enlightenment 143, 208; novels, stories, and essays (*Always Coming Home* 144–45, 199, 209, 223, 224; *Dancing at the Edge of the World* 149, 223, 224; *The Dispossessed* 141, 144, 223, 227; *Earthsea* series 33, 42, 46, 171, 203, 213, 214, 224; "Indian Uncles" 143; "The New Atlantis" 141, 144, 201, 219; "No Time to Spare" 200, 224; "A Non-Euclidean View of California" 142–43, 195, 224; "Old Music and the Slave Women" 201; *The Other Wind* 151, 202 [*see also* transformation]; *Powers*, 201 [*see also* slavery]; "Some Approaches to the Problem of the Shortage of Time" 208, 224; *The Telling* 195, 209; translation of the *Tao* 209; "Vaster Than Empires and More Slow" 211; *A Wizard of Earthsea* 171; "The Woman Without Answers" 61; "A Woman's Liberation" 201); propertarian (world) reduction 144, 209; Shevek 144, 150 (see also *The Dispossessed*); technological progress as tragedy 148; valorizing indigenous values 141
L'Engle, Madeleine: *A Wrinkle in Time* 102

Leopard Cult 125
Leopard Knocks 23, 27, 38, 125
Leopard leadership 34, 48, 50, 125, 205
Leopold, Aldo 4
The Lessons of History (Durant) 3, 115, 173–75
Letme Live 167–68, 184; see also *LaGuardia*
Levy, Michael 202, 224
Lewis, C.S.: *The Lion, the Witch, and the Wardrobe* 33
LifeGen 79–81, 86–88, 92–93, 96, 184; Towers 82, 90–92, 201
liminality 7, 12, 25, 35, 57, 72, 132–33, 136, 159, 174
Lincoln, Bruce: *Emerging from the Chrysalis* 27, 195, 224
Lindow, Sandra 4; *Dancing the Tao: Le Guin and Moral Development* 2, 65, 224; "To Heck with the Village" 197
literacy technology 169
Locus 6, 63, 109, 199, 217–18, 225, 228
Locus Award 15
Lodestar Award 15
Long Juju Man (Okorafor) 14
lookism 1, 19, 46
Lord, Karen 102; *The Best of All Possible Worlds* 102; *The Galaxy Game* 102; *Redemption in Indigo* 103
Lorde, Audre 3, 100, 115, 172, 211, 215, 224
Lovelock, James 227; Gaia Hypothesis 35, 215, 224; *The Revenge of Gaia* 211
Lyons, Gene 198, 224

Maathai, Wangari 181
Macmillan Writer's Prize for Africa 14
magic 2, 7, 9, 11, 12–13, 20, 23–25, 27, 32–33, 37–38, 42, 52–53, 57, 62–68, 73, 79, 98, 100–104, 106–7, 118, 124–29, 132, 134–37, 147–48, 155–56, 161, 173–74, 178–82, 195, 196, 197, 198, 203, 205, 206, 207, 210
magician archetype 24, 33, 125, 128–29, 136, 196
Malthus, Thomas 142, 208
Mami Wata 130, 167–68, 206
Mandela, Nelson 180
Mapping the Moral Domain (Gilligan) 23, 30, 194, 221
Margulis, Lynn 35, 224
Martin, George R.R. 75, 196
Martin-Green, Sonequa 160
Marvel Comics 153, 162, 164, 171, 174, 200, 212, 217, 219, 220, 221
Marx, Karl 57, 198, 206
Marxism 3, 15, 47, 129–30, 139, 200, 198, 199, 206, 210; dialectic 130; synthesis 129

Mashigo, Mohale 5, 224
masquerade festivals 124–126, 129, 220
masquerade societies 10, 120, 125, 136, 195, 199
masquerade theology 137–38
masquerades 3, 8, 31, 32, 35, 56, 67, 103, 108, 115–16, 118–38, 178, 186, 195, 196, 199, 204, 206, 217, 220, 221, 223, 224, 225; as ancestral spirits 121, 127–28; black parades 131; drumming 121, 123–26, 128, 205; flute music 124, 126, 128; forbidden knowledge 67; Ijele 129–30, 138, 195, 222 (*see also Lagoon*); piercing 137; unmasking 119, 122, 133, 137–38, 204, 205, 215, 217; wedding entertainment 121
"Masquerades in Sub-Saharan West African Culture" 120–122
math anxiety 104–107
maz 195
McCaffrey, Anne: "The Ship Who Sang" 136
McGoohan, Patrick: *The Prisoner* 200; *see also* surveillance
McIntosh, Peggy: "White Privilege and Male Privilege" 170, 213, 224
McKillip, Patricia: *Riddle Master of Hed* 62
Meduse 115, 117, 119, 130, 212; inspired by jellyfish 107; *see also Binti* trilogy
Méliès, Georges: *A Trip to the Moon* 211
menarche 19, 45, 101
Mendlesohn, Farah 12, 57, 222
menstruation 65, 67, 72, 84
mentorship 14, 25–30, 33–34, 39, 53, 125, 170, 222; Anatov 27; Mazi Godwin 26, 195, 209; Sugar Cream 39
messianic tradition 69
meta-human 19, 44, 57, 90, 176
meta-slavery 77, 81, 179, 200
Milestone Comics 164
military-industrial complex 201
military/militarization 17, 36, 52, 72, 80–81, 85, 96, 110, 130, 149, 174, 177, 179
Millett, Kate: *Sexual Politics* 44, 225
miscegenation 114
mitochondrial Eve 80, 200
Mohanraj, Mary Anne 15, 170
Monsters of Our Own Making: The Peculiar Pleasures of Fear (Warner) 78, 227
Moomintroll series (Jansson) 74, 196, 206, 222
Moore, C.L. 102
moral development/morality 1–4, 12–13, 17–40, 44, 51–52, 55, 58, 65, 71, 73–74, 76–79, 80, 86–89, 92–93, 96, 99, 108, 110, 118, 122, 128–30, 133–34, 136–37, 144, 146, 150, 162, 171, 173–74, 176–82, 194–96, 198, 204–5, 214, 221, 223–24
moral domain 22–23, 25, 40, 194, 221; *see also* Gilligan, Carol
moral maturity 24, 26, 31, 35, 51
Morrison, Toni 48, 102, 113, 148, 156, 180, 225; *Beloved* 148, 180, 225
Mosaic Magazine 5, 119, 194, 212, 226
Mosley, Walter 171–72
mothers 22, 44, 56, 58, 88, 93, 146, 203, 205
Mothership 155, 225
Ms. magazine 48
Mulan 46, 48
Munroe, Ororo *see* Storm
Munsch, Robert: *The Paper Bag Princess* 47
Murdock, Maureen 1, 2, 19, 21, 23, 27–28, 32, 39, 101, 197, 225; "healing the mother/daughter split" 102; "wounded masculine" 28
Murphy, Pat 14
mutants 81–82, 175, 200
Mystic Points 67; Chukwu 137
myth 27, 34, 50, 58–59, 61, 73–74, 91–92, 135, 137, 148, 199, 218
mythology 1, 57–60, 65, 72–74, 76, 82, 88, 90, 92, 96, 103, 112, 131, 148, 196, 206, 211; remythology 73–74

Nama, Adilifu 161, 162, 164, 225; *African Identities* 164; "Brave Black Worlds" 161, 225
National Center on Violence Against Women in the Black Community 54, 225
Naturale, Lauren 77, 225
Nazism 88
Nebula Award 8, 15, 103
neocolonialism 3, 51–52, 128, 143, 173, 179
neo-slavery 77, 175
"The New Atlantis" *see* Le Guin, Ursula K.
The New England Primer 61
New Fish 56, 116, 135–36, 150, 196; *see also Binti: The Night Masquerade*
Nichols, Nichelle 115, 160, 213; *see also* Uhura, Nyota
Nicholson, William 78
Nigerian science fiction 2
Nin, Anais 44
Nkrumah, Kwame 201
Nnamdi 177–78; *see also Ikenga*
nonviolent conflict resolution 134
Noor 12–13, 193, 195, 217
Nsibidi 26, 53, 71–73, 129, 147, 195, 198, 220

Obama, Barack 2154, 225
Octavia's Brood 13, 171, 219–220, 222
Okorafor, Godwin 63, 119, 195, 209; death 63
Okorafor, Helen 66, 123
Okorafor, Nnedi: airport experience 167; awards 14–15, 75–76, 85, 103, 106, 118, 127, 167, 170, 194, 200–1, 228; birth 6–7, 141, 151, 203; blue clay woman 10, 207; Clarion experience and stories 14, 50, 211–12; daughter Anyaugo 51, 10, 111, 127; descendant of African slavers 197, 199; disability 11; divorce 51; early experience with bullies 121, 124, 198; early love of reading 196; education 9–12, 74, 120, 154, 170, 179; favorite writers during childhood 74, 204; fear of car washes 123, 205; literary inspiration 10, 181, 198, 201, 205; as Nigerian immigrant 112, 203; online stories ("African Sunrise" 200, 217; "Amphibious Green" 13–14, 193, 203, 217; "Blessing in Disguise" 164, 217; "From the Lost Diary of Treefrog7" 50, 175, 194; "The Go Slow" 180, 217; "Hello Moto'" 181, 217; "Rusties" 183–84, 217); paralysis 9–10, 17, 134, 137, 213; racist harassment during childhood 158–59; as rudimentary cyborg 9–12, 14, 80; spinal surgery 9–10, 57, 76, 108, 112–113, 166, 214; as a tennis player 10, 105–6, 113, 171, 214; treeing in tennis 105
Okri, Ben 2
Okunev, Oleg 162
Okungbowa, Suyi Davies 9, 225
Olaoye, Elizabeth Olubukola 2, 218
Oliver, Mary 37, 225
Orenstein, Peggy 34–35, 225
"Organic Fantasy" 7- 8, 12, 19, 25, 28, 37, 39, 42, 72, 94, 102, 106, 117, 121, 193–97, 199, 201, 209, 217; crisis resolution 126–127
orphan archetype 24
Orwell, George: *1984* 81, 212
Otherwise Award 194, 213 225; *see also* Tiptree Award
oxytocin 190, 223

palm wine 99, 203
The Palm Wine Drinkard (Tutuola) 200, 203
Palwick, Susan: *Flying in Place* 54
pandemic 3, 142, 168, 173, 184–188, 201, 208, 212, 214–15, 222
The Parable of the Sower (Butler) 13, 114, 219
Parallax Award 14–15, 170

patriarchy 15, 18, 36, 51, 72–73, 179
Pearson, Carol S. 3, 19, 24, 31–33, 36, 39, 101, 127–29, 131, 225; *The Female Hero* 36, 225; *The Hero Within* 24, 225
petroleum industry 34–35, 128, 130, 140, 142, 151, 205, 208
Phoenix 80–83, 85–97, 155, 201–2; as the reaper 96, 202
Piaget, Jean 19, 86, 179, 196
Pilinovsky, Helen 190, 225
Pipher, Mary 3, 20, 29, 63, 101, 106, 114, 225
portal fantasy 100, 203
postcolonialism 6, 17, 56, 61, 74, 88, 108, 128, 130, 139, 158, 160, 163, 175, 195, 204, 207–8, 218–19
post conventional logic and moral development 22, 29, 134, 136, 195; *see also* Gilligan, Carol
posthuman 42, 44, 54, 93–94, 107–8, 114, 213
post-scarcity communities 140–42
post-traumatic stress disorder 2, 4, 54, 70, 76–76, 86, 113, 124, 204–5, 221–22, 227; post-traumatic play 119–20
power inequalities 8, 22, 26
Practicing Reconciliation in a Violent World (Battle) 3, 218
Prettyman, Gib 210, 226
Primate Visions (Haraway) 60, 91, 222
prison system 81, 85, 179; prison-industrial complex 52
privilege 4, 7, 6, 10, 44, 70, 69, 81, 90, 113, 119, 171, 182, 187, 214, 215
problem-solving 11, 32, 106, 166
procedural knowledge 25, 196
Prometheus 77, 96, 99, 200–1
prosthetics 10, 12, 153, 155, 158, 164–65, 193
Pullman, Phillip: *The Golden Compass* 195

"Race in Science Fiction: The Case of Afrofuturism" (Yaszek) 153, 228
racism 3, 51, 102, 154, 157–161, 169–70, 213, 218
rage 1, 28, 31, 45, 57, 68, 82, 84–86, 90, 93–94, 137–38, 156, 166, 218
Ransby, Barbara 55, 226
rape 45, 47, 52, 54–55, 58–59, 62, 66, 74, 79, 107, 110, 116, 125, 128, 174–75, 194, 224
reconciliation 3, 108, 115–16, 218
Reed, Bess 120–21, 125, 131, 142, 226
Reed, Ishmael 156
rememory 148; *see also* Morrison, Toni
Remote Control (Okorafor) 31, 182–84, 194, 217

reproductive rights and responsibilities 142
resilience 2, 8, 10–11, 24, 30, 62, 67, 98–103, 108–9, 113, 117, 222
The Revenge of Gaia (Lovelock) 212, 224
Reviving Ophelia: Saving the Selves of Adolescent Girls (Pipher) 20, 63, 101, 106, 225
The Revolution from Within (Steinem) 13, 44, 65, 227
Ride, Sally 102
Rieder, John 3, 84, 140, 226
Roddenberry, Gene 159; see also *Star Trek*
Roman Empire 175
Romero, Leonardo (illustrator) 165, 217
Roosevelt, Eleanor: "Eleven Keys for a More Fulfilling Life" 116
Rose, Tricia 156, 220
Rowling, J.K.: *Harry Potter* series 62, 69, 125, 195
Rozak, Betty 36, 226
Russ, Joanna 170; *The Female Man* 46, 85, 226; *Kittatinny* 214

sacrifice 2, 13, 24, 33, 45, 58, 60, 65, 69–72, 74, 99, 108, 110, 131, 140, 152, 160, 175, 180, 195, 225
Sahara Desert 29, 35, 40, 43, 61, 120, 146, 209
Samatar, Sofia 170
Sand, George 44
scapegoating 29, 61–64, 71, 175–76
Schalk, Sami 2–3, 9, 11, 148, 226
Schütze, Bernard: "The Grotesque and the Techno-Grotesque" 94, 226
scientists 61, 76–80, 82, 96, 109, 151, 162, 185, 200, 204, 211, 214
second wave feminism 2, 44–46, 64, 92, 141, 170
self-esteem 2, 6, 20–21, 29, 34, 39, 62–63, 98–99, 118, 158, 204, 225, 227
separate knowing 32; see also Belenky, Mary Field
The Seven Beauties of Science Fiction (Csicsery-Ronay) 93–94, 220
sexism 4, 6, 22, 50, 61, 105, 128, 154, 155, 161, 168, 171, 184, 188
sexual intimacy 18, 23, 25, 42, 50–51, 199
sexuality 43–46, 49, 94
The Shadow Speaker 16, 18, 20, 21, 24, 26, 18, 20, 22, 28, 30, 32, 36, 40, 44, 53, 54, 56, 58, 60, 62, 58, 64, 72, 78, 121, 122, 134, 142, 144, 150, 152, 154, 178, 186, 191, 176, 188, 209, 200, 206, 207, 209, 211; Chief Ette 18, 36, 38, 50, 146, 209; Dikéogu 10, 27, 50, 175–76, 195, 209 (see also "Tu-

maki"); Ejii 19, 20, 21, 24, 25, 27–28, 29–33, 35–40, 51, 53, 69, 129, 136, 146–47, 149, 166, 171, 182, 194, 199, 207, 209, 210; "My Cyborg Manifesto" 11–12, 57; Peace Bomb 37, 40; Queen Jaa 58, 152, 161, 208, 209
shamanism 26, 120, 123, 127, 221
shame 27, 30, 63–67, 70, 86, 95, 101, 115–16, 219
Shatner, William 213
Shawl, Nisi 6, 20, 131, 153, 164, 170–72, 193, 196, 211, 221, 223, 226; "The Deep End" 161, 226; *Everfair* 193, 196, 222, 226
Sheehy, Gail: *Passages* 45, 226
Shelley, Mary 3, 75–76, 78–79, 81, 83–85, 88–89, 91, 189–91, 93–94, 97, 201, 208, 222, 226–27; attends research into galvanism 78
Shelley, Percy 78, 85, 88, 189–90
Shuri series 127, 165–66, 180, 210–11, 213; conflict resolution 127–28, 166; Space Lubber 128, 166, 206
Shuri: Search for Black Panther 165, 199, 200, 205, 207, 211, 217
Shuri: 24/7 Vibranium 128, 165–66, 207, 210–11, 217
Sims, James Marion 79
slavery 6, 8, 27, 41–43, 77, 81, 110, 112, 154, 175, 179, 196, 201, 204, 208, 211; see also meta-slavery; neo-slavery
Slonczewski, Joan: *Brain Plague* 204, 226; *The Highest Frontier* 210; *The Wall Around Eden* 130
social change 129, 175, 178
social justice 13, 171, 211, 219, 220, 222–23, 226
Solomon, Rivers: *An Unkindness of Ghosts* 202, 226
soul mate 36, 46, 57, 58, 60, 80, 130
The Souls of Black Folk (Du Bois) 8, 157, 226
Soyinka, Wole 1, 14, 194
speaking truth to power 55, 147
Spiderman: Venomverse 164
Spinrad, Norman 152, 227
spiritual guides 25, 118, 143, 149–50
Spivak, Gayatri Chakravorty 1–2, 223
Star Trek 155–56, 159, 208, 213; see also Lavender, Isiah
Star Trek: Discovery 160
Star Trek: Next Generation; 194
Steinem, Gloria: *Revolution from Within* 2, 30, 44, 64, 227
Stevenson, Robert Louis: *The Strange Case of Dr. Jekyll and Mr. Hyde* 200
Stockholm Syndrome 80, 224

Stories About Stories: Fantasy and the Remaking of Myth (Attebery) 58–59, 74, 218
Storm 91, 161–62, 164–65, 206, 213
"Stormbringer" (Okorafor's unpublished novel) 175, 193
Stott, Rachel (illustrator) 165, 217
Strange Horizons 99, 198, 204, 219, 224–25, 228
Straub, Peter 7
stress management 31
Stross, Charles 74
Student Nonviolent Coordinating Committee 157
sublime 3, 67, 89, 93–97
Sun Ra 82, 91, 155, 211; as Le Sony'r Ra 82; *see also* Blount, Herman Poole
Sunny and the Mystery of Osisi 198
superheroes 11, 132, 156, 161–65, 177, 212–13, 219–21, 225, 228; Super Girl 160, 162, 212
surveillance 3, 66, 69, 81, 90, 121, 144, 183–84, 201

The Talisman (King and Straub) 7
Taoism 2, 137, 143, 209, 214
Tasmanians (Wells) 140–41
Tate, Greg 156, 220
Taylor, Keeanga-Yamahtta 15, 47, 55, 158, 220, 226–27
teaching stories 99, 101
technology 2–3, 11, 19, 37, 40, 65, 77–78, 81, 102, 111, 115, 145–46, 148–51, 153–54, 169–71, 176, 181–83, 198, 200–1, 203, 206, 210–12, 214, 221–22, 227; bit 105 (*see also* astrolabe; Binti); invasion of privacy 183–84; nanotechnology 91
Tepper, Sheri: *Raising the Stones* 130
Terr, Lenore: post-traumatic play 119–20; *Too Scared to Cry* 2, 119–20, 205, 227; *Unchained Memories* 65, 224
theocracy 130
third wave feminism 2, 39, 46, 48–49, 153, 226–27; Title 9 171
Thomas, Biyi Bandele 2
Thomas, Sheree R. 48, 54, 154, 171–72, 217, 220, 227
Tiptree Award 169, 193, 207; *see also* Otherwise Award; WisCon
To Be Real: Telling the Truth and Changing the Face of Feminism (Walker, R.) 48, 227
To the East, Blackwards see X Clan
toddler behavior 22
tradition 2, 6–8, 12, 17–22, 38, 42–47, 50–53, 58–60, 64–65, 67–69, 82, 98–102, 105–6, 112, 115, 118, 120–21, 125, 133, 135, 137, 141, 146, 150–52, 162, 170, 174, 178–80, 194–95, 197, 202, 208, 220, 223
tragedy 83, 97, 150–52, 210
transcendence 11, 34, 41, 69, 94, 134; Mikniksic 34, 196; see also *Akata Witch* series; *Book of Phoenix*
transformation 14, 34, 38, 41, 57, 67, 72, 100–2, 108, 129–30, 132, 135–36, 178, 202, 211; *see also Binti* series; *Phoenix*
transformative justice 108, 115, 219
trauma: *Betrayal Trauma* (Freyd) 221; *Trauma and Recovery* (Herman) 222; *Unchained Memories* (Terr) 227
treeing *see* Binti
treeing in tennis play *see* Okorafor, Nnedi
trickster 14, 25, 28, 99, 127, 131, 195
Trump, Donald 187, 198, 201, 207, 220
truth and reconciliation 3, 108, 115–16, 218
Turner, Nat 93
Tuskegee Institute Syphilis Study 79
Tutuola, Amos: *The Palm Wine Drinkard* 200, 203
2008 Black Writers Conference 171

Uhura, Nyota 155, 159–60, 167, 213
uli art 98–102
Uncanny magazine 154, 228
underground railroad 112, 159, 212
universal feminine 36
untouchability 50, 65, 70
utopia 33, 36, 39–40, 71–72, 84, 103, 117, 142–45, 151, 155, 157, 177, 201, 212, 220, 222–24, 226–28
utopias-in-progress 13, 36, 53, 96, 148, 159, 199

Vah 70–72
Verne, Jules: *From the Earth to the Moon* 159
Viorst, Judith 47
voice 1, 9, 11, 20–25, 27–28, 36, 48, 51, 71, 99–100, 115, 122, 195–96, 210, 221; ancestral 19, 27, 136–38, 146, 148
Volney, Constantine De Volney, Count 88; *The Ruins of Empires* 88, 201
Volta 78
vultures 67, 199

wahala 138, 167, 204, 213
Wahala Blog 119, 182, 197, 211, 217
Wakanda 162–163, 165–66
Waldo, Mark L. 77–78, 227
Walker, Alice 2–3, 46, 48, 102, 113, 126, 204, 227

Walker, Barbara G 65, 83, 96, 227
Walker, Rebecca 2, 48, 70
wanderer archetype 24, 132, 136; *see also* Pearson
war 1, 8, 17, 24, 31–33, 45, 52, 59, 62, 69, 71, 74, 81, 115–16, 140–42, 144, 146–48, 151–53, 159–63, 165, 167–68, 173, 175–77, 195, 198, 200, 202, 209–13, 219, 221; American Civil War 159, 175; Biafran Civil War 52, 176–77, 198, 209, 212, 213, 217; and consumption 176–77; World War II 33, 153, 163
war as entertainment: Arthur Kent, Scud Stud 176
Warner, Marina 59, 78, 96, 227
Warren, Elizabeth 198, 224
warrior archetype 24. 125, 128–29, 136
warrior culture 104, 109
warriors 32, 57, 176, 211; child warrior training 8, 54–56, 69, 125, 181
Watterson, Bill: *Calvin and Hobbs* 169, 227
Weil, Simone 36
Weird Fiction 203, 207, 226
Wells, H.G.: *War of the Worlds* 140, 211
What Sunny Saw in the Flames 198, 218
white privilege 162, 170–71, 213–14, 224
Whitehead, Colson: *The Underground Railroad* 211
Who Fears Death 2, 13, 50, 58–76, 85, 96, 101, 118, 124–25, 143, 170, 173–745, 177, 181, 194–96, 201, 205, 217, 220, 221, 226; Aro 67–68, 137, 199, 205, 227; Daib 66, 68–71, 73; *Ewu* 61–62, 73; *Kponyungo* 71–73, 199, 222, 223; Mwita 66–68, 70, 73, 125, 225; Najeeba 59, 65, 68, 76, 200; Onyesonwu 59–74, 124–25, 129, 135–37, 171, 174–75, 195, 199, 205; Sola 69–70; vultures 67, 199
wilderness 21, 23, 35, 51, 56, 65, 67, 75, 124–25, 135, 137, 144, 148, 199, 222, 224
Wilhelm, Kate: *Where Late the Sweet Birds Sang* 109
Wilkerson, Isabel 3, 80, 84
Williams, Adebayo 2
Wilson, G. Willow 170

windseekers 7, 10, 19, 26, 37, 38, 41–57, 66, 73, 132, 162, 168, 197, 212
WisCon 14–15, 169–70
Wisdom Ways (Fiorenza) 17, 221, 226
Wole Soyinka Award 1, 194
Wolfe, Gary K. 6, 98, 228
Wollstonecraft, Mary 76, 83, 189, 202
Womack, Ytasha 3, 81, 83, 111, 153–55, 159, 163, 165, 201, 212, 228
The Woman Warrior (Kingston) 9
woman warriors 42, 54, 66, 72, 146, 151
womanist feminism 2, 48, 113, 204, 227
women's rights 3, 8, 10, 20, 30, 38, 42–43, 46, 51, 83–84, 90, 95–117, 170, 180, 190, 194
Women's Ways of Knowing (Belenky) 20, 22, 25, 28, 32, 196, 219
Wonder Woman 163, 165, 212, 221, 227–28; 2017 movie 163
"The Word for World Is Forest" (Le Guin) 141, 143, 145, 224
World Fantasy Award 15, 75–76, 85, 201
World Reader 203

X Clan: *To the East Blackwards* 156
X-Men 77, 164, 200, 202, 213

Yahweh 60–61, 65
Yaszek, Lisa 3, 6, 153–54, 201–2, 218–20, 222–23, 227–28
Yeats, William Butler: "Leda and the Swan" 59, 228

Zahrah 19–20, 22–24, 26, 29–32, 38–39, 53–54, 69, 105, 122, 136, 171, 182, 195, 197
Zahrah the Windseeker 13–14, 18, 36, 41, 111, 118, 122, 141, 147, 150, 194, 200, 204, 210, 218; Papa Grip 26, 28; peaceful gorilla community 124, 47, 195, 210
Zamalin, Alex: *Black Utopia* 3, 82, 99, 155, 228
Zeus 198
Zipes, Jack: *Don't Bet on the Prince* 47, 194, 228

www.ingramcontent.com/pod-product-compliance
Lightning Source LLC
Chambersburg PA
CBHW032037300426
44117CB00009B/1099